Musical Meaning

Musical Meaning

Toward a Critical History

LAWRENCE KRAMER

University of California Press

BERKELEY   LOS ANGELES   LONDON

University of California Press
Berkeley and Los Angeles, California

University of California Press, Ltd.
London, England

© 2002 by the Regents of the University of California

Library of Congress Cataloging-in-Publication Data

Kramer, Lawrence, 1946–
   Musical meaning : toward a critical history / Lawrence Kramer.
      p.   cm.
   Includes bibliographical references (p.   ) and index.
   ISBN 0-520-22824-3 (cloth : alk. paper)
      1. Music—Philosophy and aesthetics.   2. Music—History and
   criticism.   3. Subjectivity in music.   4. Music, Influence of.
   I. Title.
   ML3845 .K814 2002
   781.1'7—dc21   2001027819

Manufactured in the United States of America

10   09   08   07   06   05   04   03   02   01
10   9   8   7   6   5   4   3   2   1

The paper used in this publication is both acid-free and totally chlorine-
free (TCF). It meets the minimum requirements of ANSI/NISO Z39.48–
1992 (R 1997) (Permanence of Paper). ∞

Contents

Illustrations

Figures

Musical Examples

Acknowledgments

For counsel, criticism, encouragement, help, intellectual stimulation, and more, thanks and appreciation to: Walter Bernhart, Marshall Brown, Nicholas Cook, the late Naomi Cumming, James Deaville, Samuel Floyd Jr., Matthew Head, Kim Kowalke, Richard Kurth, Claire Leonard, Nancy Leonard, Ralph Locke, Susan McClary, Vera Micznik, Albrecht Riethmüller, Steven Paul Scher, James Sellars, Ruth Solie, Rose Subotnik, Jeremy Tambling, Robert Walser, and Werner Wolf.

Earlier versions of chapters 3 and 9 appeared, respectively, in *Word and Music Studies I: Defining the Field*, ed. Walter Bernhart, Steven Paul Scher, and Werner Wolf (Amsterdam: Rodopi, 1999) and *Black Music Research Journal*, Center for Black Music Research (Chicago: Columbia College, 16 [1996]: 53–70). My thanks to the publishers for allowing me to reserve the right to reprint this material. An earlier version of chapter 6 appeared in *A Night in at the Opera: Media Representations in Opera*, ed. Jeremy Tambling (London: John Libbey and the Arts Council of England, 1994); it is reprinted here, with thanks, courtesy of the University of Luton Press. Music example 10.1 is reproduced courtesy of European American Music Corporation, again with the author's thanks.

Introduction:
Sounding Out
Musical Meaning and Modern Experience

The problem of meaning stands at the forefront of recent thinking about music. Whether music has meaning, what kinds of meaning it may have, and for whom; the relationship of musical meaning to individual subjectivity, social life, and cultural context—these questions have inspired strong feelings and sharp debate. All of them are raised anew and given a thorough shaking in *Musical Meaning*, which aims to rethink as fully as possible both how the questions are asked and how they are answered. The book celebrates meaning as a basic force in music history and an indispensable factor in how, where, and when music is heard.

In its modern form, the problem of meaning arose with the development of European music as something to be listened to "for itself" as art or entertainment rather than as something mixed in with social occasion, drama, or ritual. The music composed to be heard in this way eventually constituted a discovery that permanently altered the character and concept of music both inside and outside the European tradition. Yet although both this repertoire and the modes of listening it fostered encouraged a sense of aesthetic self-sufficiency and an idealized, unitary concept of music, a variety of exceptions and variants proliferated right alongside them to challenge the emergent model. This process has been more or less continuous, and in one respect it has been very fruitful. It has encouraged the development of both analytical devices for understanding music as autonomous art and interpretive strategies for understanding music as meaningfully engaged with language, imagery, and the wider world. In another sense, however, the debate has been fruitless, because it is not so much about the nature of music "itself" (as if there were such a thing) as about the ways in which we authorize ourselves to listen to music and to talk about it. It is obvious that in practice both sides of the debate are "right," even if in theory one is inclined

1

to prefer one side over the other—as I do myself, since most of my work has been devoted to the pursuit of musical meaning.

The underlying point of this book is that the apparent dilemma of musical meaning is actually its own solution. To see this, we need to view the dilemma itself, not in negative terms as a zero-sum game that can never actually be won, but in positive terms as a historical phenomenon. What this shift of perspective reveals is that the character of modern Western music regularly turns on the question of whether the music takes on context-related meaning in particular cases. In other words, the question of whether music has meaning becomes, precisely, the meaning of music. At least since the historical watershed just described, music has generally operated on the basis of a series of contradictory tendencies: on the one hand toward the projection of autonomy, universality, self-presence, and the sublime transcendence of specific meaning, and on the other hand toward intimations of contingency, historical concreteness, constructed and divided selfhood, and the intelligible production of specific meanings. Music presents this dual character in quasi-perceptual terms, analogously perhaps to the famous line-drawing discussed by Wittgenstein in his *Philosophical Investigations:* a figure that can be seen as either a duck or a rabbit, but not both at once.[1]

This interplay of autonomy and contingency is the general, higher-order context and condition of intelligibility for most modern Western music. It is not so much something heard as it is the vestibule through which we hear. It is a kind of template, a quasi-grammatical or a priori ambiguity to which no fixed content can be assigned. Either side of this duality may be gratifying or suffocating, vital or stale, enthralling or threatening or bewildering; either side may be ambivalent. Either may also recognize and make concessions to the other, which it is more likely to subordinate than to exclude. And either may lay claim to the same dimensions of musical experience: the expression of feeling, for example, may be grounded in concepts like form or structure or left adjacent to them, and the feelings expressed may be understood as in some sense universal or unconditional or referred to historically specific categories. The only thing fixed among these possibilities, and many more, is that virtually any act of musical composition, performance, listening, or understanding will engage some and ignore or repress others, and thus define itself by giving the interplay of autonomy and contingency a particular realization, be it ad hoc or systematic, explicit or tacit, even witting or unwitting.

The interplay itself, of course, is not unique to music, but it is perhaps more urgent and ubiquitous in music than anywhere else. As the art of the ear more than the eye, music collapses the sense of distance associated with visuality, and more broadly with the whole field of concepts, images, and words. The resulting sense of immediacy tends to feel like bodily self-presence, the intimacy of oneself with one's own embodiment. We may know the suspension between autonomy and contingency all around us, but in music we feel it in ourselves.

This last point is crucial. For it is my thesis here that the a priori ambiguity of music goes beyond the vagaries of perception to articulate one of the core conditions of subjectivity. The sense of self, too, is poised between a unique and absolute self-presence and a contingent social constructedness, and no one ever escapes from this dilemma—which, however, is also its own solution. On the one hand, certain experiences, especially the bodily urgencies of hunger and love, fight and flight, pain and desire, seem to occur beyond relativity and contingency, even to suspend or interrupt them. In a sense, the absolutely particular here seems to merge with the universal. On the other hand, all such experiences occur as parts of particular life histories whose meanings are contingent through and through. Even more, as Eric Santner has suggested, these experiences are energized by the very contingency that they seem to surmount. Their immediacy, the fruit of collapsing distance, is intensified by the secret knowledge of "its own grounding in—and thus its debt to—a contingent, 'parochial' " state of affairs.[2] What we experience as unconditional is always somewhere marked by the irrationality of its attachment to the contingent.

Music, the art of collapsing distances, plays out this paradox as nothing else can. Modern Western music has regularly been associated with depths and heights of noncontingent subjectivity; latter-day theorists have associated it with the historical, cultural, and social construction of subjectivity.[3] The claim here is that both of these associations are grounded in the iconic relationship—part symbol, part homology—between the purely musical and musically meaningful on the one hand, and the purely existential and contingently realized on the other. Posing the question of musical meaning, and above all posing it in and through music, in the lived experience of works, styles, and performances, has given music of many kinds a substantial share in the diverse, conflicted formation of subjectivity in the modern era.

The link to subjectivity rounds us back to the contradiction between pure and applied music with which these remarks began. On the one hand, music is above all that which surrounds, accompanies, suffuses, infuses; it mixes with virtually anything, words, images, movement, narrative, action, inaction, eating, drinking, sex, and death. To make anything more itself, or more anything, just add music. On the other hand, music remains entirely unaffected by the things with which it mixes, no matter how they may direct or even coerce its expressivity. Subtract them from music, or music from them, and there remains music itself, music on its own, pure music, ineffably present to sense or memory. Music adds something to other things by adding itself, but loses nothing when it takes itself away. By reason of this limitless subtractability, music has often formed the paradigm of autonomy not only in the modern system of the arts but also in the construction of subjectivity. This is the ground of pure or structural listening, the rapture of being wholly absorbed or deeply moved or touched by musical experience, revealed to oneself in the ineffability of music. Because it forms the remainder of every experience it engages, music may act as a cultural trope for the self, the subject as self-moved agency that remains when all of its attributes and experiences have been subtracted. Musical affect, expression, and association become pure forms of self-apprehension; music is known by and valued for its "transcendence" of any specific meanings ascribed to it; identity seeks to become substance in music, even though music, being more event than substance, continually eludes this desire in the act of granting it.

This subjective nucleus, however, is attended by the same pressure that, as thinkers from Hegel to Bakhtin to Lacan have insisted, impels all subjectivity: the subject is meaningless in itself alone and necessarily seeks to enunciate itself in relation to others. It seeks connection, interrelationship, in order to be. In the case of music, this dynamic dimension is registered in the potentiality for bearing ascribed meanings, meanings grounded in shared, socially mediated experience. No music, however "pure," can escape this potentiality, which can be activated by even the most casual sign, visual, verbal, or gestural—even intonational; the subtractability of music is always in counterpoint with its imprintability. As I hope to show, when ascribed meaning gives musical subjectivity a specific content, the musical remainder beyond that content becomes at the same time its support. The remainder appears only in relation to the content it exceeds and by which it is in that sense produced. In the meshes of this relationship, the remainder comes to act both as the material medium and the fantasy space or screen through which the subjective content may be enfranchised and played out.

Over the course of the past two centuries, as variously defined dualities of autonomy and contingency have tended to define the understanding of music, the terms of autonomy have increasingly tended to be upheld as primary or superior; subtractability trumps imprintability. Or at least we read that it should: "We *need* to understand music as music, as an autonomous language, if we want to grant it the power to speak of other things. . . . This is how we hear music speak: not by reducing it to some other set of circumstances—music is simply not reducible to any other circumstances, whether cultural, historical, biographical, or sexual, and any attempt to make it so has only a cartoonish reality—but by allowing it the opacity of its own voice, and then engaging that voice" on personal or "poetic" terms.[4] Part of my purpose in this book is to argue for a reversal of this value inclination, which involves criticizing the values to be dethroned without debunking or dismissing them. Concurrent with this is a critique of the assumptions about meaning, knowledge, "circumstances," and personal subjectivity that underlie the grant of an actual, rather than a figurative, autonomy in which subordinate contingent meanings must supposedly be grounded. (Clearly the stakes here extend beyond music to other forms of art and cultural practice, the involvement of which will also thread the chapters to follow.) I'm seeking to do a tricky balancing act with the debate over meaning: to uphold the semantic end, but in terms that incorporate the autonomous one; to acknowledge the historical, ideological, functional importance of the experience of autonomy in the context of a view in which the primary term is contingency. I want to take autonomy seriously by finding its indispensable place in the network of indispensably contingent practices.

In this respect the book can also be understood as a response to recent scholarship by Stanley Cavell, Lydia Goehr, Gary Tomlinson, and others, that treats music in light of the noumenal qualities that have repeatedly been ascribed to it since the turn of the nineteenth century.[5] I do not disagree with these writers in any crude way, nor do I conceive of myself as writing in opposition to them. At one level, I am simply seeking to insist on a complementarity, a historically grounded stress on music as more a means of engagement with the world than of disengagement. The chapters that follow aim to suggest some of the diverse ways in which music acknowledges the dense phenomenal life that its apparently noumenal qualities obscure. They revel in the embeddedness of music in the actual contingent conditions of life and thought, which music reflects, enhances, and in part helps to create.

At another level, though, this book does engage in a critique of the noumenal idea of music, even as the object of sophisticated historical inquiry. This level is essentially political, shaped by the democratic principle that the free public use of language is our only safeguard against destructive irrationalisms. I am always suspicious of claims to ineffability, because people who invoke the unspeakable may use it to justify unspeakable things. The mystery of music will always be cherished by music lovers, but it is best cherished when it is demystified, understood as a contingent effect, not as a first principle. My effort to do that here is not antagonistic, but part of a larger effort to inhabit some portion of the less mystical but no less gratifying field of music in the world, which is where—I couldn't hide this if I wanted to—I think music should be. The aim, as in all my work, is to achieve a nonreductionist contextualism. No cartoonish realities, please: this is a critical practice meant to affiliate music richly with things beyond itself without *either* allowing it to fade into a mere echo of those things *or* succumbing to the illusion that it has any genuine identity apart from them. Music cannot "speak" with its "own" voice until it finds a voice, or voices, among a multiplicity of others that constantly blend with, mimic, and chafe against the rest.

I am, of course, hardly alone either in regarding musical autonomy as a historical construction or in trying to understand music as a worldly activity. This project has been shared over the past decade or so with Susan McClary, Richard Leppert, and Rose Subotnik, to name just those members of my own generation with which my work has—rightly—been closely associated and to which it owes a special debt. The aim of this book is to reframe some of the questions raised by this work and to continue its initiative of investigating the intimate dynamics of culture and society, and the dynamics of intimacy in culture and society, through the lens of the arts. This is not simply a matter of using sociocultural awareness to contextualize or, even less, to depreciate the arts. It is a matter of using the arts, critically and imaginatively taken up, as tools for thought—a thought that breaks down the barriers between "art," "self," and "society," just as it does the boundaries separating the arts from each other and from speculative thought, and speculative thought from knowledge. To break down these boundaries, however, does not mean to invalidate them, but to energize them: to treat the distinctions they uphold as temporary or recurrent positions in a process—a combination of experience and reflection on experience—that is orderly without being centered, in flux without being chaotic.

Musical Meaning proposes to study the musical a priori as it plays itself out around questions of social alliance. These are questions that bear equally on the private zones of subjectivity and the public arenas of history and politics. Music has the power to give its makers and auditors alike a profound sense of their own identities, to form a kind of precious materialization of their most authentic selves, in the mode of both personal and group identity. But at the same time music has the power to alienate the sense of both types of identity by carrying its makers and auditors across thresholds of difference that at least unsettle the sense of identity and may even undo it altogether. On the one hand, music abstracts and universalizes the contingent forms of one's social and personal alliances by seeming to reach a plane beyond all contingencies; on the other hand, music falls into contingency and strands one there, alienating both itself and the listener. At one extreme the anthem, the theme song, the favorite piece, the catch-in-the-throat melody, the "little phrase" of the narrator in Proust's novel; at the other extreme the trashy, noisy, disturbing, repellent, maddening sound of other people's other music. My purpose in what follows is to track the varied forms of this dynamic across two centuries of music and to provide some sketches or outlines of how it works—and why it works so well.

The argument represents the third step in an intellectual trajectory started in two of my earlier books, as follows:

1. From *Music as Cultural Practice:* Musical meaning is understood as communicative action and therefore as embedded in a continuous texture of psychological, social, and cultural relations. Music—and in this it is no different from more explicitly semantic modes such as narration and visual depiction—means not primarily by what it says but by the way it models the symbolization of experience. (*Symbolization* here is an umbrella term covering both discourse and fantasy; communicative action, as opposed to the traditional sender-receiver model of communication, assumes the existence of interpretive transformations at every post in a general circulation of signs and meanings.) Musical meaning is understood, both in practice and in analytical reflection, not by translating music as a virtual utterance or depiction, but by grasping the dynamic relations between musical experience and its contexts.

2. From *Classical Music and Postmodern Knowledge:* The form taken by musical meaning is the construction of modes of subjectivity implicating and "condensing" larger dramas of social and cultural identity. One might say that whereas narration and depiction address the human subject by exemplifying such scenarios, the more virtual medium of music dramatizes or enacts the scenarios of subjectivity from "inside" the listener or performer. The latter does not so much identify with a distinct imaginary subject as discover a radical potentiality within his or her normal (i.e., familiar, everyday) subjectivity as that subjectivity is permeated by the music.

3. In *Musical Meaning:* This process operates by producing a specific manifestation of music's a priori ambiguity and calling on the listener (whether as performer or audience) to decide when, how, and whether to resolve the ambiguity credibly. (The degree to which particular works, styles, or events thematize or foreground the ambiguity varies widely, of course; the variation is a kind of meta-version of the ambiguity itself.) Perhaps the most familiar form of this crux is the recurring paradox of vocal music: does one regard it (now, here, today) as an indivisible musical whole

or as the setting of a text or somehow as both? Music thus addresses the subject from a (virtual, symbolic) liminal zone set between particular manifestations of autonomy and contingency. The venues for this zone may be either "internal" or "external" to the extent that these terms can be distinguished; the zones may form around boundaries of style, form, genre, performance, medium, mode of response, and so on. The listener is invited to renegotiate these boundaries: to reexperience through the music what does or does not, may or may not, belong, be included, be excluded, be incorporated in or expelled from whichever subject-position the listener chooses or is impelled to assume. (First index of the process: one's musical taste. Second index: do you move your body? Sing or hum along? Do you dance?)

This structure forms the horizon within which musical subjectivity is negotiated, but it has no fixed content and does not maintain a fixed set of values or embodiments. Each field of alternatives is socially and culturally resonant; each field continually presupposes and produces the other. All forms of autonomy harbor an immanent potential for contingent relationships and associations; all such contingencies project an autonomous musical remainder that exceeds their expressive or interpretive mandate. The two fields, however, are not finally on even terms. As we will see, although contingency and autonomy are structurally equal, their relationship is dynamically geared to the production of contingency. The "secret debt" of autonomy to contingency is always available to tip the balance.

In sum: musical meaning consists of a specific, mutual interplay between musical experience and its contexts; the form taken by this process is the production of modes or models of subjectivity carried by the music into the listener's sense of self; and the dynamics of this production consist of a renegotiation of the subject's position(s) between the historically contingent forms of experience and the experience of a transcendental perspective that claims to subsume (but is actually subsumed by) them.

Musical Meaning traces these themes by mingling theoretical chapters with case studies of the interplay of autonomy and contingency in various musical media. The emphasis in both kinds of chapter—which in any case gradually fuse—is on the way the nexus of music and meaning, both positive and negative, involves itself with the formative conditions of modern subjectivity in its diverse registers, historical, social, and symbolic. As the book proceeds, another fusion is also meant to emerge, one between thinking about meaning and subjectivity to gain insight into music, and—realizing a possibility still barely acknowledged—thinking about music to gain insight into meaning and subjectivity.

The sequence of chapters is roughly historical, running from Beethoven and Schubert to Shostakovich and Coltrane and a little beyond. It is shaped in part by a thematic undercurrent: a gradual shift in emphasis from the nineteenth century's still resonant constructions of "deep" identity and individual selfhood to the breakdown of these constructions in the century that followed. The movement into the twentieth century also involves a degree of engagement with jazz, popular music, and film and TV music as well as with the "classical" repertoire that is my primary focus. This turn reflects the proliferation of modern mass media, which both produced the distinction between "art" and "entertainment" and rendered it increasingly tenuous. One of the keystones of modern experience was the discovery that to find oneself entertained is to entertain a self, as one entertains a thought or, even better, a guest. At the same time, of course, much of the experience that modernity forced people to "entertain" was profoundly ugly. A certain millennial pressure may therefore be felt in the concluding chapters, which register the continuing need to reckon with the worst events of the newly last century, though any such reckoning itself is still far off. All of these issues need to be "sounded out" in all the multiple senses of the term: read with effort by piecemeal combination, addressed in exploratory ways for alliance and mutual understanding, grasped in the forms of echoes from an unplumbed depth, and made to sound as clearly as possible against a prevailing silence.

1
Hermeneutics
and Musical History
A Primer without Rules, an Exercise with Schubert

Hermeneutics, defined as both the theory of interpretation and "the art of understanding," began as a relatively obscure branch of German philosophy in the early nineteenth century and gradually gained more prominence in connection with twentieth-century literary criticism. As conceived by its founder, Friedrich Schleiermacher, it was strictly a text-based discipline; to music it was simply oblivious. Nonetheless, it did have a contemporary parallel in the critical reception of music, a de facto hermeneutic that treated certain musical works, in the first instance works by Beethoven, as if they had the status of texts, even though it was also generally conceded that they did not. This practice has generally been treated with tolerance at best and scorn at worst, despite its persistence to the present day. Recently, however, work on the cultural significance of music has questioned the premises of this disparaging attitude and sought to legitimize interpretive talk about music, though often in new forms. What follows is one possible outline—one interpretation—of the art of musical understanding that may result.

AUTONOMY AND MEANING

The object of musical hermeneutics is to study musical meaning, which for many people means that it is a discipline with no object at all. No ideas about music are more conventional than that music has no meaning, at least in the sense that words do, and that this lack is something to be treasured, something that helps make music special. The composer Ned Rorem speaks for many others when he claims that "music . . . is inherently meaningless in the intellectual sense of the word."[1] Music may be "meaningful" in the sense that people find it important or that it expresses emotions or serves as a medium of social connection, but it does all these things without assuming a concrete content. It bypasses both language and the systems of rational thought that depend on language. If words are involved, the music takes precedence; it expresses—is widely felt to express—more than words can say. If reason is involved, it is a reason unto itself, a purely musical logic.

Yet, however self-evident these ideas may seem, or be expected to seem, at the close of the twentieth century as I write, they have not always been so, nor, for that matter, would they always have made much sense. Like all ideas, they have a history. They are the products of a specific transformation in the development of European music, a watershed both for the concept of music and for musical repertoires. At its core, this transformation concerned the type of music widely regarded as the model of music per se, the ideally or essentially musical type. To generalize somewhat too crudely, before the last third of the eighteenth century, that music involved language; it was for singing. (With popular music, it still is.) After the first third of the nineteenth century, the prototypical music involved nothing but itself, and in particular neither text nor voice; it was purely for instrumental performance. This well-known emancipation of music from language was spurred, on the one hand, by an increasing awareness of language as a system distinct from nature in whose character music did not share. On the other hand lay the evolution of what would become the "classical" genres of symphonic and chamber music with their highly dramatic yet seemingly autonomous structures. Once those genres took hold, the possibility of autonomous music was recast as the postulate that music is in essence autonomous.

Eventually, this autonomy would become a pretext for separating musical pleasures from all "real-world" concerns, but its initial impetus was profoundly political. It served as a leading edge in the more general project of nineteenth-century aesthetics, the aim of which was to establish a sphere of personal cultivation unregulated either by state agencies or the rules of good society. (The problem, of course, is that this is easier said than done, and at the same time too easy to fantasize as done once it has merely been said. For one thing, aesthetic self-cultivation is hard to practice without already having a good deal of the social and political latitude one is supposedly seeking through it.) Music's aesthetic autonomy, however, quickly proved more problematical than anyone seems to have anticipated. The emancipation of music from language turned out to be its alienation from meaning. Texted vocal music is linked to a definite human content by default. Remove text and voice, and the link is broken; do so with music of conspicuous autonomy, and the broken link becomes something palpable, insistent, something that must be reckoned with.

For some, including weighty figures like G. W. F. Hegel and Richard Wagner, the reckoning came as the paradoxical judgment that music's autonomy rendered it incomplete. Hegel claimed that autonomous music was a chimera that teased musical amateurs out of thought; it became partially symbolic in response to their desire for meaning but continually eluded the meaning it seemed to express. Experts might be "entirely satisfied by the music itself," but music that catered to such satisfaction could "easily become utterly devoid of thought and feeling, something needing for its apprehension no previous profound cultivation of mind or heart."[2] For Wagner, music was not so much extra-verbal as pre-verbal, primitive in content rather than empty. Its progressive historical development required the complementation or penetration of music by the poetic idea. Others, however, and they were by far the majority, found means to place high aesthetic value on the semantic emptiness of music, so that the process of following an autonomous musical form with close attention was established as one of the peaks of aesthetic experience. Reversing Hegel's judgment, Eduard Hanslick declared that "unflagging attendance in keenest vigilance . . . can, in the case of intricate compositions, become intensified to the level of spiritual achievement."[3] At its most sophisticated, this attitude could subsume the process of partial symbolization described by Hegel, allowing impressions of meaning to spread like a transparent film over the surface of autonomous form.

How odd, then, that commentary about musical meaning flourished throughout the nineteenth century and persisted during the harder-nosed twentieth. Odd, too, that it operated under the peculiar condition I described earlier, which replicates the dilemma of Hegel's musical amateur: textlike meaning was regularly ascribed to music amid strenuous assurances that music had no such thing. And odd that so many of the compositional genres invented or elaborated in the nineteenth century—the tone poem, the character piece, program music—should actively seem to court this dilemma. The ubiquity of the problem suggests that something is fundamentally wrong with the core assumption that musical autonomy equals absence of meaning. If so, identifying that something might open the possibility of a musical hermeneutics no longer burdened by the foregone conclusion of its own futility or its inferiority to the purely musical. Only once that happens can the full range of music's engagements with culture become accessible. For although music minus meaning can be placed in its cultural context, it necessarily remains inert there; since meaning resides in the context alone, the music can at best be a symptom or token of some contextual element. Even the effort (for instance by Theodor Adorno) to understand musical form as a reflection or "mediation" of context necessarily chokes off the symbolizing impetus noted by Hegel. And although musical hermeneutics, like any other, can equally well ignore as uncover the interplay between a symbolic object and its context, that interplay cannot be made explicitly apparent otherwise than through acts of interpretation.

PARABLE AND PARAPHRASE

To return to the core assumption: where does the equation of autonomy and meaninglessness go wrong? In at least two places, I would say. The first is the supposition that if what music expresses is essentially nonverbal, words are helpless to elucidate it except in crude or superfluous ways. The second is the argument that because the elements of musical expression lack the capacity of words to form propositions and make specific references, musical compositions cannot have meaning in the same way that verbal ones do. Not only is each of these claims in error, but each is linked antithetically to a specific hermeneutic practice that presupposes its erroneousness—but that, as noted, has traditionally been allowed to support rather than subvert the pertinent claim.

The supposition that words become powerless in the face of the nonverbal is tantamount to a dismissal of both figurative language and illustrative narrative. Addressing the nonverbal, communicating indirectly what cannot be directly conveyed by words, is one of the most traditional functions of language, and one of the richest in terms of technique. Since antiquity this mode of language, a "figural" mode encompassing allegory, symbolism, and metaphor, has been fundamental to ethics, metaphysics, religion, and psychology, not to mention literature, all spheres it has helped as much to create as to expound. As C. S. Lewis observed, "We cannot speak, perhaps we can hardly think, of an 'inner conflict' without a metaphor; and every metaphor is an allegory in little."[4] During the nineteenth century, the expressive content of instrumental music joined the roster of mental or spiritual realities that required figural communication. The requirement was met in diverse ways, but most often perhaps by a form of parable, a brief narrative meant to convey obliquely, and only to those capable of grasping it, a higher-order concept or principle that could be conveyed fully in no other way. Basic to this technique is the understanding that the parable will seem both bald and arbitrary if applied to the music literally. What applies is not the overt representation, but the covert significance.

For example, in 1851 Wagner wrote an elaborate program in which Beethoven's *Eroica* Symphony is said to portray the self-creation of a complete human being. An exemplary masculine subject passes through phases of unrestrained force, transfiguring grief, and robust normality before achieving full selfhood through the progressive fusion of masculine and feminine principles. Evocative statements with no literal basis abound: the first movement presents a force that threatens to turn the subject into a world-crusher [*Weltzermalmer*], "a Titan wrestling with the gods"; the scherzo unburdens this force of its "destructive arrogance" [*vernichtende Übermut*] in the person of "the lovable glad man who paces hale and hearty [*wohl und wonnig*] through the fields of Nature, looks laughingly across the meadows, and winds his merry hunting-horn from woodland heights"; the finale culminates in a revelation of love that weds itself to masculine force with a "power [that] breaks itself a highway straight into . . . the inmost fortress of the man's whole heart."[5] It would be pointless as well as condescending to dismiss these statements as dated or culture bound (conditions that no statement escapes in the long run); the pressure of historical and cultural associations—the gravity of mythological allusion, the folklorish image of the Romantic hunter and his *Waldhorn*, the familiar polarity of the sexes—is precisely what gives the program, as parable, its figural effectiveness. That effectiveness, in turn, is based on the shared understanding that nothing here is meant to be taken literally, not even the core idea of androgynous self-creation, which has what might be called a greater impetus toward the literal than anything else in the text. Wagner closes with an explicit reminder that his apparently definite statements are actually indirect speech-acts, his language the language of parable: "But only in the master's tone-speech was the unspeakable to be made known, that which the word here could only just intimate within the highest self-consciousness."[6] What matters is not the "speech" of the interpreter's text, but the speechless higher understanding that the text intimates. Historically, such intimation occurred as a regular and normal response to instrumental music.

The second flawed supposition, that music's nontextual character bars it from having textlike meaning, is based on a confusion between the medium and the message. The object of interpretation in classical hermeneutics is not the word or sentence but the work, which Schleiermacher and his successor Wilhelm Dilthey regard as the place where lived experience acquires a durable form. Works, wrote Dilthey in 1900, are "the written manifestations of life."[7] Music's lack of a word- and sentence-level semantics does nothing to bar it from having meaning at the higher level of the work.

Meaning at that level depends on the treatment, arrangement, and logic of lower-level materials, a dynamic interrelationship of elements that is equally intrinsic to both verbal and musical compositions. The presence or absence of semantic value at the lower levels belongs to the medium, music or language; meaning belongs to the higher-level message conveyed by "working" the medium-specific elements into comprehensible patterns. It may be, of course, that the "work" thus constituted is not as stable as classical hermeneutics would like to believe. Both its boundaries and its meanings may be uncertain or contested, and its relationship to culture and society subject to critique. These difficulties, however, only enhance the presence of meaning as an issue or problem at this level of utterance.

Like its figural meaning, the meaning of music as, so to speak, a sounding manifestation of life has historically been associated with a traditional function of language and a corresponding set of hermeneutic practices. The function in this case was fairly obscure until recent criticism (especially by W. J. T. Mitchell) noticed its importance to the theory of representation; it goes by the rhetorical name of "ekphrasis," but as applied to musical meaning I will simply call it paraphrase. Ekphrasis is the literary representation of a pictorial representation; its aim is the ancient one of making the mind's eye see, though what is seen is not a reality but a picture. Ekphrasis is accordingly a technique of visualization, a means of training the eye. But it is also a hermeneutic technique, a means of commenting on what is visualized and therefore of training the eye to see meaningfully. The locus classicus of ekphrasis is the description of the shield of Achilles in Homer's *Iliad;* well-known modern instances include W. H. Auden's poem "The Shield of Achilles," an ironic revision of Homer, and poems by Auden and William Carlos Williams on Breughel's *Landscape with the Fall of Icarus.*[8]

The application of ekphrastic language to music rather than painting did not occur much before the early nineteenth century: not, in other words, until the autonomous instrumental work had established itself as a norm and a problem. Thereafter the verbal paraphrase of musical expression became both a mainstay of music criticism and an important literary device, with famous examples by Robert Browning, Marcel Proust, Thomas Mann, E. M. Forster, and James Baldwin, among others. By the twentieth century, paraphrase had taken over the central role formerly played by parable in musical hermeneutics, though the two modes did (and do) continually overlap. Wagner's *Eroica* parable, for example, recurrently supplements itself with touches of paraphrase, most strikingly, perhaps, in its account of the finale, where the fusion of masculine and feminine characters is identified with the progress of the theme-and-variations form.[9] Unlike parable, ekphrastic paraphrase is supposed to ground itself in literal description, or at least the fiction or convention of literal description, no matter how figurative it otherwise becomes. Like parable, however, paraphrase is not neutral. It always proceeds from the perception of a meaning that is conveyed through musical devices but not confined to them. This dimension of paraphrase is what distinguishes it from purely technical descriptions based on the idea of autonomy without meaning; in other respects the two types of description may look alike.

For example, in a widely read essay, Edward T. Cone calls attention to a pattern of disruption in a lyrical piano piece, Schubert's *Moment musical* in Ab, D. 780. The piece falls into a clear-cut A B A form, Allegretto-Trio-Allegretto; the Allegretto is itself an A B A song form in which the opening section is distorted both rhythmically and harmonically during the process of its recapitulation. Of the rhythm, Cone writes that "rhythmic irregularity, experienced in the development as an agreeable loosening of the tight proportions of the opening, has now almost destroyed the original balance. Eight bars, 2 + 2 + 4, are answered by sixteen, but they are not 4 + 4 + 8: they are 2 + 2 + 5 + 7!"[10] The second of these sentences is obviously pure technical description, though one spiked by exclamation. The first might be regarded as a more generalized form of the same thing but one colored by an interpretive impulse. It does not arrive at real paraphrase, but points in that direction; the image of destroying a balance may or may not be meant casually. This intermediate quality turns out to be carefully calculated. Cone subsequently notes that his analysis has not been "wholly objective"; in it he has "insinuated a few leading phrases to suggest . . . the kind of expression I hear in the work" (26). He then proceeds to restate his description in terms progressively closer to ekphrastic paraphrase. The process begins with the suggestion that the music "dramatizes the injection of a strange, unsettling element into an otherwise peaceful situation" with disastrous results (26), and ends with the claim that this musical action forms "a model of the effect of vice on a sensitive personality" (27), the vice referring to whatever sexual proclivities led Schubert to contract syphilis in 1822. The outcome is startling; the incremental preparation makes it seem credible.

Despite this, Cone registers a certain unease with his own paraphrase, qualifying his description as a form of "personal contact" (hence questionable for not being wholly objective) and his conclusion as "only the most tentative of hypotheses" (27). These remarks display a mild-to-medium form of what Mitchell identifies as "ekphrastic fear," one of two "moments" by which ekphrasis (here emblematic of representation in general) is continually haunted. The motive for ekphrastic fear is the sense that verbal paraphrase may work too well, that it threatens to engross and supplant the representation that it describes. The goal of the second moment, ekphrastic hope, is a positively characterized form of the same thing, a full, revelatory adequation between the verbal and nonverbal representation—ultimately, says Mitchell, a seamless "overcoming of otherness."[11]

HOPE AND FEAR

Musical hermeneutics is very familiar with both of these "moments." Ekphrastic hope appears when writing on music rises to eloquence, from the florid rhetoric of Wagner's program for the *Eroica* to Donald Tovey's precise but evocative account of how a famous horn theme emerges in the finale of Brahms's First Symphony:

> There is a moment's darkness and terror, and then day breaks. There is no more tragedy. The mode of the principal key changes to major for the last time in this symphony as the solemn trombones utter their first notes, and the horns give out a grand melody that peals through the tremolo of the muted violins like deep bells among glowing clouds.[12]

Ekphrastic fear is a pervasive feature of musical criticism, almost an enabling convention. It fosters what might be called the emphatic tentativeness exemplified by Cone, and qualifies both parable and paraphrase with assurances that they are only auxiliaries to intrinsically musical understanding. The fear of muting music with words also informs several common criticisms of musical hermeneutics: that it focuses selectively only on those aspects of music most amenable to verbal interpretation or that it gives priority to literary or other verbal forms and subordinates music to them as a dependent "other."

These criticisms, I hasten to add, are misguided. On the first point, if musical devices are really bearers of meaning, then every aspect of music is potentially available for interpretation. Meaning diffuses itself throughout its conveyances. Although no musical detail is bound to become hermeneutically active—any individual interpretation is both selective and certain to encounter, indeed to produce, things that remain opaque to it—no detail is exempt from the possibility. On the second point, if cultural or other mediations really link musical and verbal forms (among others), then music is not subordinated to the verbal just because the interpreter must perforce use words. Meaning belongs to the potential for mediation itself, that is, to communicative or expressive processes that can be realized in more than one medium. It makes no difference whether the starting point is "inside" or "outside" music; the interpretation does not locate meaning as a recoverable substance within the work, musical or otherwise, but as an activity or disposition within a cultural field.[13]

To some extent, both ekphrastic hope and ekphrastic fear are themselves misguided, the first seeking the impossible, the second fleeing the unlikely. But they also seem to be unavoidable, as if they were inseparable from the concept of representation. They are not mere errors to be dismissed, but tendencies with which musical hermeneutics must continually negotiate. It's striking, for example, how Cone, who describes Schubert's A♭ *Moment musical* with clarity and refinement rather than eloquence, opens the back door to ekphrastic hope by quoting Edmund Wilson on Oscar Wilde: "[In the end] the horror breaks out: the afflicted one must recognize himself and be recognized by other people as the odious creature he is, and his disease or disability will kill him" (28).

Ekphrastic hope and fear bear most closely on the rhetorical character of paraphrase; the problem of its content still needs to be addressed. As might be expected, the two topics interlock. As rhetoric, paraphrase assigns meaning to the sphere of immediate perception—Tovey's pealing bells, Cone's wrecked balance—as if the listener could intuit it just by following "what happens" in the music. This way of speaking rests on another version of the ideal of aesthetic autonomy that emerges at about the same time as paraphrase itself, namely the idealist view of art as the sensuous embodiment of an idea. But it is obvious that metaphors like Tovey's and formal descriptions like Cone's are highly mediated. They are the products of a long, complex process of education and acculturation. They are not so much records of immediate intuition as fictions of it, instructions for producing the illusion of it. In order to invoke the immediate, they have to make a conceptual and rhetorical leap away from it. For the most part—and not just with reference to music—this leap is not acknowledged in the paraphrase, as if it had been made naturally and without reflection (which may or may not be so). Some such omission is probably inevitable. Like the dancer who (in a famous metaphor) trips because he is thinking of his feet, the paraphrase can collapse under the burden of too much self-consciousness. And unreflective paraphrase can certainly produce real insight, as Tovey and Cone show. But there is still a problem, and the question—for any interpreter— is not whether it will arise, but when.

The problem is that unreflective paraphrase treats its conceptual and rhetorical resources as if they were universal rather than culturally embedded. This lapse is a very familiar topic in modern critical theory, which usually handles it more roughly than I will. Although the lapse may be invidious, not only intellectually but also ethically, it is sometimes nontoxic, and sometimes knowingly provisional. Even so, unless one is willing to be confined by the illusion, it is necessary to combine paraphrase, and parable, too, with a practice of reflection on the conceptual and rhetorical leaps they require. The character this reflection has to assume is clear from its purpose. The only way to avoid overinvesting in fictions of universality is to consult the contingencies of culture.

What this means in practice is the construction of paraphrases and parables that take some part of the work's cultural framework as their own context and condition of possibility. Interpretations so formed suggest, by exemplifying, the kind of sense that the work could have made in that context, under those conditions. What this expressly does not mean is that the interpretation aspires to understand the work as its maker or first audiences understood it. Nor does it mean that the interpretation will avoid using conceptual resources that postdate the work. In place of these quasi-positivist ideals, the culturally sensitive interpretation puts a concept of potential or virtual meaning. The intent is to say something consistent with what could have been said, whether or not it actually was, and in so doing to suggest how the work may have operated in, with, on, and against the life of its culture. Approached in this way, the work loses its traditional status as a bounded, prestige-laden object wedded to an individual artist, and becomes a relay in an open process of material and symbolic exchange.

LOVE AND DEATH

To exemplify this type of interpretation I will return to Schubert's A♭ *Moment musical*, but before I do, one more piece of reflection is necessary. Cultural frameworks are not stable, self-evidently meaningful objects; they are constructions pieced together by an interpreter, whose efforts presuppose some sort of ordering principle or theory, however informal. It is important to spell this out in order to avoid re-creating, at a "higher" level, misleading fictions of universality. (The notion that one can avoid this completely is itself a misleading fiction.) My chief presupposition in what follows, drawn from Michel Foucault, is that objects are constructed in culture by regularities in the way they are talked about—even when those objects are diseases: for example, syphilis.[14] Cone's interpretation skates over this point, though its divination of Schubert's illness in the music feels right; it's an inspired guess. Cone bases his paraphrase on a historical (indeed medieval) concept of vice presented as if it were universal and on a recogni-

Example 1.1. Schubert, *Moment musical* in A♭, opening figure

tion of syphilis as a physical pathology but not—despite his quotation from Wilson and another from *King Lear*—as a cultural construction. To fill these gaps, we need to hear the music in the context of the "discourse" on syphilis and to ask if their interrelationships, if any, are close enough to be significant.

For Cone, Schubert's Allegretto traces a movement from pleasurable temptation to the disastrous wages of sin, but it is also possible to hear this music as expressing a sense of suffocating paralysis from first to last. The Allegretto is pervaded by its opening figure—one can hardly call it a theme: a repeated note, upbeat to downbeat, short to long, followed by a short note a step or half-step lower (see ex. 1.1; a few variants place the short note a half-step higher). In many statements, including the first, the figure's core is a prepared appoggiatura: consonant on the upbeat, the repeated note becomes dissonant on the downbeat—something that goes bad. In other cases the "preparation" is itself dissonant, as if the upbeat had gone bad as well. In every case, the long note is harmonized as a poignant dissonance; in nearly every case it resolves to an unstable or transitional sonority. The exceptions (mm. 16, 47) are contradicted so quickly that they seem illusory. Nowhere in the piece is the long note put quite right. In every case, too, the figure as a whole is closely harmonized, embedded in a chordal texture that envelops and constrains it. In the course of the Allegretto this figure and its variants appear some twenty times, twice that if the sectional repeats are taken. No departure from it is more than a brief respite. The effect lies somewhere between pained resignation and resentful helplessness: a diffuse sense of being beset.

This same sense also pervades the work's sectional design. The middle section of the Allegretto's A B A song form itself follows an A B A pattern, the outer segments of which are dominated by variants of the opening figure. Cone is right to call this passage a "development"; it never fully achieves the contrast characteristic of song form. On the contrary: its initial action is to work the pervasive figure more deeply into the texture, transferring the figure to an inner voice where it is first mirrored, then doubled, by the bass. The first segment of this "development" also harps on the note C♭, the minor third of the tonic A♭, in the upper voice; the emphasis occurs at the beginning and end of the segment, thus forming a further level of A B A design (mm. 17–29). The remaining segments seem to leave this C♭ emphasis hanging, but it proves to be an insidious hidden presence. Its impact is such that the eventual "recapitulation" of the Allegretto's A section fails to sustain the major mode, concluding instead, as Cone observes, with an empty double octave. (Not just empty, either, but dark and dull, planted sotto voce deep in the bass.) Finally, at yet another level, the A B A form of the *Moment musical* as a whole feels subtly damaged. Its Trio, an interlude in search of a simple and amiable lyricism, is "beset" throughout by reminders of the Allegretto's implacable figure, a process that begins with the very first bar (ex. 1.2). As if transmitted by this opening, the figure's distinctive short-long, upbeat-downbeat attack on a single note returns to begin almost every subsequent phrase. Other traces of the Allegretto proliferate as well: dissonant twinges in the first half of the Trio (mm. 7, 15), a chromatically tinged episode of rhythmic irregularity in the second (mm. 22–26), the chordal cloak around the recurrent gesture throughout. Depending on performance, the result is to imbue the would-be lyricism with an undercurrent of brittleness, halfheartedness, even debility; the music seems to be putting a good face on a bad situation. The Trio's lyrical aspirations are further tinged with unreality because—pace Cone— its key, D♭, cannot take the Allegretto's A♭ major as a grounding dominant; the A♭ major is, so to speak, no longer sound.

The multiple layers of A B A (the "C♭" segment within the development within the Allegretto within the whole) thus constitute a stifling Chinese box assembly, each layer of which succumbs to infection by the infamous figure. As the source of infection, the A section of the Allegretto might even be said to illustrate a certain trope for the diseased body, tainting both the outer social world (the Trio) and its own inner core (the development) and thus growing inexorably worse (the recapitulation). This trope combines two historically distinct layers of representation: an older, that of the pariah body, reserved for the victims of leprosy, plague, syphilis; and a newer, that of what might be called the Romantic body, one susceptible to self-division and self-alienation.

My metaphor of infection, like Cone's of vice, is a guess, but one prompted by the discourse on syphilis familiar to Schubert. The disease has always been associated with ideas of ruin, decay, contamination, and debil-

Example 1.2. Schubert, *Moment musical* in A♭, beginning of Trio

ity.[15] The later nineteenth century perceived it primarily as a threat to the family and responded by a combination of social engineering and a concerted medical quest for a cure, the famous "magic bullet." The medicine of Schubert's day could do little more than describe the pathology and recommend mercury pills. Socially, the disease produced a generalized pariah status for the individual sufferer, marked especially by the characteristic outbreaks of repellent skin lesions. Emphasis fell on the victim's powerlessness to alleviate the symptoms or stop the progress of the disease, with its cycle of lesser and greater pain, remission and increasingly severe relapse. At the same time, syphilis was regarded as a punishment in kind for sexual excess. The logic was sometimes religious and sometimes social—by the late eighteenth century sexually transmitted disease was being taken as one of the discontents of civilization—but it was always retributive: the genital site of pleasure became the source of a taint that inexorably spread throughout the whole person.

Schubert suggests this profile of syphilis in a famous letter of 1824—the date of the *Moment musical,* too—not cited by Cone:

> Imagine a man whose health will never be right again, and who in sheer despair over this ever makes things worse and worse, instead of better; imagine a man, I say, whose most brilliant hopes have come to nothing, to whom the joy of love and friendship have nothing to offer but pain, at best, whose enthusiasm . . . for all things beautiful threatens to vanish. . . . 'My peace is gone, my heart is sore, I shall find it never and nevermore.' I may well sing [this] every day now, for each night, I go to bed hoping never to wake again, and each morning only tells me of yesterday's grief.[16]

The despairing cycle of night and day may give symbolic resonance to a much-noted symptomatology, a cycle of deep bone aches growing worse by night and never quite well by day. More broadly, the infection described here spreads relentlessly from the body to both the private and the social selves. The rhetoric, with its multiplication of parallel clauses, is imitative of what it describes, and bears at least a family resemblance to the rhetoric of the *Moment musical,* with its use of musical parallelisms to "taint" both the Allegretto's middle section and the Trio. Schubert also suggests a specific link between the physical and personal-social infections: his despair at the inexorability of the disease has the cruelly paradoxical effect of distributing its effects throughout every department of life.

More indirect is the suggestion of "venereal" retribution. Schubert's quotation identifies him with the protagonist of one of his own songs, the Gretchen of Goethe's *Faust:* the trusting young woman whose betrayed love has condemned her to constant physical and mental torment. If the Ab *Moment musical* conveys musical images of recurrent misery, mounting by degrees, this is the kind of love-sickness they are most likely to evoke. The title borne by the piece when it was first published, "Pleintes d'un Troubadour," suggests as much. The troubadour, too, traditionally sickens at love denied, or more exactly tends to represent love by tropes of sickness. What Schubert's remarks show is that the figurative sickness easily shades into the literal; there may be a culturally wrought alliance between love wronged and the disease contracted from a wrong love. The *Moment musical* is sufficiently excessive in its Chinese-box enclosures and repetitions of the "beset" figure to point in that direction. The music sounds sick; it ever makes things worse and worse; the hopes of its Trio come to nothing; its enthusiasm for all things beautiful threatens to vanish as it loses its grasp on the major mode. No wonder that in 1824 Schubert also became preoccupied with the idea that he had been poisoned.[17]

Once their presence is surmised, these tropes become tangible at finer and finer levels of musical detail. The Allegretto's insidious slide from major to minor is affected especially strongly. The loss of Ab major at the end exceeds what Cone calls the "starkly ambiguous" character of the final bars. The second half of the recapitulation consists simply of a lopsided pair of phrases, each stated twice in succession (Cone's 2 + 2 + 5 + 7; see ex. 1.3). The first phrase explicitly lowers C to Cb in a statement of the main figure (mm. 63, 65); the second phrase climaxes on a cadential six-four chord of Ab minor (mm. 71, 76). The closing melodic cadence unequivocally descends by step from Cb to Ab. Even though the minor triad itself does not sound at the cadence, the concluding double octave inescapably "belongs" to the minor mode. The minor is present not to the senses but as something sensed, something inwardly wrong of which the octave is the sign—be it the metaphor of a spirit in decline or the symptom of a diseased body.

Example 1.3. Schubert, *Moment musical* in A♭, second half of recapitulation

Similarly, the interior of the Allegretto's three-part "development" dramatizes a relentless deterioration consistent with both the discourse on syphilis and Schubert's description of his ruined health. Like the Trio, this middle section represents a step outside a world consigned to pain, but a step subverted by its inescapable link to that world. Framed by variants of the main figure, the section begins with a lyrical, idyllic expansion of a melodic figure heard in more poignant form in the preceding developmental A section (mm. 30–33, ex. 1.4). But everything about this passage is "wrong," off-kilter, futile. The harmony is both remote (♭VI, F♭ major written as E major) and presented only in the unstable form of six-four chords, the bass note of which carries over for two additional measures as a dominant pedal. This note is a B♮; heard in the upper voice, it forms the melodic fulcrum of the lyrical E-major phrase. But the note is also the enharmonic equivalent of C♭, the third of the tonic minor; and this note (in fact, the specific pitch) is carried over via the upbeat-downbeat juncture from the developmental A section, where it has presided over the reiterations of the main figure (mm. 29–30). We saw earlier that as the bearer of the tonic minor, the upper-voice C♭ portends the deteriorating condition just reconsidered—the loss of the tonic major at the end of the Allegretto. As B♮ in the developmental B section, the same note stands as a palpably illusory denial that the deterioration has already started and cannot be stopped. It is no wonder that the lyrical passage quickly breaks down into a less-than-idyllic counterstatement punctuated by harsh diminished-seventh chords (mm. 34–40). Every remission implies a new relapse.

But what of vice, and the allegory of temptation and fall that goes with it? Schubert's remarks seem indifferent to these categories, and the music shows no trace of the religious rhetoric that might evoke the notion—standard in the discourse of syphilis—of a just return for sin. Both the remarks and the music shift the ground of affliction from soul to self, judgment to pathos; they secularize the concept of love-poisoning. With its multiple redundancies, the music can even be heard as insisting on the dignity of the suffering it expresses, asserting the claims of the person against what Foucault called "bio-power," the social administration of mental and physical health.[18] The Allegretto's insistence on C♭/B in both its development and recapitulation may in this context seem like an act of courage or honesty, even an effort to find some constructive or aesthetic power in the very substance of misery. The piece would then be a sort of Schubertian *fleur du mal.*

Or would it? Nothing can prove it is; there is no proof in musical hermeneutics. But then, there is no proof in any hermeneutics: no certainty to connotation, irony, implication, symbol, or the like. Meanings beyond the lexical only appear when their appearance is presupposed. The trick is to align the interpreter's art of presupposition with the work of culture, which above all is the practice of presupposition as an art. Interpretation consists of neither discovering prior meanings nor inventing new ones nor even teasing out latent meanings from a stable field of possibilities, although it may do a little of each. Instead it catalyzes meaning between different perspectives, different histories, different subjectivities. Proposing a meaning is the initiating gesture of an interpretation, not its result. The meaning proposed is actualized only by being dispersed through the discursive, figurative, expressive, and pragmatic activity of interpretation itself. The result is a bounded but open-ended process that

Example 1.4. Schubert, *Moment musical* in A♭, interior of development

affirms rather than negates the possibility of alternative meanings and elicits rather than abolishes active, positive forms of nonmeaning. Reckoning with such nonsemantic "remainders" and tracing the dynamics of presupposition as each relates to music are among the chief concerns of the chapters that follow.

2
Hands On, Lights Off
The "Moonlight" Sonata and
the Birth of Sex at the Piano

In 1798 Beethoven published a piano sonata that quickly rose to the top of the classical charts and would stay there in perpetuity. Three years later he did the same thing again with even greater success. The sonatas were the ones known respectively as the "Pathetique" and the "Moonlight." The two works share both certain types of music and a certain fate. At first, both were esteemed primarily for their relentlessly passionate fast movements; eventually, their lyrical, introspective slow movements came to the fore, giving both sonatas flourishing second careers as romantic mood music. The "Pathetique" was a late bloomer in this respect. It did not become a full-fledged romantic standard until the mid-1960s, when its slow movement was adapted as the theme music for a television show, the early nighttime soap opera *Peyton Place*, based on Grace Metalious's bestselling novel of 1956, a scandalously steamy book at the time. With the "Moonlight," however, the romanticizing and eroticizing process started long before television—no later, in fact, than 1840. It has been going strong ever since.

The romantic history of the "Moonlight" Sonata is my topic in this chapter. I want to understand it as a small but significant episode in both the history of musical meaning and the history of sexuality. The two histories meet because with this sonata ascribing meaning to music became a means of ascribing sexuality to bodies, and vice versa, something made possible by understanding both the music and the bodies to be of a certain type. My discussion will accordingly focus at first more on how the music has been culturally situated than on the music itself, though at the same time it will show continually that this distinction is at best a convenient fiction. The boundary implied by the term *itself* is—itself—a product of the way musical experience is culturally situated. Although not just any music could have done the cultural work of the "Moonlight" Sonata, the sonata alone did not and could not determine most of the meanings it attracted. It could and did, however, provide an exceptionally suggestive "body" of sound to embrace the love story so often told through it.

The construction of that story was a surprisingly complex process. Its starting point was what we may take to be an accurate contemporary description of the sonata's overall design, published in the Leipzig *Allgemeine Musikalische Zeitung* (hereafter *AMZ*) in 1802. The initial reference to a "fantasy" alludes to the work's subtitle, "Sonata quasi una fantasia":

> The fantasy is from beginning to end one pure whole, rising out of the deepest emotions of the soul, carved from a solid block of marble. There cannot be a single person in any way sensitive to music who can fail to be seized by the first Adagio, led up and up and finally, deeply moved, sublimely uplifted in the Presto agitato.[1]

On this account, the sonata fulfills an aesthetic ideal important at the time, the reconciliation of untrammeled fantasy with organic unity of form, and it does so by means of an end-weighted process directed both toward and by the sublime finale. The pure whole translates itself into a compelling narrativity; the music traces out the stages of a spiritual progress on behalf of a passive listener who yields to it in a state of rapture. The reviewer leaves the content of this progress unspecified, although he may be lightly intimating that the music serves as Vergil to the listener's Dante in a quasi-redemptive ascent. What his rhetoric emphasizes, with its sequence of being seized, led ever upward, and sublimely uplifted, is the inevitability that the pure whole assumes when its ideal sculptural form is projected in time. The Adagio finds its culmination in the finale, both because an unbroken chain of feelings binds them—and this despite the lighter, more sociable middle movement, which the reviewer does not mention—and because the emotional disquiet of the Adagio, which seizes, finds its catharsis in the agitated finale, which uplifts.

Later accounts would both embellish and transform this one in at least five distinct ways. First, the end-weighting would be replaced by front-weighting; the "Moonlight" Sonata would become synonymous with its first movement. The music would still be traced to the deepest emotions of the soul, but these would tend to be concentrated in the Adagio, which would often sound self-sufficient. Second, the Adagio would become identified with a nocturnal scene, especially with a scene in which piano music, in the first instance the Adagio itself, is being performed. Third, that scene would be eroticized, with particular reference to the musical performance; the romantic love associated with this music would emanate from the piano no less than the music itself. Fourth, this love would be understood as sorrowful or renunciatory on the basis of a biographical legend. Fifth, the love lament would be replaced by its more positive form, the half-pleasurable, half-painful longing of romantic desire, especially on the verge of its fulfillment.

Despite my linear statement of them, these five interpretive trends do not form a real historical sequence. Instead they represent a figurative or conceptual sequence, an ideal narrative the separate elements of which may appear both in isolation and in various small groupings. Still, the sonata's reception does suggest a general tendency toward singling out the first movement and giving it a paradigmatic association with the night and romance, leaving open only the question of whether the romance is being forgone or foretold. That tendency can be said to have crystallized, with both romantic alternatives in place, in the two decades between Anton Schindler's Beethoven biography of 1840 and Leo Tolstoy's short story of 1859, "Family Happiness." The story contains what might be called the canonical "Moonlight" Sonata in virtually every particular, and I will use it as a point of reference in my five-point historical sketch.

Point 1. The Front-weighting. The opening Adagio of the "Moonlight" Sonata can be said to have gained its special status by taking over the attribute of sublimity that the *AMZ* critic found in the closing Presto. Music in general came late to the category of the sublime. In the early nineteenth century, writers trying to appropriate the category from nature, poetry, and painting sometimes distinguished between two musical types. On one hand, there was music that materially embodied great magnitude or great power, music that assaulted the listener's senses. On the other hand, there was music that expressed sublime states of mind without necessarily relying on such an assault. The theorist Christian Friedrich Michaelis labels these types the *objective* and *pathetic sublime,* respectively; the encyclopedist Aubin Millin speaks of the *incidental* and *essential sublime.*[2] These terms suggest a standard opposition of outer versus inner reality that tends to favor the inner, subjective, term, a preference that would prove to have broad cultural support. For Michaelis in 1805, the pathetically sublime in music resembled lyric poetry, portraying "our own nature, as we are moved, stirred, roused to emotional change and enthusiasm." For Millin in 1806, sublime feelings, which gain in impact the more one reflects on them, are "much more powerful when the artist puts us, so to speak, in the position of looking inwards into the soul, and . . . only uses external signs to show us what is going on within."

The first movement of the "Moonlight" Sonata quickly became a prime example of the pathetic sublime in music. And no wonder: the language that Michaelis and Millin apply to the category tends to form a virtual description of Beethoven's Adagio. Michaelis speaks of "the constant repetition of the same note or chord" and of "long, majestic, weighty or solemn tones" that produce "very slow movement"; Millin remarks that "when a composition is dominated by a single theme to which everything else is demonstrably beholden, there is something sublimely impressive about it." Hector Berlioz would later describe the actual Adagio in just these terms, noting the combination of "broad chords softly drawn out" in their "solemn sadness" to catch the piano's fading vibrations and the "ostinato" accompaniment that "scarcely varies from the first measure to the last."[3] The "Moonlight" Adagio thus represents the kind of music postulated or imagined as pathetically sublime. The actual music exists in a mutually reinforcing relationship with the aesthetic category.

In this role, the Adagio encapsulates at least three cardinal features: simplicity of means, profound feeling, and universal intelligibility. All three are already intimated in the *AMZ* description; the last of them is particularly noteworthy because intelligibility is precisely what the more familiar forms of the sublime nullify, including the musical version conceived by Michaelis. One might surmise that this reversal reflects the assimilation of pathetically sublime music to lyric poetry. Schiller suggests as much as early as 1794 when he argues (against Kant) that music can become a fine art rather than a merely agreeable one if the composer, like the poet and unlike the sculptor, "takes as his object the *inner* human form"; like poetry, music that articulates the form (rather than the content) of emotion "penetrates into the secret of those laws that govern the inner movements of the human heart."[4] The *AMZ* critic hears this kind of lyric-pathetic sublimity in the finale of the "Moonlight" Sonata insofar as the finale is organically related to the whole and in particular to the Adagio. In 1837, Berlioz hears the same kind of sublimity in the Adagio alone, the "poetry" of which "human language does not know how to describe" but which nonetheless expresses the mysterious form of an emotion, a fusion of sadness and tranquility, with complete immediacy. At midcentury Carl Czerny offers a more reserved form of the same trope. "This movement," he writes, "is highly poetical, and therefore perfectly comprehensible to any one" in its poignancy.[5]

Czerny's dryness lends extra credence to Berlioz's fervor, which had come to a head during a private performance by Liszt. According to his students, Liszt thought the "Moonlight" Adagio should sound "infinitely slow and dreamy"; according to Berlioz, as Liszt played for his friends, "the noble elegy . . . rose up in its sublime simplicity. . . . Each one of us trembled in silence, overcome with respect, religious terror, admiration, poetic grief; and without the healing tears that came to our aid, I think we would have suffocated."[6]

Here once again the pathetic sublime is associated with simplicity, subjective depth, and a shared understanding that overwhelms those who share it. The effect is probably more figurative than literal—Ernest Legouvé, at whose house the performance took place, gave a more restrained account of it, as did Berlioz himself in a later version—but that is just the point; the avowed purpose of Berlioz's statement (in either version) is not to record an event but to construct an ideal.[7] In the process, the Adagio is converted from an object of sublime character to what Slavoj Žižek calls a "sublime object," an object invested with a value—a glamour or charisma—in excess of any plausible rationale.[8] This new status is measured by the power of the Adagio to stand by itself. So great is its effect that there is no question of going further; simply enduring the Adagio alone requires a cathartic release of tears.

Point 2. Twilight Time. The Adagio's nocturnal associations have most obviously been supported by the sonata's much-maligned but indestructible nickname. The music is not generically a piano nocturne, a category that postdates it by a decade or more, but something about it, perhaps its blend of slow motion and prevailingly "dark" tone-color, seems to attract nocturnal imagery.[9] For Ludwig Rellstab, whose review inspired the nickname, the moonlight evoked by the sonata was that of a remote, primitive, sublime Swiss landscape. (It was not, as is often supposed, a sentimental image—mere moonshine—but something more resembling the desolate scenes of moonlight on water painted by Caspar David Friedrich.) Czerny preserves this sense of remoteness; what anyone can comprehend about the Adagio is that "it is a night scene, in which the voice of a lamenting spirit is heard at a distance." Berlioz and Tolstoy turn distance into proximity, enveloping the music in an intimate nocturnality that corresponds to its subjective power. In both cases the medium of this intimacy is the piano. Berlioz asks Liszt to play the Adagio in the twilight of a dying lamp; Liszt agrees, but asks that the lamp be extinguished altogether and plays in total darkness. His listeners are transfixed. Tolstoy's protagonist and narrator plays the Adagio in twilight on two occasions, the first time to intimate the rise of still-unacknowledged romance between herself and the man she will marry, the second to prefigure a reconciliation with him after the marriage has nearly been wrecked. The story also contains an intermediate scene in which the narrator specifically plays to her suitor by moonlight, the piano being illuminated only by a pair of candles; the same elements reappear in a scene from Wilkie Collins's contemporaneous novel *The Woman in White* (1860), although in both these cases the music is by Mozart. One might surmise that there is a figurative overlap between playing a sonata by moonlight and playing the "Moonlight" Sonata. Writing in 1857, Alexander Ulibyshev makes this connection by giving the piano quasi-invocatory powers: "As the melody sounds more brokenly, the moon discovers her pale, corpselike face and veils herself again behind the gloomy clouds hastening past."[10] In general, the "Moonlight" Adagio tended to represent a scene of musical reverie by night of which its own performance was the prime example.

Point 3. Love at the Keyboard. The piano was the audio system of the comfortable nineteenth-century household, but unlike its functional equivalents in the twentieth century—the radio, the phonograph, the CD player—its means of reproducing music included a human body, observation of which was basic to the experience of music in the home. One result, as Richard Leppert has shown, was that the nineteenth-century domestic piano became a highly charged, often transgressive locus of emotional, sexual, and psychosexual attachment.[11] Privately performed piano music was often represented, and presumably experienced, as a quasi-material medium of connection between the performer and the listener. The music enveloped the two in an intimate space oriented around the instrument, and by filling that space rendered it libidinally active; the movement of the music gave tangible form to the movement of desire.

In their Mozartian night-music scenes, for example, both Tolstoy and Collins describe a trembling, tender, musicalized atmosphere that acts like an extension of touch. "The balmy quiet," writes Collins's narrator, "that deepened ever with the deepening light, seemed to hover over us with a gentler influence still, when there stole upon it from the piano the heavenly tenderness of the music."[12] "In the half-darkness of the room," writes Tolstoy's narrator, "in every sound, in myself, I felt [my beloved's] presence. Every look, every movement of his, though I could not see them, found an echo in my heart."[13] Both scenes culminate with rays of moonlight falling into the room, an effect that is also the very condition of the scene that begins Eduard Mörike's poem "To Wilhelm Hartlaub":

> In through the window the bright moon shone;
> You sat at the piano in the twilight,
> Sunk in the dream-surge of melodies;
> I followed you afar on shadowy ground
> Where the song of hidden springs was sounding.[14]

Mörike's poem ostensibly celebrates romantic friendship, but, as so often happens, it does so in the language of romantic love, producing the sexually ambiguous intimacy that I have elsewhere called the romance of the Friend. The liquescent imagery of surging and springing carries an erotic charge typical for its historical moment, particularly in association with the shadowy recess that suggests both the darkness of sexual seclusion and the deep interiority of the loving self.[15] In an alternative version of this imagery, the beloved's piano playing moves the loving listener to tears, which measure depth of feeling by the involuntariness of its confession. In yet another nocturnal scene, this one repeated throughout her early marriage, Tolstoy's narrator plays while her husband sits at a distance, scarcely visible. But often, she says, "When he was not expecting it, I rose from the piano, went up to him, and tried to detect on his face signs of emotion—the unnatural brightness and moistness of the eyes, which he tried in vain to conceal" (46).

The Adagio of the "Moonlight" Sonata maintained a mutually reinforcing relationship with this scenario of pianistic romance, much as it did with the category of the pathetically sublime. In Berlioz's anecdote, the sound of Liszt's playing to friends in semidarkness inspired a request for the Adagio, which in turn produced a physically intense consummation by the way it filled the total darkness that followed. In the climactic scene of "Family Happiness," fullness of emotion prompts the solitary narrator to play the Adagio twice. The first time, the material-libidinal flow of the music leads to a painful awareness that her husband's place of old is empty: "The windows were open over the garden, and the familiar sounds floated through the room with a solemn sadness. At the end of the first movement I looked round instinctively. . . . He was not there" (74). The second time, the music merges with the narrator's inwardly vocalized prayer for renewal and ends with the unexpected touch of her husband's companionable hand on her shoulder. The degree to which "Family Happiness" is structured around multiple scenes of pianistic romance suggests the culturally specific capacity of such scenes to structure various aspects of subjectivity—in particular emotional responsiveness, self-development, and sexual love.

The romance scenario also informs the paradigmatic critical interpretation of the "Moonlight" Sonata given in 1859 by A. B. Marx. Marx epitomizes the sonata by its Adagio, which he hears as a renunciation of love. My wording here is meant to be exact: for Marx, the sonata does not express, but actually performs, the renunciation. The music is described as if Beethoven himself were in the process of composing it at the keyboard, and by that means enacting his renunciation in and through music. The finished Adagio emerges as the medium of an exemplary, edifying reenactment. The main theme of the movement becomes "the soft, soft song of renouncing love"; its expressive qualities testify to Beethoven's distress, its formal vicissitudes to his search for resignation. Thus "the rhythmic pulse, scarcely awakened, falters, and hesitates like the long parting look of the renouncer."[16] Thus the theme's changing harmonies trace out something like a process of mourning in the classic Freudian sense, an exhaustive going-over of all the thoughts and feelings associated with the lost loved one:

> So the theme wanders, always the same and true to itself, from the fervid C♯ Minor to the consolingly bright E Major, which must at once becloud itself to minor. There this life-step, the thoughts of which are marked by the bass, presses itself threateningly close, so that the overfilled breast almost bursts. And in painfully seething F♯ Minor the song sets forth anew; always the one thought, unchanging, with unaverted eyes it looks in the eyes of the sufferer, and the depths only echo this lament—and all longing, no matter how high and far it pleadingly gazes, sinks back in lament and dies away in the depths.

Marx's text divides subjective agency between the theme itself and the figure of Beethoven, as if to reproduce the relationship between the pianist and the intimate listener in the even more intimate, interiorized space between the pianist and the piano. The theme is said to wander, to seethe, and to gaze at the sufferer, while he, in turn, whose feelings the theme embodies, feels heartbreak and gazes back across the metaphorical space produced by the movement of his fingers. The fingers themselves are "wearily drawn across the strings," says Marx, as if to transform the keyboard into the lute or guitar of a serenading lover. The implied metaphor incidentally turns the Adagio into night music.

At the same time, Marx's own point of view is precisely that of the intimate listener, as if he, too, were present in the imaginary room where "Beethoven" is playing. His position is like Berlioz's at Liszt's 1837 performance, where, at least as the text would have it in retrospect, the intimate circle felt itself communing with the composer: "It was the spirit [*l'ombre*, the "ghostly shade"] of Beethoven, called up by the virtuoso, to whose great voice we were listening." Here, too, as also in Mörike's poem, the pianistic romance appears as an erotically tinged intimacy between men, the complement to the masculine-feminine intimacy depicted by Tolstoy and Collins. The underlying links between spirit communication, diffuse eroticism, and music making form a coherent system. Like Berlioz's virtual séance and Mörike's shadowy ground of fantasy, Marx's projection of a virtually telepathic intimacy with the spirit of Beethoven is consistent with contemporary tropes linking spectral or spirit phenomena to the mysterious depths of subjectivity on one hand and the irregularities of desire on the other. The origin of these tropes was probably the Gothic novel, whose images are progressively refined and idealized as the century proceeds, a process epitomized by the painting shown in figure 2.1, Sir Frank Dicksee's "A Reverie" (1895). Traces of the apparitional pattern are even tacitly present in the first "Moonlight" Sonata scene of "Family Happiness," where the remembered figure of the narrator's dead father helps unite her to her suitor while she plays, creating a counterpart to Dicksee's image with gender and temporal orientation reversed. But the tropes were not only literary, as Dicksee's title suggests; the era's psychology found an acute disposition to spectral delusion—"phantasmagoria"—in the kind of reverie prompted by the "Moonlight" Adagio in Berlioz, Marx, and other listeners.[17] In the right circumstances, the voice of Czerny's complaining spirit could materialize as a virtual reality or auditory hallucination.

Marx's reading also shows a certain need to limit the masculine intimacy it evokes, but only the better to uphold it. In describing the sonata's finale, Marx returns his Beethoven to a more public, conventional masculinity—the standard image of Beethoven as hero. But his treatment of this formerly sublime movement is surprisingly perfunctory. He gives it just a single straggling sentence: "And now life must be lived again, one storms up, one storms out, and rages and laments, and all the blows and all the thunder of fate shall not bow the sublime head of the consecrated one" (107). Compared to the elaborate rhetoric devoted to the Adagio, this is boilerplate. Marx actually gives more attention to the often-neglected middle movement, which he hears in strangely lachrymose terms as a virtual statement of farewell ("Leb' wohl, leb' wohl!"). It is as if Marx, and his Beethoven, was just going through the heroic motions; all his—their—emotional allegiance is with the Adagio.

Points 4 and 5. The Love Stories. Marx's interpretation is based on a nugget of biographical fact enmeshed in biographical fiction. The fact part is well known. Giulietta Guicciardi, to whom the "Moonlight" Sonata is dedicated, engaged Beethoven's romantic interest from 1801 to 1803, at which point she married someone else. This outcome was hardly a surprise and may even have been the enabling condition of Beethoven's interest; as Maynard Solomon suggests, he fell in love with socially unavailable women too regularly for mere coincidence.[18] It almost seems as if the postponement of inevitable denial was the form by which Beethoven articulated his sexual desires. If so, it is a form that both appealed to nineteenth-century habits of

Figure 2.1. Sir Frank Dicksee, *A Reverie* (1895), oil on canvas, 102.9 × 137.2 cm. Board of Trustees of the National Museums and Galleries on Merseyside (Walker Art Gallery, Liverpool).

biographical interpretation and supported an enhanced, idealized view of the romance widely supposed to lie behind the "Moonlight" Sonata, in particular its Adagio. In his 1840 biography, Schindler identified Giulietta as the "Immortal Beloved," the otherwise unknown addressee of a probably unsent letter that contains Beethoven's only serious declaration of passion for a woman. The identification was erroneous, even fabricated, but it stuck for more than thirty years, and the aura of legendary romance with which it invested Beethoven's attachment to Giulietta persisted long after her candidacy as the Immortal Beloved was discredited.

The transference of that aura to the "Moonlight" Sonata seems to have become something of a cottage industry, as both Schindler and Alexander Thayer, Beethoven's "standard" nineteenth-century biographer, complain. "Since the first edition of [my] book," wrote Schindler, "German and French pens have been at work on the affair, making it the lucrative object of romantic magazine stories. The writers of these fantasies have been fortunate in that their love story has been made even more poignant by its connection with one of the best-known of the piano sonatas, that in C sharp minor."[19] As late as 1927 and 1929, one can find both William Behrend and Romain Rolland drawing heavily on the Giulietta connection to support Marxian interpretations of the "Moonlight" Sonata, anticipated by Vincent D'Indy in 1911; Behrend even claims that Giulietta is still a plausible candidate for the role of Immortal Beloved. At about the same time, however, a modern (or modernist) counter-tradition began to emerge that would eventually succeed in dismissing these associations as "foolish legends" imposed on purely artistic forms and in banishing them to the despised realm of the "popular."[20]

For Behrend, the sonata is a "spontaneous expression" of the pain of unfulfilled love; and like Marx, Behrend finds that the Adagio's expression of this pain draws him into a quasi-telepathic intimacy with Beethoven at the piano, a sympathetic bond that in some sense replaces the one that Beethoven is mourning. There is almost a sense of rivalry between the composer's male critic and his female beloved, a feeling D'Indy had made virtually explicit with regard to the sonata in general: "[In such music] we do not think of the brunette goddess with blue eyes, or of woman in any guise; how can one see any other than the artist-creator himself, who complains, who revolts, who turns away to seek consolation?"[21] For Behrend, the Adagio projects "the lonely Master, sitting with bowed head at the piano and confiding, to his instrument, his great, deeply breathing elegy."[22] Like Marx once more, Behrend needs to find that head unbowed in the finale, but unlike Marx he is in deadly earnest about it. Although he regards the Adagio as "manly in its pain, unsentimental in expression" (76), it is apparently not manly or unsentimental enough. Only the finale "do[es] not leave us in doubt for one moment that the Master will not succumb to his suffering or grief. . . . [but] will rise hardened, doubly strengthened through his pain and [his] artist's fate" (78).

Rolland also looks to the finale for stability in the midst of passion: "As in the antique tragedies, sorrow is subdued by strength of soul."[23] Like Marx's, however, Rolland's deeper allegiance is with the Adagio, which he understands as "a confession, veracious and poignant, such as one rarely hears in music . . . [a] direct, scarcely veiled expression of pure passion" (102). Like Marx, too, Rolland refers to Giulietta to authenticate this expression, but finds that its significance lies less in its concrete historical relation to her than in the shape of the mourning process by which Beethoven detaches himself from that relation. As embodied in the music, this process satisfies Schiller's criterion for fine art; it moves from contingent passion to the underlying laws that govern passion. Beethoven's spontaneity turns out to generate its own form: "The unity that the artist does not seek in the architectonic laws of the movement or of the musical genre he finds in the law of his own passion. For all its rhapsodic form . . . the famous Adagio . . . is woven all of one piece, and exactly modeled to the beautiful, simple, veracious lines of the [melodic] idea" (105–6). Like Marx, Rolland interprets the emotional process of the Adagio as exemplary; the Adagio is less a record of profound erotic love than a school for it. Here, too, the concrete figure of the beloved woman disappears, but this time to leave behind a tangible paradigm for the experience of loving her.

Rolland's generalizing of what Behrend calls "Beethoven's love story" suggests the means by which the romance aura of the "Moonlight" Adagio expands to envelop the life stories of figures other than Beethoven: figures from Tolstoy's exemplary bourgeois wife to the young lovers of the 1937 film *Moonlight Sonata* who cross paths with Ignace Jan Paderewski (appearing as himself) to the quasi-autobiographical protagonist of Mike Figgis's film of 1999, *The Loss of Sexual Innocence*, in which only the music sustains the romantic ideal repeatedly lost in the narrative. The continuity threading these instances bears witness to the remarkable durability of nineteenth-century narrative schemas in which subjectivity is consolidated through sexual self-discovery.[24]

Equally remarkable, though, is the capacity of the "Moonlight" Sonata to encapsulate and transmit the general form of those schemas with no apparent reference to their complex cultural mediations. It is as if the music had been so saturated with romantic meanings that they have come to seem innate. For Tolstoy's narrator, Masha, as for the real-life purchasers of countless "light classical" recordings, the "Moonlight" Adagio naturally appears as the epitome of romantic mood music. Exemplary in every way, Masha is an "ordinary" person who, surprised by the course of her love story (which is nonetheless quite typical), becomes absorbed in the Adagio as a way of recognizing and understanding her own desires. In this context, the Adagio tends to shed its elegiac, renunciatory character in favor of a gathering expectancy, the sense of a still undeclared, perhaps still unrecognized love whose fulfillment may be imminent. Thus Masha's final performance seems virtually to conjure her husband Sergei out of thin air, as Liszt in Berlioz's anecdote conjures up the spirit of Beethoven for his intimate band of listeners in the dark.

A similar conjuration anchors the most literal of the "Moonlight" Sonata's biographical applications, Mary Alice Seymour's novelistic *Life and Letters of Louis Moreau Gottschalk* (1870), which uses the music—all three movements—as an explicit template for narrating Gottschalk's life. Despite what may now seem its mawkishness, this book is no mere curio.

Replete with traces of most of the "Moonlight" motifs met within this chapter, it is a relic of a once-flourishing musical culture.

Seymour finds the key to her subject's life in the exemplary coupling of love and transcendental idealism that she hears in the sonata, quite independent of any musical association between Beethoven and Gottschalk. The linkage initially manifests itself, as usual, in the Adagio: the sonata, "full of life's saddest yet richest experience, preluded by [an] *adagio* of passionate longing over love too pure for earth denied, aptly symbolizes the character and life" of the biographical subject, "whose sweet spirit and noble soul has now finished its work in the world."[25] The subject's death is essential here; the sonata figures the course of a life that is "finished" in the sense of "perfected," even though Gottschalk died prematurely.

Seymour's narrative scheme, coordinating Gottschalk's life story with the sonata as a whole, would seem to mandate a return of the Presto finale to the position of preeminence it had held briefly in 1801. That is not what happens. The "Presto" section of the book opens emblematically with a highly wrought episode centered around two performances of the Adagio. The scene is a nocturnal parlor, flickering with firelight but with its lamps unlit—shades, yet again, of Liszt's "blind" performance as recounted by Berlioz, which may well be a model here. A woman weeps at the keyboard with the sonata's score in front of her. A man enters. It is Gottschalk, who, after some intimate conversation, plays the Adagio for his companion, then segues into an improvised supplement of his own. When he finishes, he asks for light, mistakenly thinking that the music is over; after a few more moments of talk, he mysteriously leaves the room. In his absence, in an act clearly charged with diffuse eroticism, the woman plays the Adagio herself, making it "float in dreamful beauty beneath her touch." Her performance, the center of this central episode, unfurls through a long ekphrastic paragraph about the Adagio. The text begins by citing Berlioz, finds its centerpiece in the same treble-bass dialogue that so absorbed Marx ("the treble tells its passionate accents, but no human consolation can be accepted; and the deep, slow bass repeats this to the treble"), and culminates in the discovery (anticipating Behrend and Rolland) of self-sufficiency in the very strength of solitary suffering (121). As the final chord "vibrate[s]," the pianist is startled by a "deep sigh"; having overheard her finish, Gottschalk materializes behind her, as Sergei does to Masha in "Family Happiness" (another model?). More intimate talk follows, in the course of which the topics of love and marriage arise. Though these remain at the level of banter, they suggest that Gottschalk and the "beautiful pianiste" have formed a bond that symbolically reverses the loss of love mourned in the music.

The two have been have been united by their mutual absorption in the Adagio as both listeners and performers.

In the nineteenth century, the effect of the interpretive tradition shared by Seymour, Tolstoy, and the rest was to fill a serious gap in Beethoven's life and work. His reception during this era sought to establish Beethoven as the paradigmatic man and artist, through whom music itself could attain the status of the paradigmatic art. Schiller's prescription for ennobling music would be filled by interpreting Beethoven's genius as the vehicle through which music first expressed the inner laws of feeling in strict accord with musical form. To that end, a love story was needed, and one of a certain kind. It had to be a romantic story, which is to say that it had to be both idealized and "deeply" passionate. It also had to be a story compatible with the normal rituals and aspirations of bourgeois life. Tolstoy symbolizes this normality by ending "Family Happiness" with a beatification of the nuclear family core, a scene in which husband and wife unite through their mutual love and pleasure in their infant son. Mörike does the same thing in "To Wilhelm Hartlaub," which ends with the appearance of the beloved pianist's daughter. Finally, Beethoven's love story had to be unhappy, and not just for factual reasons. Beethoven was to support the ideology of domestic happiness from the outside looking in, precisely by means of the "artist's fate" that had denied him that happiness. Seymour's characters both share that fate and "transcend" it through the music that embodies it.

The Adagio of the "Moonlight" Sonata seems tailor-made to meet these requirements in musical terms. Its pathetically sublime character and investment by the aura of Giulietta Guicciardi as Immortal Beloved provide the element of romance, while its affinity with an intimate scene that could be set at the domestic piano—the darkened room, the palpable atmosphere, the charged proximity of player and listener—helps identify that romance as bourgeois. More importantly, the Adagio helps identify bourgeois life as romantic, helps to counteract the potentially stultifying respectability of the drawing room and to establish conventional courtship as a locus of profound feeling and erotic intensity. At the end of "Family Happiness," the "Moonlight" Adagio is the explicit stimulus for the searingly honest conversation between husband and wife that restores their love in a new form and saves their marriage. This music is, or becomes, a device to lend bourgeois subjectivity the risk and enchantment that its own values tend to strip from it. At bottom, the cultural work of the "Moonlight" Sonata was to make even domesticity sublime.

One aspect of this domestic sublimity is particularly noteworthy in connection with Michel Foucault's claim that the nineteenth century's extensive discourse on sexuality was the means by which the middle class gave itself a distinctive body, "a 'class' body with its [own] health, hygiene, descent, and race." According to Foucault, the discourse of sexuality mapped this body in terms of pathology, the infinite possibilities of which had to be exhaustively inventoried. Desire was literally unthinkable apart from deviance, or, to be more exact, became thinkable precisely in relation to the concept of deviance. "The potential pathology of sex, the urgent need to keep it under close watch and devise a rational technology of correction" became both the source of the bourgeois body's identity and the measure of its value. "With this investment of its own sex by a technology of power and knowledge which it itself had invented, the bourgeoisie underscored the high political price of its body, sensations, and pleasures, its well-being and survival."[26] But the pianistic romance, perhaps aided by the edifying mystique of Beethoven and the purity associated with Mozart, casts the sexuality that it articulates in a decidedly nonpathologized form, even in the neighborhood of warm same-sex feeling. The domestic piano overtly embodies a technology of power and knowledge, social as much as musical, social in being musical, but it is the instrument, in every sense, through which these things are supposed to become wholly benign. The story is different in what might be called the virtuoso public sphere, where the piano served to organize displays of social and sexual excess (see chap. 4). Tolstoy would eventually recognize that the piano could do the same thing at home, as he showed in "The Kreutzer Sonata" (1889), the story of how a bourgeois husband mistakes metaphor for reality and murders his wife because she plays duets too well. In "Family Happiness," however, the domestic piano is still the symbol of a sexuality without discord.[27]

It is in this context that Tolstoy can offer the pianistic romance of the "Moonlight" Adagio as the very antipode to a socially engineered sexual pathology. "Family Happiness" has a circular three-part structure. The first and third parts are set in the seclusion of the countryside; the first covers the idyll of Masha's courtship and early married life, the third the recovery of her marriage from its almost fatal crisis and the beginning of a new kind of idyll. All of the scenes of pianistic romance occur in these sections. The second part is set amid the sociability of the city; it traces the decay of the marriage under corrupting social influences, culminating in a near-affair between Masha and an Italian marquis. This structure, as it happens, is fully encapsulated near the beginning of the story by the scene in which Masha, at Sergei's request, first plays the "Moonlight" Adagio for him.

When she finishes, she begins the second movement, but Sergei stops her, saying "No, you don't play that right; don't go on; but the first movement was not bad." In view of later events, this impulse to stay with the Adagio, to prohibit going on, is less concerned with musical skill than with musical meaning: what Sergei wants to fend off is the sophisticated, sociable attitude embodied by the middle movement, which is a sort of minuet thrown off-kilter by repeated bouts of syncopation.

At the level of the larger plot, Masha eventually discovers that she in fact doesn't play the social game right, and doesn't want to. Only when she can herself decide not to go on with it can she rescue her failing marriage. When, after returning to the country, she decides to "go on" from the "Moonlight" Adagio only by playing it again, the gesture indicates that she has not only come home, but also come back to her true self, which lives in and through the world of the Adagio. At this point, too, the music widely heard as elegiac becomes idyllic, fulfilling its initial role in the story at a "higher" level. Tolstoy marks this fulfillment by describing the musical moment in lyrical detail, which he had not done earlier, as if it were only in combination with Masha's subjective advance that the Adagio became truly audible. This transformation of the music's character, however, does not break completely with the elegiac mode. The musical idyll is dialectical: for the newly matured Masha, the Adagio embodies both the loss of her first, romantic love and the advent of its replacement by a richer family happiness. More exactly, the Adagio both symbolizes and in part effects the transformation of one state of mind into the other: a Hegelian *Aufhebung* of romantic by familial, erotic by social love.

Although the "Moonlight" Sonata, and pianistic romance more generally, takes up only a little space in a long story, "Family Happiness" can plausibly be described as a virtual mixed-media work. The sonata's role is doubly marked and weighted: the music both symbolizes the story's structure and actually demarcates that structure. At one level, the meaning of the story simply is that of the sonata; you can't fully grasp the one unless you hear the other. The fact that the story's "Moonlight" Sonata exists only in truncated form is also telling, also significant for both what is heard and what isn't. The story even suggests that it is the capacity of the Adagio, and music like it, to mediate the protagonists' feelings for each other that lifts domestic piano playing beyond the commonplace realm of feminine accomplishment—something that Masha worries about on first playing for Sergei. The "Moonlight" Adagio typifies the realm of accomplishment but at the same time promises or threatens to break out of it. By becoming a tacit form of dialogue between lovers or partners, the music endows them with its own exemplary significance.

With "Family Happiness," Tolstoy both reflects and assists the nineteenth century's construction of the "Moonlight" Adagio as a model of identity-defining sexual love, whether incipient, lost, or dialectically regained. But in doing so, did Tolstoy, and did the era, discover something about the sonata's meaning or merely use the sonata to invent a meaning where one was needed? Inevitable though it is, this question is poorly posed. As I noted earlier, the sonata could not have determined all the meanings applied to it, but at the same time not just any sonata could have borne those particular meanings. I would suggest that this semantic gap is in principle unbridgeable. Any work of music, any object of interpretation generally, assumes some of its meanings in retrospect. There is a continual negotiation between meanings proposed by and for the object, and on historical grounds, that is, on the basis of the way people actually behave when meaning is at stake, it seems fair to say that the meanings proposed for the object always exceed those proposed by it. What needs to be asked of the "Moonlight" Sonata, therefore, is what it may have contributed to the process of its becoming as meaningful as it did. What is it about this music that encourages or at least conforms itself to the kinds of ascription it has received?

Each of the five elements of reception discussed earlier leads to a different answer. Let me conclude by taking them up in order.

The Front-weighting. The valorization of the "Moonlight" Adagio seems linked to the almost universal perception from the *AMZ* reviewer to Rolland that the music expresses the deepest emotions of the soul. The key term here is not emotion, but depth; something about this movement seems to have anointed it as the very voice of interiority. One way to ground this quality is in the movement's distinctive texture (see ex. 2.1). The Adagio can be described as a slowly evolving interplay between the treble and bass voices continuously mediated by middle-voice arpeggios. The texture is close. Except in the coda and a quasi-developmental passage in the middle, the arpeggios murmur within a narrow registral band that is continuous with the upper voice and supported on the overtones of the deep-set bass. The weave is so tight that the treble-bass interplay never assumes the external, dramatic form of dialogue; it is more like an internal monologue, an internalization of the dialogic principle. As the music ripples from bass to treble in a single unbroken motion, smoothly connecting the voices but leaving them distinct, the sonority becomes the imaginary space of an exemplary introspection. The fact that this texture never changes, except to unfurl the arpeggios briefly across a wider registral expanse, supports the impression of a singular, self-contained whole, an impression that both reflects and helps construct the character ascribed to the deeply feeling self.

This assumption of interiority by the Adagio, however, does not wholly explain either the finale's relative loss of stature or the post-*AMZ* lack of interest in the organic relationship between the two movements. A second look at the arpeggios may offer some help on these points. The first theme of the finale can be heard as an accelerated and energized form of the arpeggios that saturate the Adagio, or as a collapse of the Adagio's principal texture into its own contrastive moment. The finale theme boils up from bass to treble in a continuous surge of arpeggios. But the finale is a sonata form, which takes this arpeggiated theme as only one element in a larger synthesis, a gesture that its allusion to the Adagio repeats over the course of the whole sonata. This synthesizing impulse is consistent both with Beethoven's other work circa 1801 and with early Romantic aesthetics generally. It is not consistent, though, with the aesthetic of the Adagio, a character piece based on uniformity, not synthesis. It seems likely that Beethoven wanted to pose the problem of how to reconcile this aesthetic with that of sonata form; the subtitle "Sonata quasi una fantasia" says as much. But if, as seems to have happened, the character piece appears as exceptional rather than merely distinctive in its uniformity, as singular rather than normative, the result may be a problem without a solution: an aporia. For those who heard the Adagio as an exemplary whole, it may have been a step backward to hear it again as a mere part. At the level of cultural meaning, the tendency to isolate the Adagio betokens an impulse to preserve the nocturnal-romantic world it evokes as an unconditional imaginary space within bourgeois culture and identity.

The Shades of Night. William Behrend, after routinely dismissing the "Moonlight" label, admits that there is something inescapably nocturnal about the Adagio; I suggested a few possible reasons for this earlier. Another one may stem from a further aspect of the all-important arpeggios, which to Marx and perhaps to others suggested a lute or guitar, the instrument of a disappointed lover's imaginary serenade. Czerny's nocturnal image of a distant lamenting voice fits this suggestion as well. The pianistic reveries focused on the Adagio may indicate the relocation of the serenade in modern life, its migration to both the domestic hearth and the interior of the self. The piano serves as a kind of gateway to the interior amid the literal and figurative furniture of the middle-class household. (As an object, of course, the piano itself is the housing for a large sounding interior, some-

Example 2.1. Beethoven, Adagio from "Moonlight" Sonata, mm. 10–19

times displayed as the mysterious recess under the open lid: interior decoration.) This role is heightened in proximity to the normative scenarios of romance that support and support themselves on that furniture, including both the romance of marriage and the romance of the Friend.

The Hand of Eros. The particular pianistic quality of the "Moonlight" Adagio is readily conformable to those romances. The tempo indication of the movement is Adagio sostenuto, but Beethoven wants the sostenuto to be of a special kind. He adds a headnote stating that the Adagio must be played throughout with the greatest delicacy and "without dampers," that is, with the pedal in continuous use. (Performers on modern pianos cannot take this instruction literally, but the spirit is clear: sustain with the pedal.) The result is to foreground the sensibility of the performer's body, its receptiveness to the slightest sensation. The instruction combines delicacy, which must be produced by touch, with the continuity of sound produced by piano technology. The player's body becomes perceptible as the medium, a kind of rising channel from foot (or, with a fortepiano, knee) to hand, in which mechanically produced sound becomes feeling. To give this process both a tactile and a visual focal point, Beethoven sets the upper and middle voices within the compass of a ninth in the right hand, so that they emerge continuously from a kind of intimate, delicate touch. The hand moves in fluid, rhythmic strokes as if it were caressing the keys. It is at least possible that this way of engaging the body links the Adagio with the expressivity of the lover's serenade, and more generally with the sensitivity of the romantic body. The pianistic effects involved would have been reasonably apparent in an era that knew the music as much, if not more, by playing as by hearing it.

A related possibility is that the pianism of the Adagio produces an image of profound absorption both for the player and for an intimate observer; the absorption takes in both body and spirit and easily shades into both reverie and its more libidinal neighbor, fantasy. The meditative pace of the music, marked out by the solemn long notes of the bass, sets the scene. For most of the piece, the arpeggios and the upper-voice melody move within the compass of a right hand that itself moves only slightly when it moves at all. This hand hovers; the other drifts. When the right hand becomes more active in the central contrastive episode, the bass becomes perfectly still, a long twelve bars of dominant pedal. (The coda redoubles this stasis, fusing the pedal tone with the head of the main theme.) In intimate surroundings, the resulting display of stillness, concentration, and bodily expressivity becomes an invitation to a still deeper intimacy. Absent the surroundings, enough of the effect remains audible—in the hypnotic repetition of the arpeggios, the hovering within a narrow, crepuscular tessitura—to engage the romantic fantasy of a listener so disposed.

Love's Labour Lost. Given the dedication to Giulietta Guicciardi, the sustained minor-key mood of the Adagio, and the turbulence of the finale, the application of "Beethoven's love story" to the "Moonlight" Sonata was a foregone conclusion. The degree to which the application pervaded the sonata's reception, however, was not. Something in the music seemed to demand a story. With Beethoven, something often did. The culprit in this case was probably simple emotional extravagance, which needed a rationale if the sonata's status as a normative, canonical, even popular work was to be justified. What one French critic called its "desolate sadness" and "somber and terrible declamations" were more socially tractable when grounded as the utterances of "Juliette Guicciardi's unfortunate admirer."[28] Marx's interpretation of the Adagio helps to suggest a specific musical prompt for this process. Like most minor-key movements of its era, the Adagio moves to the relative major as a secondary key: in Marx's words "the consolingly bright E major." But this key "must immediately becloud itself to minor," something that happens after only a single bar; the "fervid" C#-minor mood infects the gesture of consolation and the stabilizing major-minor contrast is nipped in the bud. (Its ghost does return later in the movement, but too briefly to matter.) As a result, the whole course of the Adagio can be heard as imbued with a sense of obsessive brooding, as if the feelings expressed were fixated on a single object, presumably a lost one. The Giulietta story served at once to make sense of this effect, to normalize it, and to authenticate it as an expression of biographical truth.

Love's Labour Won. Other stories, however, could do similar things, as the one told by Tolstoy illustrates. If it did not prove difficult to shift the interpretive accent of the Adagio from romantic loss to romantic longing, the reason may lie partly in the ambivalence of the concepts themselves, which tend to overlap in the way they idealize their objects. As Roland Barthes has suggested, in romantic love (which he dates from Goethe's *Werther*) the image of the beloved is always more important than the person, and the two can be mourned or desired separately.[29] When Masha plays the "Moonlight" Adagio twice in succession at the end of "Family Happiness," the first performance is to mourn the image, the second to seek the person. The first bids farewell to a lost love in the music's "solemn sadness"; the second seeks a love restored in the music's fusion with inner invocatory speech: "'Restore to me all that blossomed in my heart, or teach me what to do and how to live now'" (74). Ambivalence of this sort probably needs no specific location in the music, but it is still tempting to conjecture one. The famous head of the Adagio melody, a dotted pickup and downbeat on one repeated note, is consistent with the air of not-letting-go that can seem to permeate the movement. But every time this melodic signature is heard, the movement from upbeat to downbeat brings a change of harmony. The romantic image continually metamorphoses, perhaps to declare its unyielding elusiveness, but perhaps with equal likelihood to suggest its capacity for renewal. It all depends on who's listening.

The vicissitudes of this kernel of melody effectively frame the Adagio and can stand as a parable of the sonata's semantic history. That history has not yet exhausted itself, if the continued use and marketing of the movement as romantic mood music is any indication, but it is hard not to suspect that a change is in the wind. How will the "Moonlight" Sonata metamorphose at the turn of its third century when the social and sexual ethos that supported it for so long is at best no more than a nostalgic fantasy?

Clues to an answer may come from another marketing ploy, the inclusion of the Adagio in recordings promising tranquility. In London recently, listening to Classic FM in my hotel room, I heard an ad for "Relax More," a triple CD produced by the radio station on the basis of its well-worn but apparently successful motif that classical music relaxes you. The ad (one of a series) ended with the "Moonlight" Adagio. How does one get from the erotic anguish and fervor of nineteenth-century hearings to high-toned relaxation at the start of the twenty-first? The question might also be posed apropos an American television commercial for a sleep-inducing medicine named "Sonata," which also uses the Adagio as its underscore. In one sense these usages represent no transformation at all: the music still conveys a certain middle-class ideal, or ideal image of middle-class life. It is just that now the ideal is stripped of fervor or intensity. In the context of the default musics of the present day, it may be that classical music is "relaxing" for the simple reason that it has no rhythm track; its pulse is always already idealized. In this context the arpeggios that thread the Adagio take on a new significance, dispersing the rhythmic impulse into an undulation perceived as more languid than insistent, more berceuse- than serenade-like. But *plus ça change:* in a world where middle-class heterosexuality has lost its transgressive power and much of its symbolic capital (though not, perhaps, its actual social capital), doesn't the romantic Adagio survive by suggesting the mood in which ordinary love can become extraordinary serenity, immune from a hectic, overwired, and overworked daily existence?

3
Beyond Words and Music
An Essay on Songfulness

In George Eliot's last novel, *Daniel Deronda* (1876), the hero prevents a young woman from drowning herself in the Thames. The next day, telling her story to the mother of a family with whom he has placed her, this woman, Mirah, a Jewish runaway who embodies the condition of diasporic wandering, recalls her own mother. Her recollection centers on hearing her mother sing. The musical memory grounds her sense of self by symbolically both condensing and perpetuating her entire experience of maternal love:

> I think my life began with waking up and loving my mother's face: it was so near to me, and her arms were round me, and she sang to me. One hymn she sang so often, so often: and then she taught me to sing it with her: it was the first I ever sang. They were always Hebrew hymns she sang; and because I never knew the meaning of the words they seemed full of nothing but our love and happiness. When I lay in my little bed and it was all white above me, she used to bend over me between me and the white, and sing in a sweet low voice.[1]

The mother's song marks, as its memory recapitulates, the moment in which life first assumes meaningful form. Victorian psychology tended to think of infantile consciousness as a *tabula rasa*. Here that empty space, the blank page or canvas symbolized by the "all white" above the child, becomes the ground on which the human face and voice make their first appearance and in so doing individuate the child by separating her from the void of whiteness.[2] In recognizing the face and voice of the mother, and in particular of the mother who sings, the child becomes a human subject. Paradoxically, however, this abundant provision of meaningfulness depends for its effect on a lack of meaning. The child understands the song—correctly—as full of love and happiness only because she does not understand the song at all. That understanding, or so other details in the novel suggest, would have brought a consciousness only of the exilic suffering of the Jews, which is here, in the songful lack of understanding, proleptically if only fantasmatically redeemed.[3]

I think it is fair to say that what Eliot records here, with uncommon precision, is a common experience. Isn't it true that most of us can recall, and on the basis of that recollection keenly anticipate, occasions on which song became deeply moving, not as an expressive fusion of text and music, but as a manifestation of the singing voice, just the voice, regardless of what it sang? The text on these occasions doesn't matter—is even better if unknown; song here works not by what it signifies, but by the material presence of its signifiers, which address the listener with an unusual, richly gratifying intimacy. That intimacy often seems to suggest the young child's envelopment by the face or voice of the mother, which, according to Lacanian psychoanalysis, forms an "acoustic mirror" of pleasure and identity.[4] (In theory, the maternal suggestion would be carried even if the songful voice were a man's, which may be one reason for the special charisma, each to its era, of the tenor and castrato voices. The voice of male authority and of its comic and villainous inversions is low, but that of male songfulness is high, overlapping the maternal continuum.) Often, too, this suggestion is accompanied by a formula for the voice that Eliot borrows from a famous lullaby by Alfred Tennyson: sweet and low. From this nucleus, however, vocal effects of every description, some of them extreme, may branch out independent of the role of song as enunciation. One particularly telling, because self-consciously programmatic, example can be found near the very origins of modern expressive song in the two-voice madrigal "Zefiro torna" by Monteverdi (1632), which ends with measure upon multiple measure of melismatic undulation on the word "canto": I sing.

The experience of song as enveloping voice has not, by and large, entered into theorizations of word-music relationships, which tend to assume intelligible utterance as the sine qua non of song, at least in principle. Broadly speaking, such theorizations have tended to center on either the musical expression of textual affect or meaning, the musical transformation (from assimilation to appropriation to deconstruction) of textual affect or meaning, or the relative independence of musical structure and expression from those of the text. The first type conceives of song as a special mode of utterance, the second as what Steven Paul Scher calls "composed reading," and the third as a vehicle of essentially musical expressivity in which the text serves as a supplement or point of departure.[5] One need not endorse all of these conceptions equally to feel that the assumption they share is not misguided. In most traditions, it is precisely the assumption that song is enunciation that makes song as vocalization, song as withdrawal of meaning, significant. For that very reason, however, enunciated song must continually posit the possibility of its interruption by or transformation into vocalized song. It is this possibility, constitutive of the very category of song, that has not been given its theoretical due. In what follows, I would like to take a step toward remedying this lack. My small initiative will involve a single paradigmatic song and a vocal quality that is perhaps too vague and too familiar to have attracted much study. The song is Schubert's "Heidenröslein"; the vocal quality is what, suggestively enough, is called "songfulness."

Songfulness is a fusion of vocal and musical utterance judged to be both pleasurable and suitable independent of verbal content. It is the positive quality of singing-in-itself: just singing. This description deliberately avoids listing any objectively defining features. Songfulness is one of those aesthetic qualities that seem to invite immediate recognition even while they elude definition; its indefinability is part of its character. The one who hears it may not be able to account for it, or to say for sure whether it is more an attribute of the music (which seems made for the voice) or of the performance (which saturates the music with voice), or even of the ear that hears it, but the quality nonetheless seems utterly unmistakable. There is thus, once again, a sense of immediate intimate contact between the listener and the subject behind the voice.

This contact is both an aesthetic relationship (that is, an embodied fiction) and, perhaps, an indication of the specific fantasy-structure that underlies the experience of songfulness. George Eliot's Mirah is very suggestive on this point. Her experience as the subject-listener to a primal songfulness is that of being exactly what the mother, the first Other, desires her to be. The mother renders the daughter blissful by enjoying her, taking her as the occasion of bliss; the mother continually draws close to the daughter to deliver the gift of song, which typically goes together with a loving embrace. According to Lacan, this condition of being what the mother desires, being the desire of the Other, is the very condition that structures the desire of the subject, not least by being a condition that is never in fact attainable.[6] On the evidence of Mirah's, or Eliot's, account, and of others like it, one way to understand songfulness is as the medium or support for the fantasy of attaining this unattainable bliss. In any particular case, however, this charge of fantasy may be deeply implicit, the tacit support for any number of aesthetic or expressive effects. (For those skeptical of the fantasy, the other effects may, of course, seem to stand on their own.)

Another perspective on songfulness can be gained by considering the difference between instrumental and vocal realizations of the same melody. Even without a text, the addition of voice to a melody activates a set of human relationships that an instrumental performance can only signify. As the medium of meaningful utterance, voice brings the music into a space of potential or virtual meaning even when actual meaning is left hanging; as the medium of social relationship, voice involves the listener in a potential or virtual intersubjectivity that in some circumstances may be realized in the course of song; and as a corporeal medium, voice addresses itself in its sensuous and vibratory fullness to the body of the listener, thereby offering both material pleasure and an incitement to fantasy. These effects all depend on the ability of the singing voice to envelop or suffuse both melody and text so that their independent existence is obscured. One way to define songfulness is as the condensation of this process into a quality, the conversion of the absence of textual and melodic distinctness into a positive presence. For this to happen, it may be said that the voice must be neither too "grainy" nor too brilliant. In other words, the voice must on the one hand not show too much of what Roland Barthes calls the "grain" that testifies to the singer's material uniqueness.[7] The intersubjective bond is strongest when the voice is more medium than object; Mirah does not remember her mother's voice as a timbre but as a source of intimacy. On the other hand, the voice must not display, or be required by the music to display, too much technical proficiency, which would presuppose a distanced relationship between the voice, the notes, and the text. Songfulness arises, but not reliably or predictably, in the ill-defined space between these prohibitions.[8]

Being so protean, songfulness seems not only to elude but also to resist critical or analytical understanding. Such resistance may even be one of its purposes. How, then, can we counter the resistance and address songfulness concretely? One way might be to focus on a song that by common consent both "contains" and promotes a high degree of songfulness—which leads us to our Schubertian example.

"Heidenröslein" (Little Heath-rose) was composed in 1815 to the following text by Goethe:

> Sah ein Knab' ein Röslein stehn,
> Röslein auf der Heiden,
> War so jung und morgenschön,
> Lief er schnell, es nah zu sehn,
> Sah's mit vielen Freuden.

Röslein, Röslein, Röslein rot,
Röslein auf der Heiden.

Knabe sprach: Ich breche dich,
Röslein auf der Heiden!
Röslein sprach: Ich steche dich,
Dass du ewig denkst an mich,
Und ich will's nicht leiden.
Röslein, Röslein, Röslein rot,
Röslein auf der Heiden.

Und der Wilde Knabe brach
's Röslein auf der Heiden;
Röslein wehrte sich und stach,
Half ihr doch kein Weh und Ach,
Musst' es eben leiden.
Röslein, Röslein, Röslein rot,
Röslein auf der Heiden.[9]

The poem tells a simple story, but no one would be so simple as to think it's about a flower. Obviously, it's about a girl being *de*flowered. From her point of view (which is represented in the text), the poem narrates a trauma; but neither the boy (brushing off his wounding by the thorn—no little rose can castrate him!) nor the narrator takes this trauma very seriously, and neither, it seems, does Schubert. His song is a lighthearted lyric, seemingly more concerned with the pastoral atmosphere than with the narrative action, more interested in the sonoric pleasures of repeating the word "Röslein" than in what happens to the little rose. On each of its three occurrences, Goethe's couplet refrain, the "musical" element in the poem itself, becomes the song's center of attention. A fermata sets the stage; the first line ("Röslein, Röslein, Röslein rot") draws itself out across a two-bar ritard; a second fermata turns the slowdown to a standstill as the line ends; and the second line ("Röslein auf der Heiden") breaks the stasis with a lilting two-bar statement in tempo (see ex. 3.1). In this passage the idyllic connotations of the word "Röslein" merge into the verbal and vocal "music" of its repetitions, producing an effect of pure songfulness that all but effaces the narrative line. No doubt it would be going too far to say that the effect approximates that of Gertrude Stein's circular "rose is a rose is a rose is a," but the fit is closer than one might have imagined. Songfulness such as this is uncontainable; it circulates throughout the whole song, which is carefully composed to support its circulation.

At one level, Schubert's compositional technique in "Heidenröslein"

Example 3.1. Schubert, *Heidenröslein* (complete)

Example 3.1. (continued)

affirms the song's generic form over its narrative content. The affirmation serves an ideological purpose, though not necessarily an invidious one: the song acts socially by inviting appreciation from the like-minded, not by making a statement—or, more exactly, it acts by not making a statement. The song becomes meaningful when it is recognized as an ideal instance of a familiar type, a recognition localized in the effect of songfulness. When the songfulness of the singer realizes or enhances that of the song, the result is an aesthetic pleasure that concretizes a social relationship. And because that pleasure is localized in the singing voice, listeners need not understand what is being said or pay much attention to it if they do.

Thus with "Heidenröslein" in particular: this song is a textbook example of a type very familiar to Schubert and his contemporaries, a refined form of the *volkstümliches Lied* ("popular song").[10] It is art music that is meant to sound like folk music, more or less the equivalent in song of the written-down versions of traditional fairy tales put together by the Brothers Grimm. In the generation or two preceding Schubert's, composers of German song turned to this *Volkston* ("folk tone") in order to embody an idealized unity of language and culture. By 1815, the type was beginning to acquire an overlay of nostalgia—Schubert's career as a songwriter both presumed and produced it as a dated form—but it was still, and would remain for some time, quite viable as a means of producing a sense of idealized community. The singer in this style addresses the listener in terms that evoke and confirm the purity, authenticity, and simplicity of the cultural identity they share.

If we want to understand "Heidenröslein" in the terms it suggests for itself, as a work of art that subsumes its content under a higher form and thus transcends its "surface" story of sexual predation, there is a well-established way to proceed. First, we indicate how the song's form and style conform to its genre, as we have already done; if the song is genuinely artful, something about the manner of its conformation will seem especially suitable. Second, we put the artistic results into context. In this case, we might suggest that the folk tone reflects an early Romantic preference for naturalness and spontaneity over refinement and artifice. (This formulation deliberately picks an aesthetic rather than an overtly social or political context; it is meant to reflect the way songs have typically been talked about.) Finally, we consider the song's artistry and context in relation to the details of structure and expression. In this case we would observe that the song is direct and simple in feeling; that it is in strict strophic form; that the piano accompaniment is unassuming; and that the vocal line is both grateful and catchy, a perfect gift to amateur vocalists. Everything conduces to songfulness. Sing it right, and the song will seem to sing itself.

Going a little deeper, we might also observe that the quality of songfulness in "Heidenröslein" is more than just a stylistic trait. The overall design of the song has the effect of dramatizing, while it also produces, the subordination of narrative to singing. Needless to say, given the song's genre, this design is transparently simple. It consists of a series of two-bar phrases grouped to form three sections: four bars, then six, then four again, followed by a two-bar postlude. Although the third section does not repeat the first, there is enough affinity between them to create the feeling of an A B A' format. In particular the first section ends and the third begins with lyrical phrases ("Röslein auf der Heiden" and "Röslein, Röslein, Röslein rot" respectively) set to identical harmonies and to a scalar melody that the voice leaves gapped in the first section and fills out in the third.

These outer sections both turn in self-contained lyric circles defined by the recurrence of tonic harmony. The first section introduces and prolongs the tonic (phrase 1), then cadences to it from the dominant (phrase 2); the third section reiterates the V-I cadence (phrase 1), then adds another one starting from the subdominant (phrase 2), a gesture repeated in the little postlude. Given the virtual identity of the interior cadences in this pattern, the overall effect is to suggest that the lyric stasis of each constituent phrase is mirrored and raised to a higher order in the symmetry of the whole. The suggestion is redoubled when the second section of the song is taken into account. This middle section is where the bulk of the poem's narrative is enunciated—resumed, in fact, after the first section has interrupted it for lyrical reflection on "Röslein auf der Heiden." In keeping with its narrative impetus, the section is all dynamism; it consists of an extended cadence to the dominant, an action initiated in its second bar and completed in its sixth. If the outer sections are all suspension, this one is all suspense. But its suspense is tightly contained, reduced to a mere interpolation between the identical V-I phrases of the outer sections and the larger lyrical symmetry that they support. Repeated strophically, the design of the song consists precisely of enacting this containment three times over. As a counterplot to the narrative of the text, the song "narrates" the ascent of its own songfulness.

Further details could be explored at finer levels of technique, but in essence they would do no more than fill out the picture—in this case a picture of "Heidenröslein" as a little gem of a song, the value of which lies in this very littleness and in the seemingly artless and naive songfulness that it makes possible. (That the artlessness is only seeming would not be ironic, except perhaps in a highly refined Schlegelian sense; the song conforms to the traditional topos of the art that hides art.)[11] The only thing left out of the picture would be any serious reference to the narrative, or, in other words, to what the text, and therefore the song, might mean. As already noted, this exclusion is built right into the musical design, which in large part coincides with the process by which the song's intelligibility as enunciation becomes inessential to its effect. Meaning would figure, if it figured at all, only as a pretext for the song's expression of feeling, which in this case is keyed not to action but to atmosphere. And even that expression of feeling would tend to be subsumed under the more inclusive and fantasy-laden effect of songfulness.

The exclusion of meaning lies at the root of this process. It frees the music from the limitations of mundane circumstances and transfers emphasis to the unqualified, decontextualized sound of the singing voice. It might be said to convert the imaginary space unoccupied by meaning into the site of unfettered fantasy. But what if the exclusion left a listener dissatisfied, uncomfortable with the virtual dismissal of narrative meaning, or of meaning in general? (The fantasy does, after all, point to the unattainable.) What if even the song itself intimated a similar dissatisfaction? Might there be something about the song that doesn't fit what we think we know about it so far—not necessarily something obtrusive, but something one might notice without even being aware of doing so?

In answer we might observe that this song has a single high note, one of several high Gs, that would give some amateur singers a bit of trouble. It is the longest note in the song, it is completely exposed, and it occurs at what is expressively the song's very heart, where the singer slows down to linger over the phrase "Röslein rot." The note is also supposed to be sung very softly, which makes it all the harder. The problem is not that the note threatens to be unsingable—the high G is of course at the upper limit of the normal range; it does not present a glaring difficulty—but that an amateur singer might have trouble making it sound smooth, pure, and natural. The note would put such a singer under a slight strain, and the strain would be audible, even if only slightly.

It turns out, then, that the folk tone of "Heidenröslein" has a catch in it, almost literally a catch in the throat. Furthermore, it is clear that this catch has been strategically planted, although whether Schubert planted it by design or simply welcomed it when it came along is impossible to determine. Either way, the sensitive high note does not fit quite comfortably into the folk tone, and its presence, or more exactly its role, is a small puzzle. This is not just any note, but the note on which the song's whole effect pivots, the very acme of songfulness. It might even be said to form the climax of a series of increasingly prominent high Gs marking formal turning-points: a little yelp at "Heiden" (m. 4), an irrepressible-seeming cry at "Freuden" (m. 8, changed to the antithetical "leiden" after the first strophe), and then the long-breathed tone completing the key phrase "Röslein rot" (m. 10). Why, in a song that otherwise keeps to the voice's comfortable middle range, focus so intently on this one high G?

To suggest an answer, we might begin by looking more closely—that is, listening more keenly—to the effect that the note has on the folk tone. Obviously the effect is not to abolish the prevailing folksong atmosphere, but to put it under a certain pressure, almost to put it in quotation marks. When we hear the high note, we can hear the demands of art music imposing themselves in the carefree realm of folk music. Thanks to the high note, the folk tone becomes self-conscious. The song no longer glides blithely across an acknowledged but tacit gap between the appearance of spontaneous artlessness and the reality of sophisticated art, but instead lets the gap resonate. The pretense of naivete evolves in such a way that the pretense itself can become audible. That, perhaps, is why the crucial note is no mere vocal fillip, but the endpoint of a carefully wrought yet unobtrusive series of high Gs. As the series unfolds, the qualities of naturalness, spontaneity, and naivete begin to unveil themselves as the elements of a collective fantasy. In each strophe the completion of the series brings the fantasy to the brink of disenchantment, then renews it with the lilting postlude.

In the terms of Schiller's famous dichotomy, with a touch of Derrida added, the song thus shuttles undecidably between the naive and the sentimental. The irony that does not appear when we accept "Heidenröslein" as a little gem now begins to cast its shadow, even if only lightly. Heard sympathetically, the song might be said to express a touching nostalgia for the simple life, a life free of modern perplexities. The nostalgia even extends to the fantasy that supports it; no longer secure in the power to suspend disbelief, the fantasy proper begins to displace the world it evokes as the object of a certain social desire. Heard more skeptically, the song could be accused of trying to fool itself, and us, by its pretense of innocence; its charm is meretricious.

The ramifications of these alternatives are wider than they may seem, as an episode from the song's later reception may suggest. During World War II, Alfred Hitchcock made a movie called *Lifeboat* about the aftermath of a German submarine attack on a merchant ship. Clambering onto a lifeboat, the Allied survivors discover that the U-boat has also been sunk, and take what seems to be a workaday German sailor on board. With a subtle blend of seamanship and deception, the German, who is revealed in turn to be a surgeon, the U-boat's captain, and a Nazi, makes his rescuers his dependents and effectively takes control of their boat. At the height of his power, which includes the establishment of friendly feelings between himself and some of the others, he sits rowing at the prow and sings German songs. The first of these is mainly ironic, an index of his dominance; the third and last, lapsing under dialogue, mainly serves narrative continuity. The second stands apart—and the second is "Heidenröslein."

In this way the plot of the movie comes to pivot on Schubert's songfulness. Because all but one of the other characters don't understand its words, "Heidenröslein" marks its singer as alien. But because song per se does not, ideally speaking, need to be understood, the same song generates a sense of intimacy and community, even of romance. The truth of the matter could go either way, and in some sense goes both ways. For the time being, the song evokes a simpler, purer world than the war-torn world of the characters, but this nostalgia, in its very effectiveness, is really a way of warning the film spectators that things are not what they seem. Shortly afterward, the German captain commits a ruthless murder, for which he in turn is savagely killed by his shipmates. His singing of the medley with "Heidenröslein" turns out to have been a reminder of the way the Nazis gave their own peculiar twist to German culture's longing for a simpler, purer world. Yet the songs, in their songfulness, remain stubbornly and disconcertingly beautiful.

There is, of course, no direct path from Schubert to the Nazis, but there is an indirect one, and I suspect that the actor playing the German officer found it in this particular song. The actor was a real German, Walter Slezak, who was both a staunch anti-Nazi and the son of Leo Slezak, one of the great Wagnerian tenors of the early twentieth century. When Slezak sings "Heidenröslein" in character, in his own light lyric tenor (and with trouble on the high Gs), he symbolically reenacts the alienation of his own heritage to people like the man he plays. In so doing, he becomes the very embodiment of the danger inherent in all *volkstümlich* innocence, the danger that someone may try to translate the aesthetic effect of cultural purity into political or social reality.

That danger, meanwhile, is by no means foreign to Schubert's song. It's time now to remember Goethe's poem, the point of which is that girls like the little red rose have got to yield to the sexual insistence of boys, and that even if this involves a certain violence there is no use making a fuss about it. That's life. Schubert's song takes this cynical-worldly view and makes positive pleasure of it; the prevailing mood of the music, its warm, lilting lyricism, is responsive to the beauty of the rose but perfectly indifferent to her suffering. As it happens, this indifference falters only at one point, and it is the very point we have been discussing: the portion of the refrain where the voice slows down singing "Röslein, Röslein, Röslein rot" and completes the phrase on the lingering high G. The note freezes the musical action, as if the singer were feeling regret or compassion for the rose—but the moment passes, the song drops back into the folk tone, the pleasure of the boy's triumph resumes, and the pressure of narrative meaning is released. Songfulness prevails.

As I have suggested elsewhere, the degree to which the music of this passage makes restitution to the poem's narrative varies greatly with the performance of the singer, particularly with the handling of the ritard on the last of its three appearances.[12] Some encroachment of narrative force on pure vocal utterance is, nonetheless, assured. But the intricate dialectic of sense and non-sense, of the transparency of the poetic signified and the materiality of the vocal signifier, is not yet finished, even in so simple a song as this. (Songs love to exceed their apparent simplicity.) The high G is perfectly calibrated to sound pure, beautiful, and tranquil when sung well; it provides a moment at which the expressive artistry of the singer can fuse with the generic artistry of the song. At the very moment, then, that narrative restitution is activated, a contrary impetus reaffirms song as the occasion of a socially grounded intimacy between the singer and the listener in which meaning plays at best an auxiliary role.

This contradiction, like the others in "Heidenröslein," can be said to articulate with exceptional clarity a tension that belongs to song in general. Formally and generically, song is a form of meaningful utterance that varies between two modes of presentation: a vernacular mode, in which words and music seem to have a simple, simultaneous existence, and a cultivated mode, in which the music responds to the meaning of an independent, usually preexistent text. Formally and generically, song in either mode is motivated by what its words express, even if the music expresses something more or something else, and even if the music, considered apart from the words, has independent aesthetic interest. Kofi Agawu's challenging statement that the music of a song need have no relation to its text is right in principle but wrong in practice; at least since the Renaissance, solo song has defined itself as a means of expression tied to the words it enunciates.[13] Despite which, however, song harbors a powerful contrary tendency that can take the fore at any moment, either through the agency of a singer or by the invitation of a composer. The very techniques by which song becomes meaningful utterance often lead to at least a partial loss of meaning; songfulness makes meaning extraneous, if not downright superfluous.

Songfulness, it is important to add, is not the only source of this loss of meaning. It may, in fact, be considered the complement of what I have elsewhere called overvocalization, "the purposeful effacement of text by voice" associated with "emotional and metaphysical extremes, blurrings of ego boundaries, and [instability] of identity."[14] As technique, overvocalization is often the result of melisma or sustained vocalic tones, but the same is sometimes true of songfulness as well; the two modes of meaning loss cannot necessarily be distinguished on technical grounds. What separates them is a blend of purpose and circumstance. Overvocalization projects meaning loss as the outcome of a rupture, a wrenching of song beyond the symbolizing terrain of language and even of conception, and therefore beyond the type of regulated subjectivity mandated on that terrain by the laws of what

Lacan calls the symbolic order. Songfulness projects meaning loss as the outcome of a relative indifference to meaning, a kind of higher carelessness or forgetfulness that simply does not avail itself of the symbolic, allows the symbolic to lie unused even if its words may still be heard clearly. Songfulness does not exactly constitute a resistance to or escape from the symbolic, but an interlude of imperviousness to it. And whereas overvocalization is extraordinary, or at least a convention for signifying the extraordinary, songfulness is a condition that shows no need of the extraordinary; it is, in fact, the ideal ordinariness of song.

A quite different complementarity conjoins songfulness with incantation, a topic that will shortly round us back to George Eliot's *Daniel Deronda*. In some situations it is important that sung words be heard as highly meaningful whether or not their particular meaning is apprehended. What matters is that certain specific words be clearly enunciated in song; what the ear fastens on is not the content but the performance of the enunciation. Incantation in this sense is the parallel in song to what Mikhail Bakhtin calls "authoritative discourse":

> The authoritative word demands that we acknowledge it, that we make it our own; it binds us, quite independent of any power it may have to persuade us internally; we encounter it with its authority already fused to it. The authoritative word is located in a distanced zone, organically connected with a past that is felt to be hierarchically higher. It is, so to speak, the word of the fathers. Its authority was already *acknowledged* in the past. It is *a prior* discourse . . . . It is given (it sounds) in lofty spheres, not those of familiar contact. Its language is a special (as it were, hieratic) language. It can be profaned.[15]

The authoritative *(avtoritetnoe)* quality described here is hard to distinguish from the authoritarian, the sheerly dictatorial. The slippage is part of Bakhtin's point, the context for which is life in his homeland, Stalinist Russia. But to make the point, Bakhtin lets another one go unmade; his description fails (or declines) to recognize that the authoritative word may be both the object of desire and the source of rapture for those who receive it—which is not to say that the desire may not be suspect and the rapture dangerous. It is precisely this ecstatic side of authoritative discourse that is addressed by incantation. Authoritative song both embodies the ecstasy—the spiritual and/or libidinal dimension of the symbolic—and in the ideal case produces it in the listener.

Daniel Deronda, Mirah's future husband, discovers the ideal case when he goes to a service in a Leipzig synagogue. Raised as a Christian gentleman, Deronda has been born a Jew. His visit to the synagogue acts as one of a series of intimations of his "true" identity, which he does not know; the fulcrum of the experience is the incantation of the liturgy. The passage requires extended quotation:

> [Deronda knew] he was chiefly hearing Psalms and Old Testament passages or phrases, [but] gave himself up to that strongest effect of chanted liturgies which is independent of detailed verbal meaning—like the effect of an Allegri's *Miserere* or a Palestrina's *Magnificat*. The most powerful feeling with a liturgy is the prayer that seeks for nothing special, but is a yearning to escape from the limitations of our own weakness and an invocation of all Good to enter and abide with us . . . [a] yearning and [an] exultation gathering their force from the sense of communion in a form which has expressed them both, for long generations of fellow-men. . . . This evening all were one for Deronda: the chant of the *Chazan's* or Reader's grand wide-ranging voice with its passage from monotony to sudden cries, the outburst of the sweet boys' voices from the little quire, the devotional swaying of men's bodies backwards and forwards, the very commonness of the building and shabbiness of a scene where a national faith, which had penetrated the thinking of half the world, and moulded the splendid forms of that world's religion, was finding a remote, obscure echo: all were blent for him as one expression of a binding history, tragic and yet glorious. He wondered at the strength of his feeling; it seemed beyond the occasion—what one might imagine to be a divine influx. (416–17)

Eliot's description illustrates the power of incantation to give the authoritative word a tangible, rapture-inducing form. Incantation initiates Deronda into the bliss of the symbolic as songfulness initiated the infant Mirah into a bliss that precedes and surrounds the symbolic. (The gender differentiation in this contrast is, of course, a familiar symbolic effect with a story of its own.) But the experience also shows more. Through incantation, Deronda is prompted to receive with ecstasy an authoritative word, a whole symbolic tradition, of which he still knows little and to which he does not (to the best of his knowledge) belong. The power of incantation is not only one of inclusion, but one of election.

A good way to explain this seemingly autonomous power is to find it symptomatic of a fundamental relationship between voice and the symbolic. Slavoj Žižek has suggested that at some point in collective and personal memory, the symbolic, here represented as the Law, depends on a supplementation by voice: "It is only the *voice* that confers on the Law its performative dimension, that is, makes it operative: without this support in the senseless voice (voice *qua* object), Law would be a piece of powerless writing obliging no one."[16] Voice, on this account, becomes the animating link between principle and person by making it a link between person and person, an effect that persists subliminally no matter how impersonal the principle may elsewhere become. Experiences like Deronda's would suggest that incantation is a means for restoring and reaffirming this primordial link. Incantation induces ecstasy when the listener hears it as giving voice to the Law—and at the same time hears the voice giving itself expressly to him. The sense of personal address is a point of contact between incantation and songfulness, and of contrast to overvocalization, which tends to disrupt or abandon structures of address.

The experience of incantation is also one that reforges the link between the person and a historical community, which is one reason Eliot's presentation of it involves Judaic material. The autonomous power of incantation poses the threat of seizing the listener for the "wrong" community, as it does Deronda, whose Jewishness becomes powerfully emblematic in this context, Judaism being the traditional paradigm of the wrong community for Christian Europe. Eliot, a philosemite, takes Deronda's "wrong" but ultimately right absorption by the synagogue service as an ideal model for the general experience of incantational ecstasy, which, she suggests, always carries the listener to a beyond that ruptures as much as it affirms the symbolic. For that reason, she represents the song itself as beautiful, sensuously gratifying, and rhythmically absorbing, though she is also careful to establish a Christian parallel by invoking Allegri and Palestrina. To those, however, who resist Eliot's open form of rapture and demand a strict reinscription within the bounds of a known (or idealized) community, the wrong incantation will—must—seem ugly, offputting, even repellent. It is no wonder that Jewish cantillation, that "sense-and-sound confounding gurgle, yodel, and cackle," was a focal point for the revulsion of the most musical of antisemites among Eliot's contemporaries: Richard Wagner.[17]

The threads passing from Mirah's lullabies through Schubert's "Heiden-röslein" to Deronda's incantations can be taken to radiate from a single central point. Song, they would seem to suggest, characteristically positions a meaningful conjunction of words and music among multiple potential modes of meaning loss, including those not specified or even imagined here. From this, however, it by no means follows that meaning should take a lesser role in the understanding of song. On the contrary, it remains the very nucleus of song. But any understanding of song does need to take account of how and why meaning is so regularly cast off. Let me conclude as I began, with an illustrative anecdote—one that balances the imaginary suffering of George Eliot's Mirah with a suffering all too real. Not long ago, in a corridor of the New York City subway, a shabby figure leaned against the wall and sang to passersby for whatever coins they might choose to toss his way. What he sang, very badly, was an oldish and fatuously optimistic pop standard called "High Hopes." The contradiction between the song and the singer was both arresting and, if one paused to think about it, perplexing. What was this man doing? Was he suggesting that he had high hopes of getting charity from those who heard him? Was he showing that he had high hopes of getting straight despite the apparent hopelessness of his condition? Was he naively or ironically contrasting his own hopelessness to the high hopes of the song or of the more fortunate people who heard him sing? Or was he, after all, paying no attention to these questions and doing the only thing needed to make contact with a sympathetic stranger: just singing?

4
Franz Liszt and the
Virtuoso Public Sphere
Sight and Sound in the Rise of Mass Entertainment

From classical times through the eighteenth century, the power of Western music to move its listeners was generally personified by a singer. The archetype was most often Orpheus, coincidentally so for both the creators of Florentine opera and for Shakespeare, whose mythographic account is exemplary:

> The poet
> Did feign that Orpheus drew trees, stones, and floods,
> Since nought so stockish, hard and full of rage
> But music for the time doth change his nature.
>
> (*The Merchant of Venice*, V.i.79–82)

Charismatic singers of both sexes have kept the figure alive to the present day in both opera and popular song, helped out by both literature and film. During most of the nineteenth century, however, and part of the twentieth, the Orphean singer had both company and a rival in the person of the virtuoso pianist. The archetype was Franz Liszt, as legendary a figure in his own way as Orpheus—Hans Christian Andersen dubbed him "the Orpheus of our day" in 1840[1]—and one who is repeatedly described as enslaving, dominating, and overwhelming his audiences. "I have seen quiet Copenhageners," Andersen writes,

> with Danish autumnal coolness in their veins, become political bacchantes at his playing. The mathematician has grown giddy at the echoing fingers and the reckoning of the sounds. Young disciples of Hegel (and among those the really gifted and not merely the lightheaded) . . . perceived in [Liszt's] sea of music the wave-like advances of knowledge toward the shore of perfection.[2]

Even Johannes Brahms, who detested Liszt as a composer, conceded that

"Whoever has not heard Liszt really has nothing to say. Liszt came first. . . . His piano playing was something unique, incomparable, and inimitable."[3]

Liszt may not exactly have invented the virtuoso pianist, but he did define the model that subsequent virtuosos have been expected either to emulate or to reject. Surpassing his own model, Niccolò Paganini, Liszt seems to have been one of the first to realize how a star could be born from the marriage of technical wizardry and sexual magnetism. During his concert career in the 1830s and 1840s, he became the first performing musician to command the adoration of a mass public, and therefore to establish music as a popular entertainment medium—a problematical development, because many musicians, paradoxically including Liszt himself, were simultaneously trying to establish music as a fine art.

This last point introduces a quality that sets the Lisztian virtuoso sharply apart from the Orphean singer. The virtuoso is riddled with ambivalence. He can be identified equally well with the extremes of transcendental expressiveness and cheap, flashy display. Unlike the singer, he cannot choose between modesty and show (a key aesthetic issue in Liszt's day and earlier); he cannot, so to speak, be either Orpheus or a siren, but must always be both. Unlike the singer's, his instrument carries no metaphysical privilege; it is a machine that must be both manually operated and yet spiritualized.[4] Unlike the singer, whose instrument is invisible, the virtuoso must show what he does and thus so court the charge that showing is all he does. He thus becomes a magnet for the multiple ambivalences that have haunted the concept of appearance itself at least since Plato—in relation to the body, theatricality, deception, rhetoric, and the like. Thus Felix Mendelssohn found Liszt's virtuosity both "ignorant" and "uncleanly" when it involved taking liberties with works by Beethoven and Bach, but elsewhere conceded that he had "not heard any performer whose musical perceptions extend to the very tips of his fingers and emanate from them directly, as Liszt's do."[5] The virtuoso's hands, to bring out the metaphors, are alternately dirty and mesmerizing—terms that may only seem antithetical. "Liszt's way in everything," Mendelssohn grumbled astutely, "is a perpetual fluctuation between scandal and apotheosis."[6] For Hans Christian Andersen, Liszt's aura of celebrity opens the ears of dull bourgeois listeners to musical genius; for Heinrich Heine, it exposes Liszt's charisma as the product of clever merchandising.[7] For Sir Charles Hallé, a conductor and pianist who first heard him in the 1830s, Liszt is "all sunshine and dazzling splendour, subjugating his hearers with a power that none could withstand"; for Frederic Chopin the splendor dissolves too easily into glitz, and Liszt into a sideshow figure who will "one day . . . even be a deputy—perhaps even king of Abyssinia or of the Congo" while "the motives of his compositions . . . will be consigned to the newspapers."[8] The Lisztian virtuoso lives between two worlds, where no Orphean singer can safely go.

What follows is an attempt to sketch out some of the cultural meanings of this disconcertingly charismatic figure. What were the culture-specific grounds of the piano virtuoso's ambivalence and what forms did it typically assume? What kind of social event was the virtuoso concert and what kind of relationship did it establish between the performer and the audience? What was the specifically musical significance of the virtuoso and what was the relationship of virtuosity to the music played and composed by the virtuoso—both before and after those functions were separated in the mid-nineteenth century? Canvassing these questions will require an examination of several topics related more by a historically grounded semantic adjacency than by straight-line logic: the vexed relationship between virtuosity and visuality; the development of a visually oriented "public sphere" in which virtuosity helped form a series of epoch-making connections between mass entertainment, the construction of subjectivity, and the birth of stardom; and the attempt to reconcile virtuosity with the ideal of "autonomous" classical composition, a project represented here by Liszt's own B-Minor Sonata.

Descriptions like Mendelssohn's and Andersen's, Hallé's and Chopin's, can offer some insight on these matters, and I will be reading them, and others, rather closely to that end. Their rhetoric may be revealing if it is taken more seriously than usual, on the principle that the social vitality of language dulled by time or familiarity can be partly restored by refurbishing its tarnished tropes.[9] A more indirect and speculative first approach, however, may be helpful in setting the stage.

VISION

In my student days I was especially fond of Brahms's B♭ Piano Concerto and went to several concerts to hear it. On one occasion, however, what impressed me most was not something I heard but something I saw. In several climactic passages, especially in the second movement, the "extra" Allegro Appassionato with its "elemental enjoyment of its own rage," the pianist was drowned out by the orchestra.[10] The orchestration, as I knew, makes this almost inevitable, but the pianist was fighting the inevitable with everything he had. He was making theater of it, hamming it up, and the sight of him riveted my gaze as he flogged the keyboard apparently without making a sound. The effect struck me as both comical and uncanny. It was as if the pianist had suddenly become a kind of involuntary mime, becoming less articulate as he meant to become more voluble. The scene has always stuck with me; later on I came to associate it with a horrifico-comic episode in Thomas Mann's *The Magic Mountain* when a character willfully seeks to give an oration next to a waterfall that utterly drowns him out. More importantly, this little scene of quasi-Brechtian alienation brought home to me the element of visual drama housed within any such pianistic performance but normally supposed to be subsumed by it. The pianist's inadvertent pantomime acted as a visual excess that momentarily reduced both the performance and the music to absurdity. In doing so, however, it also highlighted the ever present possibility of just that absurdity. Being silenced is not required, and neither is the orchestra. A highly demanding solo piano part, even one as pointedly unflashy and artistically serious as Brahms's, is always poised on the brink of visual excess. And that is where Liszt comes in. The possibility of going over the brink of visual excess is basic to the virtuoso role that he embodied and largely invented. It would thus make sense both descriptively and historically to sum up my "alienation effect" by saying that it momentarily turned the pianist into a caricature of a Lisztian virtuoso.

The visuality of Liszt—one of the most sketched, cartooned, painted, and photographed artists of the nineteenth century—is well enough known, encapsulated by Robert Schumann's often-quoted remark, "If Liszt played behind the scenes, a great deal of poetry would be lost."[11] Schumann does not say what this visual poetry consists of, but he does perhaps intimate it elsewhere in his article. Liszt is playing Weber's *Konzertstück*:

> Beginning the piece with a force and grandeur that made one think of an attack on a battlefield, he carried this on with continually increasing power up to the passage where the player, as it were, places himself at the head of the orchestra, leading it forward in triumph. Here indeed he resembled the great commander [Napoleon] to whom he has been compared in personal appearance, and the tempestuous applause that greeted him was not unlike an adoring *Vive l'Empereur!*[12]

The similes in this passage progressively translate the musical event into a visual display, an epiphanic *tableau vivant*. (The underlying trope may even invoke this popular genre of dress-up performance.) The initial "attack on a battlefield" is ambiguously suggestive of both sounds and scenes, but it is anchored in qualitative terms—force, grandeur, power—with familiar auditory associations. The description of the climactic passage shifts to purely visual language, though the referent remains auditory. The mark of auditory climax is a two-step heightening of visual specificity: at the peak of his bravura, Liszt figuratively steps forward crowned with military sublimity, at which point his musical "generalship" merges with his quasi-pictorial appearance as a double for Napoleon leading his troops.[13] Schumann's description goes beyond merely supplying a series of narrative images to evoke a performance the reader cannot hear. The *musical* power of the performance is consummated in a *visual* transformation that "promotes" Liszt from the embodiment of broadly Napoleonic virtues to the virtual image of Napoleon himself. The musical performance, though implicitly, achieves its full effectiveness in a certain visual excess. Confirmed by the "speaking" applause (the adoring "*Vive l'Empereur*"), that excess assumes a symbolic form immediately afterward as Schumann recalls the triumphant Liszt being presented unexpectedly with a bouquet of flowers and spends several apparently irrelevant sentences justifying the presentation. Both visual excess and floral symbolism will come up again very shortly, as, later on, will the trope of the virtuoso as an adored absolute ruler.

Schumann seems ready to take the sort of visual apotheosis he describes at face value, even though he privately acknowledged that Liszt has "something of the showoff in him, too much."[14] Chopin, in his remark about Liszt becoming king of Abyssinia or the Congo, found only vulgar exhibitionism in the same thing. The image of Liszt in cultural drag, equally available to embody official Europe, an exotic earthly paradise (as Abyssinia was thought to be), or the "primitive" black-African jungle, uses the grotesque literalism of a satirical cartoon to connect the narcissism of the star performer with the fantasies of a mass public.[15] Either way, star quality, as the worn-out metaphor implies, is something that catches the eye.

For some observers, however, Liszt's playing represented not the triumph of visuality but a triumph over it. Charles Hallé's metaphors carry this implication if they are taken seriously; if Liszt is all sunshine and dazzling splendor, he must figuratively disappear into his own light, which is blinding to look at. Hallé goes on to say that "one of the transcendent merits of his playing was the crystal-like clearness which never failed for a moment even in the most complicated and, to anybody else, impossible passages; it was as if he had photographed them in the minutest detail upon the ear of his listener."[16] Reversing the effect of Schumann's, Hallé's metaphors displace the visual into the auditory. They suggest in particular that Liszt imparted to sound the otherwise purely visual power of perfect correspondence between reality and representation, the contemporary criterion for which was the supposedly unimpeachable fidelity of the camera.[17] The effect of this correspondence was to reveal otherwise invisible truths; photographed on the ear, music played by

Liszt revealed itself with an otherwise inaudible degree of clarity and detail. The "transcendent merit" of such playing was to annul or even reverse the relation of conception and performance, original and copy. The music became crystal-clear only when Liszt made it ring like crystal. Heinrich Heine makes a similar point, based, like Hallé's, on Liszt's "transcendental" technique, which subordinates the sight of performance to the sound of a musical epiphany: "[Others] shine by the dexterity with which they manipulate the stringed wood, but with Liszt one no longer thinks of difficulty overcome—the instrument disappears and the music reveals itself."[18]

Heine, however, juxtaposes this purely musical revelation with an acute awareness of Liszt's face and bearing at the keyboard. Elsewhere, he testifies to the ambivalence produced by the mixing of sight and sound when Liszt performs:

> When he sits at the piano and has brushed his hair back over his brow several times, and begins to improvise, then he often rages all too madly over the ivory keys and there sounds a wilderness of heaven-storming ideas, between which here and there the sweetest flowers spread their fragrance, so that one feels at once anxious and blessed, but yet still more anxious.[19]

Liszt's repeated gesture of brushing back his hair acts for Heine as a small but compelling visual excess from which the process of virtuoso improvisation seems to spring. The gesture was one of Liszt's most widely noticed and imitated mannerisms. For Heine its ritualized quality and seductive emphasis on the performer's body anticipates both the inspired irrationality of the impending performance and the listener's ambivalent response. Once marked by this gesture, the music can never fully reveal itself. The visual excess sticks to it, and translates for the listener into a corresponding excess of anxiety over blessedness.

The French critic Ernest Legouvé did not share Heine's equivocal attitude toward Liszt, but he did share the perception of the virtuoso forelock as a site of visual excess from which ambivalence radiated. He set about working through the problem with a pair of the key tropes of the era, theatricality and nationality, the first of which will concern us later:

> Liszt's attitude at the piano, like that of a pythoness, has been re-marked again and again. Constantly tossing back his long hair, his lips quivering, his nostrils palpitating, he swept the auditorium with the glance of a smiling master. He had some little trick of the comedian in his manner, but he was not that. He was a Hungarian; a Hungarian in two aspects, at once Magyar and Tzigane. True son of the race that dances to the clanking of its spurs.[20]

Like Schumann's, Legouvé's epitomizing images reduce music to the noise-making that supports a triumphant sight, but with a twist: his dancing Liszt is imbued with Otherness ancient and modern, compounded of the oracular trance of the priestess of Apollo and the furious energy, backed by clanking spurs, of a half-gypsy warrior.

Liszt's particular identity as a piano virtuoso seems to have forced on his era the general question of the relationship of visuality to music. Richard Leppert has argued compellingly that the sight of music making is just as important in forming the social meaning of music as musical sound and that in the nineteenth century the piano is preeminent in this process.[21] Recognizing this can help underwrite a reinterpretation of the twin styles that seem to have driven nineteenth-century pianism, one devoted to performative display and the other to the realization of the composed work. The first style sets up a dynamic interplay between the visuality of solo performance and the sound of music; it courts visual excess and foregrounds the performer's body. The second style concentrates on the musical work alone; it minimizes the visuality of performance, reducing it to a necessary but insignificant by-product of the main business of making music. The first style is typical of pianistic virtuosity, which produces what we would now call a mixed-media event; to the extent that it includes fidelity to the work, it dramatizes the dependence of that fidelity on the genius of the performer. The second style is typical of the pianist as executant, faithful equally to the letter of the composition and the spirit of the composer; to the extent that it includes expressive styles of performance, it requires that these be limited and in a sense authorized by reverence for the music or the composer. As my descriptions imply, these styles are related not by simple opposition but by a dialectic, the dynamism of which helps continuously sustain the ambivalence surrounding the central figure of the virtuoso.[22]

Both styles can be illustrated by recalling another well-known anecdote. Hector Berlioz was appalled when he heard Liszt play the Adagio from Beethoven's "Moonlight" Sonata with liberal rubato and added trills and tremolos, but he was deeply moved when Liszt played the same movement with the utmost fidelity. The second performance (at Legouvé's home) is the one discussed in chapter 2, the one that, by Liszt's own request, took place in total darkness. Leave it to Liszt: he could show off even when no one could see him. But as this particular bit of showmanship seems to recognize, Liszt's association with visuality is at least partly responsible for the persistent suspicion attached to him even by many of his admirers, and for the curbs put on his prestige from his own day to ours. For nineteenth-century commentators, both pro and con, the question of how far Liszt would go visually is almost always pressing. When Liszt and his music alike are said to be flashy, vulgar, or concerned with mere "effect," they are being accused of wanting to be seen too much.

Thus Heine recalls Liszt being showered on stage with bouquets, plucking a red camellia from one of them, and putting the flower in his lapel. For Heine, the camellia contrastively evokes the "red camellias of a hero's blood" worn by soldiers in the audience just returned from Africa, whom the audience ignores to treat Liszt as the successor of Napoleon—a more questionable succession in Heine's view than in Schumann's.[23] The symbolism of the episode is almost too good to be true. But whether it was Heine's invention or Liszt's, the effect is the same: the blood-red camellia is a kind of epitomizing stain in the field of vision; it symbolizes the symbolism of visual excess in Liszt's style of performance.

It may be rewarding to dwell a little longer on this detail, allowing oneself, like Heine, to be drawn back to it. The camellia can be regarded as what Slavoj Žižek, following Jacques Lacan, calls the stain of the Real: the mark of a desire too disruptive to be represented and therefore one that manifests itself only as a blot or extrusion within representation.[24] The doubling of Liszt's camellia by the camellias of blood, aside from its political irony, may suggest that the stain here marks a bizarrely literal translation of a desire acknowledged to be at stake in the virtuoso concert, the desire to penetrate to the interior of the person, to touch the life of the inner self. Political irony no longer aside, the image thus helps locate the virtuoso concert as one place where this dimension of self is produced, paradoxically linked to flagrant display, and posed against a different, more purely public form of selfhood marked by the sacrificial lack of any pretension to inwardness. Heine's irony, typically hard to decipher, seems to register an uneasy awareness that a revolution in mass psychology is in progress. As we will see, the desire to be touched at the quick—touched personally—by the star performer is basic to the dynamics of modern mass entertainment that Liszt's virtuoso career helped to launch.

FEUX FOLLETS

The heightened visuality epitomized by the camellia seems to have struck many people not just as a feature of Liszt's performance style and social persona, but as a quality he imparted to the music he played. Heine had felt the same thing about Liszt's model, Paganini, and developed a trope of musical "second sight" to describe it. He later applied the trope in more developed, more ambivalent form to Liszt: "I avow . . . how very fond I am of Liszt, but his music does not affect my mind agreeably, the more so that I'm a Sunday's child and see the ghosts that other people only hear, so that every tone his hand strikes from the piano raises a corresponding sound-image in my spirit, in short, the music becomes visible in my inner eye."[25] Heine's urbane language is not to be taken at face value, but it nonetheless testifies to an uncanny persistence of vision where none belongs. When Liszt plays, the seemingly obvious boundary between sight and sound becomes uncertain. Unlike Charles Hallé's later image of a photographed sound, Heine's "sound-image" *(Klangfigur)* is a visual form: not a reproduction of the music but a ghostly double that transforms it and renders it uncanny. One way to sense the cultural relevance of this trope is to fast-forward from Heine in 1837 to find an older, less flamboyant Liszt still evoking similar impressions. Amy Fay, an American pianist who studied with Liszt in the 1870s, also experienced his playing as a transposition from sound to sight and used spectral imagery to describe it: "It does not seem as if it were mere music you were listening to, but as if he had called up a real living *form,* and you saw it breathing before your face and eyes. It gives *me* almost a ghostly feeling to hear him."[26] Fay goes Heine one better: where he describes a ghostlike visual double to the music, she turns the music itself into the visible ghost.

Fay's description of literally coming face to face with that ghost points to a further dimension of the visuality associated with Liszt. For commentator after commentator, Liszt's playing drew attention to his face, where the expressive content of the music took on visual form—in particular the form of a synchronous visual excess that proved the authenticity of the musical expression. Fay herself draws attention to this tendency, again recalling her study with Liszt in 1873: "It is as interesting to see him as it is to hear him, for his face changes with every modulation of the piece, and he looks exactly as he is playing."[27] Things had been much the same some thirty years earlier, when a Paris reviewer observed: "M. Liszt is not only a pianist, he is above all an actor. . . . Everything he plays is reflected in his face."[28]

This effect, obviously encouraged by Liszt's keyboard manner, is probably the source of what might be called the facial rhetoric of later generations of virtuosos. Heine suggests that by 1841 Liszt had moderated the violent physical expressivity of his earlier manner and shifted its emphasis from the body as a whole to the face. As we will see, descriptions of Liszt's playing after this shift (essentially a change in the site of visual excess) often retrace the shift itself as a sublimating movement between Liszt's body or hands and his face; the rhetoric of facial expression, of "countenance," made possible a variety of idealizing constructions of virtuosity that for some listeners made the dialectic of the twin pianisms irrelevant. By "looking exactly as he [was] playing," Liszt could simultaneously both unleash his charismatic physical presence—the face is a body part that changes with emotion—and assert the symbolic value of his performance—the face is a kind of sign where subjective states are negotiated. Eventually, of course, the virtuoso's facial rhetoric would become conventional, no more or less compelling than a pop singer's mouthing of a hand-held mike. As a part of the Liszt persona, however, putting a face on the music seems to have been irresistibly appealing. Even Eduard Hanslick, who dismissed Liszt's symphonic poems as "a kind of vision-promoting medicine," yielded to this visual pleasure when Liszt played: "Not only does one listen with breathless attention to his playing; one also observes it in the fine lines of his face."[29] After describing Liszt's flashing eyes and the tilt of his noble head in some detail, Hanslick concludes (a touch defensively) that "all this has the utmost fascination for his listeners."[30]

For some listeners, Liszt's facial rhetoric seems to have produced a kind of listening gaze to which it revealed new modes of musical response, new forms of musical meaning. When Liszt played in 1854 for the young Marian Evans (soon to become George Eliot), she noted the absence of his legendary physical extravagance, but found it sublimated in the expressive mobility of his face:

> I sat near him so I could see both his hands and face. For the first time in my life I heard real inspiration—for the first time I heard the true tones of the piano. He played one of his own compositions, one of a series of religious fantasies. There was nothing strange or excessive about his manner. His manipulation of the instrument was quiet and easy, and his face was simply grand—the lips compressed and the head thrown a little backward. When the music expressed quiet rapture or devotion, a sweet smile flitted over his features; when it was triumphant, the nostrils dilated.[31]

Heine's co-presence of sound and ghostly sight here becomes a repeated ascent from sound to spiritualized sight. The meaning of the music lies less in its own expressive content than in the process of Liszt's visual translation; the sounds of his tones become "true" as the sight of his face verifies them. The listening gaze attunes itself to the slightest alterations of Liszt's features, which generate a surplus of significance (and of signification) by virtue of their synchrony with the music. The face transfigures the music that transfigures it; the effect, in the words of another English observer, is playing in which "genius give[s] elevation to art."[32] The aesthetic of expression (so to speak, the default mode) gives way to an aesthetic of witnessing, the receptive ear to the listening gaze.

Hans Christian Andersen had a similar experience in 1840. The result in his case was a full-blown visual narrative—a pantomime—of passage from the demonic to the divine:

> As [Liszt] sat at the piano, the first impression of his personality and the trace of strong passions upon his pale countenance made me imagine that he might be a demon banished into the instrument from which his tones streamed forth. They came from his blood, from his thoughts; he was a demon who had to free his soul by playing; he was under the torture; his blood flowed, and his nerves quivered. But as he played the demon disappeared. I saw the pale countenance assume a nobler, more beautiful expression. The divine soul flashed from his eyes, from every feature; he grew handsome—handsome as life and inspiration can make one.[33]

For Andersen, the spiritualizing movement from sound to sight exists at two levels. Liszt's mere appearance summons up the listening gaze, which forms the synchrony of the virtuoso's pale countenance and streaming tones into an allegorical image. The course of the performance then realizes the terms of the allegory in "ascending" form. What this involves is the metamorphosis of a face linked to the lower body—a pulsating mass of blood, nerves, and corporealized thought, identified with and contained by the instrument, which is also a rack—to a face linked only to the soul, for which it has become a transparent medium. What this does not involve is music, which Andersen, unlike Eliot, does not even bother to mention. The concluding description no longer even has an auditory referent.[34] For this observer, hearing Liszt play becomes an entirely visual experience. True to form, the crowning epiphany registers in the bulge of visual excess: the diffusion of the gleam of Liszt's eye to every feature and the change of countenance that makes him superlatively handsome.

Andersen's loss of listening in the gaze may help to explain why Liszt's visuality provoked dismay as well as admiration. It might be supposed that the synchrony of sight and sound could favor either term as circumstances dictated, but in actuality—and not just by chance—sight tended to predominate. (Its power to do so would be proved again in the twentieth century by the subordination of movie music to the film image.) The reasons for this may have something to do with the broad cultural authority invested in semantic (pictorial or narrative) versus purportedly nonsemantic (strictly musical) forms—a topic that will return in chapter 7. More narrowly, the reasons seem to rest with the then (and still) current conception of music as a weakly nonvisual medium, that is, as a medium unable to withstand a visuality it is felt to transcend. An idealized mode of visuality like facial rhetoric could suspend the dialectics of virtuosity, but not forever, and not for everyone.

To those who valued music above all, Liszt was at bottom antimusical, and this not despite his genius as a performer, but because of it. The post-Enlightenment idealization of music tended to represent it as the transcendental antagonist of the visual, which stood in for the whole phenomenal world. Goethe, though not always the best source on musical matters, captured this emerging ideal very well in a passage from his *Wilhelm Meister's Apprenticeship* (1796):

> In oratorios and concerts, the form of the musician constantly disturbs us; true music is intended for the ear alone; a fine voice is the most universal thing that can be figured; and while the narrow individual that uses it presents himself before the eye, he cannot fail to destroy the pure effect of that universality. . . . On the same principles, [instrumentalists] should as much as possible be hidden; because, by the mechanical exertions, by the mean and always awkward gestures of the performers, our feelings are so much dispersed and perplexed.[35]

The sight of the performer disturbs the effect of universality by displaying both the material awkwardness of music-making and the more metaphysical awkwardness of being confined *(eingeschränkt)* to individual existence. The virtuoso alters the equation by embracing these qualities where he could surmount them and by turning them into sources of social and psychological power. As Hallé and Heine testified, Liszt was felt to be uniquely capable of disappearing behind the music he played; his "blind" performance of the "Moonlight" Adagio as commemorated by Berlioz is both the perfect realization of the antivisual ideal and its reductio ad absurdum. But Liszt, and this is what made him so disconcerting, was constantly seen—literally seen—to discard the ideal of invisibility for its negation, and to do so willfully, with a palpable arrogance of power. The seductions of vision seemed to betray him into sacrificing universality for a narrow individuality, even if his gestures elevated meanness and awkwardness into a nearly irresistible charisma.

Heine's description of the immediate movement from the virtuoso's hand to the mind's eye makes a similar point: the movement elides the music altogether. Nor is the music all that disappears. With it disappears the self-possession of the listener, who becomes uncannily subject to the performer's quasi-hypnotic control. Reflecting in 1911 on the Lisztian magnetism of a later virtuoso, Ignace Jan Paderewski, James Huneker recalls attending "recitals . . . where I sat and wondered if I really *heard;* or was Paderewski just going through the motions and not really touching the keys?" The experience reminds him of a story he had written in which a pianist figured as a mesmerizer. He sat at his instrument in a silent, crowded hall and worked his magic . . . . The scene modulates into madness. People are transported. And in all the rumour and storm, the master sits at the keyboard but does *not* play.[36]

The scene provides a literal rendition of the lurking anxiety that the music—any music—produced by the virtuoso is only a pretext, a mask and a medium for the frenzy of collective idolatry.

Even darker implications thread a cognate scene from a more celebrated literary source, Thomas Mann's novel *Buddenbrooks* (1901):

> Christian sat down at the little harmonium that stood in the dining-room and imitated a piano virtuoso. He pretended to toss back his hair, rubbed his hands, and looked around the room; then, without a sound . . . he bent quite over and began to belabour the bass, played unbelievable passages, threw himself back in ecstasy at the ceiling, and banged the key-board in a triumphant finale.[37]

This dead-on Liszt impersonation is comic at first, but quickly turns serious; the player, the ne'er-do-well and artist manqué Christian Buddenbrook, breaks off abruptly "as though a mask had fallen over his features" and stands silent "as if he were listening to some kind of uncanny noise." The musical emptiness of his pantomime embodies a vacancy of spirit that its comic bravura cannot mask for long. The vacancy will eventually make Christian modulate into madness. Cut off from the music that could validate it—the music that Christian can hear only as an uncanny noise—virtuoso performance is revealed as charlatanism, its charisma enthralling but destructive.

Some of Liszt's antagonists were willing to tolerate such charisma as a by-product of performance, but denounced it fiercely as an effect of composition. Hanslick is a case in point. He regarded Liszt's piano pieces as worthless except when Liszt himself played them, which was all right because he also regarded them as mere vehicles for Liszt's self-display. But Liszt's symphonic music, which demanded to be heard as an instance of musical art, was contaminated by its visual and literary devices. Courting the particular, it became meretricious. Brahms and Joseph Joachim took similar positions, Joachim railing against Liszt's "vulgar use of sacred forms" and "repulsive coquetting with the noblest feelings for the sake of effect," and Brahms claiming that "The prodigy, the itinerant virtuoso, and the man of fashion ruined the composer before he had even started."[38]

HARMONIES DU SOIR

These last remarks specifically target theatricality, the mode of visuality felt to be the most antimusical of all. (It is Christian Buddenbrook's favorite.) According to Friedrich Nietzsche, "the emergence of the actor" in music during the nineteenth century threatens to turn music into "an art of lying" subject to the whims of popular taste: "a capital event that invites thought, and perhaps also fear. In a formula: 'Wagner and Liszt.'"[39] At stake here is a contradiction between the means and ends of producing the century's technically difficult and spiritually ambitious art music. The music is supposed to possess independent symbolic value and cultural authority, but it can be transmitted to a wide audience only by means of public spectacles that threaten to subordinate music to the histrionics of performance. With music involving soloists, the danger comes mainly from the charismatic performer who takes control of the audience's emotions and debases music by associating it with the visual, the uncanny, and the bodily. The performer as faithful executant is the countervailing figure, but the technical difficulty now expected of music seeking canonical status exerts a continuing pressure in the direction of virtuosity. With symphonic music, the danger comes mainly from compositional practices that build theatrical associations into the music itself. "Absolute music" is the countervailing force, but one with notoriously ill-defined boundaries, beset both by the encroachment of programmatic tendencies on the symphonic genre and by the theatrical-virtuosic demands of writing for orchestras of ever increasing size and instrumental range. (Chamber music seems to have been left out of this dialectic, perhaps because its traditional emphasis on ensemble worked against too much virtuosity, perhaps because it had not yet fully migrated from the home to the concert hall.)[40]

Liszt is the emblematic villain in both the performing and the composing arenas, and is no doubt guilty as charged. Perhaps his most disconcerting effect in either venue was to suggest that music itself, despite the reverence being claimed for it, is surprisingly fragile as a symbolic medium. What threatens its integrity is not some grave historical turn of events, but its seemingly innate disposition to mix self-effacingly with other media. The material, the bodily, the visual, the narrative, the theatrical—all of them were readily able both to degrade music by their presence and, as objects of imitation, to corrupt it in their absence. Like the popular audience, music is a sucker for a good show.

Liszt's virtuoso career helped produce this dilemma, but not simply because Liszt had a flair for theatrics ("M. Liszt . . . is above all an actor") and astonishing pianistic gifts, though of course he had both. The virtuoso concert can be understood historically as part of a long series of performance genres devised to attract a large public. Many of these genres originated in the social and cultural turmoil of Paris during the Restoration and July Monarchy, but the effects of this local development have been widespread and long lasting; each new genre has its own historical development, and the network of genres can be said to form the genealogy of modern mass entertainment. My focus is on the small group of genres that form the immediate prehistory of the Lisztian virtuoso concert and that are linked to the concert through the process of displacement. The term "displacement" is to be understood here in two not entirely congruent senses, one emphasizing process, the other history. The widely used processive sense derives ultimately from Freud; it refers to a pattern of containment in which the disruptive activities and energies actually present in one situation become only virtually or symbolically present in another. The more recent historical sense comes from Foucault; it refers to a pattern of cultural amnesia in which the origins of one situation in another are wholly or partially forgotten on behalf of the later form.[41]

The Restoration regime in France promoted itself heavily by staging fêtes and public spectacles, perhaps prompted by wishful or cynical memories of the great *Fête de la fédération* of 1790, the mass celebration of which had briefly seemed to unite and renew the nation.[42] The focus could be relatively narrow, as in the supervision and financing of the Paris Opéra by state officials, or all-encompassing, as in the coronation of Charles X in 1825, a grandiose combination of religious ceremony, arts festival, and political circus. A prostrate Charles in white satin was anointed with a special coronation chrism secreted away since the Terror; there were stagings of a Three Tenors–style operatic gala and a new, specially commissioned opera by Rossini, *Il Viaggio a Rheims*; just before the actual coronation Charles freed fifty prisoners, and the day after he applied the "king's touch" to cure the scrofula of a hundred and twenty-one people.[43] Countervailing forces rooted in popular sentiment were, however, already at work, making notable breakthroughs in the triumphs of Victor Hugo's antireactionary play *Hernani* early in 1830 and, two years earlier, of Auber and Scribe's opera *La Muette de Portici*, which was widely understood as celebrating the spirit of popular revolt from the stage of the Paris Opéra itself.[44]

Once the monarchy had fallen, a popular reappropriation of festivity took place on several fronts, though only after several years of social and economic misery. Carnival, which had been discontinued during the Empire and Restoration, revived with a vengeance; along with it came a carnival impulse that spilled over the traditional calendar and resulted in year-round public balls. These were explicitly perceived by contemporary observers as displacements of revolutionary energy. Like the Paris Arcades that had already flourished during the Restoration, the balls were marked by the unregulated mixing of social classes, but they themselves were free of the pretext and regulation of commerce; they existed for pleasure alone. The balls were driven by overt social and sexual energies associated with specific forms of music and dance. The dance was the cancan: not the cleaned-up Offenbach version, but a wild, grossly erotic dance apparently based on an Algerian model and introduced during the cholera epidemic of 1832 as a defiant mixture of celebration of life and willful *danse macabre.* The music was that of a popular orchestra conductor—a bandleader, really, like a time traveler from the swing era: Philippe Musard.[45]

The *Bals Musard* were large events involving crowds of two or three thousand people and orchestras of at least forty hand-picked musicians. Like the cancan, which they often featured, the balls struck contemporary observers as overflowing with displaced energies: "[The people] dance, they galop, they waltz with ardor, with passion, the way they would fight if we had a war, the way they would love if people today still had poetry in their hearts."[46] The dancing was driven by a music of seemingly demonic power, music that provoked what was widely described as orgiastic frenzy; one account of "the delusory madness created by Musard with his devilish violins" is forced to beggar mythological superlatives: "A witches' Sabbath, a revolt of giants, eruptions of Vesuvius hardly manage to give the vaguest idea of these dizzying surges. Nothing, not even a raging ocean could have stopped Musard's infernal *galop* once it had started."[47] The well-known caricature of Liszt virtually levitating on the dizzying surges of his famous *Galop chromatique* (which, said one contemporary, "causes all nerves to vibrate")[48] could well come to mind here. So, too, could his legendary effect on the women in his audience; the *Bals Musard* were particularly notable for their release of uncontrolled female sexuality. For Ludwig Rellstab in 1843, "the ever wilder *galop* presents a horrible picture of Bacchanalian wantonness. In this dance the rhythm grows faster, and eventually the females look like racing Maenads—with glowing cheeks, breathless heaving chests, panting lips, and hair that has come undone and is flying."[49] The displacement here is obvious enough. More remarkable than Rellstab's sexual imagery per se is the logic that produces sex *as* imagery. The musical rhythm and the women's dancing bodies are perfectly synchronous, and their synchrony produces sexual pleasure as public spectacle.

Heine in 1837 also notes the association between the era's dance craze and unbridled female sexuality, both of which he associates in turn with Liszt's pianism. Conflating the public ball with the soirée, he describes the women of July Monarchy Paris as dancing like the Wilis, the brides of German folklore who have died before their wedding day, and who therefore "have the unsatisfied desire for dancing so deep in their hearts that each night they rise from their graves, gather in bands on the highways, and abandon themselves to the wildest dancing." Here, as in Heine's and Amy Fay's accounts of Liszt's playing, supernatural imagery indicates the ecstatic loss of ordinary, self-possessed subjectivity. Death becomes the symbol of enhanced life. When Heine goes on to specify the dance music, its source turns out to be a fictitious Liszt:

> It all began with music. Franz Liszt had allowed himself to be drawn to the piano. He pushed his hair back over his impressive brow, and waged one of his most brilliant melodic battles. Even the keys seemed to bleed. . . . Everywhere in the hall—pallid faces, heaving bosoms, subdued breathing during the pauses, and at last tumultuous applause. Women always behave as if intoxicated when Liszt plays. With frantic delight the Wilis of the salon then abandoned themselves to the dance.[50]

Liszt here assumes a quasi-demonic, quasi-mesmeric power to compel synchronies between music and the body, starting with his own. The image of the bleeding keys is particularly telling; it seems to combine suggestions of displaced revolutionary ardor (also contained in the figure of melodic battles), an uncanny mixture of animate and inanimate forms consistent with the figure of the Wilis, and the traditional sign of lost virginity. Equally suggestive is the implicitly causal sequence that runs from the brilliance of Liszt's playing—once more anticipated by the sight of his tossing hair—to the eroticized response of the audience to the self-abandon of the dance.

As Heine's fictionalized scene suggests, the item that follows the public ball on the dance card of festival displacements is the virtuoso concert. When the real Liszt took the stage, he gave a kind of one-man *Bal Musard*, condensing the music and the dance into a single person. The public balls had already stylized or symbolically reenacted at least two defining features of carnival; Liszt repeated this gesture on a still "higher" level in keeping with the general trend of the European "civilizing process" toward increasing regulation of bodies and behavior.[51]

The first of these carnival features is untrammeled physical expressiveness. According to Mikhail Bakhtin, popular festivity is rooted in the pleasures and pains of the "grotesque body," with particular emphasis on the "material bodily lower stratum"; at stake here is not just an indifference to the body's dignity but a violence toward its boundaries.[52] Dancing in a milling crowd constitutes a displaced form of this violence, which reappears figuratively in images of depersonalized frenzy—the Bacchantes and the Wilis. The physical frenzy of Liszt's early keyboard manner seems to have constituted a symbolic boundary breech; the physically more constrained audience could gain a carnivalesque pleasure by identifying with the wildly impulsive body of the performer. Like Rellstab's racing Maenads, the members of the audience were sutured into this identification by the music, but at the same time they achieved a "civilized" distance from it by the displacement of acting into looking. (In the de facto hierarchy of transcendence, acting was to looking as looking was to listening.) Any leftover identification could be translated into the furor of Lisztomania, which extended the festivity of performance through a series of secondary symbolizations and social rituals.

Even after Liszt had "sublimated" his performance practice by focusing more on facial rhetoric, the cultural memory of his original body rhetoric persisted. Preserved in countless descriptions and caricatures, the carnivalesque body of the younger Liszt formed the horizon against which the facial expressiveness of the older was perceived. The face, where the "finer" feelings—and the feelings of "finer" people—had been found legible at least since the invention of sensibility in the eighteenth century, thus gained a powerful tacit connection to the passions of the body. ("His whole face changes and gleams, and grows majestic," wrote one observer, "revealing the master-spirit as his hands caress while they master the keys.")[53] Not even a distaste, like Hanslick's, for the music Liszt was playing could immunize a listener from the resulting fascinations of the playing itself. The influence of this model on later performing musicians both "classical" and popular is almost impossible to overestimate. The freely offered sight of the performer's face or body possessed by music creates the conditions for a virtual intimacy that may be even more ecstatic and symbolically resonant than the "real" thing.

The second carnivalesque feature of the virtuoso concert is the coexistence of exaltation and debasement, a specific form of the ambivalence that has surrounded Liszt in general. In Bakhtinian carnival, ambivalence takes the form of travesty, the parodistic debasement or "discrowning" of all that is serious, official, or exalted, which, nonetheless, persists in its inverted forms. In the public ball, "discrowning" translates into the mixture of social classes that allows bodily and specifically erotic energies to be released with impunity. The lower social strata can dispense with deference to their betters, who, in turn, can live out their fantasies of low life; as one upper-crust contemporary wrote, "[people at Musard] might meet their valet or their groom; wonderful! It is possible to dance in front of such people without compromising oneself."[54] The virtuoso concert produces a considerably rarified but structurally similar duality by oscillating between two types of music, one frenetic, bravura, or "demonic," the other tender, sentimental, or pious. Heine, Schumann, Eliot, and Andersen, among many others, remark on some version of this oscillation. Their remarks tend to intimate an underlying narrative to the performance itself, an "ideal type" that is most explicitly concretized in Andersen. (It is also the substance of Heine's famous account of a performance by Paganini.)[55] The narrative carries the performer through debasement or demonization to exaltation or the reverse, usually with emphasis on the expressive synchrony between the music and the performer's body.

The most recent incarnation of this exaltation-debasement narrative is the climactic sequence of the 1996 film *Shine,* in which the virtuoso pianist collapses into madness after a performance of Rachmaninoff's Third Concerto. The first two movements are ruled by exaltation, conveyed by the self-assured movements of the pianist's hands, the calm look on his face, and the smoothness of his long hair, which, however, shows a progressive tendency to come undone. With the finale, debasement gradually takes over. The hands, for the most part, remain exalted, spinning out the music in a whirlwind of virtuosity. But the face begins to grimace and sweat profusely, the hair to become a streaming, unruly tangle—a tendency climaxed by a long facial close-up in slow motion with the music reduced to silence, replaced by the faint thudding of the keys and something like a heartbeat heard against a faint rumble. The muting and slow motion even overtake a shot of the hands before the music returns, now counterpointed against the player's contorted face.

There is a striking overlap between this film sequence and a famous cartoon narrative of Liszt published in 1873 (fig. 4.1).[56] The cartoon is framed by nearly identical images of the calmly smiling virtuoso making a humble bow, as if to acknowledge the exaltation-debasement narrative as conventional or performative. In between, his playing successively evokes what the accompanying captions identify as introspection, religious inspiration, the brooding of Hamlet and Faust, memories of lost youth, and Dante's Inferno. These changes are tracked by the progressive arrangement and derangement of Liszt's posture, facial rhetoric, and above all of his long hair, the perennial vehicle of his visual excess, which develops (in a slightly jumbled sequence) from a smooth coiffure to a streaming, unruly tangle. Here as elsewhere, Liszt's hair functions as *le trait unaire* ("the unary trait"), Jacques Lacan's term for a contingent detail that serves as the support and vehicle of someone's personal magnetism. Enveloped by his commanding personality, Liszt's hair becomes a *trait*—a stroke, a feature, a characteristic touch—possessed of fascination and allure. In *Shine*, the hair of the actor impersonating the pianist David Helfgott acts like a contrary trait, marking the collapse of personality by provoking visual displeasure.[57] Unlike Helfgott, Liszt can personify the emotional extremes of the exaltation-debasement narrative without being destroyed by them. That he can do so is in some sense the definition of his power as a virtuoso.

The cartoon also helps pinpoint the key element through which the virtuoso concert displaces and reconfigures carnival festivity and the public ball. The visual narrative represents the piano by only a barely visible patch of keyboard; like Andersen's text, it submerges the music in the spectacle of the musician. What the virtuoso concert introduces is precisely this: the mediation of carnivalesque energies by the charismatic presence of a single central figure. Bakhtinian carnival has no leader or cynosure; it is all body and no head, "theater without footlights." Despite his celebrity, Philippe Musard disappears behind the music of his own "devilish violins" and the social and sexual fervor of the dance. But Liszt's performances put him front and center; they are not just performances by Liszt but performances of him. The virtuoso self he performs, moreover, is not ultimately defined by either technical genius or expressive depth, but by an incandescent power to act as a surrogate for the social transformation of the audience. Thus Andersen describes how on Liszt's entry into the concert hall "a sunbeam flashed across each face, as though every eye were seeing a dear, beloved friend." When this universal intimate plays, he emits "a sea of sound, which in its very agitation is a mirror for the life task of each burning heart."[58]

The operation of this all-embracing intimacy was often expressed through the trope of kingship, which offers a means to grasp the social and psychological issues at stake in the experience. Liszt was continually identified with royalty *(Vive l'Empereur!)*, and himself famously adopted a variant of the phrase "noblesse oblige"—"génie oblige"—as a personal motto. A well-known anecdote even has him getting away with a public rebuke to the Czar of Russia when the latter talked too much during a performance. One key to understanding this identification is the relationship of royalty to public ceremony, something exemplified earlier in the coronation of Charles X. Traditionally, such ceremony depends on the authority and sometimes on the person of the king. The tradition identifies the king's body with the state; in Lacanian-Žižekian terms, the king embodies the big Other, the symbolic order of law and language in which the people

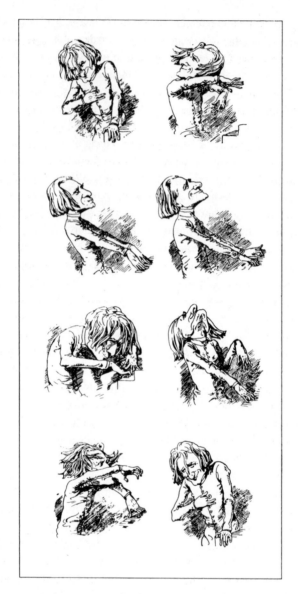

Figure 4.1. János Jánko, "Liszt at the Keyboard" (cartoon series), from *Borsszem Janko* (6 April 1873). Yale Art Gallery.

are enrolled as the king's subjects and through which, in the broader sense of the term, all subjectivity must be formed.[59] In public ceremony, pleasure belongs to the big Other, who gives it out in return for discipline. In a sense, even the king in his personal body is subject to this rule; poor Charles X provoked disapproval during his coronation festivities by publicly fidgeting during the performance of Rossini's *Il Viaggio a Rheims*.[60] The antithesis of this relationship appears not in republican ceremony— the French revolutionary festivals of the 1790s, for instance, especially during the Terror, were incipiently totalitarian[61]—but in Bakhtinian carnival. Carnival disjoins pleasure from discipline. It steals pleasure from the Other and scatters it freely across the lines of social hierarchy. Pleasure during carnival belongs to everyone—and to no one, which is one reason why carnival traditionally involves both displays of mock royalty and the inversion rites of discrowning.

The virtuoso concert combines the contradictory functions of ceremony and carnival. On the one hand it exacts disciplined attention from the audience along with awe at the performer's preternatural skill. On the other it frees the audience to take personal pleasure in the spectacle of the virtuoso's face and body, which becomes a medium of both identification and desire. The star takes the place of king as cynosure, but unlike the king, he offers himself as someone on whom one can freely feast one's eyes. The music simultaneously absorbs the charisma of this figure and infuses him with it. Meanwhile it also reserves a kernel of independent interest for the attentive ear, something that often makes itself felt as a sense of disconnection between the sight and sound of virtuoso performance, as if it were impossible to believe that two hands could produce Andersen's "sea of sound." Liszt, not by accident, was the first pianist to make sure the audience could see his hands, along with the rest of him.

The point of the concert is thus to create a pleasure that both belongs to the audience and yet retains a connection to the big Other. The shift from king to genius as source and cynosure does not constitute a dethroning of the big Other, but a shift between different versions, different embodiments, of the Other. In the virtuoso version, the unbridgeable distance between ruler and subject becomes unstable, dialectical, and intimate. (It also, as Heine noted, becomes a concealed commodity, a perfect instance of Marx's roughly contemporary concept of the commodity fetish.) The audience belongs to the Other, the virtuoso as king, whom it idolizes, but the virtuoso-as-Other belongs to the audience, which he lives to please.

This reversal produces the core paradox of the virtuoso, precursor of the object of fan adulation, the star. The virtuoso reaches sublime heights of performance by virtue of having some quality, some combination of talent and sex appeal, that the audience member does not have and never can. Yet for that very reason the virtuoso connects the audience member to the latter's own pleasure and the interior of his or her own identity. The star gives of himself and in so doing gives the fan nothing less than the fan's "true" self, which would otherwise be strangely lacking. "No artist in the world," wrote one admirer, "understands better than Liszt how to survey at a glance the character and the most hidden recesses in the hearts of his audience. This very fact is the cause of his wonderful effects, and will secure them to him always."[62] The perception of this capacity in Liszt was probably responsible in part for the unusually vivid aura of "personality" that enveloped him and for his legendary ability to "master" an audience just by appearing on stage. In his novel of 1999, *The Ground beneath Her Feet*, Salman Rushdie assigns the same capacity to his latter-day Orpheus and Eurydice, the rock stars Ormus Cama and Vina Apsara, at the height of their powers: "When they walked into rooms, hand in hand and glowing, people fell silent, in awe. . . . The long-dimmed torrent of their joy poured over anyone within range, drowning strangers in unlooked-for happiness."[63]

The star's gift frequently takes the material form of the souvenir object, a little concretization of visual excess by which an audience member can take possession of the star, the embodied Other. Liszt's long hair, the object of commentary by almost all contemporary observers, formed a virtual invitation to his fans to consume bits and pieces of him as charms, talismans, fetishes. Hair in the nineteenth century was perhaps the primary means of giving bodily energies and desires a public and visual form. An exchange of locks could substitute for physical intimacies; the simple fact that hair could be seen, even though women generally wore theirs bound, offered a locus for gazes and fantasies in an era in which bodily display was hampered by heavy clothing and regimented by strict dress codes. The open pursuit of star souvenirs has tended to be guided by heterosexual norms, so most of the fans seeking symbolic bits of Liszt and his successors have been women. Fan behavior may be deemed odd, but it is not supposed to be queer; men looked at Liszt's hair, but women tried to get locks of it. They also snapped up the gloves, handkerchiefs, and snuff boxes he discarded in order to provoke them, wore his broken piano strings as bracelets, and even scavenged his coffee dregs and cigar butts. Similarly, during Jenny Lind's American tour of 1850 men could buy—aside from Jenny Lind sofas, sausages, and pancakes—strands of hair purportedly lifted from the star's hairbrush by the hotel chambermaids who hawked them.[64] The fan-star relationship embedded in souvenir objects, however, is not necessarily limited by gender.

Born of the Lisztian virtuoso, star souvenirs form a further expression of his characteristic ambivalence. At one level they are worthless castoffs, mere waste products of the concert and the virtuoso body. At another, their connection with that body invests them with a fragment of its charisma on the model of the king's touch. Debased in symbolic value, they shine with the stain of the Real. Thrilling to the fan, they strike others as trivial, silly, or disgusting. The souvenirs thus display the same combination of exaltation and debasement that helps identify the virtuoso performance as a displaced form of both ceremony and carnival. One of the nineteenth century's important discoveries was that audiences would accept mass produced objects as equivalents to actual souvenirs, investing commodities with charismatic value by the simple act of paying too much for them. Artificial souvenirs also had the virtue of neutralizing or reversing the gender limitation. When Liszt toured Vienna and Pest in 1839, one could buy little pastries in the shape of a grand piano iced with the name "Liszt."[65] Earlier confections included little Paganinis and Rossinis made of sugar.[66] During the American tour of the danseuse Fanny Elsser in 1840–42, "Shops peddled Fanny Elsser brand boots, garters, stockings, corsets, parasols, cigars, shoe polish, shaving soap, and champagne"[67]—champagne aside, a virtual catalogue of fetishistic part objects for both men and women in the form of bodily appurtenances. Twentieth-century fan magazines and tabloids would achieve similar results by combining photographs of celebrities with erotic narratives about them.

The fan's souvenir, however, whether real or ersatz, has the symbolic side effect of depleting the object of adoration. The body of the virtuoso is expended in performance on behalf of the spectator. The recital narrative is like a high-wire act without a net; its form presupposes the possibility of interruption by something like the climactic sequence of *Shine*. This is the flip side of the formula "génie oblige." The virtuoso is a Prometheus as well as an Orpheus—both, by the way, the subjects of symphonic poems by Liszt in the 1850s; he steals the Other's pleasure by becoming permeated by it and offers it to the audience via the total abnegation of his mundane self. Liszt's humble bow presents the artist-king as the servant of the audience, and his facial and bodily rhetorics enact his symbolic sacrifice. The post-concert mobbing of the star, something that also seems to have originated with Liszt, suggests the audience's quasi-bacchantic acceptance of the offering. The virtuoso enables himself to be consumed by the music so that in the process he may be consumed as the Other by the audience. The practice is symbolic; the rapture it induces is real. In the twentieth century, films of virtuoso performance often concentrate on the rapid blur of the pianist's seemingly disembodied hands, which become the cinematic equivalent of the souvenir as they fill the screen, the imaginary core of the virtuoso's power. This dismemberment by camera corresponds closely to nineteenth-century sketches in which the virtuoso sprouts extra hands or fingers to signify virtual motion. The virtuoso cannot keep his body to himself.

EROICA

For musical idealists like Hanslick, Brahms, and Joachim, the apparatus of virtuoso worship provides ample debasement of music but no exaltation. What is bothersome to them about star-quality virtuosity, however, is not its end but its means. They, too, would like to relocate the Other through music, but they want the Other's place to be in the composer or the music itself, not in the performer or performance. It is for this reason that their main animus is directed against music composed for virtuoso "effect" rather than against the performer who conquers technical difficulties, a figure on whom composers in general had begun to rely. Once virtuoso technique becomes prerequisite, the question of showiness shifts its ground. The composer who writes merely for "effect" is just a showy performer in disguise, hopelessly tainted by the distasteful star syndrome: "in a formula: 'Wagner and Liszt.'"

What is at stake in this formula is again the strange ease by which music becomes complicit in its own degradation. Liszt's piano music has often been taken as a model of this complicity because its performance requires a Lisztian virtuoso, which is not far from requiring the reanimation of Liszt himself. A recent feature article from the Sunday *New York Times* is suggestive on this point, which involves both the musical quarrel between sound and sight and the uncanny conversion of the one to the other. The article aims to find something of value in Liszt's later, more "serious" work, but it begins with a sharp attack full of familiar tropes: "Here's [Liszt] the man: a strutting, manipulative, priapic rock star for the Romantics. . . . Here's the piano music: all flying fingers and crossing hands and empty virtuosity, thorny thickets of 32nd notes that sound of fury signifying nothing."[68] Both the man and the music are said to be all show, then rebuked with an allusion to Shakespeare, presumably a showman with substance. The music—the actual music, not just its performance—is rhetorically identified with empty visual display. Yet the emptiness fills with what Fay called the semblance of "a real living form," the more disconcertingly because the form is no longer living. The flying fingers and crossing hands demanded by the music were originally Liszt's own, and legendary for it. The pianist who supplies such fingers and hands today is condemned to be a Liszt impersonator, the sight of whom, half "priapic" and half mechanical, is coextensive with the music's expressive content.

The idealist position cannot stand the view. It locates musical pleasure in disciplined listening, which it associates with the cultural authority and transcendental value of music. What it wants from music is ceremony without carnival, regardless of the cost in strict social and aesthetic regulation. When Joachim writes Liszt in 1857 to say that the latter's music "contradicts everything with which the spirits of our great ones have nourished my mind from my earliest youth," he sets the stakes as high as he can, putting both heritage and selfhood at risk. In fact, he rises with no sense of disparity from aesthetic judgment to apocalyptic fantasy. He imagines what he calls the unthinkable, the catastrophic loss of "all that I feel music to be," and informs Liszt that "your strains would not fill one corner of the vast waste of nothingness."[69] According to Žižek, this sort of terrifying void is what appears when the symbolic order breaks down.[70] Joachim's fantasy, therefore, is tantamount to the statement that he would rather have no big Other at all than have one touched, let alone embodied, by Liszt.

The irony is that Liszt himself was also a musical idealist, very much concerned with the relationship between virtuosity and the concept of the musical work, and on his own terms very much aware that composition was a venue for the quarrel over who should stand musically for the big Other. One of his first long-term projects after abandoning his virtuoso career to concentrate on composing was to address this problem in a series of major works, his two piano concertos and the Piano Sonata in B Minor. The sonata can serve to illustrate.

Liszt's formal initiative in this work, as in the concertos, is very well known. All three pieces assimilate the independent movements of a typical sonata or concerto into one continuous movement threaded with thematic cross-references, and all conceive the enveloping mega-movement along the lines of first-movement sonata form. The resulting model of a steadily evolving unity quickly developed an influential life of its own in musical aesthetics. In the context of pianistic virtuosity, however, this complex cyclical structure is less an object of aesthetic contemplation than the script of an elevated mode of performance. Its continual self-reference and self-transformation form a running intellectual parallel to the pianist's display of instrumental technique and the associated qualities of brilliance, power,

Example 4.1. Liszt, Sonata in B minor, opening passage

Example 4.1. (continued)

and sensitivity. The structure, like the sonority, is a conduit opened between the charisma of an original genius and the audience's hunger to receive it.

But such charisma has its reasons, which are perhaps most evident in the layout of the B-Minor Sonata. The main body of the work is framed by the statement and recapitulation of a short passage that baldly presents the thematic material from which the whole will germinate (ex. 4.1). The passage combines the roles (and the tempos) of introduction and exposition and is clearly set apart by pregnant pauses. Taken by itself, this frame constitutes a strong assertion of the confluence of rationality with the work's virtuosity. No matter how extravagant they become, the concurrent metamorphoses of constructive and pianistic technique remain perspicuously related to the primary passage, which stands as both an origin and an end.

Nor do matters stop here. The three elements presented in the primary passage—a semi-scalar descent in octaves, a declamatory theme (also in octaves), and an agitated percussive theme deep in the bass—are all introduced off the tonic, and subsequently recapitulated either at the tonic (the descent, the percussive theme) or over it (the declamatory theme). The main body of the work thus presents itself, not merely as a free elaboration of its germinal themes, but as a purposeful transformation of them. The virtuosic display, at both levels, appears as the means by which the constructive and expressive energies latent in the core themes are released, enjoyed, exhausted, and finally channeled into a stable and intelligible form. The percussive theme is the decisive element in this process. Introduced as a terse model and sequence starting on the third scale degree, the theme returns at the end as an extended tonic pedal, thus rationalizing both its role in the work and its position in the bass (ex. 4.2; compare with ex. 4.1). This gesture—which also incorporates a shift in mode from minor to major and a shift in dynamics from loud to soft—opens the recapitulation of the primary passage and initiates a reversal of its original thematic order. Such a reversal would be exceptional in a standard sonata, but in this "sonata deformation" its clear-cut symmetry constitutes another claim to rationality, tightening the frame and emphasizing the conjunction of performative display and constructive technique.[71] This conjunction also sounds in the harmony, which is definitive but not cut to standard cadential patterns.[72]

The sonata also constitutes a composed script for the bipolar narrative of furor and sentiment typical of Liszt's virtuoso performances. Throughout the work, extended virtuosic passages alternate with briefer passages of extreme simplicity. This alternation now seeks to act as both an emotional disposition (its role in the virtuoso concert) and a vehicle of form; the relationship between the two types of passage becomes rational, organic, and dynamic, rather than—or as well as—sensational or transgressive. In either incarnation, this relationship can be said to trope on the traditional duality of the sublime and the beautiful by cutting out the middle ground between them. The virtuoso is a figure at the limits, the subject of the extremes, scandal and apotheosis. What the sonata adds by suggesting an organic link between these terms is an intimation that the limit, the extreme, has itself become the source of a higher order, a transcendental reason. Like the virtuoso performance, moreover, the sonata realizes its formative principle of excess in visual, even pictorial, as well as musical terms. The compositional alternation of virtuosic and simplistic passages makes available a performative alternation between the sublimity of frantic hand and/or bodily motion, and the beauty of a stillness from which the performer imbues the simple notes with the fullness of his surplus feeling. The result once again is that the virtuoso—the virtuoso that the sonata constructs as its ideal executant—models, embodies, and in a sense suffers the "deepest," most "authentic" dimensions of the audience's subjectivity.

In conclusion, and in imitation of the sonata, we can return to a germinal idea stated at the outset: the title of this chapter. According to Jürgen Habermas, a distinct sphere of public opinion and "rational-critical debate" developed in the clubs, salons, and literary and journalistic press of eighteenth-century England, France, and Germany, initiating a process of trans-

Example 4.2. Liszt, Sonata in B minor, closing passage with reverse recapitulation of opening

(continued)

Example 4.2. (continued)

formation that can be traced to the present day.[73] This "bourgeois public sphere" was resistant to top-down forms of political domination, in part because its only allegiance was to reason, and in part because it was inclusive of (indeed, creative of) a large "public": no matter how restrictive it was in practice, in principle any interested party could have access to it. The public thus defined formed the nucleus of the ever larger mass publics of later eras. Habermas sees the development of the paid-admission concert as a direct extension of the public sphere, a relationship that can be extended further until it reaches Liszt. The virtuoso practice that Liszt pioneered can be understood as an effort to appropriate the social effects of the bourgeois public sphere for (musical) art. Mingling aesthetics, entertainment, and social transformation, virtuoso performance both summons a large public into being and pleasurably resists social domination by replacing it with the masterful but self-expending charisma of the artist. Staid citizens become "political bacchantes" in the virtuoso sphere because what they find there— rightly or wrongly, escaping or succumbing to the hidden hand of celebrity commodification—is the gift of a social power and personal vitality that, or so it seems, was already theirs to begin with.

5
Rethinking Schumann's *Carnaval*
Identity, Meaning, and the Social Order

This chapter is a rewritten (not merely revised) version of an essay that first appeared in 1993 in the pioneering feminist collection *Musicology and Difference*, edited by Ruth Solie, a volume with its own sort of carnivalesque exuberance in which I was glad to share. My argument there was that in *Carnaval* Schumann drew on the traditions of European festive practice to stretch and exceed the conventional bounds of gender as his age understood them. I would still say so, but in the years since, I've come to think that the subject needs and deserves a more fully historicized treatment, and a more problematized one. The original essay also drew some stimulating criticisms from Leo Treitler, which, although I don't agree with them, prompted me to rethink and clarify certain issues of musical meaning that flow directly into the mainstream of this book. It is no doubt just a coincidence that I am writing this prefatory note during Mardi Gras, 1999.

MOTIVES AND METAPHORS

Robert Schumann's *Carnaval* (1834–35) lived up to its billing for his contemporaries, who—so they tell us—heard this cycle of twenty-one short piano pieces as a poetic expression of the carnival spirit. Franz Liszt, for example, one of the work's earliest performers, described it as "reveal[ing] a colorful masquerade of artists whose groups are treated so directly, so energetically and vividly, that by remarkably reproducing their physiognomies and capturing their most lively gestures it must count among the richest and most successful works of the author."[1] Later generations tended to take a drier approach. In his magisterial *Nineteenth-Century Music* (1980), Carl Dahlhaus sees the poetic impulse in Schumann as a sign of provinciality, though, to be sure, a "provinciality of the highest order":

Schumann's character pieces have a poetry permeated by the spirit of Jean Paul, a poetry of literary and even autobiographical allusions, of mottos and eloquent titles that sometimes appear to mean more than they actually say. From the standpoint of social history, we have no trouble categorizing this poetry as the aesthetic of a narrowly circumscribed coterie.[2]

Using *Carnaval* as his example, Dahlhaus sharply separates the "sociohistorical" from the "aesthetic" and "structural." Schumann's subtitle refers to scenes on four notes; Dahlhaus suggests that this "meager melodic substance could yield a web of motives" spanning and unifying the cycle because the motives of romantic piano music, in contrast to themes, are fundamentally rhythmic:

> Almost invariably, the motive has a distinctive rhythm while the pitch content remains open and variable. Thus the "four notes," instead of quickly cloying by frequent repetition and manipulation, merely serve as an initial impetus to the pieces. At the same time, the pitch content, by merely alluding to the opening of the movement, could be taken up again and again without courting monotony or "unpoetic" pedantry.[3]

Fine though this analysis is, one may wonder at Dahlhaus's assumption that it is somehow less addressed to a "narrowly circumscribed coterie" than the titles and musical anagrams of Schumann's piece. The problem is compounded by the fact that carnival itself, far from being a provincial affair, was in the 1830s still a major social form with a significant capacity to disrupt settled routines. If Dahlhaus chooses to forget this—and he does so, of course, not just from personal inclination but because he is writing from within an academic discipline that mandates the forgetting—the effect and perhaps the purpose is to protect the music from the disruptive effects of its own meanings. These are meanings that mock and symbolically unseat the norms of social, intellectual, and sexual authority, or, more exactly, scoff at the very idea of such norms. The aim of this chapter is to remember how and why they did that: to renew their carnival license. Yet to pursue that aim will also raise the question of the deeper motives for revoking the license, not just by critics of one mind with Dahlhaus, but by the very music that enjoys it.

Schumann uses the famous design of *Carnaval*, a quasi-improvisatory skein of short, sometimes fragmentary, sometimes clustered or interconnected pieces, as a general metaphor of carnival festivity. The style and technique of the particular pieces ramify this metaphor, continually inviting the listener to think about the interrelations of festivity, art, identity, and gender. The frolic plays out on three broad platforms:

1. The disunity of the socially constructed self. As conceptualized by Mikhail Bakhtin, carnival is "a minimally ritualized antiritual, a festive celebration of the . . . gaps and holes in all the mappings of the world laid out in systematic theologies, legal codes, normative poetics, and class hierarchies."[4] Carnival festivity temporarily frees its participants from the demand that they organize their physical and emotional lives into a coherent, restrained totality. This normative self splinters amid the general outbreak of buffoonery, playacting, and masquerade; its component parts assume the guise of separate characters, or, more exactly, caricatures, personifications of excess or impulse. Caught up in the anarchic scene, the reveler is free to identify with any or all of these figures. *Carnaval* uses cartoonish, highly stylized textures and overt cross-references among pieces to project this free play of identification and comment on it. The result is a kind of affirmative fragmentation well described by Carl Kossmaly in the earliest full-dress critical essay on Schumann's piano music (1844): "[These] 'musical genre pictures' . . . are a genuine, fresh, fantastic masquerade, boisterous and colorful, full of high jinks and intrigue . . . a wild crowd of chaotically thronging figures [and] tones of wanton pleasure."[5]

2. Cross-dressing and the mobility of gender. Carnival free play, particularly in masquerade, invites the free crossing of gender boundaries. Cross-dressing by both men and women gives each gender a chance to appropriate the qualities culturally ascribed to—and reserved for—the other, qualities that in everyday life would mostly have to be hidden or disavowed. *Carnaval* explicitly focuses its vision of carnival through the lens of gender, using the interplay among its masculine and feminine character sketches to re-create and reinterpret the gender-crossing of masquerade. In the music, as sometimes in the festivity, mobility of gender is both the vehicle and the symbol of mobility of identity in general.

3. The woman in the mirror. This particular loosening of subjective boundaries had another nineteenth-century venue to which *Carnaval* may be drawn. The music recurrently seems to form mirror images: juxtapositions of the same complete idea in slightly different voicings, the second of which estranges, softens, or idealizes the first in the course of reflecting it in full. Technically, each pair of "images" consists of the symmetrical repetition of a section or a melodic strain with a slight but telling difference of articulation. (With sections, the repetition usually arises where a contrast would be more normative.) As with an actual mirror, the reflection must not only be recognized "as" the original (a cognitive act) but also identified with it (an imaginary, figurative act); the music to some degree replicates the psychology of this process. (Those sympathetic to Lacanian psychoanalysis will see in this a fundamental fantasy-structure put to a historically specific use.) Culturally, this mirror imaging presents itself as a feminine activity, in keeping with nineteenth-century tropes associating self-reflection with feminine self-creation; masculine modes of identity are supposed to be more fixed and less visible, more "internal." A woman gazing into an actual mirror, pool, or other reflective surface is the most familiar trope for the process. This is not to say, however, that a listener can or should hear the musical mirrorings as explicit metaphors of women in the looking glass, but that both forms of reflection are instances of the same underlying activity of culture-specific self-invention. I will return to this topic later.

Schumann's techniques of mirroring point to an ambivalent fantasy of gender mobility for which carnival is the metaphor and *Carnaval* the medium. The question once again refers to the stability of identity in general: if the masculine composer finds pleasure in feminine masks, how sure can he be that his own masculinity is not a mere mask as well? Is there redress from imaginary cross-dressing? And mirroring is not the only issue. As Naomi Schor has suggested, modern European culture consistently encoded the art of the miniature, the art of the detail, as feminine. This code was quite explicitly applied to music, and to piano pieces in particular.[6] In constructing a piece out of miniatures—*scénes mignonnes* he called them, "tiny scenes," "cute scenes"—Schumann was following a standard paradigm for "feminine" art. He would later apply the same paradigm to his *Blumenstück*, Op. 17 (1838), tracing the piece to an increasingly feminine tendency in his style and describing it to Clara Schumann as "a set of little things, . . . of which I have so many, assembled in a pretty way"; Kossmaly also describes the piece along these lines.[7]

Carnaval presses the point with its numerous feminine character sketches and frequent use of very short motives to "capture physiognomies and gestures"; Liszt put the cycle as a whole in feminine dress by describing it as "so charming, so bejeweled . . . so variously and harmoniously put together."[8] Yet in linking his miniatures through an enveloping "web of motives" to create a larger unity, and in closing the cycle of miniatures with a sonata-like recapitulation of themes drawn from the opening, Schumann also follows a traditionally "masculine" paradigm: the standard of mastery in which variegated details are structured into a unified whole. This "bisexuality" in Schumann's role as the composer of *Carnaval* is a mainspring of the cycle's musical action. The music constitutes an effort—though not, finally, a sustainable effort—to affirm unrestricted gender mobility as a source of social and artistic value.[9]

Before examining this effort in *Carnaval* itself, we need to examine its motives, which are both personal—that is, psychosexual—and cultural.

Male artists in nineteenth-century Europe increasingly found their masculinity at odds with their calling. The role of artist, traditionally marked by the achievement of virile mastery within a limited, quasi-artisanal sphere, was changing in dramatic and contradictory ways. Mastery now required the charismatic, hypertrophied virility of a Dickens, a Liszt, a Wagner, as the artist was asked to become a star, a cult figure who miraculously surmounted the fragmentation of modern society. At the same time, the artist's creativity, the modern version of his artisanal skill, was understood to derive from a volatility of emotion and responsiveness to sensation that were markedly feminine in character. With growing transparency, the artist's public masculinity was understood to be the product of a private femininity embodied in his art.[10]

A brief comparison of two famous poems can serve to measure the extent of this feminization. In the fifth of his *Roman Elegies*, written in 1790, Goethe identified artistic with erotic mastery. Referring to his mistress, Christiane Vulpius, he wrote:

> Oftmals hab ich auch schon in ihren Armen gedichtet
> Und das Hexameters Mass leise mit fingernder Hand
> Ihr auf die Rücken gezahlt.   (15–17)

> [Often I have even made poetry in her arms, and the hexameter's measure softly, with fingering hand, counted on her back.][11]

Goethe was only joking, of course, but among men this sort of joke makes a serious claim: the fingering hand, the artist's hand, acts with the power and pleasure of the phallus. When the Vicomte de Valmont, the male lead in Choderlos de Laclos's contemporaneous novel *Les Liaisons Dangereuses* (1782), does something quite similar, there is no doubt at all about what it means: "I have been using [Emilie] as a desk upon which to write my fair devotee—to whom I find it most amusing I should send a letter written in bed, in the arms, almost, of a trollop (broken off, too, while I committed a downright infidelity), in which I give her an exact account of my situation and my conduct."[12]

Quite a different claim informs Yeats's "Adam's Curse," written in 1902. The subject is poetry:

> I said, "A line will take us hours maybe;
> Yet if it does not seem a moment's thought,
> Our stitching and unstitching has been naught."   (4–6)

That beautiful mild woman . . .
Replied, "To be born woman is to know—
Although they do not talk of it at school—
That we must labour to be beautiful." (15, 18–20)[13]

Art here comes, not from working on women, but from women's work: the quintessential women's work of needlepoint and self-adornment. Yeats's image of stitching and unstitching even suggests a parallel to the work of the paradigmatic female artist, Penelope, who continually weaves and unweaves a hero's shroud, thus articulating, in her own terms, the plot of the *Odyssey*.

Inevitably, the feminization of art provoked a defensive reaction. Many male artists sought to recuperate the masculinity of their calling; to that end, they began to take the control or repudiation of femininity as a primary cultural mission. Any man, wrote Nietzsche, who denies "the abysmal antagonism, the necessity of a forever hostile tension" between gender principles, "will probably prove too 'short' for all the basic questions of life . . . unable to penetrate *any* depth."[14] The depiction of dangerous women in opera, fiction, painting, and film emerged as a popular means of "penetrating" life's questions by "acknowledging," that is, constructing and mastering, the antagonism of gender. The fact that many of these portrayals are nuanced or ambivalent does not cancel out the antagonism that the nuance or ambivalence is asked to mitigate; the mitigation is itself a means of constructing the antagonism. Nor is crude misogyny a requirement. The aesthetic medium can escape being feminized simply by representing femininity as a problem, an enigma, a thing in itself.

In this context, *Carnaval* figures as an unusually free-spirited work, perhaps composed as much to advance as to comply with the process of feminization, which was still nascent in 1834. Certainly, Schumann was predisposed to welcome this trend. As a young man he seemed strongly if intermittently drawn to fantasies of gender mobility and feminine identification. An essay from June 1828 celebrates "genial" youths (i.e., those who combine creative genius with social geniality) for their oscillation between gender positions, "now soft and gentle like virgins, now strong and wild like a lion woken from its slumber."[15] The same oscillation invests a poem from the end of the same year with what Peter Ostwald calls "the flavor of bisexual fantasy":

Und wie den Jüngling wild der Jüngling liebt,
Und wie er ihn umarmt, and wie er mit ihm weint,
So bist Du jetzt; einst warst du mir Geliebte,

Jetzt bist Du mir Geliebter.
Und aus den Blüthen deiner Liebe
Wand sich die Freundschaft sanft hervor.[16]

> [And as one youth wildly loves the other youth, and as he embraces him, and as they weep together, so are you now; once you were my feminine beloved, now you are my masculine beloved. And from the blossoms of your love, friendship wafts forth softly.]

A letter written two years later (to the composer's mother, no less) characterizes intense male friendships in similar terms: "With [Semmel] my love has been more masculine, firm, well-behaved; with Rosen it is more talkative, girlish, full of feeling."[17]

Schumann was deeply attracted by the idea of partnership, shading into fusion, with a woman artist. The idea was part of what drew him to the pianist Ernestine von Fricken, Clara Wieck's predecessor as his fiancée, and to Clara herself. A recurrent topic in the Schumanns' courtship and early marriage, this symbiosis found its most striking musical expression in Robert's piano suite *Humoreske* (1839), which incorporates a theme from a Romance by Clara as an inaudible inner voice. The theme is written out on a separate line between the right and left hand staves but remains unplayed; it is meant to be heard beyond or through the sounding music as the secret inner voice of a compound subject. On receiving the score of Clara's Romance, Robert wrote her that "Each of your ideas comes from my own soul, just as I must thank you for all the music I write. . . . When did you write the [Romance]? In March I had a similar idea; you will find it in the *Humoreske*. Our mutual sympathy is absolutely remarkable."[18]

A scattering of remarks from letters and diaries also shows Schumann associating either music or his own musical creativity with feminine personae. Small verbal details give a fantasy-enriched form to familiar metaphors, from the feminine gender of music itself to the classical image of the work of art as brainchild:

> It's amazing that there are no female composers. . . . Women could perhaps be regarded as the frozen, firm embodiments of music. (1828)

> Music is the feminine friend who can best communicate everything that we feel internally. (1838)

> I've put on my frilly dress and composed thirty cute little things from which I've selected about twelve and called them "Scenes from Childhood." (1838)

> [After orchestrating the *Spring Symphony*] I feel like a young woman

who has just given birth—so relieved and happy, but also sick and sore. (1841)[19]

Recognition of Schumann's feminine personae can help clarify some problematical features in two of his best-known song cycles. *Dichterliebe* (1840), a chronicle of lost love, famously ends with a contradiction. In the last song, *Die alten bösen Lieder*, the jilted poet assumes a hypervirile posture and repudiates both femininity and art. The song, however, dissolves into the lyrical, feminine-identified piano postlude of the earlier *Am leuchtenden Sommermorgen*, which becomes the basis of an extended postlude for the cycle as whole. On the most obvious reading, the dissolve indicates that the poet is still in love; his anger is a disavowal that fails as we listen. Perhaps, though, we should take this dissolve to suggest that the creative imperative, associated in the earlier song with the whispering and talking flowers of the summer morning, is stronger than any romantic imperative. "Do not," the flowers have said, "be angry [*böse*] with our sister,/You sorrowful, pale man." In framing this admonition poetically, the speaker also heeds it, a speech act redoubled—and revealed—by the poignant music that envelops it. The last song begins by trying to revoke this concession, then thinks better of it. What is revoked instead by the return of the earlier music is the exaggerated masculinity that forms an impediment to art.

Along similar lines, the notorious *Frauenliebe und -leben* (1840) might be understood not only as a patriarchal dream of feminine worshipfulness, but also as a fantasy of feminine identification that courts the extremes of dependency, passivity, and masochism. Franz Brendel, Schumann's successor as editor of the *Neue Zeitschrift für Musik*, came close to this suggestion when he remarked that "in th[is] song cycle . . . [Schumann] expressed the deepest inwardness, the intimate life of a female sensibility. The heart has been revealed without mediation in these songs; one looks straight into the soul."[20] Schumann's "expression" of feminine inwardness, as Ruth Solie has suggested, is actually a construction of the cyclical time to which a woman's life was conventionally assigned. The songs tend to be "rounded" by piano postludes and/or closing recapitulations of opening stanzas; the cycle as a whole is rounded by a piano postlude that recapitulates the music of the first song.[21] Yet while framing the protagonist's identity as the exemplary wife and mother, an ideal object, this practice of involution also helps seal in Schumann's transgressive identification with her as a fantasmatic subject.

Carnaval suggests a contrary extreme. Its prominent feminine roleplaying avoids even the appearance of conventionality or respectability, the better to celebrate its composer's own creative energies in their most innovative and unorthodox vein. In 1828, Schumann had written admiringly about the "free, loveable nonchalance *[Nachlässigheit]*" of "genial girls";[22] six years later he drew on the carnivalesque impersonation of that nonchalance—nineteenth-century "girl power"—to help construct an earthy, oppositional model of the musician's social role. On at least one occasion as a young man, Schumann seems to have made this connection personally in a festive setting. In February 1830, after a week of nonstop revelry, he went to a masked ball where he apparently played a cross-dressed role in an all-male theatrical skit.[23] In light of his later remark about musical childbirth, it may be suggestive that he took "the mother's part," though the suggestion should obviously not be pressed too hard.

CARNIVAL UNLEASHED

The miniatures of *Carnaval* are largely of two types: dances or marches and character sketches. This generic division loosely corresponds to what Mikhail Bakhtin identifies as two major dimensions of popular festivity.[24] The dances and marches, all of them vigorous, suggest the release of pent-up bodily energies; the character sketches, mercurial and caricature-like, suggest the collapse of social and psychological boundaries at the prompting of masquerade. Schumann's musical free-for-all encourages the types to mix, but in general the dances and marches serve as a horizon of possibility against which the character sketches crystallize and dissipate in quick succession.

Above all else, these sketches constitute musical skits, impersonations, "take-offs" of one person by another. Schumann underlines the point by freely taking his sketch subjects both from life and from the improvised theater of Italian commedia dell'arte. All the sketches are equally ventriloquistic, even—or especially—when Schumann himself is the subject. All the sketches project a persona that belongs to both the self and the other. As a series, moreover, the sketches in their crazy-quilt diversity challenge the notion that there is a single self behind all the masks. This challenge was particularly important to eighteenth-century masquerade, which, as Terry Castle observes, embodied a "devaluation of unitary notions of the self, as radical in its own way as the more abstract demystifications in the writings of Hume."[25] Eighteenth-century festive practices and their survivals in nineteenth-century German university life were probably Schumann's models in *Carnaval,* as they had been a few years earlier in *Papillons,* the close of which corresponds to the closing episode of Jean-Paul Richter's novel *Die Flegeljahre* (Adolescent years): a masked ball.

In affirming the nonunitary self, Schumann gives his "own" self an exemplary volatility. Both his musical signature and his poetic projection as the introvert-extrovert alter egos Eusebius and Florestan come to the fore in *Carnaval*, but only in the most elusive, most imponderable of terms. The "Schumann" identity weds itself to so many enigmatic ciphers and stylized personae that it, not they, comes to seem secondary, esoteric, and illusory. Brendel was disconcerted by this aspect of *Carnaval*, which he took to mark the actual disappearance of Schumann's subjectivity. Although he finds the work "interesting" in its attempt to draw character portraits, he is bothered that the characters appear only "in disguise." He faults the music for an artifice that amounts to insincerity, complaining that it is "entirely removed from the realm of spontaneous artistic creation."[26]

Carnaval is famously based on a group of three- and four-note mottoes printed in the score in double whole notes under the title *Sphinxes*. Each motto contains all the German musical letters found in Schumann's name: S. C. H. A. (E♭-C-B-A), his musical signature; A. S. C. H. (A-E♭-C-B); and As. C. H. (A♭-C-B). The two mottoes that spell "Asch" refer to the hometown of Ernestine von Fricken, who appears in the cast of *Carnaval* as "Estrella." The Sphinxes indicate that the Asch mottoes are anagrammatical masks for the musical signature without explaining why (sphinxes never do). The implication, however, is the same as the one Schumann expressed in a letter: "I have just discovered that the name ASCH is very musical and contains letters that also occur in my name. They were musical symbols."[27] The anagrams are thus both genuinely esoteric (they conceal Ernestine's identity as woman and artist together with Schumann's impulse to absorb it) and fictitiously esoteric: any performer or score reader, and many listeners, can follow their vicissitudes. They also suggest the indeterminacy of gender that permeates the cycle: Egyptian sphinxes are male (S. C. H. A.?), Theban sphinxes female (A. S. C. H. / As. C. H.?). The most famous of the latter posed a riddle (solved by Oedipus) to which the answer was "a man."

The Asch mottoes alone do constructive work in *Carnaval*. The musical signature can be felt only as something missing, a lost or perhaps imaginary origin; all identity here is substitute identity. A trace of the signature does perhaps surface in *Eusebius*, which places it near the core of Schumann's creativity. Yet the signature there is deeply recondite, almost a mirage, in telling contrast to the Asch motives, which are always perfectly clear. The enciphered notes are present in a jumble, never crystallizing into a melodic figure. The music does, however, dwell with sphinxlike patience on S, the tonic first degree. In the first and fifth measures, S gleams out by skipping over a melody in undulating steps; meanwhile the first eight-measure phrase prolongs S continuously in the middle voice, where it oscillates with its upper and lower neighbors. As example 5.1 shows, a cryptographic epiphany flickers by in measure 6. As the middle-voice upper neighbor resolves to Eb (S), A sounds in the bass against an oscillation between C and H in the treble; the four notes draw together in dissonant knot that has to be untied with reference to S. The gesture, which is repeated several times, can be heard—but only by someone armed with the score and a will to out-fox the sphinx—as an inchoate, half chimerical form of the originary motto S. C. H. A.

Even more chimerical is the role of the musical signature in the skittish *A. S. C. H.___ S. C. H. A. (Lettres Dansantes).* The title acts as a riddle, for neither of the mottoes it names appears in the piece. The answer comes in fragments. The melody line of the first measure consists of "dancing let-ters" that form a palindrome, As-C-H-C-As, on the Asch motto *not* named in the title, here heard for the first time in the cycle. As for S. C. H. A., it once again appears only via its initial *S,* this time as a harmony. Like *Eusebius,* the piece is in Eb, here a key that continually "dances" over a dominant pedal without finding—or seeking—a cadence; the close, again as in *Eusebius,* is on the tonic six-four. A. S. C. H. thus disappears into its alter ego; S. C. H. A. fails (on schedule) to appear. In a sense, the most accurate cipher in the title is the empty dash; like the nonunitary self, the dancing letters have no stable reference point, no fixed abode.

In this connection it is important to note that the musical anagrams of *Carnaval* are not musical motives—rhythmically articulate short figures—that happen to coincide with ciphers. They are merely, as Schumann's sub-title indicates, sequences of notes that are variously worked into the larger melodic units—real motives and themes—with which most of the pieces in the cycle begin. The sphinxes have no discrete musical identity; they are real ciphers notated in and by music. Their appearance in the score, the faceless rows of double whole notes, underlines their esotericism: they do not even look like music. What they denote, moreover, is not so much a dis-crete set of referents as the anagrammatical process itself, which in this context embodies the carnivalesque extreme of impersonation. The notes assume varied forms throughout the cycle, but they have no primary form, no grounding "self," an absence underlined by the silence of the S. C. H. A. signature.

That absence is remediable only if the Sphinxes are played, which rarely happens. Playing them, according to Slavoj Žižek, improperly exposes the uncanny and discomfiting "preontological" substrate of the music, "like seeing a dead squid on the table, no longer alive and gracefully moving in

Example 5.1. Schumann, *Eusebius* (from *Carnaval*), mm. 5–6

Eusebius

the water." Yet the score gives no indication that they are *not* to be played, and the fact that playing them is the only way to hear the S. C. H. A. motto suggests that the sphinxes are more, or other, than ugly little "impossible" objects. As played, precisely as nonmusic, they form an uncanny admonition: the search for a symbolic reality behind the imaginary series of carnival masks will lead only to a suspension of vitality, a sphinxlike stoniness or the larval immobility of the Hawk moth, otherwise known as Sphinx.[28]

Schumann's closest approach to a definite symbolic presence in *Carnaval* emerges in the paired pieces named for his dual personae, Eusebius the dreamer and Florestan the man of action. "Definite" in this context, however, is a decidedly relative term. *Eusebius* is more like a study in the blurring of definitions. It is in A B A form, but its B section is no more than a recapitulation of most of A: slower, texturally enriched, and continuously pedaled rather than unpedaled, but the same music. The second A section continues with the slower "teneramente" tempo; it recapitulates the same music as B but restores the original texture. Anticipating *Lettres Dansantes*, though in a limpid, lyrical vein, the piece is also oriented around an unstable chord, the tonic six-four, on which it ends. The only full cadence—a languid "feminine" cadence drawn out over a full measure—comes at the close of the B section. Thus the "final" cadence is displaced to the interior of the piece, where it is blurred into the harmonies preceding it, while the precadential six-four chord is displaced to the end, which it robs of finality. Meanwhile, above the free-floating harmony the melody murmurs continuously in irregular rhythmic groupings, a sinuosity without a shape. If his piece is any measure, Eusebius is neither a self-sufficient nor firmly bounded figure; he is more alter than ego.

Florestan, in case we were expecting Schumann's virile other side to do something resolute, is if anything even more vertiginous. Agitated and passionate, the piece begins with a dominant minor-ninth chord that once again "resolves" to the tonic six-four; the same dominant, this time without pretense of resolution, returns to supply the end. In the closing passages the chord is even stripped repeatedly of its root, which would also have formed the bass note of the nonarriving tonic six-four. Meanwhile, two interpolations have arisen to suggest that harmonic open-endedness is the least of Florestan's worries. The first tentatively alludes to a theme from the opening number of Schumann's *Papillons*; the second actually quotes the theme, which is also identified in the score. As the theme crystallizes, we are invited to remember that *Papillons* impersonates the main characters of Jean-Paul's novel *Die Flegeljahre*, Walt and Vult, whose relationship parallels that of Eusebius and Florestan. Florestan can thus be said to contain Vult, and Schumann Jean-Paul, as an inner double. Nor is that all. The interpolated theme is played, not at its original tempo, but at the Adagio tempo we have just heard in *Eusebius*. The effect is introspective, almost dreamy; it suggests that Florestan may also be said to contain Eusebius as an inner double. That Eusebius is decentered, open-ended, and himself doubled between pedaled and unpedaled musical images carries the whirligig of identities to a giddy extreme, the more so if one connects the "Eusebian" aspect of Schumann's Florestan to the brooding of his counterpart in Beethoven's *Fidelio*. Far from encapsulating and stabilizing Schumann's identity, *Eusebius* and *Florestan* propose that identity is a delusion. There are no selves, only impersonations.

The subjective mobility and lack of boundaries projected by *Eusebius* and *Florestan* have a distinctly feminine cast in nineteenth-century culture, though one more often dreaded than courted. The era invested women with extraordinary metamorphic powers, perhaps as a reflection of the dramatic changes in character imputed to them as a result of changes in age, sexual condition, and marital status. The theme proliferated throughout the arts, increasingly so as the century progressed, encompassing a host of literary and pictorial mermaids, lamias, nymphs, coquettes, prostitutes, actresses, and singers, together with their real-life counterparts and such musical exemplars as the flower maidens of Wagner's *Parsifal* (not to mention Kundry) and the elusive, angelic-demonic object of the *idée fixe* in Berlioz's *Symphonie fantastique*.[29] In his comment on *Kinderszenen*, Schumann gives the trope of loose-fitting femininity its domestic form, identifying with both woman and child in order to create an overabundance of pretty things; Brendel's comment on *Frauenliebe* invokes the inner permeability of the feminine subject in suggesting that Schumann has completely gotten under a woman's skin; Liszt consistently describes the mercurial side of Schumann's music in terms that suggest without specifying midcentury stereotypes of femininity: "exceptional grace," "a certain charm," "a hundred touches of coquetry, enjoyment, passion, love, blindness, and dizziness."[30]

Nietzsche would later pick up on the general subjective volatility of Schumann's style as a derisory feminine trait: "Schumann . . . was essentially a *petty* taste . . . constantly stepping aside, shyly withdrawing, a noble weakling wallowing in utterly anonymous bliss and pain, a sort of girl."[31] Schumann's Asch mottoes in *Carnaval*, with their "stepping aside" into an esoteric persona with feminine associations, their sphinxlike anagrammatical play with the absent signature motto, extend the connotation of feminine shape-shifting over the cycle as a whole. If masquerade is the paramount image here, then cross-dressing is the paramount form of masquerade, the symbolic means of gaining access to the feminine powers of self-multiplication and self-creation. And here the character sketches come into their own, together with a hermeneutic call, heeded by Brendel, Kossmaly, and Liszt, to give the characters their full ascriptive play.

Two episodes in *Carnaval* make musical cross-dressing especially prominent. The first centers on *Coquette*, the piece that follows the pairing of *Eusebius* and *Florestan*. *Coquette* mingles a "flirtatious" figure with broad lyrical gestures; its texture is as stereotypically feminine as that of *Florestan* is masculine. The texture, however, also signals the play of a female impersonator. Wide melodic leaps to the upper register link *Coquette* to both *Florestan* and the earlier *Arlequin*; its characteristic rhythm states that of *Arlequin* in reverse (see ex. 5.2). Better yet, *Coquette* begins by partly resolving the open-ended harmonies that thread *Eusebius* and *Florestan*. Picking up the dominant with which *Florestan* ends, *Coquette* "coquettishly" diverts it with a V–VI deceptive cadence, then proceeds to cadence on its own tonic, B♭, the very sonority to which the final E♭ six-four of *Eusebius* failed to progress.

Schumann's masculine personae thus coalesce under a feminine sign. More, they coalesce under a misogynist sign, or at least a satirical one; coquettishness implies vanity, sexual teasing, triviality. These qualities, however, are revalued in the context of carnival, which invites us to understand the coquette as a quintessential impersonator, an unrivaled roleplayer as acrobatic with her identity as Harlequin is with his body. The teasing is philosophical—carnival as Humean critique: is the Coquette a disguise that fits both Florestan and Eusebius and thus offers them an imaginary unity—as Schumann? Or is the true coquette the musically cross-

Example 5.2. Schumann, opening passages of *Arlequin, Florestan,* and *Coquette* (from *Carnaval*)

a.

b.

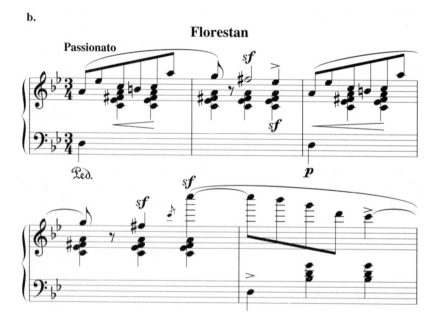

dressing Schumann who even as himself can appear only in disguise as Florestan or Eusebius?

The second episode of musical cross-dressing involves a trio of pieces, *Chiarina* (Clara Wieck), *Chopin,* and *Estrella.* In this instance, the feminine character sketches are strikingly virile and Florestan-like. *Chiarina* is impassioned, shot through with *agitato* rhythms; *Estrella* is vigorous and striding,

Example 5.2. (continued)

c.

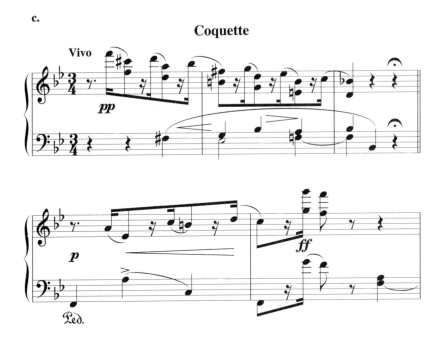

Coquette

almost swaggering. As transvestite skits, these pieces might suggest several different sorts of fantasy. Chiarina and Estrella, both modeled on girls still in their teens, might retain a "boyish" energy that they have not yet been taught to repress, though Schumann has been; they might offer a point of identification with the loveable nonchalance that the young Schumann admired in genial girls; or they might provide feminine masks that enhance and gratify a fictitiously secret masculinity that they only half conceal.

The whirligig of genders and identities turns the other way in *Chopin,* a faux-nocturne that mediates between *Chiarina* and *Estrella* with studied effeminacy. *Chopin* inverts the gender masquerade of the pieces that frame it by both satirizing and imitating the supposed effeminacy of its model, turning Chopin into a feminine persona for the masculine Schumann who impersonates him in drop-dead note-perfect style. (The real Chopin was not amused.) This is the early Chopin, whom Schumann described in 1841 as having "comported himself as though overstrewn with spangles, gold trinkets, and pearls"[32]—a carnivalesque display of feminine role-playing if ever there was one; the description ironically echoes Liszt's description of *Carnaval* as charming and bejeweled. At the same time, *Chopin* is so perfectly "Chopinesque" that Schumann's own persona risks disappearing into it, as if it were really Chopin here who has the upper hand.

The images in *Chiarina, Chopin,* and *Estrella* have a specific historical character that needs to be recognized. Fifty years after *Carnaval* the figures of the "mannish" woman and the effeminate male would become medical categories betokening—in the influential formulation of Richard von Krafft-Ebing's *Psychopathia Sexualis* (1886)—perversion and degeneracy. They would represent threats to the social order from outside, but an outside understood as identical with the inside of the psyche. Schumann's depictions of similar figures in *Carnaval* are nothing of the kind. They are realizations of performative possibilities within the social order that carry critical and utopian force, and may be resisted because of it. They are, as Liszt observed, the masks of a band of artists, for whose relationship to the social order carnival is the appropriate metaphor. The medium of their social performances might even be the very pianos used to impersonate them; since all three figures are pianists, the character pieces may at one level represent their keyboard manners, one aspect of which is the ability to disregard the boundaries of gender.

The pieces in this group are linked musically in ways both plain (a characteristic rhythm permeating *Chiarina* and *Estrella;* a telltale melodic cross-reference) and fancy (ambiguous play with F-minor harmonies in all three). *Chiarina* consists entirely of reiterations of a figure built around a dotted rhythm; the outer sections of *Estrella* state an augmented form of the same figure in every other pair of measures. The core gesture, a repercussive leap, is ascending in the one piece, descending in the other (ex. 5.3). The opening phrase of *Chiarina* also finds a distinct melodic echo in the opening of *Estrella,* the latter's descending minor sixth, Ab-C, inverting the former's ascending minor third on the same notes. As to harmony, the opening four-measure phrase of *Chiarina* begins on an F-minor chord that turns out to be a subdominant, progressing to a full "feminine" cadence in a tonic C minor. The parallel phrase of *Estrella* also begins on an F-minor chord; this one turns out to be a tonic, progressing to a full "feminine" cadence via a dominant C major. The harmonic progressions involved are quite similar; they are probably most apparent to a score-reading performer, who sees the switch from three to four flats and whose left hand executes similar (initially all but identical) leaps in both pieces. *Chopin* anticipates *Estrella's* role-reversal of F and C at a particularly expressive moment near its close, but only within the confines of Ab, the relative major of F minor. We are free to read this anticipation as suggesting either that *Estrella* and *Chiarina*

Example 5.3. Schumann, opening passages of *Chiarina* and *Estrella* (from *Carnaval*)

a.

Chiarina

b.

Estrella

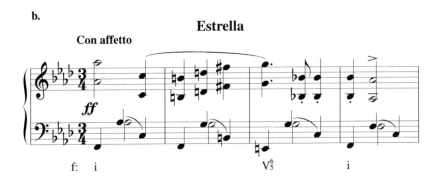

can be linked only through the mediation of a masculine (but feminized) inner double, or that the energies latent in *Chopin* can be realized only through a pair of feminine (but masculinized) outer doubles.

The pairing of *Chiarina* and *Estrella* is replayed near the end of the cycle with the mediating figure withdrawn. In *Aveu* the key shifts to F minor, but the pitches of the anagram are the same as those of *Chiarina* and the rhythm is also agitated, with a similar little stutter over the C (so who makes the avowal? to whom?). The anagram at the beginning of *Promenade* is virtually identical to its counterpart in *Estrella* in both pitch and breadth of gesture, though, again, the key adds a flat (it's Db), thus preserving the tonal relation of the earlier pair (so who goes promenading? with whom?). Neither the quality nor the location of gender is allowed to settle anywhere in this nexus of pieces.

INTERMEZZO: A THEORETICAL DETOUR

The reciprocities of *Chiarina* and *Estrella* and their later echo in *Aveu* and *Promenade* also suggest a set of mirror images, which leads us to the third term of my argument. It is a term, however, that requires some mulling over in advance. I will shortly propose that *Carnaval* sets up musical mirror relations that belong to a larger family of mirror tropes current during much of the nineteenth century. Leo Treitler has objected to this idea on the grounds that it assumes too many mental operations on the listener's part between musical details and concepts and that the supposed presence of mirror tropes in the musical codes of Schumann's era remains moot. This critique rests on two frequently held but mistaken assumptions: first, that a hermeneutically ascribed meaning must, if valid, be produced and embodied by technical details as a self-present intuition for "the listener"; and, second, that to ascribe such a meaning supposes it to be a positive encoded presence in the work or the context.[33]

The erroneousness of these assumptions is reflected in the order of their statement in Treitler's text, which is best answered by mirror-reversal, or crab-canon, if you like. Treitler's movement from embodied to encoded meaning goes from effect to cause; a bona fide meaning can be apprehended as embodied because it is encoded. Although the act of interpretation, which cannot recover the past exactly, will inevitably add something, what it adds must be subsumable under the original meaning; anything more is just an interpretive fiction. This straight-line logic, however, leaves out the dense and unpredictable layer of mediation which necessarily intervenes between the work, musical or otherwise, and any meanings ascribed to it at any time, under any circumstances. Interpretation arises in the first place precisely because meaning is not firmly encoded in the work (or style or event), musical or otherwise; the meaning is not the cause of the interpretation, but its effect.

What is objectively "present" in the work (style, event) is not a specific meaning but the availability or potentiality of meanings that may or may not be ascribed, or may be ascribed by indirection. A meaning that is ascribed has not necessarily been grasped intuitively in past or present acts of listening, and may never be so grasped, at least not fully. The meaning in question is not a message, something that can be encoded and decoded. It is a kind of action, a sometimes virtual, sometimes actual piece of cultural work that may (or may only) become available in indirect, figurative, penumbral forms. As chapter 7 will argue more fully, such meaning is produced from "above," not "below": it isn't the technical musical detail that suggests the idea of mirroring (i.e., suggests it in logic, whatever the case in fact), but the idea that ascriptively constitutes the musical detail as mirror-like. Semantic potentiality is mobilized and "validated" by mediating between the work and the ascription. This is so, moreover, regardless of whether the interpreter is a contemporary or an heir of the work's cultural context. Although some such meanings may become, or may once have become, immediate, others may not; and some may occur to the mind's ear, or to musical memory, or the score-reading eye, or acts of musical performance rather than or prior to occurring in the listening ear. Listening is not the sum total of musical experience, just its indispensable core.

CARNIVAL REFLECTED

Mirror reflection in the nineteenth century supports a trope of slightly estranged self-perception linked with mobility of self-fashioning. Compare the case of Chiarina and Estrella, in relation to both each other and their impersonator, with a case from a very different area of life in the 1830s—but one only seemingly from far afield. Henriette d'Angeville, who in 1838 became the first woman mountaineer to climb Mont Blanc, insisted on carrying a looking glass with her on the climb: "a truly *feminine* article," she wrote, "which I would none the less recommend to anyone contemplating an expedition at altitude (even a captain of dragoons!). For one may use it to examine the skin to see what ravages the mountain air has wrought and remedy them by rubbing gently with cucumber pomade."[34] Practical though it may be, the larger importance of the mirror here is social, its background the resistance D'Angeville had to contend with. The mirror serves as a trope for constructing, playing with, and identifying with imaginary self-reflections: "at altitude," in the freedom regularly associated with the mountains, a woman looking in the mirror may act just like a captain of dragoons, who, in the same situation, will find it in his best interest to act just like a woman. Just so then with Chiarina and Estrella in the imaginary press of Schumann's carnival.

As D'Angeville's text suggests, the nineteenth-century mirror increasingly becomes the space reserved for women's subjectivity rather than, as was traditional, the sign of their vanity. By gazing into the depths of the mirror, women can enjoy, explore, and to some degree construct their own identities. They can spot damage and repair it. They can even do for themselves affirmatively what men do to them appropriatively: gaze with a pleasure that constructs the thing it sees.[35] Not that this is an unmixed blessing. The association of feminine identity with visual pleasure is a masculine convention. The mirror preserves rather than resists male control unless the reflected image becomes too absorbing, in which case the mirror arouses male hostility—and desire—by making the woman psychologically and sexually impenetrable. The speaker of Arthur Symons's poem "Laus Virginitatis" (1887), murmuring "I to myself suffice" to her mirror-image, is a woman self-enclosed in just these terms:

> The mirror of men's eyes delights me less,
> O mirror, than the friend I find in thee.[36]

As a masculine fantasy, this dreamy self-sufficiency forms a covertly anxious antithesis to the more playful, distanced notion of self-fashioning intimated by D'Angeville.

Still, male artists do sometimes acknowledge the authority of the woman in the mirror without much seeking to limit it. Wagner, for one, gives heroic dignity to the newly awakened Brünnhilde as she defers being caught up by Siegfried's desire—which she will soon have to recognize as her own:

> Sahst du dein Bild im klaren Bach?
> Hat es dich Frohen erfreut?
> Rührtest zur Woge das Wasser du auf;
> zerflösse die klare Fläche des Bachs:
> dein Bild sähst du nicht mehr.
>
> > [Have you seen your image in the clear stream? Joyous one, has it rejoiced you? Had you stirred the water to waves, the stream's clear surface would have broken up, you would no more have seen your image.]
>
> (*Siegfried*, Act 3)

Meanwhile women artists take up the mirror themselves for a variety of creative, that is, self-creative, uses. Lucy Snowe, the protagonist of Charlotte Brontë's novel *Villette* (1853), negotiates with mirrors repeatedly. At the turning point of her story, and amid the confusions of an outdoor masquerade, she "secretly and chiefly long[s] to come on [a] circular mirror of crystal, and surprise the moon glassing therein her pearly front." At the end, when Lucy attains a Woolfian room of her own, its centerpiece is precisely "[a] small round table [that] shone like the mirror over [the] hearth."[37] In "The Other Side of the Mirror" (1908), Mary Elizabeth Coleridge engages in a kind of psychotherapy based literally on the necessity of facing herself. Sitting before her glass, she deliberately conjures up an image "wild / With more than womanly despair," disfigured by unacknowledged or forbidden feelings of anguish or thwarted desire. Coleridge engages this disfigured image in order to dispel it together with the conventional "fairer vision" that it displaces, leaving a free "crystal surface" behind in which a more authentic self may—just may—appear.[38]

Other women are drawn to the art of reflection rather than driven to it. Mary Cassatt's idyllic painting, *Mother and Child* (ca. 1905; fig. 5.1) interprets the mirror as the means by which feminine identity is passed from mother to daughter; the affectionate scene offers a tacit alternative to the Oedipal rivalry typical of male models of cultural transmission. The sunflower at the mother's breast unites nurture with both procreative power and adornment, that is, with both nature and art. The mirrors, large and small, model Cassatt's own art of figure painting, which becomes a cultural projection of the feminine reproductive power also symbolized by the position of the naked child on her mother's lap. Clementina, Lady Hawarden's photographic study of her grown daughter at the mirror (ca. 1861–62; fig. 5.2) similarly locates the power of feminine self-fashioning in two reproductive media, large and small, the daughter's mirror and the mother's camera lens. The mother receives back the intense glow of natural light burnishing the exposed flesh of the daughter's shoulder, uniting her own bodily creativity with the medium of her art; the daughter receives an amorphous space of fantasy and imagination, her image in the mirror enveloped in a kind of dreamy twilight while a fringe of light barely brushes the reflected shoulder. The image of external world looms faintly beyond, but only out of focus, as a blur.[39]

Writing to Clara Wieck in 1836, Schumann adumbrates his own version of the scene in Cassatt's painting and Hawarden's photograph. "My future," he tells her, "seems more secure now . . . but I still have to accomplish a great deal just to achieve what you can see anytime you happen to step in front of a mirror—in the meantime you too will want to remain an artist. . . . You will carry your own weight, work with me, and share my joys and sorrows."[40] Addressing Clara with the intimate "du" for the first time in their correspondence, as if the term had been vacated by the recent event of his mother's death, Schumann takes the woman/artist in the mirror as the model for the construction of his own subjectivity. His fantasy of Clara's self-sufficiency suggests that, as a woman's, her body image is whole while his is still fragmentary, as if he had been frozen in a moment of psychosexual prematurity, prior to the Lacanian "mirror-stage" of jubilant (if ultimately false) self-recognition. Schumann does not present himself, however, as revealing a personal pathology, but as acknowledging a social structure that gives a particular historical value to tropes of self-reflection along gender lines. Reflective self-fashioning is the form in which

Figure 5.1. Mary Cassatt, *Mother and Child* (c. 1905), oil on canvas, 36¼ × 29 in. Chester Dale Collection, the National Gallery of Art, Washington, D.C.

the feminine mobility noted earlier assumes a relatively stable and determinate form. Part of the work that Schumann feels he has to accomplish is the musical structuring of this process, which also loosens its ties to literal gender formations and becomes available for symbolic articulation.

The musical mirror images of *Carnaval*—slightly estranged repetitions of melodic or sectional wholes—try to do just that. On the largest scale, *Carnaval* as a whole projects a mirror image, its first half being ruled by the A. S. C. H. motto and its second half by As. C. H., with *Lettres Dansantes* effecting the transition. Within the fold of this mirror further reflections proliferate; in several cases the effect is overdetermined, with a larger symmetry enclosing a smaller. Both within and among pieces, the cycle is a musical hall of mirrors, a sound space of feminine pleasure and liberty. Already cited as an instance of mirroring among pieces is the network formed by *Chiarina, Estrella, Aveu,* and *Promenade;* of mirroring within pieces, the internal reflection formed in *Eusebius* by using continuous pedal

Figure 5.2. Clementina, Lady Hawarden, photograph of Clementina Maude (1861–62). V. & A. Picture Library, Victoria and Albert Museum, London.

in the B section to repeat, enhance, and render more fluid much of the unpedaled A section. The B section even produces a "true" mirror reversal by beginning with the second part of A and ending with the first; the subsequent reprise of A does the same thing as it rounds off the piece in the slower "mirroring" tempo.[41]

Reconaissance behaves in similar ways, thereby mirroring both *Eusebius* and itself. The A sections, in A♭ Major, present their theme over a foursquare inner-voice staccato; the B section, in B Major, weaves the same theme over and under a syncopated inner-voice legato. In a subtle reversal of *Eusebius*, where the "mirror" of the B section carries the melody to the next higher register, *Reconnaisance* carries it to the next lower; the resulting close texture gives the impression of a reflective rather than a limpid inwardness, despite—or underlying—the lively tempo. This mirroring between sections can be taken as a higher-order form of mirroring within the sections, perhaps even one with a paradigmatic dynamism. In the A sections, the right-hand staccato doubles the theme at the lower octave in rapid repeated notes. The effect is less an actual than a potential mirroring, an embodiment of the glittering and skittering energy that mirroring momentarily stabilizes. The B section enacts that stabilization, continuously mirroring statements in the treble with overlapping statements in the bass. The overlaps, their close counterpoint combined with the close texture, cause the statements to blur into each other at the borders, much as figure and image do in Lady Hawarden's photograph of her daughter in mirror-reverie. At the same time, the syncopated inner voices of the B section keep the stabilizing step off balance, continuously refreshing it with speculative energy. The title *Reconaissance* suggests recognition, acknowledgment, and exploration, the object of which, we may surmise, is the feminine depth of reflection itself.

Perhaps the most explicit mirror piece in *Carnaval* is *Replique*, the richly ambiguous title of which can refer to a musical repeat, artistic replica, theatrical cue, and riposte or response. The piece is an abbreviated variant of *Coquette*, which it follows like a stray coda. *Replique* not only mirrors *Coquette* directly, in the process coaxing the woman-mirror trope into the open, but also, like *Reconaissance,* redoubles the mirroring process within itself. In this case, the internal mirroring again involves thematic repetition between different voices.

Replique begins by mirroring in the upper voice a sprightly little figure (marked *poco con grazia*) first heard in the inner voice at the opening and close of *Coquette*. A reprise of that opening/close follows immediately, remirroring the figure in its original inner-voice position under a restatement of *Coquette's* main theme (X, ex. 5.4). Next the figure assumes a new form that also appears first in the upper voice to be mirrored immediately in the inner voice under the *Coquette* theme (Y, ex. 5.4). Then a metamorphosis happens: the sprightly figure undergoes a lyrical expansion, once more heard first in the upper voice and mirrored immediately in the inner voice, this time under a new form of the *Coquette* theme (Z, ex. 5.4; at the close the lyrical melody leaps into the upper voice to coincide with the transformed *Coquette* theme, which is now rising instead of falling). And that, but for a repeat of the whole process, is that. In *Replique*, mirroring becomes an explicitly creative activity: three mirror images make up the whole of the piece, itself a mirror image; the series of mirror images effects a transformation of expressive character both within *Replique* and between *Replique* and *Coquette*. In this creative or generative aspect, mirroring claims cultural power for the "feminine" artistry of the Coquette who (with greater freedom than the Florestan and Eusebius she absorbs and displaces)

Example 5.4. Schumann, *Replique* (complete; from *Carnaval*)

plays with her replicas: for the metamorphoses, changes of mask, and changes of costume embodied in the sequence of themes. Concurrently, by always moving from the upper to the inner voice, the mirroring of *Replique* evokes the peculiar sense of enchanted remoteness by which the mirror creates an alternative to the world of men. Whenever the *Coquette* theme appears, the mirrored figure becomes more elusive—more fluid and imaginary. *Replique*, too, envisions a room of one's own.

CARNIVAL REINED IN

In the ideal world, Schumann would have been able to sustain the impetus of *Replique* indefinitely. In the real world, probably no nineteenth-century man could contemplate the feminine with complete equanimity, not even the Schumann of *Carnaval*. Late in the cycle, the free play of gender that animates masquerade is arrested; *Pantalon et Columbine* sets masculine and feminine roles in drastic opposition under the goad of male sexual desire. The Pantaloon of Italian pantomime is an old skirt-chaser (literally: he really chases), a greedy, lecherous, and cuckolded figure whose costume usually includes a prominent phallus. Columbine, pretty and saucy, is forever eluding his clutches. In what amounts to a parody of *Reconaissance*, which precedes it, *Pantalon et Columbine* stages a farcical battle of the sexes in alternating sections of staccato and legato. The fast patter and clatter of the one suggests the lecher's frenzied pursuit, the slower sinuous twirl of the other his quarry's lyrical self-assurance. (Columbine's legato even hints at a perhaps narcissistic self-reflectivity; much of its texture is closely imitative.) The piece concludes with Columbine's articulation gradually overtaking and retarding Pantaloon's (ex. 5.5), as if, in a fulfillment of standard-issue masculine anxieties, she were appropriating his phallus for uses of her own. At the end she seems to emerge intact in the form of an unresolved inner-voice note that keeps sounding after the rest of the music abruptly stops, then to make a quick exit in a mocking echo of Pantaloon's staccato motion—a fine instance of capturing physiognomy and gesture. Columbine, indeed, is always cutting Pantaloon short. Her entrances twice prevent him from stating the consequent of a 4 + 4 measure period, and her closing dissolution of his texture not only thwarts the same consequent but derails symmetrical phrasing altogether.[42]

The catastrophe of the purloined phallus cries out for a retort, and Schumann soon provides one in *Paganini*. This appropriately virtuosic piece projects an antithesis to the image of the reflective, feminized artist. It gives us the artist as mesmerizer, the charismatic master of improvisation who

Example 5.5. Schumann, closing passage of *Pantalon et Columbine* (from *Carnaval*)

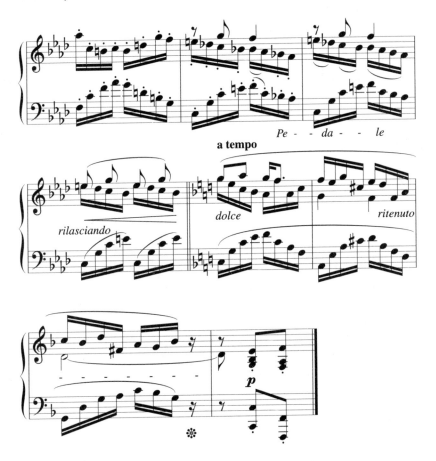

possesses the inordinately phallic power of—in Schumann's words—"subjecting the public, of lifting it, sustaining it, and letting it fall again."[43] This phallic bravado is particularly obtrusive because *Paganini* is framed, but in no sense contained, by two renditions of a dance piece, *Valse Allemande*. The waltz seeks to manage the outbreak of sexual anxiety by sublimating the conflict of articulations found in *Pantalon et Columbine*. Columbine's slower legato now syncopates the rhythmic motto of *Coquette*, foregrounding both structural and representational continuity within *Carnaval* as a cycle. Pantaloon's faster staccato now meshes with social ritual, moving in step with the vigorous waltz rhythm and rounding off the dance with a

Example 5.6. Schumann, excerpt from *Paganini* (from *Carnaval*)

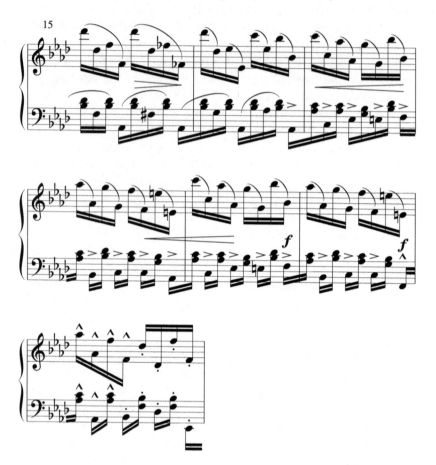

robust cadence. *Valse Allemande* also arranges its legato and staccato segments in notably symmetrical periods, as if to rectify or undo the collapse
of symmetrical phrasing in *Pantalon et Columbine*. By these means the
waltz recasts the sexual as the aesthetic, commotion as custom, contention
as balance. *Paganini*, however, rejects these efforts to temporize. With
renewed exaggeration, it appropriates both the staccato and legato articulations on behalf of its formidable masculine mystique. It even reverses the
earlier collapse of Pantaloon's staccato into Columbine's legato (ex. 5.6).
Paganini, in short, retrieves the purloined phallus from Columbine.

Paganini confirms that the sexual opposition of *Pantalon et Columbine*
cannot be assimilated to the fluctuations of masquerade. Ripples of unease

continue; the second *Valse Allemande* takes a faster tempo than the first and drops the repeat of its second half. It edges toward the hectic as if its fabric of sublimation were beginning to unravel. (Or is this a disturbance of reflection: "The mirror crack'd from side to side;/'The curse is come upon me,' cried/The Lady of Shalott"?[44] Compare *Eusebius*, which sustains a fantasy of reflective depth by repeating itself more slowly.) Once beset by masculine anxiety, *Carnaval* seems compelled to water down the festive imagery that has guided it so far. Carnival as the scene of masquerade, where subjective unity is cast away or recast in the crucible of gender, dwindles into a means to *épater le bourgeois*. As I noted earlier, the concluding *Marche des Davidsbündler contre les Philistins* evolves into a recapitulation of themes from the opening *Préambule* to close the cycle in quasi-sonata style. Free play and insouciant heterogeneity are thus reduced to an organized procession—a circus parade with Schumann as ringmaster. The music remains rambunctious enough to affront any number of Philistines, but it also joins them by growing deaf to the music of masquerade, of shape shifting, of gender in free fall.

Deaf—or almost deaf. The *Marche* also introduces a peculiar new element, a seventeenth-century theme that is labeled as such in the score. Kossmaly heard this quotation as a carnivalesque transformation: the "old-fashioned, narrow-minded, and genuinely philistine" tune, "Der Grossvatertanz" (The grandfather's dance), "introduces a grotesque contrast and produces a genuinely comic rococo effect"—what amounts to another change of mask.[45] Another contemporary, Adolph Schubring, suggests that the tune has an infectious charm despite (or because of) being old-fashioned; the thought of "olden times" evokes the cultural memory of the "bridal processions and weddings" at which the "Der Grossvatertanz" was traditionally played.[46] At once ironic and nostalgic, the old tune invites us to imagine a social world less rigid than anything the nineteenth century has to offer, a world less privatized, less insulated from wild ruckus. The tune reverts to the utopian dimension of masquerade; it marks the site where the untrammeled, feminine-inspired spirit of carnival has been lost, and where it may still linger, though only as a somewhat distanced "rococo comic effect."

This deconstructive fillip occurs twice during the *Marche*, each time to be met with a master musician's answer: sublimation by thematic metamorphosis. The music may be high spirited, but it means business. Meanwhile, the march keeps bustling forth in a kind of giant accelerando until it dwarfs the miniatures whose energies it is supposed to celebrate. By thus turning conclusively to the security of pure music, Schumann anticipates

Dahlhaus's gesture of protecting *Carnaval* from its own meanings. The intent to do so is announced forcefully by the virtuosic keyboard-spanning outburst of "Pause," which leads to the concluding march. This is music that means only itself, or more exactly that in announcing the end of carnival, more halt than mere pause, retracts into itself. Some insight on this retraction can be gleaned from *Paganini*. If that piece really suggests a recuperation of the purloined phallus, then it is important to observe that the phallus is musical, that it belongs to the virtuoso whose mastery of music is absolute. By reflecting on itself as a medium, the music masculinizes even self-reflection and withdraws from the arena of gender- and identity-mobility; a stable self remains in the person of the master musician. At this point *Carnaval* enters the virtuoso public sphere in all its masculine bravado. *Paganini, Pause,* and the lengthy *Marche* all make a point of displaying virtuoso technique, unlike most of the rest of the cycle, which in any case varies in its degree of difficulty. There is even a movement from figurative to literal virtuosity: the pianist as imaginary violinist, still caught up in carnival impersonation, gives way to the pianist proper. The music thus performs its own course correction. The bottom line is that without the stability of purely musical form and technique, without the possibility of intelligible meaninglessness, *Carnaval* cannot acquire the value of art— something possible only if it approaches the "greater forms."

POSTLUDE: VICTORIA'S SECRET

In Robert Browning's long dramatic monologue *Fifine at the Fair* (1872), a married and supposedly domesticated Don Juan tries to justify his sudden infatuation with a Gypsy dancer. To find a model for his feelings, he turns to nothing other than Schumann's *Carnaval*, which prompts him to see the world at large as a tumultuous, promiscuous masquerade:

> Howe'er it came to pass, I soon was far to fetch—
> Gone off in company with [Schumann's] music!
> . . . .
> And what I gazed upon was a prodigious Fair,
> Concourse immense of men and women, crowned or casqued,
> Turbaned or tiar'd, wreathed, plumed, hatted or wigged, but masked—
> Always masked—. . . . On each hand,
> I soon became aware, flocked the infinitude
> Of passions, loves and hates, man pampers till his mood
> Becomes himself, the whole sole face we name him by.[47]

Browning's version of carnival is seamier than Schumann's, but the community of idea and feeling is evident. Browning also follows Schumann in evoking the appeal of gender mobility, though he reverts to heterosexual norms far sooner than Schumann does. The irresistible Fifine appears first, not as a person, but as a transvestite persona, a "squalid girl" who sheds her petticoats to reveal a "gamesome boy" (sec. 3). The real Fifine simply reverses the transvestite roles, appearing in a pageboy costume cut down to reveal her breasts (sec. 15). Like Schumann's coquette, Browning's Fifine models a creative vitality that is both shameless and limitless, a vitality the composer and the poet themselves cannot quite muster.

Browning's interpretation of *Carnaval* supplies an effective foil to Leo Treitler's complaint that

> despite frequent appeals to the dialogic nature of the historian's enterprise, participants in past cultures that are the objects of investigation are not asked their opinions of the ingenious work of today's interpreters. . . . In the absence of that, the gesture toward historicization, the notion that understanding music depends on understanding it in its social and cultural situation, while intuitively appealing after the failure of the opposite doctrine, remains unconsummated.[48]

The effectiveness of Browning's "replique," however, may not lie where Treitler seems to look for it. Like the other participants of past cultures consulted here, Browning helps "consummate" a later interpretive project not by the content of his interpretations, but by its resources, the imagistic and semantic crossovers that it implies between the music and other discourses and cultural practices. Browning shows the vitality of carnival and transvestite imagery as contemporary mediations for hearing this music, but he does so in terms required of anyone at any time: he combines ascriptive parable and paraphrase (for the terms, see chap. 1) in ways that sometimes localize meaning in technical details and sometimes diffuse it over the music as a whole. Browning is no less dependent on the stock of possible rather than actual meanings than a later critic who might have to recover them— though even a contemporary, of course, can be blind to certain live possibilities, and all meaning is legitimately subject to reframing as a result of conceptual developments that postdate it.

Browning moves with no sense of discomfort between technical and semantic issues. His speaker plays through all of *Carnaval* and comments on it as an amateur pianist, remarking on fingering problems ("abductor of the thumb,/Taxed by those tenths' and twelfths' unconscionable stretch"; sec. 93), the prevalence of flat keys, and contrasts of staccato and legato.[49] At the same time he finds social meaning in the cycle's "web of motives," which he experiences as a living process: "I somehow played the piece:

remarked on each old theme/I' the new dress. . . . how faded phrase grew fine/And palled perfection" (sec. 92). Like the carnival vision that it prompts, the music works toward "victories over the commonplace" and assumes a bite that is likened in true carnival style to the taste of a briny pickle. Browning does not try to read the music determinatively against a stable cultural context or background, which is at best a ramshackle fiction, but to enfranchise the dynamic, dialogical, and reciprocal transformations worked between different parts of the cultural field. He speaks out of his engagement with the music as one who plays and as one who imagines. Kossmaly, Brendel, and Liszt were also willing to do that, and in so doing to establish a model of practice, if not of critical method, that is well worth reviving. This kind of interpretive language is inextricably a part of the world of the music. Without it, indeed, there is no such world.

6
Glottis Envy
The Marx Brothers' A Night at the Opera

Cav-Pag. Near the end of *The Godfather, Part 3* (1990), the critically unsuccessful final movie in Francis Ford Coppola's Mafia trilogy, a performance of Mascagni's *Cavallieria Rusticana* is intercut with lurid scenes of gangland murder. The sequence is an homage to the famous climax of the first *Godfather* (1972), which intercuts its similar violence with a christening ceremony. Part of the problem with the later version is that the gangland plot is already quite "operatic" enough; there is no real contrast, certainly nothing as potent as the first movie's florid juxtaposition of the sacred and the profane. Another problem is that the disruption of the opera, threatened in the film's narrative and actually carried out by its intercutting technique, has a comic edge, also backed by movie memory. When I saw Coppola's Cav, I could not help thinking of the antics of a group of zany Pags: the real danger was not the possible assassination of the tenor, but the remembered appearance of Chico and Harpo Marx making a mess of Verdi's *Il Trovatore* in the Marx Brothers' 1935 classic *A Night at the Opera*. In the world of movie fantasy, these operatic hit men make the Corleone clan look like amateurs.

Opera and/as the Movies; or, Dueling Banjos. But why put a hit out on opera in the first place? And why is it such an easy target? Why has the Marx Brothers' romp become legendary? Perhaps opera and the movies—Hollywood movies—are just too much alike. They notoriously share a passion for the extravagant, the supercharged, the larger-than-life; for big stars with big egos; for passion, betrayal, sex, and death to the *n*th degree; for fetishistic absorption in body parts and appurtenances. They would have to be rivals: perhaps even Oedipal rivals. It is hard to imagine the Babylonian crowd scenes of *Intolerance* without the public spectacles of *Lohengrin* and *Aida,* or the burning of Atlanta in *Gone with the Wind* without the confla-grations in *Die Walküre* and *Götterdämerung,* or the production numbers of Busby Berkeley without the Gypsy camp of *Il Trovatore.* And Holly-wood's long preoccupation with female sexuality and feminine sacrifice is virtually unthinkable without *Lucia di Lammermoor, Tristan und Isolde,* and *Madama Butterfly.* Throughout movie history, cultural pretension has involved operatic grandiosity. As a genre, grand opera, at least, is the father of the movies—or at least the godfather.

This particular genealogy, however, unfolds across a stretch of the "great divide" between elite and popular culture, with all its socioeconomic bag-gage, that had begun to emerge by the turn of the twentieth century.[1] It is by now a commonplace that this high-low division stemmed in part from the rise of mass media and the interlinking of modern subjectivity with the new technologies of communication. Walter Benjamin's classic account, the much-cited "The Work of Art in the Age of Mechanical Reproduction" (1936), describes the result as a loss of "aura," the quality of singularity per-ceived as something numinous.[2] Aura arises from the "unique existence [of an object or event] at the place where it happens to be" (220), and persists in the quality of distance situated between the original object or event and its reproduction. Mechanical reproducibility collapses this distance and throws into question the very concept of an immediate, self-present origin. Benjamin's prime instance of the mechanical arts is film, which he specifi-cally contrasts to the stage play. Where the spectator in the theater must "respect the performance as an integral whole" (228), the film editor splices together discontinuous shots to represent events that may never have taken place at all, but may be infinitely repeated on the illusory plane of the film screen. "For the first time . . . man has to operate with his whole living per-son, yet forgetting its aura" (229). The film industry responds to this "shriveling of the aura" with an "artificial build-up of the 'personality' out-side the studio" (230); the aura of the actor gives way to the infectious but always suspect glamour of the star.

Benjamin says nothing about opera. Although he mentions sound film once or twice, sound, and particularly music, are tacitly assumed to lack the-oretical value. (The assumption is not surprising; see chap. 7.)[3] By rectifying this omission, we may be able to start specifying what's at stake in the opera-movie rivalry. Theory may have something to learn from eavesdropping.

The difference between aura and glamour is key here; it bears impor-tantly on the ways in which opera and the movies channel the desires of their audiences. Social as well as sensory issues are at stake in the basic observation, which reiterate the social and aesthetic tensions between music and visuality encountered in chapter 4. Part of the prestige of opera lay in its ability to wed transcendental sound—especially the intangible object of desire manifested in the high operatic voices of tenor and soprano—to visual pleasure.[4] This pleasure was mediated by the stage spectacle and focused on the perception of the singer as a virtuoso; the magnetism of the virtuoso body more than compensated for any deficiencies found in the personal one. The aura of live performance was channeled into the representation of the virtuoso body as a medium for a unique voice perceived in its most acute transitoriness: *this* voice in *this* aria on *this* night at the opera.

In their first few decades, of course, movies could do nothing remotely like this. No matter how sumptuous their visual display, the immateriality of the film image intruded a sense of lack; even a department-store show window, an entertainment medium to which the movie is an heir, was more auratic, even if it was more obviously a commodity form. Virtually from the outset of the film era, this lack prompted a search for sound—a search, that is, for music, not for speech. (The popularity of "talking pictures" actually came as a surprise to much of Hollywood.)[5] Key here, as in the genealogy of the virtuoso, is the effect of synchrony. The live music that accompanied silent films was too perceptibly a kind of prosthesis. Even at its most lavish—the grander silent-movie palaces employed symphony orchestras to evoke an operatic atmosphere, often by means of operatic pastiche—the music was "muted" by its palpable material separation from the cinematic images it haloed. Only with the development of the soundtrack could movie music merge itself seamlessly with the spectacle on screen. Synchronous sound permitted both orchestral and vocal sonority to be taken into the system of filmic desire; opera's numinous intangible, with all its cultural and aesthetic prestige, could be annexed to the sphere of visually sumptuous mass culture. As an invisible source of music, a kind of endlessly reproducible Bayreuth orchestra pit in perfect synchrony with the image, the soundtrack allowed the movies to rival opera as a source of rapture. Anyone who wished to (and some who didn't) could now find presence, depth, and feeling pervading the screen. The synchronous soundtrack let glamour pass as aura. It made opera obsolete.

La Forza del Destino. Someone, of course, still had to break the news to opera, and it was probably inevitable that a movie would come along, sooner rather than later, to do the job. Clearly this was an offer the Marx Brothers couldn't refuse. And what better way to do it than by bringing down the house—or at least the set—on *Il Trovatore*, the most Hollywoodish of canonical grand operas?

Il Trovatore comes so close to doing itself in that the brothers' demolition might seem like a mercy killing; the movie audience gets to hear the opera's four best tunes and has a barrel of laughs in the process. Like Harpo, however, *A Night at the Opera* is strangely affectionate toward what it demolishes. It takes apart—dare one say deconstructs?—the opera in order to claim both theatrical and social superiority for itself, for the Hollywood movie, but its claims turn out to depend on the opera in intimate and unexpected ways. Not a mercy killing, then: a love death.

Anything You Can Do . . . A Night at the Opera claims that an entertaining movie, even a zany Marx Brothers movie, can tell a more moving, catch-in-the-throat musical love story than an edifying opera. Not that the Brothers particularly sought to yoke their comic mayhem to a serious love plot; the plot was imposed at the behest of the producer Irving Thalberg as a box-office necessity. Unruffled, the brothers responded subversively, surrounding the saccharine romance with visual and verbal reminders of the sexuality that it high-mindedly represses. (Desire is blind, unconscious, urgent, hungry, they tell us, as a sleeping Harpo gropes the nearest chambermaid in the famous stateroom scene. Heterosexuality is an operatic charade, they tell us, as a simpering Harpo cross-dresses as both Nedda and Azucena.) Less predictably, the brothers also subvert the romance by treating it with a grave, almost tender seriousness. They behave as if its conventional triangle—clean-cut hero, smarmy villain, and sweet, plucky girl—constituted an uncanny repetition of the lurid, lethal triangle of *Il Trovatore*. The film, in fact, ends by merging the two triangles on the operatic stage.

This integration of comedy and romance may stem in part from the directorial hand of Sam Wood. "Unlike others," observes one Hollywood historian, "[Wood] does not neglect the supporting cast and the intervening musical and romantic sequences which . . . Thalberg considered necessary."[6] But the Marx Brothers may have had something more urgent than production values in mind, as some remarks by Stanley Cavell suggest:

> I asked myself why it was, when the Marx Brothers' thoughts turned
> to opera, that they proposed (or inspired others to propose to them) . . .
> *Il Trovatore* as their example. . . . Then one remembers that the Marx
> Brothers [like Manrico and di Luna] are brothers, and . . . considers
> that these brothers, famous for their absurdities, may be taking on,

as a grand enemy, the famously dark fixations of *Trovatore* that just about anyone regards as exemplary of the supposed absurdities of grand opera; and so considers that their competition with that darkness, absurd only in its terrible lack of necessity, is to use the power of the film to achieve the happy ending in which the right tenor gets the part [of Manrico], the film concluding triumphantly with the opera's most famous, ecstatically melancholy duet.[7]

Cavell's argument is persuasive, but it stops short of recognizing a contradiction—a welcome one—in the film's inversion of the opera's darkness. The power of the film turns out to depend on the power of opera, even to embody an aspiration to the condition of opera. The film's conclusion is "triumphant" only insofar as it is—absurdly—operatic.

On reflection, then, *A Night at the Opera* seems both to depend on and to yearn for the very operatic pleasures it claims to surpass, and to do so precisely in relation to erotic love. The marks of this operatic nostalgia punctuate the film. Near the beginning, we see the mute Harpo dressed as if to play Canio in *Pagliacci* and pretending to "sing" something climactic in front of a mirror. (The loss of aura, says Benjamin, "is basically the same kind of estrangement felt before one's own image in the mirror" [230].) Toward the middle, Groucho supplies the missing vocal part, intoning "Ridi, Pagliacco" several times in an ambivalent gesture of self-reference. And the concluding love duet frames—incorporates, assimilates—the reprise of a comic "duet" from early in the movie in which Groucho and Chico "make" a contract by tearing it up clause by clause. Operatic love and vaudeville ridicule join "musically" to rip the fabric of an absurd society—as Harpo has literally ripped the fabric of a backdrop in escaping from the opera manager and his police henchman during the performance of *Trovatore*.

Se vuol ballare. This conjuncture also underwrites and complicates the film's social claims. *A Night at the Opera* reels off a pie-in-the-face fantasy minus the pie: a fantasy of exploiting the exploiters, of humbling the smug plutocracy of the Great Depression, a mob of opera patrons by definition. "Mr. Driftwood," says the Margaret Dumont character who, as always, is Groucho's mark, "three months ago you promised to put me into society. In all that time you've done nothing but draw a very handsome salary." "You think that's nothing, huh?" Groucho retorts. "How many men do you suppose are drawing a very handsome salary nowadays?" The exchange takes place at a pricey restaurant, and not by chance. This movie is constantly hungry, obsessed with food. The rich, it seems to be saying, can afford to take oral pleasure in expensive song, but poor people have to eat before they can sing. The pleasures of song can never fill an empty belly.

The fantasy of aggression against the "haves" finds its obverse in a fantasy of identification with the "have-nots." An opposition unfolds between the lifeless, rigid, morally bankrupt dominant classes and the vital, mobile, emotionally wealthy masses of the dominated. This fantasmatic play—strangely tender-minded in light of the brothers' nihilistic credo: roughly speaking, if it moves, mock it—comes to a head in the interplay of opera and the movies. The brothers' assault on *Il Trovatore* forms a demonstration that opera in America is the true property, not of the "New York Opera Company," its WASP upper-crust patrons, and its German manager, but of the working-class Italian immigrants in whose culture this opera is grounded. (For "Italian," read also "Jewish," like the Marx brothers themselves. Given the date of the movie, the celebration of these two immigrant groups may have a political edge; no less a critic than Mussolini himself picked out the Marx Brothers as the embodiments of anti-Fascist society.)

The "downward" shift in ethnicity and social class gives the operatic voice a demotic, democratic inflection, and allows *A Night at the Opera* to take as its primary object of desire precisely the intangible bliss manifested through the melancholy ecstasy of that voice. The narrative goal of the film is to find the operatic voice for, and in, its young lovers: opera singers, as it happens, a soprano and a tenor, destined for a love duet. To be "found," the operatic voice must be wrested away from plutocratic control and reconnected to its repressed origin in the energies of popular culture. The film identifies those energies with carnival festivity and sexual desire. It finds them among the masses of its immigrants, with whom Chico, Harpo, and the tenor, Riccardo, mingle on the steerage deck of a steamship—the very womb of immigrant America. The brothers disembark to wreck the opera in order to save it *for* the people and *from* itself. They redeem opera from its plutocratic appropriation by giving it a night at the movies.

At the end of that night, the social and theatrical/romantic fantasies coalesce. The young lovers, Rosa and Riccardo, bring the movie to its "triumphant" conclusion by singing their "ecstatically melancholy" duet, "Sconto col sangue" from the last act of *Trovatore*. The duet is actually sung twice, first within the opera, highlighting the melancholy, then as an encore, highlighting the ecstasy. The repetition allows a shift in focus from the opera plot to the film plot; the original duet marks the parting of Leonora and Manrico, the encore the union of Rosa and Riccardo. This reorientation need not be taken at face value (and won't be, later on), but it does support an all-important change in audience address. It allows the encore to be directed *through* the snobbish opera audience *to* the melting-pot movie audience. It is as if the opera house were dissolving into the movie palace, whose lights, indeed, come on just after the encore ends.

Fixing (up) the Tenor. The mutual desire of Rosa and Riccardo is indistinguishable from their vocal rapport. Riccardo, however, is overshadowed by a more famous but less talented rival, Lassparri, who is also in pursuit of Rosa. This Bad Tenor represents the ultimate in narcissistic snobbery. (He enters the movie by viciously beating Harpo, the moral equivalent of taking candy from a baby.) Although Rosa finds him repellent, he successfully keeps her apart from Riccardo until he is debased and Riccardo elevated by the Marx Brothers' anarchic antics.

Two logics govern this process of complementary abasement and elevation, cultural logics that go well beyond the confines of either film or opera. One is the logic of carnival, as theorized by Mikhail Bakhtin, in which the dominated masses renew their vital energies by celebrating the material, bodily basis of life and by ritually flouting official culture, defying its rules and degrading its representatives. The other logic is that of castration, in which authority and charisma are symbolized by the phallus and governed by the symbolic possessor of the phallus.[8]

These logics intertwine throughout the film and merge at the moment when the disruption of *Il Trovatore* reaches its peak. The moment caps an outbreak of carnivalesque anarchy with the ritual (and only half-figurative) castration of Lassparri, the Bad Tenor. Thereafter the phallus is delivered to Riccardo, enabling him to sing his duet with Rosa. The film takes this symbolic transfer of phallic power seriously, or at least deadpans it, but its seriousness is neither naive nor credulous. Although it blithely upholds a phallocentric order of things, *A Night at the Opera* also shows that order to be pure artifice, something no more (but then again, no less) substantial than Groucho's greasepaint moustache. The logic of castration here is always implicitly a logic of carnival, as its primary symbol—namely a salami—all but explicitly proclaims.[9]

The two logics come into clearest focus at three moments, two seemingly marginal, one obviously central. Spaced fairly evenly, these center on a triad of indecorous material-bodily events: a whack, a peep, and a squeal.

Taking a whack. Early in the film, Chico and Harpo meet each other in the opera house and rush into a fervid embrace. Each at once proceeds to pull a

salami out of his clothing and offer it to the other with a grin. Like all phallic allusions in the movie, this exchange is at once a jibe at phallic posturing,
a flouting of (hetero)sexual norms, and a real source of privilege. Harpo,
however, does not really know what to do with phallic privileges—or perhaps he knows exactly what to do with them. Ever-regressive, he disrupts
the signification of the phallus by grabbing a handy axe and violently
whacking off the end of his salami. This "castration," startling though it is,
is also perfectly reasonable, as Harpo proves by doing the perfectly obvious:
he eats his salami. To be more exact, he picks up the end piece in one hand,
takes a bite, picks up the still semiphallic remainder in the other hand, con-
templates it a moment, then takes a bite of that, too.

Before a salami is a phallus, Harpo reveals, it is just something to eat.
(The logical *before* is here a temporal *after*). Before objects effect signification, they affect satisfaction. The interchangeability of symbolic and bodily
values, of phallic power and oral pleasure, and of the oral pleasure of speech
and song and the oral pleasure of eating (on which Harpo, the mute, always
harps) is basic to the movie, which reiterates it often. The movie, indeed,
constitutes a kind of extended reiteration of this scene, but in reverse. In
order to take possession of the operatic voice, the Good Tenor Riccardo must
pass through the carnival celebrated by the immigrants in steerage, a scene
of gustatory pleasure that merges with the release of both social and sexual
energy. Thereafter the Good Tenor must receive the phallus liberated by the
castration of his rival amid an operatic reprise of the shipboard festivity.
Harpo moves from phallus to antipasto; Riccardo moves from the pasta to
the phallus.

Taking a peep. There is plenty of pasta in steerage: huge heaping plates of
spaghetti also piled high with breads and vegetables: a cornucopia. It is after
cleaning his plate (as Chico and Harpo do theirs) that Riccardo moves to the
center of festivity. He translates the oral pleasure of satisfying his hunger
into the oral pleasure of singing, sparking a dance of all the people with a
lively number, "Cosi-Cosa," in operetta style. (This style, anticipated in an
earlier, premonitory love duet between Riccardo and Rosa, mediates
between folk music—the immigrants are singing "Santa Lucia" as
Riccardo, Chico, and Harpo come on deck—and operatic art music.)

As the people dance to Riccardo's song, they transform the random press
of close-packed, jostling, hungry bodies into the choreography of a mass
courtship ritual. The moving force behind this ritual is masculine desire, and
its object soon comes literally into view. On the fringes of the dance, a man

is seen making a suggestion to a woman. Properly shocked, she refuses, only to accept a moment later with a radiant smile. At that moment the camera closes in on the swirling skirts of women in the dance. One woman is singled out—or her lower body is, carnival-style. (According to Bakhtin, carnival revels in "the material bodily lower stratum.")[10] As the shot becomes a closeup, the woman's skirt swirls up once to reveal her legs and again, swirling higher, to offer a frontal view of her panties. At once there is a jump-cut back to the middle distance; the sight/site of the female genitals marks the limit of phallic representation and provokes masculine dread as well as desire.

When Riccardo gains possession of the operatic voice, its phallic power will allow him to identify the object of desire glimpsed here with the whole person of Rosa and to transfer the intensity of sexual passion into the vibratory friction of shared song. In the meantime, the camera's eye combines a voyeuristic peep with a peek at the truth: the focal point of masculine desire is also its vanishing point; the phallus is required to counteract the vanishing, but the phallus, like the camera, is an apparatus, something as easy to pass around or slice up as a piece of salami, or to decompose into the slither of an overflowing plate of spaghetti. At the site/sight of the female genitals the castrated salami becomes a horn of plenty, but still, here, a muted horn, a mute horn, even if the spectator is momentarily horny: and it is the voicing of this muteness, the blowing of this horn, that will come [*sic*] to perfect the movie's night at the opera.

Fixing the Tenor II: The Squeal. The abasement of Lassparri and subsequent elevation of Riccardo is the most elaborate routine in the movie, the real heart—but that is not the right organ—of the matter. As usual, the assault is led by Harpo. It follows on a carnivalization of the scene in the Gypsy camp that opens Act II of *Il Trovatore*. As the scene unfolds, Harpo and Chico slip into it dressed as Gypsies, in flight from the stage manager and detective, who also dress as Gypsies in order to pursue. The movie and opera plots implode on each other; like the steerage deck, the opera stage mixes up its Gypsy outcasts and the outlaw Marx Brothers into a heady brew. The opera goes on without missing a beat—or with Chico giving the beat, a Gypsy at the anvils—even as Harpo turns the performance into a circus act with giant rope swings and a twirl on a high bar. The erotics of the steerage carnival reappear as Harpo proceeds to rip off the skirts of female Gypsies while Groucho makes approving noises from (for?) the audience: "Now we're getting somewhere." Opera cannot be disturbed by such sexual dis-

play because opera, a striptease for the voice, *is* sexual display. Opera cannot be disturbed by the whirligig of carnival because opera, at bottom, *is*
carnival.

Lassparri disagrees. He tries to restore order with his performance of
"Mal regendo," the narrative in which Manrico tells Azucena of his battle
with the Count di Luna. Continually interrupted by the dropping of "inappropriate" scrims (not to mention Harpo's swinging by on a rope to snatch
his wig) Lassparri's singing climaxes with his castration. In an irony that
virtually no one in the movie audience would grasp, but which the movie is
too opera-mad to pass up, this outcome reverses that of the sung narrative,
which recalls how Manrico, his blade flashing above di Luna's body, feels
impelled not to strike. As we know from the salami, Harpo feels no such
compunctions.

Another operatic allusion sets up the event. The first scrim to break up
Lassparri's performance shows a pushcart, forcibly placing Lassparri in the
immigrant world he disdains. The second scrim shows a battleship dwarfed
by its own grossly phallic gun barrel: *Il Trovatore* meets *Madama Butterfly*
as Lassparri becomes the cocksure despoiler Pinkerton. The joke once again
mocks phallic display as imposture but without thereby undermining the
power of the phallus itself—a power soon to be felt through the voice of the
Good Tenor. As Lassparri embarks on the high A that concludes his aria, the
house lights go out. The note continues for a moment, then stops; then a
high-pitched squeal pierces the darkness. A speaking voice cries out, "Don't
you do—"; the lights go up; Lassparri is gone.

The opera soon continues with Riccardo as Manrico. Harpo and Chico
keep Lassparri bound and—significantly—gagged in a box above the stage.
When by chance they tumble down, the manager cries, "Lassparri, where
have you been?" "Been?" comes the reply, "Do you know what they did to
me?" What they did will soon be obvious. To castrate the Bad Tenor is not
to make a castrato—a sexually ambiguous "monster" with a charismatic
voice—but to make a mute. Hence Lassparri's special hatred of Harpo.
Deprived of the phallus, Lassparri loses the operatic voice; when he tries to
recoup his discomfiture by strutting on stage for an encore, he is booed back
into the wings before he can open his mouth. Chico anticipates this outcome
while Lassparri is still captive in the box—a carnivalized version of both
opera box and coffin. As Riccardo's voice merges with Rosa's in their ecstatically melancholy duet, dominating the vocal texture with the same high
note (A♭ for A) on which Lassparri has been cut off, Chico makes a fist with
his thumb sticking out. Positioning the fist directly over Lassparri's groin,
he jerks his thumb in the direction of the voice and says, "Hear that? That's

real singing!" The gesture simultaneously reprises Lassparri's castration (pulls him off), toys with his official sexuality (a man pulls—jerks—him off, he gets off during the opera), affirms the phallic character of Riccardo's operatic voice, and reaffirms the sexual subtext of the love duet. If Irving Thalberg had only known . . .

Cherchez la femme. But she has become hard to find. Rosa, whom the camera fetishizes in the person of Kitty Carlisle, tends to get lost in all this, as, indeed, does Leonora in the love duet, most of her part being a florid ornamentation of Manrico's. When the phallus is at stake, even the most adored woman is a mere adjunct. Both Rosa and her apparent opposite, Groucho's dowager nemesis, are alibis; they provide the Marx Brothers' horseplay with the pretense of social utility, sublimating a downscale version of antinomian modernism (transvaluation of all values, disorganization of all the senses) with the facades of romance and satire. If anyone can withstand this, it is not the ingénue but the dowager, at least as played by Margaret Dumont, who, like opera, remains serenely impervious to being repeatedly debunked (and whom Groucho can never quite upstage). Even so, the Marx Brothers quickly devour each new pretense, each adjunct, just as Harpo (who else?) chugs down a pitcher of water even though it washes away his disguise of the moment, a false beard. Each lost pretense releases more farcical energy; the women are sported like Harpo's beard.[11]

Encore, encore . . . But in this movie, what isn't? Certainly not the Good Tenor and the clunky mechanisms of his Hollywood romance, which it makes no more sense to ratify than to dismiss. One answer (Harpo will have another, and a better) is "Sconto col sangue," the farewell duet of the lovers in *Il Trovatore.* We need now to reread the double appearance of this duet from a less idealizing perspective than before.

Heard as an encore, "Sconto col sangue" completes a process of decontextualization that leaves it meaningless, and in so doing establishes its peculiar value. The encored duet no longer refers to anything but itself. It has already been extracted from the opera; the scene from which it comes has been played in the movie as autonomous, the one intact remnant of the unstrung performance, and the encore, played in front of the curtain, is unconnected with the scene. The encore now further "extracts" itself from the plot of the movie, the happy lovers of which are united in the sad song of final farewell. By thus shedding both its operatic and cinematic supports (despite shifting from the one to the other, as noted previously), the duet allows its pleasures to become purely musical in the sense that singsong or tuneless humming is purely musical. It offers an "idiotic" gratification: a sound truly enjoyed for its own sake because, as Slavoj Žižek might suggest, what is enjoyed in it is an unspeakable pleasure that cannot be symbolized.[12] The music, in this strange condition, becomes almost the only thing in the movie that cannot be assimilated to carnivalesque anarchy: not because it presents a countervailing ideal (which is what it might seem to do at first blush), but because it itself shares in the same anarchic spirit. The duet produces a pleasure without boundary or location, beyond the satirical debasement of the social conditions of its production, beyond the cardboard-cutout lovers—who, of course, are only lip-synching the song, the words of which presumably mean nothing to most of the movie audience—and beyond the fact that the final duet is probably there in the first place only as a studio-mandated hedge against the Marx Brothers' take-no-prisoners brand of comedy. Welcome, at long last, to Absolute Music—Harpo sez.

Garbo talks? But what does Harpo do? The infantile Harpo, mute because he lives outside the phallic order upheld by speech and ruled by the operatic voice, embodies a truth that Riccardo and Rosa disavow through their love duet, despite the melancholy of its text. This is the truth that desire can never be satisfied. It is therefore the further truth that the "triumphant" end of the movie is an illusion. Operatic voice and cinematic vision may make it a seductive illusion, but outside the theater the world remains hungry and the melodramatic fate of Verdi's lovers is more lifelike than is comfortable to admit.

As his name declares, Harpo, too, is musical, but his musicality serves the wistfulness of lack rather than the fantasy of plenitude. Harpo has a harp solo in *A Night at the Opera* that is regularly derided as sentimental. Certainly, when he plays his instrument, he is serious, even heartfelt; you can read it in his face. But he is not, for all that, out of character. At the climax of his solo, played mainly for the children in steerage, his natural peers, Harpo supplies his own version of the operatic voice whose absence marks his entry into the movie. It is a version that makes no claims, asserts no power or privilege, only yields to the passing pleasure of the music while keeping its celestial rhetoric down to earth. Garbo may talk all she likes. Harpo whistles.

7
Hercules' Hautboys
Mixed Media and Musical Meaning

This chapter and the next form a couple. The aim of this one is to ask what can be learned about musical meaning from the phenomenon of mixed media; the aim of the next is to ask, conversely, what can be learned about mixed media from the phenomenon of musical meaning. Like the questions, the answers represent two sides of the same coin. This chapter will suggest that mixed media specifies both the general form and the historical basis of musical meaning, and with them the means for music to enter the culture-wide stream of communicative actions and exchanges. The next chapter will suggest that musical meaning always exceeds its specification by mixed media, but in a way that vitally supports what it exceeds and helps position mixed media, too, in the general communicative economy. The two chapters also carry a pair of tutelary deities, whose symbolic roles will quickly become clear: another couple, though improperly mated, and both on journeys with no clear end.

OBVERSE: M
                U
                S
                I MAGE TEXT
                C

Music has by and large been cut off from the communications system by which meaning in Western cultures is produced. Of necessity, language is the dominant force in that system. As Hans-Georg Gadamer argues—and it is hard to disagree—"Language is not just one of man's possessions in the world, but on it depends the fact that man has a world at all."[1] No such demiurgical claim could be made for music; it would be inconceivable except as metaphor, which testifies to the truth of Gadamer's statement. On the other hand, language is forever failing to grasp the world it creates. It cannot do without supplements. The most important of these, and one whose importance has grown steadily since the eighteenth century, is the visual image.

According to both Gilles Deleuze and W. J. T. Mitchell, the general Western system of meaning operates on the basis of an opposition between language and visuality, or, more exactly, between the verbal and pictorial description of reality. According to Deleuze, "speaking and seeing, or rather statements and visibilities, are pure Elements, a priori conditions under which all ideas are formulated and behavior displayed, at some moment or another."[2] At the level of communicative action, this historical a priori plays itself out in the interplay of telling and showing, diegesis and mimesis, the statement and picturing of states of affairs. Mitchell associates this interplay with what he calls the *imagetext*, a term that may refer, according to context, either to specific juxtapositions of text and image or to the general condition of their interrelatedness. According to Mitchell, "the interaction of pictures and texts is constitutive of representation as such: all media are mixed media, and all representations are heterogeneous; there are no 'purely' visual and verbal arts, though the impulse to purify media is one of the central utopian gestures of modernism."[3] Music has no place on this map, and its absence is perhaps most remarkable for not being remarkable at all. Mitchell suggests that texts address images as their Other, and vice versa; music is beyond the pale. Because of the essentially mixed character of the imagetext, however, the otherness internal to it is relatively limited. In a much stronger and more "improper" sense, the imagetext as a whole takes music as its Other—a role that music knows all too well.

In *Classical Music and Postmodern Knowledge*, I argued that this separation of music and the imagetext is a historical construction prominent especially since the mid-eighteenth century, and that it has been misused to isolate music from meaning and from the real-world contingencies in which meaning is embedded.[4] Chapter 1 of this book carried that argument forward and proposed that the misuse turns on a confusion between the properties of expressive media and those of expressive works, styles, or events. It simply does not follow that because music is an initially nonsemantic medium that the products of the medium cannot engage meaning or do cultural work. Music and the imagetext are, as a matter of historical record, more partners than Others. Each breaches the boundaries of the other as an ordinary event all the time. This is most obvious from the phenomenon of mixed media, which is actually the primary form of music both historically and epistemologically; purely instrumental music is the exception, not the rule, notwithstanding the conceptual tendency (dating from the early nineteenth century) to take it as the paradigm for music as such, the musical *Ding-an-sich.*

Nonetheless, the exclusion of music from the imagetext is not simply an error that can be made to disappear. It is a real historical formation with a lengthy past and considerable powers of endurance. Once produced, it continually reinstates itself, if only as a formal condition through which meaning can emerge through acts of boundary crossing. One must recognize its force by historicizing, not merely denying, its vision of music as a resistance to or surmounting of meaning, and through it of real-world contingencies. Instead of a contrary vision of progress, where the ideal of autonomy gives way to one of mediation, there is a scene of continual negotiation in which what it means to mean or not mean in a given circumstance takes on both musical and sociocultural significance. Similarly, instead of passing from a "false" conception of music as the Other of the imagetext to a "true" conception of music as an integral part of a more general communicative economy, there emerges a set of dynamic relations between the two conceptions as each is realized in experience. By always keeping both conceptions in play, we can recognize, if not quite reconcile, both the rooted intuition that music makes sense, it is something we can follow, something we "get," and the equally rooted conviction that music is something that eludes our rationalizations and often carries us away in both body and spirit.

By exploring the recognition that most music is actually produced in alliance with the imagetext, and that all music can be adapted for mixed-media use, it becomes possible to recast the whole question of musical meaning. The key to this recasting is the process that Gadamer calls application, the transference of meaning from one frame of reference to another.[5] The model is judicial—how, for example, can a law written in the past be construed to make sense in the present?—but its own applicability covers a much wider field, including musical mixed media. Unlike texts or images, which generally seem to "have" meaning regardless of their circumstances, music tends to "get" meaning (i.e., semantic, not formal meaning) only from the process of application itself, which is to say, as an effect of being applied to texts or images. That is why the music-imagetext boundary is so important. Music is the art that questions meaning; therefore its meaning is always in question. Nonetheless, because music sets "statements" and accompanies "visibilities" all the time, it assumes meaning all the time. Where music does not literally combine with the imagetexts of other aesthetic media (from poetry to theater to dance to film and video), it follows verbal or visual mediations to inform social and religious ritual, festivity, romance, or the improvised musicalization of everyday life. These combinatory forms are everywhere, are commonplace; it may be their very familiarity, joined with the tendency to overvalue unattended music, that encourages us to think of them as secondary. What would happen if we defamiliarized this application of music to the imagetext and the concurrent realization of meaning in music? What would happen if we redescribed it as something remarkable and strange—which, in fact, is what it is? Here is an instance I find especially suggestive because in it, as often happens, the musical meaning precedes the music itself.

HERCULES' HAUTBOYS

In Act IV of Shakespeare's *Antony and Cleopatra,* just before the tragic downfalls begin in earnest, a group of Antony's soldiers hears music under the stage: "Hark!" "Music i' th' air." "Under the earth." "It signs well, does it not?" "No." "Peace, I say! What should this mean?" "'Tis the God Hercules, whom Antony loved,/Now leaves him" (IV.iii.12–16).[6] What should this music sound like? It might be martial or mournful, simple or complex, coherent or fragmentary; it might sound faintly throughout, or gradually fade, or seem to come and go; it might be played by hautboys (early oboes, harsher than modern instruments) as Shakespeare himself specifies (though he does not say how many, or whether they should be accompanied) or by any other instruments a stage director chooses. The music, in fact, can sound in a multitude of ways, but in one important sense, the way it sounds does not matter. Unless the audience finds it glaringly inappropriate, the music, whatever it sounds like, will carry the meanings proposed for it by the scene. It will do so, moreover, with seeming immediacy, as if the meaning were simply there in the music, as palpable as the sound itself. Whatever the music's concrete textural and topical qualities, they will mold themselves to fit the interpretive occasion.

In the process they will also partly constitute the meaning they assume. If the music here is martial, Hercules may seem to be leaving Antony with resolution; if mournful, with reluctance. In any case, the audience, probably without a second thought, will find a way to hear the music as the scene tells them to—and in so doing enrich or transform the scene. At the same time, however, they may also hear more than they are told to. The music may exceed the meaning that informs it, and the excess may either stand by itself or add some new meaning to the scene or both. A dialogue of two hautboys, for instance (i' th' air, under the earth) could equally well embody the separation of Antony and Hercules and act out its own melodic drama in little. Like the soldiers, the audience will find that the music both makes sense in context and continually eludes a final reckoning.

One thing that makes this scene exemplary is the self-reflexive structure by which the audience mirrors the soldiers' act of interpretation. The two interpretive levels dramatize different ways of producing musical meaning within a context of overall commonality. Consider the commonality first. Both levels suggest that musical meaning is not something unusual but the ordinary result of applying music to the imagetext; both involve recouping an apparent exception, a music that seems to escape or challenge the possibility of such application. Both levels suggest that the meaning thus produced, like the music heard in the scene, has no single or fixed location. The meaning emerges in the music on the basis of something in the imagetext, and at the same time emerges in the imagetext on the basis of something in the music. The temporality of the process is unclear; the meaning is everywhere at once.

Both levels, too, suggest the distinctive character of musical meaning. Because it stands outside the imagetext, music is semantically absorptive, or, to change the metaphor, a semantic chameleon. Under certain common conditions, it becomes replete with meanings ascribed to it on the basis of the imagetext, while also holding over a remainder that exceeds those meanings. At the same time both the ascriptive process and the remainder will affect the imagetext in kind. This process may also work in reverse, though its reciprocity is limited by the power or privilege of the imagetext to set the terms of meaning. That conceded, the music can modify the semantic agenda by conveying meanings of its own into the imagetext, which also holds over a remainder that exceeds them. This happens most readily, though, when it involves quotation, stylistic allusion, parody, or the social typecasting of style or genre: that is, when it is less the music "itself" that contributes meaning than traces of the lore surrounding it—traces, that is, of earlier ascriptions. When the music-imagetext relationship is unclear or enigmatic, the music is likely to feel out of place, creating (perhaps designedly) a kind of semantic suspense that can be resolved only by interpretive mediation. The music in this case can even feel intrusive or discomfiting—precisely the effect that Antony's soldiers try to rectify by connecting what they hear to what they recognize as Antony's tragedy.

The conditions for producing these effects are also evident from the example. First, the perceiver must take some cognizance of what the imagetext says or shows; this cognizance need not be articulate or even articulated, and exact or detailed understanding is not necessary. This criterion may seem trivial or obvious at first, as well as loose to a fault; its import will become evident shortly. Second, the music must not provoke a judgment of glaring inappropriateness. No positive judgment of appropriateness is required; many kinds of loose fit can be accommodated. The music may, however, seem to be misapplied ironically ("It signs well, does it not?" "No."), in which case it implicitly postulates an alternative imagetext to which it belongs, but which does not appear. "Irony" here covers a wide range of discontinuities and equivocations, some of them quite subtle or implicit; a kind of nimbus of alternative imagetexts is perhaps more the rule than the exception. The looseness of these conditions provides ample latitude for the remainders that the mixed-media application cannot fully incorporate. It also makes the conditions easy to meet: and once they are met, musical meaning arises with no sense that something external is being imposed. The meaning is not a prosthetic attachment; the music is infused with it. In the "metatheatrical" mirror of the scene from *Antony*, both the soldiers and the audience make this discovery, which in this case takes the form of prophecy or revelation. The process is not impeded even by a reflective awareness of its operation (a common effect most often felt when one tries and fails to resist it, moved in spite of oneself) although in other circumstances reflective awareness can support a sense of distance or alienation (see chap. 10).

The soldiers' interpretive level, though, differs from the audience's in its means of ascription. The soldiers talk things over and decide to hear the music through the mediation of a certain utterance. Their act of ascription is informal but explicit, and it depends on the interpreters' ability to formulate the mediating utterance themselves. The audience engages in no such procedure. It simply imparts meaning to the music on the basis of the scene, which happens to include the soldiers' ascription. That ascription leads to a particular outcome, but if the soldiers' last line had been "I know not" instead of "'Tis the god Hercules . . . ," the audience would still have imparted meaning to the music on the basis of the scene. They may even still do so, hearing both what the soldiers hear and something more. The off-stage sonority of the music, for example, especially of strident hautboys, may suggest the mysterious fatality of destiny that brings these ordinary men to the margins of great historical events. The audience, in other words, hears the music through the tacit mediation of the scene, the value of which for the purpose is assumed in advance. For the soldiers, the ground of meaning is a mutual interpretive agreement. For the audience, it is the joint presence of the imagetext and applied music bundled together as constituent parts of the play: that is, of the work, grasped in its classical hermeneutic function of giving lived experience a durable form (see chap. 1). It so happens, though it need not have, that the soldiers' interpretation also treats the music as if it were already applied; at least on one reading, the soldiers act as if they were overhearing the music for another scene, that of Hercules' departure. The requested music might well evoke the imaginary scene, since hautboys were often used to accompany dumb shows (mimed narrative) on the Elizabethan stage. For dramatic purposes, this *mise-en-abime* (the soldiers hear applied music; the audience hears them hear it) may be meant to suggest something about the way legends are formed or histories written. For present purposes, it may be taken to embody the semantic power of music in mixed media.

IN THE LOOP

How can we account for the sources of that power and describe its typical effects? The answer, broadly speaking, depends on the perception that music is the dynamic force in mixed media, the embodiment of agency and energy, and that its dynamism is primarily a manifestation of the musical remainder. Concretizing this answer will require reconsiderations of three key topics: music's semantic qualities, its relationship to the sign, and its material character as sound. The results should make it possible to go a step further and begin to account for the semantic power of music heard apart from mixed media.

1. Semantics. The relationship of music and the imagetext both is and is not semantically hierarchical. As Nicholas Cook has argued in his study of what he calls musical multimedia, traditional models have tended to be rigidly hierarchical, assuming that music simply expresses a meaning fully present elsewhere, usually in a text.[7] Cook argues compellingly that this view does not do justice to the complexity of actual mixed media, where, as he says, meaning is not reproduced, but constructed (97). His own alternative, however, a notion of free, variably hierarchical negotiation among the media, does not quite do justice to the historical and cultural force of the imagetext, which does enjoy a semantic authority that music is denied, nor again to the deeply felt values, pro and con, that attach to that denial. What's needed is a way to recognize semantic priority in the imagetext without conceding primacy to it. And here we encounter the deferred importance of the loose criterion of cognizance described earlier. The semantic process in musical mixed media does not start with a deep, definite, hermeneutically divined meaning but with a meaning-generating surface: an ensemble of statements made, tropes used, images formed, events represented—all that is not expendable in making sense of the passage, whatever sense is made. The presence of this signifying surface both instigates semantic movement and identifies/legitimates it as such. The function by which the imagetext sets the semantic agenda is thus a historical-cultural one, a criterion for establishing meaning in general. It does not require the imagetext to have a stable sense, or a particular sense, but merely to make some sort of sense in advance of hermeneutic interventions.[8]

Music applied to such a semantic field not only informs but also consolidates it; what was semantically loose becomes close-knit. The weave between music and the imagetext is closer than any between image and text alone. In general, the music of a song seems more fused with its text than an illustration of a text is with the text it illustrates; the score on a soundtrack seems more knit into the cinematic image than a voice-over narration. One measure of this strong interconnection is the dramatic power of leitmotifs and theme songs, that is, the capacity of music to infuse present imagetexts not only with musical meaning but also with reminiscences—musicalized traces—of former imagetexts.

More than just conveying this "lore" (as I called it earlier), music activates and reinterprets it. At the close of George Gershwin's opera *Porgy and Bess* (1935), the full orchestra recalls the opening phrase of "Bess, You Is My Woman Now." The phrase subsumes both the pleasure of the original love duet and the pathos of its lightly scored orchestral reminiscence, heard just a few moments earlier as Porgy discovers that Bess has deserted him. The climactic statement, together with its segue into Porgy's own leitmotif, precariously situates the narrative resolution—Porgy's departure for New York in search of his runaway beloved—between visionary heroism and willful delusion. In Francis Ford Coppola's film *Apocalypse Now* (1979), attack helicopters in Vietnam become travesty Valkyries courtesy of the music on the soundtrack, Wagner's "Ride of the Valkyries." The effect is not simply—not primarily—conceptual. The armored choppers seem to look and move differently than they would otherwise, to be both more terrifying and more grotesque. The music will convey this effect whether it and its lore are recognized or not; but these things are also part of the story. Lt. Col. Kilgore, the aptly named commander of the squadron, actually broadcasts "The Ride of the Valkyries" from loudspeakers attached to the helicopters: "We'll come in low, out of the rising sun, and about a mile out we'll put on the music . . . Yeah, I use Wagner—scares the hell out of the slopes. My boys love it!" The full force of the allusion remains esoteric for those who don't know the *Ring* cycle or the implications of associating

Wagner with a racially charged triumphalism, but a wider semantic circle has nonetheless been drawn. For whatever it might mean, the spectacle of dark forms swarming out of the rising sun becomes Wagnerian.

These instances also exemplify the diffuse, unstable temporal structure of musical mixed media. Logically speaking, meaning flows from the image-text to the music. For example, the imagetext has to signal us to refer certain music to messengers of death, and to tell us whether the messengers are Valkyries or helicopter gunships. Our actual experience, however, tends to proceed contrariwise, from the music to the imagetext. The sense of ebullient fatality—heroic in Wagner, monstrous and/or "Wagnerian" in Coppola—seems to pour into the operatic or cinematic scene from the pulse-pounding music. The meaning-bearing music seems both to blend with the imagetext and envelop it, both to saturate and exceed it. The process can even leapfrog from one imagetext to another: a listener to *Die Walküre* who knows *Apocalypse Now* might well find Wagner's scene assuming or revealing the deluded brutality evoked by Coppola's.

In sum: musical meaning in mixed media is experienced in inverted form; it runs on a loop. The music seems to emit a meaning that it actually returns, and what it returns, it enriches and transforms. This outcome depends on, and at the same time suspends, the "normal" relation of music and the imagetext outside the mixed media context. From the standpoint of the imagetext, music has greater communicative immediacy, though less communicative power. Music, indeed, is one of the defining modes of an immediacy that the imagetext has to exclude in order to stabilize itself, to enable its generalizing, abstracting, and speculative capacities, even at the cost of an ambivalent fascination with the excluded and excluding other. But as soon as meaning effectively runs from the imagetext to music along the semantic loop, the music seems to convey that meaning to and through the imagetext in preconceptual, prerepresentational form. As soon as a listener knows how "Bess, You Is My Woman Now" sounds musically, the music can embody what the phrase means—a complex blend of reassurance, rescue, and appropriation—without any further help from the words. As soon as a listener knows that the off-stage music haunting Antony's soldiers is the sound of the departing god, the sound of the music is the sound of the god's departure.

The semantic loop is the formal means by which music asserts its unrivaled capacity for mixture and through which it appears as an active, almost drive-like tendency to mix with and inform that which initially excludes it. For a classic recognition of this quality, combined with a significant misrecognition of its structure, we can turn to one of the chief architects of the nineteenth century's elevation of music to aesthetic preeminence, Arthur Schopenhauer:

> The close relation music has to the true nature of things explains the fact that, when music appropriate to any scene, action, event, or environment is played, it seems to reveal to us its most secret meaning, and appears to be the most accurate and distinct commentary on it.[9]

The logic of this statement pivots on the concept of appropriateness, and points up the importance of the purely negative version of the concept—no judgment of inappropriateness—discussed earlier. If the music assumes its revelatory value only when it is appropriate, the meaning it reveals must be consistent with those already embedded in the scene, action, etc.—that is, in the imagetext—to which it is applied. The essence revealed by the music is thus always posited for it in advance; the revelation consists of the music's returning the meaning in enhanced form along the loop structure. Schopenhauer is thus "mistaken" only in the productive sense that he accepts the phenomenal value of the loop as a metaphysical one. In that, however, he is only letting music do what it is supposed to do in his cultural field—and ours. Music has, is endowed with, the special capacity to assume "appropriateness" at need and to express it as a palpable, dynamic, living quality—in Schopenhauer's terms, the Will, the "true nature of things."

This helps explain how and why the music-imagetext relationship may be complex, nuanced, ironic, ambiguous, and so on. It is not a simple question of matching meaning to music, like fabric swatches, but of meshing the two together and rearticulating both. For example, in Jane Campion's 1996 film *Portrait of a Lady*, based on the Henry James novel, excerpts from the variations movement of Schubert's D-Minor String Quartet (D. 810) are used recurrently to convey the wracking emotional outcome of the heroine's marriage. The music's gapped melodic lines, registral extremity, and continuous pulsation readily take the ascriptive print and saturate the film images with what then seems to be the music's own meaning, a sense of thwarted passion by which the self is consumed. But to someone who knows that these variations are based on the song "Death and the Maiden," a new vein of meaning is tapped: the music transforms the disastrous marriage of the heroine, Isabel Archer, from a modern social dilemma into an inexorable fatal encounter, both medieval and timeless, between Death and the Maiden. To someone who also reinserts the film music into the variation process from which it comes, the formal dimension of the music further becomes an "accurate and distinct commentary" on the fatality that the narrative describes: the inescapable repetition of a living death not just despite, but in and through, all efforts to change it. In this context there is symbolic resonance in the purely formal fact that the quartet music attaches only to Isabel's film image; she never hears it. Her "deafness" turns the "Death and the Maiden" episodes into ironic realizations of some words from an earlier scene, found in the novel as well as the film, in which she does hear some music by Schubert—for piano—and is moved by it, only to be handed a portent: "I'm afraid there are moments in life when even Schubert has nothing to say to us."[10] At the nadir of Isabel's experience, the quartet music will recur with "nothing to say" to her because, in its disconsolate insistence, it speaks for or even *as* her. It dissolves her identity, and with it her cherished illusions of autonomy and freedom, into an impalpable and mythic substrate in which she is a mere puppet. On several of these occasions this collapse is seconded visually by the presence of mirror images of Isabel that she does or cannot see, visual doppelgängers to match her musical ones.

2. *Signs.* Another way to understand the semantic loop is to think of it in terms of classical semiotics. The communicative power of signs is intimately bound up with a series of absences. As Jacques Derrida has particularly emphasized, the sign, to be a sign, must be potentially intelligible in the absence of every particular referent, sender, and receiver.[11] The sign must be capable of surviving the perishable circumstances in which it is produced. This absence-in-principle is often felt to haunt the sign and to form the measure of discontent with the necessary and ubiquitous process of representation. Thus Derrida recalls that Plato found emblematic significance in the fact that the Greek word *sema* means both sign and tomb, and that Hegel identified the sign with the Egyptian pyramid, the tomb into which "a foreign soul has been deposited."[12] In the semantic loop, however, music can partly restore as presence the absence of referent and person posited by the sign. When the imagetext mixes with music under the aegis of the work, the music acts as a semi-material embodiment of the meanings ascribed to it on the basis of that mixture. In particular, since music is constitutively referred to states of feeling, which is to say, of subjectivity, what the music in this circumstance embodies is the lived presence that is excluded from the sign.

Explicit recognitions of this effect begin no later than the early nineteenth century. Thomas De Quincey, for example, recalling opera nights in London in 1802, writes that "a chorus &c. of elaborate harmony, displayed before me, as in a piece of arras-work, the whole of my past life—not as if recalled by an act of memory, but as if present and incarnated in the music."[13] De Quincey's language suggests that music has the capacity to bring the allegorical power of visual imaging (the arras-work) to life through a kind of higher-order ekphrasis (see chap. 1) that takes the form of intuition rather than of speech—an effect echoed in the sacramental overtones of "present and incarnated."

It has to be added, though, that this embodiment comes only at the sacrifice of the monumentality of the sign, so that the presence offered by the music is almost always imbued with a sense of its own ephemerality. Music restores the loss inscribed in the sign only at the cost of reliving it. Musical sound changes with the vicissitudes of performance and recording technology, and its presences are fluid, fragmentary, and indefinite even when they crystallize most sharply (on this point, see chap. 12). For De Quincey, the musical mirroring of his past life depends not on any correlation between his own experience and the content of operatic scenes (with his favorite soprano "pour[ing] her passionate soul forth as Andromache, at the tomb of Hector, &c"—the "&c" speaks volumes), but on his pleasure in forming a semantic loop between a certain sonority—a favorite voice, an orchestral texture neither brass- nor string-heavy—and his sense of identity. This is a process that paradoxically works by erasing the concrete biographical content on which that sense is usually founded. Once musicalized, the past life is "no longer painful to look on . . . the detail of its incidents removed, or blended in some hazy abstraction; and its passions exalted, spiritualized, and sublimed."[14] The erasure allows De Quincey to identify with the music as the "incarnation" of a historically specific mode of subjectivity defined by its capacity to "spiritualize" error and suffering through expression and representation. (In this light, the example of Andromache at the tomb of Hector is not so arbitrary after all.) The sense of presence translates the underlying process of identification into an illusion or fiction that is both durable and transitory. De Quincey has it repeatedly for (as he says) the price of a gallery ticket, but he has it only for a single season, and even then must supplement it by drinking laudanum—tincture of opium.[15]

Music in this light might conjecturally be said to act like a sign fragment, the signifier of a veiled or unrealized signified. It is not a full sign because it lacks both a referent and a signified, but it is not merely an "empty sign" (in Kevin Barry's phrase) because it could at any moment have either or both.[16] In the suggestive metaphors of Hegel's semiotics, such a sign-fragment would be a receptacle for a "strange soul" to which its connection is not immediately intuitable, but the presence of which is strongly felt. But one must above all not conclude from this that music lacks meaning. On the contrary, the semantic fragmentation forms one basis of music's semantic absorptiveness. The absence of meaning at the level of virtual utterance is the medium in which meaning arises at the level of the semantic loop. Hegel's criterion for the sign, that it assume a meaning foreign to its own nature, is precisely the one that music pointedly does not meet, or at least gives the illusion of not meeting. Music heard as meaningful does not seem to transmit a meaning that it signifies but to assume a meaning that it exemplifies—"as if present and incarnated."

Insofar as music thus becomes a virtual presence to be addressed or shared, it does not act as a sign, despite being highly meaningful. This is not to say there are no musical signs, but such as there are belong to a small number of highly conventionalized gestures imbued with a slight sense of distance—a pastoral drone, a trumpet call, an amen cadence; they are local elements embedded in a larger field of meaning that is not the signified of the music's signifiers. It is for this reason that the music can at one level be understood without reference to the imagetext—mysteriously be both "intelligible" and "untranslatable" as Claude Levi-Strauss put it—and nonetheless be semantically animated by ascriptions of meaning.[17] The effect of these relationships is in line with Heinrich Heine's account of music as a kind of aesthetic Persephone with an identity divided between separate realms: "It stands like a twilight mediator between spirit and matter; it is related to both yet different from both; it is spirit, but spirit needing measure; it is matter, but matter with no need of space."[18]

3. Sounds. As both Heine's figure and Levi-Strauss's remark suggest, musicalized presence is not simply something numinous and indivisible, though it can sometimes seem that way. A further perspective on it can be drawn from recent work on the role of ambient sound as a continuous support and background for perception in general. "As human beings," writes Bruce R. Smith,

> we are surrounded—and filled—by a continuous field of sound, by sounds outside our bodies as well as by metabolic sounds within. It is out of this continuous chaos of sounds, Michel Serres remarks, that meanings emerge: "Background noise is the ground of our perception, absolutely uninterrupted, it is our perennial sustenance, the element of the software of our logic. It is the residue and the cesspool of our messages. No life without heat, no matter, neither; no warmth without air, no logos without noise."[19]

Although its character is historically contingent, some form of murmuring sonorous envelope forms the general field from which communication in sound is cut or crystallized into articulation. By some accounts (see chap. 3) this envelope also acts as the still operative remnant of an "acoustic mirror" in which infants first begin to recognize their identity as subjects.[20]

At the same time, however, the sonorous envelope acts as the locus of the visual field, which continuously situates things seen in relation to sound sources and looks weirdly alienated otherwise; hence the imagetext, too, is surrounded and filled by sound. This audiovisual relationship may even resist deafness. As Oliver Sacks has noted, those who become deaf tend to substitute the perception of vibration for audition and often "hear" phantom sounds associated closely with what they see. In his memoir *Deafness*, David Wright records that his loss of hearing "was difficult to perceive because from the very first my eyes had unconsciously begun to translate motion into sound." The "phantasmal" character of this sound appears only when a cousin, "in a moment of inspiration, covered his mouth with his hand when he spoke. Silence! Once and for all I understood that when I could not see I could not hear."[21]

For present purposes, the most salient feature of the sonorous envelope is that it is filled with nonsignifying matter but nonetheless exists in a dynamic relationship to signification. The locus of this relationship is a body of sound that, like Heine's twilight mediator, shuttles between the borderless mass of noises and articulate utterance. This mediatory sound embraces everything that, whether literally or figuratively, makes up the sphere of musicality, from natural or instrumental sounds taken for music to the flow of intonation that runs through speech to ritualized vocalization and songfulness. To the extent that such musicality is heard as expressive or constructed, it bears on signification; to the extent that it is received as material, visceral, or merely sensory, it bears on the nonsignifying realm uniting the body to the world. These "bearings" are rarely experienced as alternatives; their mutual implication is almost unbreakable. Shuttling between "logos" and "noise," musicality thus embodies the general flow of communicative energy into which nonsignifying sound is funneled and from which language and imagery, description and depiction, are precipitated. In the semantic looping of mixed media this intermediacy comes to life, becoming a felt process with a specific charge of pleasure and knowledge: the rustle of the sonorous envelope becomes palpable at the same time as the articulation or delineation of meaning within its folds. Whenever we respond to experience with music or musicality we invoke this effect, and in so doing supply both music and musical mixed media with their prototypical mode of being. It is perhaps with this in mind that Wallace Stevens, in a poem ostensibly about the power of language to shape perception, pauses to speculate that if there were "a change immenser than/A poet's metaphors in which being would/Come true," it would be found at "a point in the fire of music."[22]

ASCRIPTION AND VIRTUALITY

The semantic loop has historically been the primary means of concretizing the perception of music as presence, whether in excess of the sign or as twilight mediator. The next stage of my argument is to suggest that the loop structure is the prototype of free-standing musical interpretation, that is, of hermeneutic response. The mixed-media work, as we've seen, tends to obviate any immediate need for further interpretation, but it also, as in the case of Antony's soldiers, shows how further interpretation can be done. Both the semantic loop and the direct ascription of meaning are means of clarifying and concretizing music's "anthropomorphic" character as a virtual subjectivity that its own textures and processes can be taken to evoke, model, reveal, impose, transform, and so on. This is a subjectivity, moreover, that is felt, identified with—in contrast to its counterparts in the imagetext—as if from the inside out. This point of identification (Lacan calls it the quilting point, the point where the subject and the signifier are stitched together) allows musical subjectivity to feel universal, which is to say, it supports that important (and continuing) cultural trope.[23] But the virtual subjectivity of music is in practice always contingent and historically specific, and therefore poses the problem, or offers the opportunity, of encountering it in terms that recognize (but do not necessarily synthesize) both its limited generality and one's own.

This contingency links musical subjectivity with the wider reality, the constructed and imagined world, within which it occurs. The basis of this link is once again the dynamics of ascription, which may be said to derive its fullness of semantic infusion not only from the immediacy deficit of the imagetext but also from its own grounding in everyday forms of sense making that carry our sense of the world. These sense-making techniques form an interpretive parallel or dimension to what Pierre Bourdieu calls the habitus, the loose ensemble of dispositions, the repertoire of "structuring structures," that allows the members of a community to respond effectively to changing circumstances without following explicit rules.[24] It is the interpretive habitus more than the immediate object of interpretation that is the source of meaning. The scene of Antony's soldiers makes this evident by its express portrayal of the shared, social character of musical understanding.

How do the semantic loops within a mixed-media work compare with ascriptions of musical meaning made by listeners like Antony's soldiers who act on their own initiative? This question involves more than just instrumental music; texted music, even mixed-media music, may be addressed in this way as long as it is treated as autonomous, as an indivisible whole that can be heard "for itself." The soldiers' conversation gives a good idea of what such explicit ascription is like. In the first instance it is improvisatory, figurative, unregulated, and socially negotiated—all qualities typical of the habitus, though the interpretive process may eventually venture beyond or even reject habitus-based modes of common sense. The ascriptive process also shows significant powers of synoptic condensation, the construction of a kind of portmanteau image through which a larger fund of meanings can be epitomized without necessarily being made explicit. As Stevens puts it, there emerges

> a point in the fire of music where
> Dazzle yields to a clarity and we observe,
>
> And observing is completing and we are content,
> In a world that shrinks to an immediate whole,
>
> That we do not need to understand.[25]

Understanding can be deferred because the clarifying point temporarily replaces it, forming a symbolic place holder that is the antithesis of zero—De Quincey's living arras-work.

The combination of this synoptic energy with habitus-based forms of sense making allows explicit ascription to replicate the semantic fullness of the mixed-media work, though inevitably with a lesser degree of felt immediacy. The interpreter acts on the same basis as a songwriter, opera composer, or choreographer, or as a stage or film director choosing incidental or soundtrack music—all of whom, in turn, act like someone choosing music for a social or religious ceremony or else just whistling, humming, or singing along with the experience of the moment. In a figurative sense, every interpretation is a sketch for a mixed-media construction.

One step beyond this "sketch" lies the effect of virtuality. One of the commonest ways of listening to music is to "associate" mental images with it—of scenes, narratives, styles, ideas, turns of phrase, and so on. Explicit ascriptions of musical meaning always bear at least the traces or seeds of this process, and may be thoroughly informed by it. One never gets too far away from Antony's soldiers. Even the most autonomous music may thus be edged, at least intermittently, toward the condition of applied music.[26] Of course, the most generally approved kind of listening is more ascetic than this, supposedly focused just on the music itself. Yet the two kinds of listening are hard to keep apart, and both involve an identification or partnership with a virtual-subject position that stands as the music's addressee or interlocutor. Some element of imaginary application, of fantasy looping, lies at the core of all but the most rigorously disciplined, not to say chastised, listening.

E. M. Forster wins his way to this recognition, if only implicitly, in an exceptionally nuanced discussion of the problem, an essay slyly entitled "Not Listening to Music" (1939). Forster is ostensibly talking about two kinds of music, one that provokes nonmusical associations and one that doesn't, but he notes that the two sorts "melt into each other all the time," and it quickly becomes clear that what is really at stake is two modes of listening. Forster is personally most attuned to the associative mode; as a young man, he says, "I thought that music must be the better for having a meaning," and adds, "I still think so, but am less clear as to what a 'meaning' is." On the one hand, "[in many cases] music reminds me of something non-musical, and I fancy that to do so is part of its job." On the other hand, the associative process can lapse into pure fantasizing in which the music is lost, so that Forster gives higher value to structural listening. The premise that enfranchised fantasy leaves the music behind is subject to question, but even more important is that Forster does not suggest that structural listening escapes the question of meaning. On the contrary: the question persists, but in a changed and perhaps enhanced form. Music, he says, is not abstract; "It is not like mathematics, even when it uses them. . . . [It] certainly [has] a message, but what on earth is it? I shall get tied up trying to say. There's an insistence in music . . . a sense that it's trying to push across at us something which is neither an aesthetic pattern nor a sermon. That's what I listen for specially." Part of the urgency of this listening resonates with the date of the essay; as Europe heads toward catastrophe, music "seems to be more 'real' than anything, and to survive when the rest of civilization decays. I am always thinking of it with relief. It can never be ruined or nationalized."[27] The thinking may be as wishful as it is relieving, but the thought is consistent with the then century-old desire to cultivate an independent ethical sphere through musical aesthetics.

More broadly still, Forster's concept of "insistence" is of a piece with Schopenhauer's revelatory dynamism, and in this case it works by rejecting, not the "message" that the music is trying to "push across," but a pair of inadequate media for that message: pure pattern and didactic speech. The conditions of associative listening—the conviction of not-yet articulated meaning, suggestions about its possible articulation, and a subject position through which the whole process passes—are all preserved and sublimated. Forster's initial metaphor for structural listening is telling in this regard:

"Professional critics can listen to a piece as consistently and steadily as if they were reading a chapter in a novel" (126).[28]

Forster also affords some insight into what is at stake in the apparent opposition of associative and structural listening. He repeatedly suggests that the latter provides a special sort of intimacy, which one can win by disciplining one's attention and avoiding all "wool-gathering" even of the "superior" variety. The intimacy may be with the sounds themselves— "the closer we can get up to them the better"—or with the untranslatable "message" of the music, which lies "nearer the center of reality" than associative meaning, or with the composer, in this case Beethoven, to whom Forster gains a direct "physical approach" when playing—badly—his piano music: "I grow familiar with his tricks, his impatience, his sudden softnesses" (130). These characterizations of structural listening suggest something grounded more in an ideal of tutelage than in utopian or escapist aesthetics. Such listening is a formation of what Freud called the ego ideal, a mode of action in which compliance or conformance to the ideal ("[my performances] compel me to attend—no woolgathering or thinking myself clever here") is rewarded with pleasure approaching bliss. Whatever the meaning, or lack thereof, in particular works or occasions of music, music in Western society tends to "mean" both the enforcement of this essentially masochistic ideal—masochistic in that it identifies obedience with pleasure and affirms itself by claiming to will its own obedience—and its rejection on behalf of the activities of a more enfranchised, socially invested subject, the non-ideal practice of meaning to which Forster is powerfully drawn but apologetically writes off as woolgathering. What is at stake in this dialogics or dialectics of obedience and enfranchisement is not just the musically identified ideal and its contrary but two major currents of cultural practice, each of which forms the object of an ethic and a "care" in Michel Foucault's sense of organized inspection and cultivation.[29]

When Forster's "woolgathering" becomes explicit musical hermeneutics, its primary role in social life is to make music a medium of alliance: to promote collaboration, establish a socially resonant interplay of consensus and contention, and form or enrich intimacy or group identity. The speech acts on which this process depends are often elliptical and indirect, and often the byproducts of making aesthetic or performative judgments. In the chemistry of ascription, meaning in small doses can have large effects. More introspectively, the ascription of musical meaning forms or enhances identificatory bonds between the listener, the music, and, however tacitly, the worldly contexts of both. ("The climax of the first movement of the Appassionata," writes Forster, "[the 'piu allegro'] seems to me sexual"

[128], thus without fanfare turning the very end of the movement into an extended orgasm, a display of literally conclusive, perhaps violent, perhaps tragic sexuality. Tacit here is the question of sexual orientation, which declares itself more plainly, though still indirectly, a few sentences later when Forster invokes Hugo Wolf's setting of Goethe's homoerotic "Ganymed" and praises its gift of "stratosphere beyond stratosphere.") In these roles, the ascriptive process becomes indispensable to music making and musical communication. It consists in the way we really talk about music in the pragmatics of performance and social exchange and the closer bonds of shared experience, even when that experience is nominally solitary. Part of the meaning of any work of music is constituted by the history—a history still largely unwritten—of the ascriptions it receives and ways it returns them. In everyday practice, backed by the habitus, explicit ascription plays a large role in determining how we hear the music we share and what we "hear it as," whatever its formal features may be. Antony's soldiers can determine how to hear the music that haunts them because they know that gods sometimes speak in music, that divine speech translates as portent, and that portents concern great men. Put into words, the soldiers' knowledge shapes them into a community of listeners as we watch. The satisfaction they find in producing a viable ascription mirrors the satisfaction the theater audience finds in receiving one.

THE SUBLIME OBJECT OF MUSICAL MEANING

What, then, does the phenomenon of mixed media show about musical meaning? First of all that musical meaning is continuous with meaning in general—an idea that is only surprising because we are so used to thinking the opposite without enough surprise. We make sense of music as we make sense of life. And since we make sense of life only amid a dense network of social, cultural, and historical forces, musical meaning inevitably bears the traces, and sometimes the blazons, of those forces. The initial position of music outside the imagetext sets up a universalizing and abstracting impetus, but the semantic looping of music through the weave of the imagetext sets up a countervailing impetus toward contingent perception and historically informed understanding. Tradition has tended to foreground the first of these processes; critical musicology tries to foreground the second without forgetting the first. It tries to speak from and for the liminal zones traced out by semantic loops.

Another showing is that meaning does not come directly from something "in" the music, but from an interplay between ascribing a kernel of meaning to the music and unfolding the possibilities of experiencing the music—hearing it, performing it, describing it, imagining it—with that ascription as a guide. Musical meaning is awakened by animating the structure of application that constitutively links (but also separates) music and the imagetext. Through some combination of parable and paraphrase (see chap. 1), and with or without the help of titles, texts, programs, or other designators, the interpreter proposes an imagetext (full or sketchy, realized or latent, intuitive or reflective) through which the music (with or without tangles) may loop.[30]

The key question about musical meaning, then, is not whether it can be ascribed; it is ascribed all the time. Cook even says that we're impelled to ascribe it—to turn "[musical] experience into a story . . . to share our experience of music with others and even (if it makes sense to say so) with ourselves" (267–68). The impulse, I would add, is built right into the music-imagetext system and plays itself out across a continuous spectrum of practices ranging from a few impromptu words to full-blown hermeneutic forays. No: the key question is what kinds of meaning we want to ascribe, what meanings best conform to, extend, or challenge our general practices of sense making. The answer does not require either a strong dependence on the formal properties of music, let alone control by them, or reliance on a generic, vaguely humanistic vocabulary uninformed by theory, culture, and history. On the contrary: the formal properties of music are amenable to a wide range of ascriptions, which may at any rate home in on only a few salient details, and the range of interpretive vocabularies is at least as wide as the potentiality for mixed-media applications.

This is not to deny that music, like the imagetext, is always already pervaded by the effects of a multiplicity of communicative actions and cultural practices. On the contrary, as we've seen, semantic looping is a key means by which music (as style, tune, work, gesture) continuously refreshes itself with cultural lore. Nonetheless, in the concrete instance, be it the actuality of mixed media or the virtuality of ekphrastic response, the semantic engagements of music have to be activated by a specific interpretive practice that locates a meaning on the immediate "surface" of the imagetext. The meaning need not be definite, but the location must. The establishment of this semantic location, to repeat a point that cannot be stressed too much, is a broad cultural mandate, through which the effects of communicative energy are constituted and legitimated as meaning. The meaning thus activated is sure to have, and likely to assert, multiple, complex, and unforeseeable affiliations, but it must have only the one location. What gives the music-imagetext relation, whether actual or virtual, its characteristic dynamic form is the capacity of the music to work on the meaning initiated at that location in two ways at once, on the one hand enhancing and transforming it in the process of semantic looping and on the other hand concentrating other, unrealized possibilities in the musical remainder, which also upholds the connection of sonority to the nonsignifying field of general sonority. Music thus contributes to the "construction" of meaning by continually enacting its own intermediacy between the imagetext and the sonorous envelope. There is no equivalent to this process in word-image mixtures, but the meaning it produces behaves with the same versatility that meaning characteristically shows within the imagetext. Once the process starts, meaning may spring up anywhere and branch out everywhere—and would not be meaning if it didn't.

These observations remove the sticking point in traditional considerations of musical meaning, which tend to shut down interpretation where the signifying capacity of musical details leaves off. If interpretation must rest strictly on such formal details (supposing them to have some kind of "objective" status), the relative semantic poverty of the details considered in themselves becomes an insurmountable problem. Either the interpretation must falsify itself by exceeding the details, or hobble itself by working only with the limited vocabulary that can be coordinated with the details, something nearly impossible to do in practice. In other words the interpretation must either be "hopelessly subjective" or hopelessly meager. An understanding of the continuity between applied and hermeneutic meaning in music, however, can help clear up this problem. It can show that the gap between meaning and detail in music is not a barrier to interpretation but the very condition of its possibility. What interpretation carries over from mixed-media application is the productive power of the ascriptive process, by which the music both absorbs meaning and returns it in new or heightened form. The musical details produce meaning precisely by exemplifying a meaning that exceeds them.

This last point is crucial. Although one may in practice take cues from certain details, musical hermeneutics is radically ascriptive. The ascription imparts meaning to the musical details that exemplify it, and does so regardless of whether those details originally suggested the ascription. The ascription has a life of its own. It virtually always produces an interpretation that exceeds the musical details, that cannot in any strict way be derived from them. The interpretation is not, and cannot be, built up systematically from atomic units of signification or computed as the sum of component meanings with independent sources of validation. The details must, so to speak, be energized by ascription before they become meaningful, at which point alone they can attract descriptions that are topically, conceptually, and expressively rich.

In this way the details undergo a process of sublimation in the sense given the term by Slavoj Žižek. They are animated by being inserted in a field of symbolization that they may affect, even transform, but that deploys them—or rather in which we deploy them—to ends that regarded in themselves they cannot encompass. The sublime object is "an ordinary, everyday object that undergoes a kind of transubstantiation and starts to function, in the symbolic economy of the subject, as an embodiment" of the impossible-unattainable substance of enjoyment. Such an object "is able to subsist only in shadow . . . as something latent, implicit, evoked; as soon as we try to cast aside the shadow to reveal the substance, the object itself dissolves."[31] Just a few notes can evoke a musical world, but the world vanishes when one tries to reduce it to the notes. The activity of interpretation serves to defer that reduction by enveloping the music in the shadow (or, as Heine says, the twilight) of something latent, implicit, evoked.

The ascriptive character of musical hermeneutics thus renders music's lack of a rich referential system irrelevant to the question of meaning. The fact that music does not belong to the imagetext is not only no bar to its having meaning, but a precondition of it. The bearing of "unjustifiable" meanings is not a problem with musical semantics but its normal and familiar mode of being, exemplified and enjoyed by but not restricted to the overt semantic looping of the mixed-media work. Musical meaning emerges along a continuum of ordinary, effective processes of ascription that are basic to the shared experience of music, as they are to shared experience in general. The continuum runs from the simple, unreflective act of forming an impression to the sublime transubstantiation that "elevates" the ordinary object yet is itself rooted in the ordinary conduct of mental and social life.

THE POLITICS OF INTERPRETATION

None of this, of course, means that in interpreting music one can say just anything, even assuming that anyone seriously wanted such a license. The fear that one might, which is to say, the fear of subjectivity, is in any case based on the misconception that subjectivity itself is arbitrary, a kind of innate principle of eccentricity or deviation. Interpretive statements win an initial credibility precisely because they are subjective, that is, because they are culturally and socially conditioned, context-sensitive, and the product of education and dialogue. Subjectivity is regulated by the range of subject-positions available within a speech community. It is not to be understood as a condition of self-enclosed private existence, but as a condition of public relatedness, a position—or series of positions—in a network of practices and representations. The wild subjectivity feared by those who identify rationality with objectivity is not, to be sure, a mere phantasm, but it consists not in the inevitability of personal idiosyncrasy but in mistaken positional choice. No one can act outside of a subject position; the attempt to do so is one definition of delirium, psychosis, madness.

Nonetheless, it is not clear how what one says from inside a subject position is to be regulated and contested. Subject positions supply the means of interpretation and influence its ends, but they do not determine its content. Except under constraint—and sometimes even then—the subject speaks *from* the position, not merely *for* it. The result, as Leo Treitler complains in one of his feistiest essays, is that no one seems to know the rules of the game: rules of interpretation that are sound, reliable, and explicit.[32]

The problem, though I confess I don't find it a problem, is that no such rules are possible. Interpretation is a type of practical knowledge, taught primarily by example and highly sensitive to particular circumstances. The forces that bind it are not those of rule but those of habitus; there is simply no way to formalize it or reduce it to a technique. The statements that constitute it are likely to be as laden with tropes and as open to interpretation as the object they address. Although an interpretation mediates between its object and the general communicative economy, the plausibility of its mediation is established only ex post facto as the interpretation itself is elaborated, discussed, and put to use. Interpretation joins one communicative stream with another so that meaning can run through both.

This is not to say, however, that interpretation is a purely pragmatic enterprise, any more than it is a purely fanciful one. It necessarily operates in collaboration and negotiation with the shared presuppositions and modes of utterance that ground it, among which there is always an implicit standard of reason. The hermeneutic attitude, at least in the tradition I am trying to construct here, might even be characterized—interpreted—as an attempt to orchestrate (without seeking to reconcile) imagination, rhetorical invention, and a post-Enlightenment ideal of independent, skeptical reason. Hermeneutics is in that sense hopelessly political. Its exaltation of the ad hoc, which includes its embrace of historical particularity, is not only its modus operandi but also its means of avoiding the tyranny of fixed ideas, whether in the form of dogmatic beliefs or of the esoteric, mythographic, or—for lack of a better word—paranoid systems that also support themselves by producing interpretations. Hermeneutics insists on its independence from semiotics on the one hand and axiomatics on the other for both conceptual and ethical reasons. The conceptual point is to recognize the capacity of "lived experience" to alter or construct the presuppositions through which it becomes intelligible. The ethical point is to enrich and enhance that very capacity, without which the "lived" character of the experience becomes sterile and the framing presuppositions coercive.

In the language of recent studies of the evolution of complexity and consciousness, hermeneutically generated meaning might be identified as an "emergent" property; Cook, for example, uses the figure of emergence to designate the process whereby meaning in musical "multimedia" is constructed rather than produced (82–86). According to N. Katherine Hayles, an emergent property is one that "cannot be found in a system's individual components or their additive properties but that arises, often unpredictably, from the *interaction* of the system's components. Emergent properties appear on the global level of the system, not the local level of the system's parts."[33] This way of speaking about questions of meaning is potentially revealing as long as its metaphorical dimension is kept in mind. Strictly speaking, an emergent property is the result of a structured interactivity involving recursive processes; it is not only an unpredictable outcome but a "blind" one. An interpretation, by contrast, is the result of human choice, agency, and desire, all crisscrossed with cultural suasions and semantic plurality. The interpreter cannot (yet) be plausibly described as a function within a system of "distributed cognition" (a system in which intelligence is pervasively but not necessarily uniformly diffused), in part because interpretation cannot—or not yet, but my bet is on the "not"—be reduced to a "structured interactivity" and in part because it cannot be limited to cognition. This last point will return below, as will the notion of emergence.

THE NEST

How does the explicit interpretation of music compare with that of texts and pictures? How is the value of interpretation affected by the loss of a rich representational content in its object? The typical answer is of course in the negative: musical interpretation is at best severely limited, at worst illusory. My answer, on the contrary, is that with music the apparent loss of initial content strips away the illusion that representation and meaning are necessarily, or even typically, coextensive. The apparently defective case is actually the defining one. Not only does music not lack meaning: musical meaning is the paradigm of meaning in general.

This claim will probably always seem counterintuitive on first acquaintance; the interpretation of a text or picture, after all, usually reflects its contents in some way. Yet even with the imagetext, the contents of a complex representation never fully determine its meaning. To arrive at meaning, one must redescribe, resignify, place in context, put into relation, and in so doing one always exceeds what can be strictly derived from the representation's semantic units. The units do not even fully "have" their own meanings until they are referred to a higher-order meaning, an organizing process or pattern. Statements may be understood and images recognized, but texts and pictures have to be interpreted. The activity of interpretation invests the work in question with a dynamic quality, as if the deployment of its contents were a kind of virtual behavior addressed to the interpreter; this quality corresponds to the "lived experience" in the classical hermeneutic formula met with earlier: the work as lived experience in durable form. Something of the character of this process is captured in a remark made by Ludwig Wittgenstein in a somewhat different connection. "What I hold fast to," he wrote, "is not a proposition [Satz], but a nest of propositions."[34] The metaphor of the nest gives condensed expression to the core paradox of interpretation. It suggests that meaning is the outcome of mere improvised assemblage, a gathering up of diverse bits and pieces; but once made, the assemblage may hold together as a secure, enveloping home.

A revealing illustration of this process appears in Robert Browning's comments in *Fifine at the Fair* on Schumann's *Pantalon et Columbine*. This is the only double character portrait in Schumann's *Carnaval,* and as we saw in chapter 5, the textures of its contrasting sections can be associated with the frenzy of lecherous pursuit and the allure of flirtatious resistance. When Browning wrote his passage, however, he misremembered Schumann's title. As a result his Pantaloon and Columbine switch musical textures:

> [I] played through that movement, you prefer
> Where dance and shuffle past . . . Columbine, Pantaloon:
> She, toe-tips and *staccato,*—*legato,* shakes his poll
> And shambles in pursuit, the senior.[35]

In its ascriptive form, Browning's error is identical to the "correct" interpretation, which follows the order of Schumann's title. In a sense, the two readings are equally plausible, since technical details can accurately be adduced to support each. The conclusion most often drawn from this is that the music, in its own right, really has no semantic meaning in the first place. What this fails to recognize, and what the music, and music in general, paradigmatically demonstrates, is that where hermeneutics is at stake, meaning is always in the second place. No matter how many cues it receives or clues it follows, interpretation always works from back to front.[36]

Modern Western music embodies this process at its most explicit, and in so doing gives tangible form to its considerable social energies. Music is continually felt to convey meanings that it cannot plausibly be said to encode. The independence of representation and interpretation here reaches its peak—but the peak is where it started from. Music nearly always has potential meaning in an intersubjective or cultural sense, even if it rarely has meaning in a simple enunciatory sense. And once this meaning is acknowledged, once it is accepted as a common experience rather than dismissed because it lacks the apparent security of the imagetext, it cuts across and counterbalances the imagetext's cultural dominance. Musical meaning discloses what the imagetext's richness of representational content necessarily dissembles: the radically ascriptive nature of all interpretation. It embodies the recognition—the problem, the opportunity, the danger, the pleasure—that meaning is improvised, not reproduced, performed, not revealed.

Nor is it the case, as some (e.g., Roger Scruton) argue, that the inevitable gaps between verbal meaning and musical effect—the remainders beyond ascription—posit an essential and purely musical meaning beyond the avowed program of a piece like "La Mer," or, more generally, beyond the words applied to any piece, even by the piece itself.[37] This point of view also underlies defenses of music's relative autonomy, which take the nonsemantic remainders as guarantees of immunity from the social and contextual forces that are acknowledged to affect the music elsewhere.[38] What these views fail to recognize is that the remainders cannot be stabilized within the musical work, and that they actually serve to support rather than to subvert ascriptions of musical meaning. The gap between music and meaning is an instance of the more general constitutive gap between any set of discrete signs and its discursive, performative, interpretive globalization. As I suggested earlier, all interpretation involves such remainders, such semantic gaps, without which it cannot proceed. Interpretation is not simply a conceptual activity but a dynamic one, invested with social and psychological energies, even libidinal energy. The gap or remainder is the locus of interpretive dynamics, interpretive desire; interpretation both assumes and reproduces it as a condition of possibility and an active incentive. Interpretation arises to bridge a gap or adjust for an excess, but never to close the gap or smooth out the excess; interpretation preserves these noncongruities in order to continue the production of meaning just as fantasy maintains a distance from its objects in order to continue the production of desire.[39] Similarly, purely instrumental music and musical mixed media presume and produce each other. "Pure" music is precipitated out of the media mixture in order to be partly reabsorbed by it, just as the medium-based opposition of music and imagetext is constantly reinstated in order to be broken down.

Ideally speaking, all these processes rest on a conceptual openness that is hard to characterize in terms other than paradoxical, even oxymoronic: relaxed yet disciplined, spontaneously mediated, finite but unbounded. The aim of this openness is to achieve a vital connection with the remainder, something perhaps best approached on the ground of the figurative practice discussed in chapter 1, namely ekphrasis. Speculating on the relation of texts and pictures, the art historian Hubert Damisch envisions a mode of description that inverts ekphrasis as a mirror does writing:

> I am less interested in having painting "speak," using different histori-cal tools, than in reflecting on what makes us speak in it. . . . The Littré Dictionary says that description is a way of rejoining, through linguistic means, the silence or mutism of painting. Thus a description must fi-nally arrive at silence. And this is a complete paradox. One uses the detour of language in order to encounter muteness. It's an idea of description that is completely different from the notion that it should substitute itself for the object—because it's an idea that description should be used to find that which escapes description, what stumps it. . . . Every description should make the work function more intensely, more actively—it should reactivate the work by providing a new point of departure. . . . For me, silence is at the very heart of description.[40]

Like the paradoxes at the head of this paragraph, the "complete paradox" of Damisch's evocative statement recognizes that the remainder is irreducibly ambiguous: always both gap *and* excess, lack *and* substance, it is a positive kernel of non-sense that keeps us coming back to the artwork.

In its "mutism," the pictorial remainder serves as what Lacanian theo-rists call the *objet petit a*, a little thing—any little thing—that embodies the lack that triggers and sustains desire, and thus acts as the tangible source of ekphrastic hope and fear.[41] The musical remainder is the same kind of thing, but its position outside the imagetext gives it a greater immediacy and a dif-ferent character. Unlike pictorial silence, the musical remainder is not an impersonal opacity, but a form of address and a medium of intimacy. It forms the kernel of the virtual subjectivity that music can readily assume, at least for modern Western listeners.

Within the historical boundaries of that virtuality, the relation between the musical remainder and the imagetext might even be said to model the relation between the living subject and the imagetext, that is, to posit the feeling of an antecedent subjectivity constantly required to translate itself into words and images. This subjectivity can only appear, perhaps only exist, as the horizon of its own translations, best discerned when the latter display their inevitable instability and inadequacy. The musical remainder adds a tangible and tangibly inward form, enhancing one virtuality with another. It has to be added, though, that its virtuality does not make musical subjectivity merely an ersatz or pseudosubjectivity, though it may become one for other reasons.[42] "Actual" subjectivity is impossible to distinguish clearly from the emergent product of such virtualities, and musical subjectivity is, so to speak, the most actual of the virtual by virtue of music's dynamic relation to the imagetext. Actual subjectivity might be described as the emergence of the capacity to interpret, which is to say, to supplement and perhaps to surpass emergence as a generative process. One function of music is continually to restage this progression.

The underlying structure of subjective "translation" also runs between images and statements (and even between image and image, statement and statement) but to a considerably lesser degree imposed by the sign function that regulates the imagetext much more rigidly than it does music. The imagetext upholds a calculability that music always exceeds, but to which that very excess incessantly drives it to return. Music and subjectivity share the same loop; music is virtually subjective because subjectivity is virtually musical.

8
The Voice of Persephone
Musical Meaning and Mixed Media

If the last chapter is right, musical meaning finds both its source and its structure in the phenomenon of mixed media. The source and the structure are coextensive. Insofar as the structure involves an interplay of meaning and nonmeaning, semantic ascription and nonsemantic remainder, the a priori semantic ambiguity of Western music can be said to be produced historically by the use of music to supplement and suffuse texts and images. The "a priori" is installed retrospectively by its contingent, concrete, dynamic realizations. That's why an understanding of how music works in the context of mixed media can supply a general model of musical meaning. The construction of this model, however, leaves open the converse question of how mixed media works in the context of music. In other words, we may know how mixed media bears on musical meaning, but the question of how music bears on meaning in mixed media, and the meaning *of* mixed media, is still open. The current chapter is meant to examine that question, the proverbial other side of the coin. In the process, it will lead once again to a recognition of the pivotal role of the musical remainder. Its efforts will therefore run counter to most mixed-media theorizing, which has tended to concentrate on the production of meaning either through cross-media analogies or, more rarely (as in Nicholas Cook's important recent study) through cross-media differences.[1] There is nothing to object to in this— quite the contrary; but there is something to be gained by examining what it leaves out.

In dealing with applied music in the last chapter, I suggested that music-imagetext combinations may occur both aesthetically, via mixed-media forms, and performatively, via social ritual, festivity, and other "musicalized" events. This distinction, while of course neither rigid nor rigorous, tends to be marked by a difference in the character assumed by musical meaning. In the event-based sociocultural forms of applied music, remainders tend to be forgotten, elided by the sense of inclusion and participation. We have seen something of this effect in dealing with the virtuoso concert in chapter 4. The excitement of shared absorption in an event tends to cast remainders out, which is part of the pleasure gained but also part of the danger fostered when the "remainders" are embodied in groups of people. In mixed-media forms, however, the remainders often make themselves palpably felt. The tangible presentation of mixture itself is part of the mixed-media effect, which often makes a heterogeneous address to the perceiver and leaves moot the question of which medium, if any, is currently primary.

Here, too, however, the effect tends to be marked by a difference, in this case prompted by whether one is more focused on the content or the form of the music-imagetext mixture. A focus on content, that is, on the production of meaning, tends to elide the remainder much as the participatory event does. The remainder acts as a support for the sense of successful ascription; it operates more as medium than as message, giving tangible presence to imaginary or symbolic constructions. Nonsemantic itself, the remainder supports the realization of the music's semantic potential by sustaining interpretive desire. By contrast, a focus on form, that is, on the production of media mixture per se, highlights the remainder and invites a recognition of its value and effect. Music added to text or image adds its dynamism and body to their semantic value, but the musical remainder, again through the force of interpretive desire, works against the semantic tendency toward closure and completion. The remainder makes sure that musical meaning overruns the semantic borders set out for it and, more broadly, set out for the mixed-media work as a whole. The focus on content allows musical meaning to expand, like the sound of Hercules' hautboys as it migrates from place to place. The focus on form—and of course this distinction is often even more tenuous than the term "focus" allows—prevents imagetextual meaning from contracting. Like a free-floating voice it calls up further horizons and locations of meaning "i' th' air," "under the earth."

REVERSE: IMAGEM$_U$S^{I}CTEXT

I have recently been much struck with the idea that a concern with mixture and its contrary, the purity that is not or may not be mixed, is basic to the culture and politics of the modern era, an era now seemingly in its twilight. Socially, in connection with ideas of race and nationality, purity has been perhaps the most virulent idea of the past century. Countless deaths and degradations have been issued in its name. The same era, however, has also entertained ideals of aesthetic purity, from a redemptivist view of art to various forms of the ideal of aesthetic autonomy, that for some have supplied a principle of opposition to the totalitarian idea of social purity. That claim, for example, is eloquently staked by E. M. Forster in an essay of 1949 with the willfully anachronistic title, "Art for Art's Sake"; the work of art, he writes, "is the only material object in the universe that may possess internal harmony. . . . It achieves something which has often been promised by society, but always delusively."[2] The harmony that Forster speaks of, however, is a quality of the work of art in its traditional, singular forms: the pure work of literature, of music, of plastic representation. But Forster is writing in an era increasingly dominated by composite forms, mixed forms, from collage to cinema, in which internal harmony may be moot at best. What social implication or analogy might have occurred to him had he thought of that, or thought through it to a recognition that many of the traditional forms, from illustrated books to vocal music, are also mixtures?

To be sure, the social and aesthetic venues of the opposition between purity and mixture have a certain degree of independence. But they also have overlaps, metaphorical links, mutual implications that deserve to be explored. There is a sense in which the interpretation of social processes in the modern era and after must involve both theorizing purity—or more exactly theorizing impurity, the condition of mixture without which purity itself is unthinkable—and theorizing mixed media. The activity of theorizing, I should add at once, does not imply any claim to "have" a full-fledged theory, which is perhaps a chimera in any case. It claims only the root sense of the word "theory," a work of contemplation, a "viewing" that holds detachment and absorption in precarious balance. In what follows, I will be trying to theorize mixed media in this sense.

The concept of mixed media is much more recent than the thing itself. The recognition of mixture as a fundamental element in certain communicative and expressive forms seems to flow out of a recent epistemic watershed; it emerges at the same time as a new break with the past renders modernity a historical epoch, itself more past than present. The terms of this break are already pregnant with questions of mixture. In the first phase of what we can at least metaphorize as a historical sequence, late modernity is understood to be traumatized by a condition of general heterogeneity, corresponding to the loss of a former purity or synthesis. Thereafter, what might be called early postmodernity is understood to reveal that the supposed trauma is not traumatic at all, no declination from a prior and higher order, but a manifestation of the true and perfectly viable order of things. A new *cogito* emerges, the latest of many: I mix, therefore I am. The grandiose nineteenth-century idea of the *Gesamtkunstwerk* unexpectedly gets a new lease on life from a heady mix of mixes: economic and social globalization; the workaday development of composite media based on new technologies—film, video, information processing on screen and on line; the collapse of normative identities in favor of a continual juxtaposition of social, sexual, racial, and conceptual alternatives; the erosion of the distinction between a "high" culture grounded in autonomous modes of expression and the polyglot, promiscuous world of "popular" culture. One result is the recognition I wished upon Forster, that mixture is ubiquitous. It needs to be understood, not only as a trademark feature of modernity and postmodernity, but also as a factor basic to the communicative and expressive forms of cultural formation in general.

This understanding, as I have already implied, may be approached either via the social dimension of mixture, involving questions of purity, difference, and order (the "harmony" that transforms mixture into an organic whole), or via the formal dimension, involving composite agencies of communication or expression. In what follows, I concentrate primarily on the latter, although in ways that continually implicate the former. I will not be concerned, however, with typologies or gradations of mixture based on genre, choice of media, or the relative degree of distinctness or fusion of different media strands. Such taxonomic schemes, however interesting, are always exceeded by the complexity of actual mixtures. My concern is with the phenomenon of mixture in general, not with its range of exemplars. I will proceed on the assumption that the same kinds of mixture can be realized in different material or discursive forms, just as the same story can be told by different means—by picturing, narration, dramatization, and so on. Similar mixtures may also take place within a single medium as a result of heterogeneity in style or genre; the theory of mixed media is a theory of mixture first, and media second. The key question is not what mixes with what, but the character that mixture assumes when it is perceived as a virtual process: a fusion, a collision, a temptation, a danger, an adventure, a detour, a hierarchy, a free-for-all, and so on, or, of course, some mixture of these things. These possibilities of characterizing mixture are not purely formal or ad hoc, but emerge from cultural and social contexts in which characteristic types of mixture have symbolic import and ideological weight.

These contexts, it should be added, have a finite historical scope, and so does mixture itself, which is not a transcendental category. One of its alternatives in particular has become so important that it must at least be acknowledged before we proceed. Mixture is not the same thing as assortment, the collection of diversities; for there to be mixture, a boundary must be crossed. The boundary may be social, ethical, cultural, psychological, formal, or all of the above, but whatever its consistency, crossing it must be consequential. Assortment, by contrast, has no consequence, or more exactly is its own consequence. One of the defining features of modern mass culture has been the provision of multiple sites of contained but abundant assortment for both commodity display and entertainment, activities that have increasingly tended to merge with each other.[3] Many older forms have persisted despite the accumulation of newer ones; the list runs from newspapers and magazines to collectable images (photographs, videotapes, CD-ROMs), radio and television, shopping emporiums from arcades to malls to superstores, and the World Wide Web. Starting around the middle of the eighteenth century, assortment developed right alongside the synthesizing forms of the aesthetic, which it both modeled and travestied. Perhaps the magazine, in its compound meaning of storehouse, store, stock, and disposable publication, is the master metaphor of assortment; perhaps a mall is only a magazine in social and material space, the Web only the magazine of virtual space. Mixture, which always carries with it an ad hoc theory of impurity or impropriety, is the negation of assortment—a negation in the Hegelian sense, a liberatory movement away from the given, but one that, in the classic forms of mixed media, is often obscured by the manifest appropriateness with which the media have been mixed, rendered aesthetically "valid" by acts of synthesis, however qualified or ironic these may be in some cases.

It is important to distinguish, therefore, between assortment art, familiar mainly from avant-garde traditions of film, performance, and museum installation, and mixed-media art, which tends to occur in more traditional forms. (These generic distinctions, of course, cannot be rigidly maintained.) Assortments gather signs from different media into a kind of general signifying environment that to some degree exceeds and obscures the contribution of its components. Mixed media require a more structured, more potentially problematic interaction. Assortments have ingredients where mixtures have agencies, allow extras where mixtures produce remainders. What I will identify as the mixed-media effect operates with a distinctive double or circular movement in which the recognition of mixture per se entails a perception of intersecting media, and the perception of intersecting media yields the paradigmatic effect of mixture, the crossing or negotiation of boundaries. The resemblance to the ascriptive loop of musical meaning (see chap. 7) is not coincidental.

This process is often the locus for unresolved social and cultural tensions as well as for the release of vital social and cultural energies. Or at least it has been: the days of mixed media as a dominant form may be numbered. The globalization of commerce and culture may steadily be turning assortment into the underlying form of everyday life; mixture, and its correlative, the aesthetic, may go on the shelf as part of the worldwide assortment and lose their power as models and ideals. But the social tensions addressed, both well and badly, by those models have not diminished; on the contrary. The assortment principle potentially heightens these tensions by giving them, as it gives everything, a niche, which in this case may merely mask a force that cannot be contained. The possibility emerges of an ever-expanding assortment or niche culture in which diverse enclaves repeat within their "equally valid" borders the kinds of othering and claims to authenticity once deployed by single dominant groups against a large range of subalterns. The proliferation of identities, shibboleths, and cultural phantoms increasingly combines the speed of postmodern communication with the fervor of premodern conviction—a heady and combustible brew. At the level of aesthetics and representation, if the terms still apply, the effect of the assortment principle is to normalize heterogeneity so relentlessly that it becomes a means of inhibiting rather than producing interaction. In a sense then, the study of mixed media is both timely and anachronistic: timely because the issue of mixture at every level is, if anything, less resolved now than ever, and anachronistic because the rise of the assortment principle gives even the most sophisticated media mixtures a nostalgic quality.

THE SONIC DRIVE

Throughout the history of modern mixture, music has played a special role as the medium of mixture par excellence. In some sense, a theory of mixture is always also a theory of music. Texts and images may be amenable to mixture, but music seems actively to seek it. As I have suggested before (both in this book and elsewhere), music is famous, not to say notorious, for its capacity to mix with other forms—to mix, indeed, with anything and everything, something from which even the most autonomous-seeming music is not exempt. Music is almost always part of a mixture, a something added or blended into another circumstance, the source of a solution, suspension, or precipitate. At the level of social engineering, music is filler, the antidote to abhorred vacuums in elevators, shopping malls, and telephone holds. At a more communicative level, a level where it is meant to be heard, not just sensed, music is something like the material substance of intimacy, the tangibility of relatedness. (When I hear a melody, Rousseau once wrote, I am aware of the presence of another like myself, a sentient being.)[4] Music, often with terrific libidinal or affective or rhetorical force, is preeminently that which mixes, the master solvent among the arts. Add music to a sequence of images, and the images assume a quasi-narrative or -lyric order, rhythm, impetus, together with a sense of depth or resonance. Associate music with an image, idea, character, phrase, or circumstance with even a slight persistence or emphasis, and the music thereafter will have the power to embody that correlative in the latter's absence, to become a force of memory, possession, or yearning for possession.

At the same time, however, music poses a profound threat to the heterogeneity of mixture. In yet another realization of its a priori ambiguity, the music that mixes with everything becomes that which cannot properly mix with anything. In its sheer absorptive power, music can seem to envelop and incorporate anything with which it mixes, to distill the mixture into a graspable but indescribable essence. In film and musical theater (including opera), music often seems to encapsulate large stretches of narrative or trajectories of character in a single melody, song, texture, or even phrase, often one that acquires more essentializing power each time it is repeated. This essentializing capacity is one reason why music as a pure, isolated phenomenon becomes, during the modern era, a primary defense against the experience of heterogeneity. Music becomes pure, purity becomes musical—and therefore exquisitely vulnerable to each new turn of mixture, which, depending on context, can debase music or revitalize it with dizzying speed.

The mediating term between these antithetical qualities of music is the musical remainder, which, like music in general, plays a special role in the expressive economy of mixed media. Although there is always a mutual remainder between image and text and between music and imagetext, the musical remainder is more immediate and palpable than any other. It is so virtually by definition, given the immediacy effect that constitutively divides music from the imagetext. Vocal music, for example, may by tradition either efface itself before its words or efface the words, but it may also, again by tradition, both allow the words to be heard and still be regarded as being in some way beyond them. Songs are not usually loved for their texts, but precisely for exceeding them in some way.

In film, likewise, music is traditionally supposed to stay in the background, but even when it does it may siphon off attention from the image, and it is more than capable of intruding on the image it is supposed to supplement, stealing the scene by infringing on its visual consistency. In Fritz Lang's classic *M* (1931), the music of Grieg's "In the Halls of the Mountain King" (from the incidental music to Ibsen's *Peer Gynt*) is almost as much a character as the protagonist, a child-murderer played by Peter Lorre. It is something like the murderer's unconscious made palpable, a materialization of the compulsion that, we later learn, he experiences inside himself as an alter ego, a force, and a voice.

Here as elsewhere, however, the relationship to the film image is complicated by whether the music is diegetic (part of the story), extradiegetic (outside the story), or, at different times, both. In *M*, "In the Halls of the Mountain King" accompanies the opening title sequence, after which there is no further extradiegetic music at all until the closing frames, when the title music briefly returns. In the interim, Grieg's piece invades the diegetic space as the motto that the murderer compulsively whistles while he works. The whistling, however, is uncannily detached from the character whose presence it announces and whose true nature it indecipherably encodes. We hear it first while the camera shows us his back or his hands; later we see him begin it in fleeting profile—never full face—and hurry off screen. In the film's central section, when the murderer wanders the streets as both hunter and hunted, the tune is repeatedly heard off camera, while he remains out of view. At one point it is even heard impossibly, emanating from nowhere as we see him (through a thick screen of foliage) vainly try to stifle the sound by covering his face. The music, at first evoking a timeless mythic underworld from the safe distance of high culture, suddenly finds itself thrust into the streets of a modern urban underworld where the enemy is not a troll but a psychotic killer who can't be recognized because he looks so ordinary. In this new context the tune becomes meaningless as music. It is a pure symptom, an obscene private ritual, a secret from the outset between the audience and the murderer, whom it binds too closely together. The tune's original meaning, however, does not disappear with its original context; it remains a secret that the audience shares, but only in the defamiliarized form of an enigma.

The musical remainder has a kind of negative existence in which it is familiar but trivial. Some sort of remainder must be the basis on which the same music can be applied to different texts or images—Ibsen's world or Fritz Lang's—or be suitable for different occasions. No single text, image, or situation can exhaust the music's potential for meaning or wholly "saturate" its formal qualities. What I would like to do is recognize the remainder, not just as this sort of abstract logical necessity, but as something with a positive existence and character of its own. The remainder is a fragment of musical meaninglessness that is the indispensable condition for producing musical meaning in mixed media—and perhaps in general.

The musical remainder appears most openly when the "fit" between music and the imagetext seems or comes to seem questionable, and when, therefore, mixture itself becomes a tangible process and problem. This is not a question of the music being different or having an independent character, but of its cutting across or away from an apparently coherent system of sameness and difference. Like the opposition of music and the imagetext, to which it is related, this coalescence of disruption and remainder is as much a historical as a "grammatical" phenomenon. At bottom, the models for media mixture are social formations of hierarchy or ideal equality, which thus tend to survive in art even long after they have crumbled in reality. With some exceptions, such as the realization of songfulness or certain gen-res of eighteenth-century opera, music is expected to yield at some level to the referential authority of the imagetext, even if it is also expected or per-mitted to "transcend" it. The musical remainder tends to embody some-thing at odds with the normative good order grounded in the imagetext, which is not necessarily to say that the remainder can exist apart from the order, the coherent mixture, that it resists, eludes, escapes, mocks, inverts, or the like. What the remainder can do is embody the historicity, the con-tingency, of that normative order, and therefore its openness to reinterpre-tation, critique, or change, precisely by embodying what the order must exclude in order to sustain itself. In this role the musical remainder may also epitomize other incommensurables lying elsewhere in the work.

In Alfred Hitchcock's movie *Rear Window* (1954), for example, the voyeuristic hero (Jimmy Stewart) discovers a wife murderer living in an apartment across the courtyard from his own. The soundtrack is saturated by background noise heard through his open window, a babble of music, street sounds, and voices. Most of the music can be referred to characters in the mise-en-scène, who are listening to it on the radio or performing it, usually in some romantic or erotic connection. The voices, too, identifiably belong to these people—all, as Slavoj Žižek notes, except one: "the voice of an unidentified soprano practicing scales."[5] This unlocated, unlocatable voice will simply not mix in the film's diegesis, but it is not exactly extradiegetic, either—it is, after all, coming from somewhere within the apartment complex. It cuts through both the film as mimesis and the film as cinematic presentation. This voice is apparitional: it haunts the film like the voice of the dead wife or, more broadly, of the feminine sexuality to which, according to Žižek, the hero is just as hostile as the villain. (It is interesting in this connection that the film does contain two other unlocalized vocal sounds, the traces of unheard voices: whistled operatic melodies and a woman's terrified scream in the night.) More interested in watching passions than in having them, the surly hero fends off the advances of a "perfect" woman (Grace Kelly) for as long as possible. The film introduces this "love interest" as a shadow falling across his face at just the moment when the phantom soprano voice reaches its highest notes.

Later, the hero, whose left foot cannot support his weight because his leg is in a cast, blinds the villain with flashbulbs as the camera cuts back and forth between them. Each man carries one of the wounds of Oedipus, so that the two put together stand as one in opposition to the riddling feminine principle, the silken voice of the sphinx, who in this case fools Oedipus with her riddles, although he never realizes it. Practicing scales, the voice of the phantom soprano inhabits a primary musical order that transcends the psychosexual disorder filling the apartment complex—that walled and gated city. The operatic voice pierces the story in which it has no part and exposes the story as soap opera. The mandatory happy end for all, accompanied by blaring diegetic music, is presented as sheer narrative fabrication and ends with a castration joke: a shot panning from the hero, now with both legs broken, up Grace Kelly's very intact legs to her smiling face, the sphinx as ingenue.

OTHER VOICES, OTHER WORLDS

Another way to describe the musical remainder exemplified by this Hitchcockian voice from elsewhere is to say that it appears when one medium (the imagetext) is no longer allowed to determine the boundaries of another (music). These terms are suggested both by the status of music as the other of the imagetext and by Jacques Derrida's classic essay "Tympan," which turns a critical ear to the effort of Western philosophy to "think its other."[6] For Derrida, to think one's other is to set the boundaries between what is and is not oneself or one's own, and at the same time what should and should not be oneself or one's own. To think one's other is to control the difference between what is proper to oneself and what is not. The effect of doing so, however, is paradoxically to miss what is truly other. The other that I define is, precisely, the other that can be defined by me; one might say that such an other is proper to me. But the other that I cannot define, the other that defies my power of definition, goes unrecognized in this conceptual regime, which is not to say that it goes without acting there.

In "Tympan," Derrida investigates these relationships in terms of speaking, singing, listening, and hearing, which is why I spoke of his turning a critical ear and why I find this essay particularly suggestive in theorizing the musical remainder in mixed media. Approaching his subject obliquely, Derrida suggests that the nomenclature applied to the anatomy of the ear inscribes the project of philosophy on the organ by which one is meant to hear the other speak—or sing. The result is that one hears only oneself. The tympanic membrane, the "drum" of the eardrum, forms the border between the "labyrinth" of the inner ear and the auditory "canal" leading to the surface of the body. The drum controls and harmonizes the "inner" and "outer" vibrations that follow when a sound strikes it.

Derrida asks how it is possible to pierce this literally self-centered system. He asks this through that which is other to his own text, an extended quotation from Michel Leiris's autobiographical work "Biffures" (Cancellations). Leiris's text is inscribed in the margin of Derrida's. Thus piercing the proper text, the other text speaks of piercing the ear by a spiral or corkscrew motion. This motion is both wandering and purposive; it may be either organic or mechanical, appealing or disgusting; it may aim either to penetrate a hidden depth or to emerge from one into the light. Leiris connects these alternatives by associating two words: *Persephone*, heard awry as if to name the goddess as a piercing sound, "perce-phoné," and *perce-oreille*, the French word for "earwig," the insect that pierces the pits of fruits and is sometimes said to enter the human ear and attack the tympanum. Leiris also speaks of the perce-phonic singing voice as what Derrida might elsewhere call a supplement. He conjectures that the voice in singing "presents itself as the translation, in a purely sonorous idiom, of that which could not be said by means of words." We are back, then, at the ear-piercing voice of Hitchcock's soprano practicing scales—a voice returning, Persephone-like, from the underworlds of death and unconscious desire. But from Hitchcock's soprano we may take the suggestion that the "translation" effect that Leiris describes becomes activated, becomes the mixed-media effect I have been trying to theorize, only when the voice disengages itself from the coherent system of forms and meanings to which it was supposed to have belonged. If we listen obliquely, suggests Derrida in turn, we may really be able to hear well, which in this case means to hear improperly.

The percephonic voice—percephony—that asks to be heard this way is a personification of the remainder in its most active, desire-invested form. Like the mirror in relation to *Carnaval*, discussed in chapter 5, it is a figure whose significance lies somewhere between its concrete form as a trope and its symptomatic relation to an underlying process of acculturation and subject formation. This intermediacy is itself part of what percephonic voice makes audible, as a brief sampler of modern instances, pieced together from diverse sources, can help suggest.

Schoenberg's "Herzgewächse" (Heartflora; 1911, for soprano, celesta, harmonium, and harp, is a brief setting of a poem by Maurice Maeterlinck; the poem recounts a sexually ambiguous allegory of rebirth, the rise of a single lily in a ruined garden. The setting concludes as the voice attains, then relinquishes, an extreme high note that marks the vanishing point of voice in song and renders what remains uncanny, impersonal, almost inhuman. The note is the F far above the treble staff, sustained *pppp*. And it signifies: this is the high note of the Queen of the Night's famous revenge aria in Mozart's *The Magic Flute*. Schoenberg's moment of percephonic voice transforms the enlightenment succubus into a symbolist angel.

Stravinsky's *Perséphone* (1934, rev. 1949), for speaker, tenor, chorus, children's chorus, and orchestra, sets a text by André Gide in which Persephone's return to the underworld is a voluntary act of compassion. But the music's intimation of percephony is scored against the grain. Stravinsky's Persephone is less a moral agent than a mysterious mediator between fullness and lack, almost a personification of Heine's concept of music as a "twilight mediator" between spirit and matter (chap. 7). The key to her identity is her voice, which is both full and lacking. Full, because it is the only voice in the cantata with a single identity; the tenor acts both as narrator, outside the time of the story, and as several characters in the story, while the chorus represents both the society of the living and the shades of the dead. Lacking, because Persephone, again unlike the tenor and the chorus, has no musical voice, only a dramatic one; she speaks, but she never sings. Her musical voice is "heard" only in the pastoral lyricism that pervades the work as a whole. Its literal absence suggests that she has always already "sacrificed" some part of herself, that part of her has belonged to the underworld from the beginning. Her singularity is paradoxically grounded in this self-division. It is not only her duty but also her desire that divides her between the realms of world and underworld and does so regardless of either the contingent events of the story or the moral rationale by which Gide glosses them.[7]

Rodgers and Hammerstein's musical *South Pacific* (1949) addresses the experience of (white) Americans faced with new cultural and racial boundaries in the Pacific theater of World War II. As the genre dictates, the primary form of boundary crossing is romantic, as the all-American heroine Nellie Forbush acknowledges when she sings "I'm in Love with a Wonderful Guy." The object of her love is a French planter, who, she will soon be upset to discover, is also the father of two interracial children. The song both recognizes her dawning love for this man and tries to reconcile it with her sense of national identity. The lyrics link her feelings both to Fourth of July festivity and to the social and natural fertility of the American heartland, the "amber waves of grain" of another famous song. Her opening words describe her as "corny as Kansas in August"; the pun on "corny" links the aw-shucks authenticity of middle-American romantic sentiment with the traditional pastoral image of the flourishing earth, thus establishing Nellie as one of Persephone's sisters. But the climax of the song carries this implied identity to a degree of intensity—"extreme" is not quite the right word here—that can no longer be securely contained by the national and racial limits of the musical's love stories. Nellie concludes by approaching the song's title phrase with a crescendo consisting of four repetitions of the phrase "I'm in love" sung to the same snatch of melody. This little mantra easily absorbs as much fullness of voice and force of expression as the singer can pour into it; if there is an element of self-persuasion or resistance in the need for repetition, the unconstrained voice quickly masks it. Thanks to this breakaway outburst, the voice of Persephone (resurrected from the corn) momentarily takes over the song. It sounds out, however, less in the outburst itself than in the unarticulated interval between the voice confined by ideology and the voice released by its own exuberance, suggesting an explosive, transracial, transnational, even impersonal force of libido that the whole musical otherwise exists to tame.[8]

Finally, on the last day of her life, Salman Rushdie's "Vina Divina," the "legendary popular singer Vina Apsara" (heroine of the novel *The Ground beneath Her Feet*) sings both Amore and Eurydice in the finale of Gluck's opera *Orfeo*. Literally swallowed by the earth during a quake, Vina becomes a Eurydice-like quest object herself, and more: "This posthumous goddess, this underground post-Vina, queen of the underworld, supplanting dread Persephone on her throne, grew into something simply overwhelming. . . . Dying when the world shook, by her death she shook the world."[9] Vina is figuratively what Persephone is literally, a true diva. Her voice both overruns boundaries and emanates from behind a boundary that no one who hears it can cross.

But why do all these voices belong to women? Perhaps it needn't be so in every case (Walt Whitman, for one, heard male Persephones in bel canto tenors), but it does seem that percephonic voice is paradigmatically feminine, regardless of its actual source or sonority. Although the usual reasons apply—the symbolic tradition makes femininity the medium of otherness; the ultimate reference of both boundary and desire is the maternal voice and body—another answer may seem more compelling, if more conjectural. At moments of boundary disruption, in terror or ecstasy, voice defies gravity: it rises in a cry, regardless of whether the body soars or falls. The tessitura of voice in extremis is "naturally" feminine, or at least "unnaturally" masculine (the falsetto, the castrato). The location of this voice (or more exactly its never-quite-attainable goal) is symbolized by the figure of Persephone and her sisters regardless of how individual moments of percephony sound.[10]

Percephonic voice, however, is not always audible and may even be most piercing in its silence, which is often the tone of its deepest underworld roots. Steve Reich's composition *Different Trains* (1988) evokes the rail transport of people across both the United States and Europe during the Holocaust; the music incorporates the recorded sounds of these different trains, on one type of which the young Reich, on the other the young condemned by the Reich, then traveled. The work also combines music for string quartet (both live and taped) with taped speech culled from Reich's governess and a pullman porter on the one hand, and a group of holocaust survivors on the other. The music for string quartet forms melodic motives by transcribing the pitch profiles of small samples of the recorded speech. The result is a peculiar, not to say uncanny eloquence, not of either the recorded or the melodic voices in themselves, but of the gap between them.

The unspeaking but articulate voice of this gap (also present in the gaps between sampled phrases and full speech, recorded retrospective voices and the actual voices of the past) marks the inevitable loss of what is most individual about the recorded voices, the kernel of identity that the melodic transcriptions can never fully capture. The same melodic phrases could be drawn from virtually anyone's voice, and while this breadth of reference gives the phrases symbolic resonance, allowing them to stand for whole generations, it also demonstrates the frightening ease with which the most intimate quality of a person can be abstracted and depersonalized, a process that the work itself cannot help repeating over and over. It is the potential anonymity of the era's voices, or, what amounts to the same thing, the fading echo of their identities, that most palpably unites the American passenger cars and Nazi cattle cars, and reminds us that the travelers and the victims were consigned to different trains on the basis of sheer chance. The music can do no more to counter the rule of such (mis)chance than to record the blind contingency of its operation. "While [my train] trips," Reich observes, "were exciting and romantic at the time, I now look back and think that, if I had been in Europe during this period, as a Jew I would have had to ride very different trains. With this in mind I wanted to make a piece that would accurately reflect the whole situation."[11] Anything better may be impossible. According to Nietzsche, at least, to escape the rule of chance, or at least the agonizing thought that it is perhaps the only rule, "one would have to have been already a guest in the underworld and beyond all surfaces, sat at Persephone's table and played dice with the goddess herself."[12]

A DIFFERENT THRESHOLD, ANOTHER TRAIN

From this conclusion, theory may come as a relief. What, then, does musical meaning—and musical meaninglessness—show about mixed media? Above all, that conjunctions of music and the imagetext entail a negotiation between the relatively unified, ascriptively full effects of coherent mixture and the strange insistence of the musical remainder—a dialogue, or pair of monologues, that acts out an historically concrete version of the a priori ambiguity of music. The process of mixture involves an attempt by one medium, usually the imagetext, to think its other, and a response in which, however indirectly or implicitly, the other, usually music, thinks for itself. The musical remainder is often obscure or marginal, forgotten in the mutual reinforcement of each medium by the other, but it is always there, always capable of emerging as the most compelling, most revealing, most chastening or animating force in the mixture.

This process can be paraphrased in social terms as, roughly speaking, an interplay of ideology and impulse. As the dynamic element in media mixture, music edges toward a metaphorical identification with a primary social energy. Its sensuous and rhythmic character readily comes to embody the drive quality of social relationships. If Freud was right to suggest that social groups form around the sharing of ego ideals (personality types that the subject seeks to resemble), then music most readily supplies the impulsive, noncognitive dimension of that sharing, the palpable force supporting the given rationale of cohesion.[13] But the a priori ambiguity of music entails that it serves this purpose only as the remainder left over from its own expression of the social rationale. Music's drive character is inseparable from its expressive quality; each of the two terms is produced as that which exceeds full representation by the other. Music assumes its impetus to solidarity only insofar as it invites, encourages, even insists on ascriptive practices that invest it with meaning. In this doubleness, music might be said to form the aesthetic equivalent of the liminal zones in culture that, according to Mary Douglas, are symbolized by the permeable zones of the body and that constitute the key sites for the articulation of both purity and danger, solidarity and transgression, identity and difference.[14] Music, however, recasts the liminal zones by subsuming the ethical category of purity under the aesthetic one of pleasure, which, in turn, partly fuses with danger instead of cleanly opposing it. The law-based antithesis of purity and danger becomes the pleasure-based ambivalence of autonomy and contingency.

THE VOICE OF PERCEPHONY

By way of illustration and conclusion, I offer a pair of small case studies drawn from the televisual equivalent of lyric poetry: the opening title sequences of two TV series. The genre interests me because it often encapsulates the fantasies underlying the shows' narrative formulas without the need to rationalize them or bring them to closure. The examples interest me because both involve their fantasies with percephonic images, faint traces of the corkscrew motion that moves between the underworld to the upper world while belonging to neither.

The X-Files chronicles the paranoid quest of FBI agent Fox Mulder to expose the truth about both paranormal phenomena and a grand conspiracy involving extraterrestrial life and the U.S. government. Mulder's credulity is supposedly held in check by the scientific skepticism of his partner, Dana Scully, but since the show's plot lines almost always endorse Mulder's theories, the real significance of the partnership lies elsewhere. The opening sequence helps to suggest where.

The visuals begin with a thickly drawn X that fills the screen; the show's title appears in small lettering. The sequence of images is deliberately obfuscatory, but it slowly crystallizes into a narrative pattern. It starts with a series of topical shots intercut with blowups of Mulder's and Scully's ID cards: a UFO seen in sequential stills, a hand hovering over a radar screen, a mysterious sphere pierced by spermlike tentacles of light; a dissolve from the sphere to a silently screaming face subjected to curvilinear distortion, like the face in Edvard Munch's painting *The Scream;* a ghost passing down a corridor. A group of sequential stills then shows the two agents crossing a threshold with anxious faces and guns drawn, themselves rendered ghostly by their dim surroundings and the sudden glare of a flashlight in the viewer's eyes; their movements are discontinuous but smoothly segued together. As the two draw close and their image clarifies, the screen bleaches away. It goes blank; then the whiteness condenses into a paper doll–like figure of a man whirling downward (away from the screen surface) into a dark handprint that fills the background. The image suggests someone, presumably Mulder, falling into the hands of fate or of some puppet master, and also alludes to the imagery of neurotic obsessiveness of Hitchcock's film *Vertigo*. (Is there also perhaps a hint of *Alice in Wonderland*?) As the fall ends, an opening eye fills the screen; it is followed by what it presumably sees, a mountain ridge under a sky crossed by fast-moving clouds—preternatural storm clouds. The high place is presumably in Roswell, New Mexico, the supposed site of a UFO crash and government cover-up in 1947. It is identified as the traditional site of visionary revelation and fulfilled quest not only by the eye-opening image that precedes it, but also by a written legend that ends the visuals by flashing like a neon sign across the sky: "The Truth Is Out There."[15]

To this sequence the music (by Mark Snow) opposes an image of endless nonprogressive movement, an antinarrative. The signature theme consists of nothing but the slightly varied repetition of the same melodic idea, each statement of which closes with an accented short-long repetition of the same note, the expectancy-laden fifth scale degree; the closing figure echoes throughout at different points in the musical texture. The theme has a "spooky," hollow character created by emphasis on leaps of a fourth and fifth and by a tone color that sounds like unison whistling—whistling in the dark or in the wind, whistling a happy tune to keep from feeling afraid. The accompaniment is a basso ostinato that really sounds obstinate: paired statements of a motive rising quickly by fourth and fifth to be met head-on by a stinging dissonant accent. The net effect is complex: at once an impression of the obsessional element in Mulder's relentlessly goal-directed quest and, with the constant harping by the melody on the fifth degree and the bass on the dissonant sting, the impression of an expectancy never satisfied and never meant to be, of the obsession as self-sustaining, unfolding not in an effort to find the truth but to defer finding it, to make sure that the truth is indeed still "out there." Hence the role of Scully, whose partnership and deep personal tie to Mulder (which, however, is never eroticized) is based on her doubts. Scully provides Mulder with the formal convention of deferral. If he could convince her of everything, the quest would be over—which, at bottom, is not to be desired. (In its fifth season, the program finally offered answers to some of the puzzles of its long-running conspiracy plot—but against the tacit resistance of Mulder, shown spending most of his time playing basketball or otherwise scoffing and brooding. Roles reverse as Scully insists that the truth is out there, holding the place that Mulder will reclaim—and she relinquish—in subsequent episodes. Two years later, with Scully almost a convert as the agents reinvestigate their first case, Mulder disappears, apparently joining a group of alien abductees. He finds, even becomes, the truth out there, but cannot share it with his partner—so the narrative continues.)[16]

The contradiction between the symptomatic ritual of the music and the narrative line of the visuals is manifested in positive form by the gaps in each—in the narrative, by the unrepresented but perceptible breaks in the agents' motion during the threshold-crossing segment, then by the white screen that follows; in the music, by recurrent pregnant pauses between statements of the leitmotivic signature theme, the last note of which seems always to trail away into an indistinct distance. These gaps are *biffures:* they mark the true X in the X files, the algebraic unknown that is in principle knowable, but whose knowability is canceled, crossed out, by the X of a fantasy that is inconclusive because it is inconclusible. The gaps posit what Lacan called the Real, the unavowable true desire of the subject: Mulder and Scully linked forever in their division, a postmodern Don Quixote and his feminine Sancho Panza who is also part Dulcinea.

NYPD Blue, which identifies itself as a "police drama," spins out its opening sequence across a similar gap.[17] Although deliberately overloaded with information (the pandemonium of the big city), the sequence is spare and transparent in form. At first the music (by Mike Post) seems synchronous with the visuals; each follows a clear-cut A B A pattern in tandem with the other. The music to the first A section consists of a faint lyric background and a torrent of what sounds like massed drums beating, although it is actually a kind of mega- or meta-drum set produced by complex sampling techniques. The visuals begin with a speeding elevated train rushing at the viewer through the night like the vengeful spirit of *The Great Train Robbery.* A rapid succession of urban images follows, the camera swiveling and jerking as it presents them. Some of the images suggest potential violence with sharp edges and jagged perspectives; others seem more innocent. They are interspersed with brief shots of the show's regular characters in medium closeup. Taken together, the music and visuals reinvent a cluster of well-worn metaphors: the great modern city as jungle, as machine, as social cacophony mirrored by a sonic one.

The next phase, the B section, offers relief from this pandemonium, even something like redemption. The images become more innocent (one even shows children playing); the camerawork softens into slow motion; the reassuring presence of the show's characters is enhanced by their own slow-motion appearance (replacing snapshots with portraits) and by subtitles joining the actors' names to their faces. ("Real or fictitious," the titles seem to say, "these people can be trusted; their charisma is what you need, and all you need.") One slow-motion image even explicitly sublimates the threat of violence into aesthetic contemplation: it shows a building being demolished as if gracefully, the camera speed "thinking" the other of violence as something shaped, contained, controlled. The music, meanwhile, has reversed polarity; the drum-like pounding has faded into the background and the lyric melody come to the fore. Sung on the English horn, the melody has a distinctly pastoral air. Michael Beckerman has suggested that it is a "subliminal recollection" of one of Mike Post's favorite pieces, the Largo from Dvořák's "New World" Symphony, "with its English horn evoking the wide and peaceful prairies";[18] another resonance may be with the *alte Weise* with which the English horn opens the third act of Wagner's *Tristan und Isolde*. Like these other bittersweet Arcadian melodies, the English horn theme here evokes a distant or lost world. The theme corresponds to nothing in the urban scene, yet its presence seems to draw that scene, at least wishfully, toward a vision of harmony in the broad sense of the term.

This transcendental moment, however, proves to be fleeting. The last section is a reprise of the first, a return to the danger and confusion of the city, the pounding drums, the speeding train. From a narrative standpoint, this return is necessary; the city must supply the wrongs that each week's story tries to put right. But the return is complete only in the music. Although the visuals reprise the normal motion and mercurial camera techniques of the A section, the images take on a new dimension. (As with *The X-Files*, the visuals tend toward a narrative that the music tends to repudiate.) Where daylight dominated before, lyrically composed nocturnal scenes appear; the swiveling of the camera turns the multicolored lights of the city into beautiful abstractions, visual continuations of the angelic music that has now been lost. The first nocturnal image even defers the moment of loss, its lyricism holding on to the English horn melody for a single poignant moment, almost literally the blink of an eye, before the drumming resumes. From here the section pivots on another benign explosion, that of firecrackers over a brightly illuminated street, to the scene of a Chinese New Year celebration. The sweetness of the nocturnal lyricism is abandoned, but not its play of colors and lights; the urban anarchy of the A section metamorphoses into festive license.

The climax of this scene is a glimpse of a man energetically drumming. The image completes a new coalescence of music and visuals sparked by the firecrackers, but it also introduces a new disjunction. It turns the drumming man into the symbolic, quasi-diegetic source of the music, and in so doing reinterprets the music's own drumming; the threat of antisocial violence reappears as an organized expression of social energy. Like the show itself, the sequence seems to find its goal in this outcome. But the outcome (as in the show) is unstable: as always, there is a musical remainder, and this one demands a reckoning. The drumming continues, suddenly sweeping the visuals into its track. The sequence ends as darkness returns and the train that opened the A section plunges at high speed into a subway tunnel, which appears as if seen from the front of the head car. Closure comes with a reversal of perspective: the viewer who began by seeing the onrushing train now sees from it. The music may now suggest the emblematic rumble of that train from either perspective, but its energy has become autonomous, its symbolic boundaries impossible to fix. The viewer thus plunges along with the train into an urban labyrinth to the depths of who knows what tympanum.

In spite of which, everything is going to be all right, or so the sequence would have you believe. The music may hammer on, but the viewer has the Ariadne's thread to this labyrinth, even if he or she has never heard of Theseus or Ariadne. There is no blow, no cry, that can pierce the city's tympanum with a sound it cannot assimilate. The music just signals your excitement. The good police and the show's producers have thought the city's other; you don't have to worry about it. Only watch.

In spite of which, again, the tangible effect of mixture arises and persists in the shifting relationships between music and image. Not that anyone necessarily wanted or planned this, but there it is. And in this process— not in the music's violence, which has been thought and packaged as a proper other, but in the vicissitudes that make this thinking and packaging itself audible—there arises the possibility of learning what, in particular, is oblique, improper, and piercing with respect to this system of representations. We might understand the "philosophy" of *NYPD Blue* as involving the sublimation of a certain urban disorder, a process that operates in multiple registers, narrative, imagistic, musical, and ultimately social. The unthought other of that philosophy might be surmised as a disorder beyond the reach of sublimation, something unspeakable and debasing that seems to haunt modern constructions of urban space regardless of actual safety or danger. (The labyrinth of streets and cellars in *M* and the warren of apartments in *Rear Window* harbor the same threat.) This disorder can be neither imaged nor sounded directly, as the sequence acknowledges by portraying only the city, never the crime that threatens it. But the dread and fascination of the unthought other do find a concrete realization as the symbolic link between the drumming man and the drumming music breaks down and the viewer is flung headlong into the tunnel of the underworld—to which, and from which, the vertiginous voice of Persephone spirals its endless way.

9
Powers of Blackness
Jazz and the Blues in Modern Concert Music

One of the great emblematic moments in the history of movies occurs early in the first "talking picture," *The Jazz Singer* (1927), when the star, Al Jolson, steps out of character after doing a musical number and speaks a few lines he had made famous on the vaudeville stage: "Wait a minute—wait a minute—you ain't heard nothing yet." As Michael Rogin observes, "These first words of feature movie speech, a kind of performative, announce—you ain't heard nothing yet—the birth of sound movies and the death of silent film."[1] But the film is also emblematic in another way. The images used to promote and memorialize it virtually all show the star in blackface. Jolson blacks up for two of the film's key scenes, including the sensationally popular finale in which he sinks to his knees with outstretched arms to climax his singing of "Mammy." And this moment emblematizes, perhaps even emblematized for its original audiences, a scenario basic to American modernity.

As Rogin suggests, blackface in *The Jazz Singer* dramatizes the power of European immigrants, represented by their pariah figure par excellence, a Jew, to assimilate into the social mainstream by establishing their difference from America's blacks. In principle, only a white face can wear a black mask. That the proving ground of this not-entirely-accurate principle should be music is no accident. According to Sampson Raphaelson, author of the play on which the film was based, the most adequate symbol of "the vital chaos of America's soul" was jazz. By jazz, though, Raphaelson did not mean the "primitive" music of African Americans, but the "sophisticated" transformations of it wrought by Jewish American entertainers: "Jazz is Irving Berlin, Al Jolson, George Gershwin, Sophie Tucker."[2] The result, says Rogin, "unnoticed in all the critical commentary, is that [*The Jazz Singer*] contains no jazz"[3]—only minstrelsy.

The social-musical drama thus played out overtly in the field of mass entertainment was also being played out more covertly in the field of high art. Modern music, and music in relation to modernity, could not escape the often disavowed presence of "raggy time" music in either field. The aim of this chapter is to examine the encounter between some of the music of black America—ragtime, blues, and jazz—and white modernist concert music in both the United States and France, circa 1909–31, with a later codicil from England. The encounter was both rich and strange, and it produced a large handful of now canonical or near-canonical concert works. During the inter-war period it was crucial to the definition of musical modernism itself, especially in the United States, though that is not the story usually told about it. It was also, and this virtually at every turn, haunted by ambivalence about the musics on which it drew, with which it mingled on terms compounded of pleasure, envy, condescension, anxiety, and celebration. To describe the result by saying that there is no jazz in the jazz-singing pieces of modernism would be going too far, but such jazz—or blues, or ragtime—as these pieces offer is marked and filtered by the network of race relations that, both silently and noisily, pervaded (and pervades) social life. As I hope to show, it is *not* going too far to describe the results as a kind of minstrelsy, a continuation of blackface by other means.

This is not, of course, to say that the concert pieces in question are *nothing but* racial echo chambers, any more than the music of Berlin, Gershwin, et al. is *nothing but* an appropriation of "real" jazz. All of this music engages a host of other social and cultural issues, as well as musically intramural issues of stylistic and formal enterprise. But when the forms and styles involved have, as these do, a long history of racial encoding, they cannot easily be extricated from the problems of domination and desire, purity and danger, pleasure and identity. Tracking these problems becomes tendentious only when the messy, ambivalent process of constructing social hierarchies is misconstrued as a simple, unconflicted, unproblematic structure.

My thesis about minstrelsy is admittedly more problematic. The original blackface minstrelsy, after all, was crude, obscene, and egregiously racist, a carnivalesque debasement of the black male as Other, the social site where the racial anxieties of nineteenth-century white Americans became (their) self-pleasuring. These qualities were softened, but hardly eliminated, when minstrelsy moved into vaudeville around the turn of the twentieth century. Nothing of the kind can be said of black-inflected modernist concert music. On the contrary: the encounter of musical modernism with jazz and blues in particular might be said to have produced a site at which dominant white cultures were unusually hospitable to African-American cultural energies, and this well in advance of parallel encounters in popular music, which could not fully accomplish the same thing until the 1960s. My thesis, however, is concerned not with what minstrelsy signified but with what it did, not with its perpetuation of racist stereotypes but with its deployment of racial positions. Toni Morrison similarly abstracts the function from the content of minstrelsy in order to delineate a permanent racial subtext in American literature:

> In minstrelsy, a layer of blackness applied to a white face released it from law. Just as entertainers, through or by association with blackface, could render permissible topics that otherwise would have been taboo, so American writers were able to employ an imagined Africanist persona to articulate and imaginatively act out the forbidden in American culture.[4]

What Morrison presents as rhetoric also scans as history; her analogy tacitly recognizes a kind of Africanist continuum running from the vernacular of minstrelsy to the high art of literary form.

DECONSTRUCTING RECONSTRUCTION

The social and cultural motives for giving concert music an Africanist dimension obviously differed by nation, although not as widely as might first appear. The United States had to contend both with the traumatic history of slavery, civil war, and Reconstruction and with the long tradition of popular entertainment—from Daddy "Jim Crow" Rice to *The Jazz Singer*—fascinated with, not to say obsessed with, blackness. France was a leading player in the long European scramble for Africa itself, the colonial adventure that put control over African lands and peoples at the very heart of modern national destiny. On both sides of the Atlantic, what presented itself as a musical question of stylistic authenticity tacitly invoked social questions of what might be called colonial administration—in France of Africa, and in America of Africans.

In the United States, the overt issue was how to make American art a reflection of American national identity without also making it provincial. In literature, the issue had come to the fore at least as early as 1841 in Ralph Waldo Emerson's essay "The Poet." Emerson already recognizes, although in passing, the necessity of encountering in art those ever present others who, in America, are not really other at all:

We have yet had no genius . . . which knew the value of our incomparable materials, and saw [in them] . . . another carnival of the gods he
admires so much in Homer. . . . Our log-rolling, our stumps and their
politics, our fisheries, our Negroes and Indians . . . the northern trade,
the southern planting, the western clearing . . . are yet unsung.[5]

In concert music, the demand for a national style inflected by "our Negroes
and Indians" famously crystallized around the figure of Antonin Dvořák,
whose three-year stay in America (1892–95) witnessed the appearance of
both his "New World" Symphony and the statement that certain American
critics (but not Dvořák himself) would come to broadcast as a clarion call:

> I suggested that inspiration for truly national music might be derived
> from the negro melodies or Indian chants. I was led to take this view
> partly by the fact that the so-called plantation songs are indeed the
> most striking and appealing melodies that have yet been found on this
> side of the water, but largely by the observation that this seems to be
> recognized, though often unconsciously, by most Americans.[6]

Dvořák's own contribution to "truly national" American music turned out,
ironically, to be a refined form of blackface. As William Austin reports, in
1893 Dvořák arranged Stephen Foster's "Old Folks at Home" for two solo
singers, mixed chorus, and orchestra.[7] The soloists and chorus at the first
performance—apparently the only performance the piece would have for
roughly a century—were all African Americans; Dvořák conducted with a
special ebony baton.

Yet if Dvořák's "Old Folks" recycles the sentimental plantation stereo-
type with well-intentioned naïveté, his observation that Americans in the
1890s tended to recognize the value of "negro melodies" only unconsciously still strikes home. It points to the catch-22 that undermined, but in
so doing also defined, the whole project of constructing an American
national style on an Africanist basis. For the white Americans who generally controlled the country's cultural and ideological formations, America
was fundamentally a white nation. An American national style, accordingly, could not ground American identity in the powers of blackness. The
Africanist presence must be marginalized or disavowed, lest the whole culture of the country be creolized. As Austin observes, one of Dvořák's critical acolytes, James Huneker, eventually came to spell out this imperative
with brutal directness:

> If we are to have true American music it will not stem from "darky"
> roots, especially as the most original music of the kind thus far written

is by Stephen Foster, a white man. The influence of Dvořák's American music has been evil; ragtime is the popular pabulum now. I need hardly add that the negro is not the original race of our country.[8]

Writing in 1920, Huneker voices an ideological mandate that is especially urgent during the long post-Reconstruction era, when, according to Rogin, the United States gradually came to exchange one form of internal division for another.[9] The nation that was once two nations, south and north, slave and free, now faced the problem of unifying itself culturally after the trauma of political unification by civil war. This second unity could be achieved only by the paradoxical means of once more becoming two nations, black and white. The firm establishment of a black subaltern group served to configure and stabilize the social order of true, white America.

For those less panicked than Huneker, the problem of a national style in music came to turn on questions, not of exclusion, but of subordination. Among the musics that "most Americans" could be counted on to recognize as truly American, "though often unconsciously," those that carried a black sound were preeminent. Huneker notwithstanding, this was even true of Stephen Foster's "Ethiopian" minstrel songs, which were widely if erroneously thought to reflect African American sources; even W. E. B. Du Bois thought that "the songs of white America [had] been decisively influenced by the slave songs or [had] incorporated whole phrases of Negro melody, as 'Swanee River' and 'Old Black Joe.'"[10] The national style had no choice but to reflect these realities. But to be truly American, it would have to reflect them in a way that reproduced musically the all-important social relationship between black America and white America.

To that end, there evolved a body of techniques by which the texture of a concert piece could embed the sounds of black music but at the same time imbue them with an aura of distance, sometimes slight but always telling. So embedded, the black sounds surrender part of their immediacy. They function as citations, framed references to a low vernacular idiom, vital but perilous—the idiom of the Other. The effect is the same whether the citations merely inflect or wholly saturate the musical texture. The texture, meanwhile, attains to the national style precisely in the act of citation: in other words, not by identifying with the powers of blackness, but by enclosing them.

In other words still, the citations function as what Toni Morrison calls "Africanisms": signs of blackness against which the subject of the dominant culture can seek to define itself as white—"white" here meaning normative, race-free, universal. Africanisms, writes Morrison, establish "the denotative and connotative blackness that African peoples have come to signify, as well as the entire range of views, assumptions, readings, and misreadings that accompany Eurocentric learning about these people" (6–7). Because Africanisms are discursive formations, anyone can use them, including black people, just as black troupes could practice blackface minstrelsy after the Civil War. Resistant, "signifying" usages are possible, too, but my impression is that they are tellingly rare in modernist concert music.[11] At any rate, the primary subject of Africanist discourse, the subject who fantasizes being in control of it, is a subject that produces itself as white by differing from what it constructs as blackness.

Musical Africanisms are generally supposed to occupy an ex-centric position, to stand outside the essence of the artwork even as their presence defines the character of the artwork. This ex-centricity, combined with good old-fashioned eccentricity, is already full blown in the first major work by a now canonical American composer to make substantial use of Africanisms. The work is the First Piano Sonata of Charles Ives, composed between 1902 and 1909. Massive and deeply earnest, the sonata is laid out in a five-part arch form. The even-numbered movements, with fast basic tempos, are ragtime pieces that Ives thought of as scherzos. Mixing up their ragtime with both hymn tunes and nonvernacular materials, they show the polystylistic heterogeneity that is Ives's stylistic trademark. In contrast, the odd-numbered movements, with slow basic tempos, show Ives coming as close as he ever would to the style of Lisztian Romantic pianism. By Ivesian standards, the texture both within and among these movements is strikingly homogeneous. Although hymn tunes do appear, as well as the barroom ditty "How Dry I Am," they rarely stand out as they do in the ragtimes; the vernacular elements are closely worked into the texture and abstracted and subsumed into a sustained process of thematic transformation. Together, the three slow movements form a continuum broken only by the ragtime scherzos; powerfully goal directed, they build from and around a tiny germinal motive, a descending minor second and minor third, that sounds at both the beginning and the end of the whole. As Wilfrid Mellers observes, the motive "develops not through tonal conflict and resolution, but with . . . evolutionary, polymodal, polyharmonic, polyrhythmic freedom."[12] The evolutionary process culminates near the close of the last movement with the motive swept up into a resounding, long drawn-out apotheosis. Like the similar climax near the close of Ives's Second String Quartet, this one suggests the ecstatic conclusion of an arduous contemplative process, the revelation at the end of a spiritual quest.

The ragtime movements lie outside the trajectory of that quest, at best suggesting a distraction from its rigors, at worst a dark defile of temptation through which the quester has to pass. The movements are raucous and frenzied, far removed from the classic rags of Scott Joplin and James Scott. Their blackness, such as it is, is mediated and disfigured by blackface, all but overtly figured in the cacophonous, carnivalesque atmosphere. Ives's own commentary traces the origin of these movements to his undergraduate days at Yale, and to music he heard—and occasionally played—at Poli's Theater in New Haven as an accompaniment to the songs of blackface comedians. (Ives used to spell the pianist, George Felsburg, when the latter wanted "to go out for five minutes and get a glass of beer, or a dozen glasses."[13] Hence perhaps the unregenerate appearance of "How Dry I Am" in the second movement—to be redeemed in the fifth.) More generally, Ives characterizes ragtime itself as "something like wearing a derby hat on the back of the head, a shuffling lilt of a happy soul just let out of a Baptist church in old Alabama."[14] In other words, ragtime is a new way of conjuring up that loose-limbed dandy of the old minstrel shows, Zip Coon. The dark defile is a site of racialized fantasy, a fantasy that helps ground the presumptively race-free quest romance of the odd-numbered movements.

In keeping with Mikhail Bakhtin's theorization of the carnivalesque, the ragtime scherzos of the First Sonata debunk something normally revered in order to celebrate gross bodily pleasure and momentary release from social regulation.[15] The debunking here is directed at the hymn tunes, which are mocked and distorted by being ragged, in direct contrast to their sublimation in the movements of the spiritual continuum. The pleasure that results is wild and giddy, and a welcome relief from the strenuous sobriety that surrounds it, but it is also potentially monstrous—a duality Eric Lott finds typical of blackface, which both desires and fears the "black" pleasures it claims to imitate.[16] Latent throughout the second movement, the monstrosity simply erupts at the start of the fourth: a protracted spell of noisy, grinding, motoric rhythms, a kind of sonic abyss that eventually spews forth a rag.

Although Africanist distance can generally be taken to imply racialized fantasy, neither need go to the extremes found in the First Sonata. Ives offers a less drastic but no less instructive form of both in a piece started about the same time the sonata was finished. Originally entitled "An Elegy for Stephen Foster," "An Elegy to Our Forefathers" became the first movement of Ives's Second Orchestral set. In slow tempo, it begins with the basses singing the rocking minor-third motive, "I'm Coming," from Foster's "Old Black Joe." Overlaid with a dense instrumental blur and the faint tolling of bells, the basses intone the motive incessantly. Thus muffled,

"I'm coming" will form the accompaniment to a long elegiac melody, the utterance of which is the sole business of the piece. Heard by itself, however, before the melody starts and long after it stops, the "I'm coming" motive is not an accompaniment at all but a singular, static presence; it is simply there. When the melody arises, the motive assumes the value of an ostinato and grounds the articulation of the melodic upper voices. But when the melody stops, the motive is once more simply there.

Ives's choice of "Old Black Joe" is an Africanism; it invokes Foster in Du Bois's manner, as an authentic conduit of Negro melody. Although there may be some truth to William Austin's claim that Ives generally uses Foster's Ethiopian tunes without regard to their words, the "Elegy" also quotes the chorus from "Massa's in de Cold, Cold Ground" as a postlude to its own melody, making the associations with slavery hard to ignore.[17] As the bass of an elegy to our forefathers, the weary voice of the old slave stands exactly where it should, at the basis of the nation's history. Yet it is the purpose of the elegy to sublimate that black basis into a higher, "race-free," universal spirit. Austin describes the process clearly, though his reading of it remains race blind, or rather, race deaf:

> The main melody, begun by a soft trumpet and second violins, presents the Foster motive . . . and continues into the phrase "for my head . . ." But now a pun takes over: all these notes belong equally to the chorus of the Sunday-school hymn "Renar" by William Bradbury, "Yes, Jesus loves me, yes Jesus loves me, the Bible tells me so." As Ives's melody continues, Bradbury more and more dominates Foster, as if all mourning for Foster or any other forefather were dissolved in childlike faith. (327)

Ives's old black Joe never gets to enter the promised land. His "I'm coming" is an origin in the most rigorous sense, significant in itself only in relation to what it becomes. It finds its musical end in becoming an ostinato to the main melody; it finds its spiritual and historical end in becoming the old black voice that configures and stabilizes the voices of pious white children. The threshold of this becoming is the first melodic moment of the piece, when "I'm Coming" rises from the depths on the trumpet and at once surrenders itself to the process of transfiguration.

Through its Africanist distance, Ives's "I'm coming" invokes racialized fantasies of sentimental benevolence and noble resignation. In the first instance it looks back uncannily to the pairing of Tom and Little Eva in *Uncle Tom's Cabin*. In the second it looks forward to the role of "Ol' Man River" in *Showboat*—but with no Paul Robeson to mark the tune with the resistant grain of his voice.

"OUR BLUES"

With the advent of what might be called jazz-age modernism, and the quest for symphonic jazz that surfaced during the 1920s and early 1930s, mainstream musical Africanism can be said to have combined the semiotics of Ives's First Sonata and the structural usage of his "Elegy." Jazz, of course, was widely taken to signify modernity, urban energy and alienation, and sexuality, along with American identity. Concert music, desiring all these things, but not too much of them, sought to absorb jazz without at the same time becoming jazz, to enclose it without identifying with it. Despite quarrels over priority and musical value, this project was able to draw on a close agreement in principle between critical reception and compositional practice. The agreement, in turn, could draw on a polite veil of racial silence behind which to conceal, at least by halves, the uncomfortable social inversion that put white music into a relation of dependent craving on black music. The point, as Carol Oja observes, was not lost on George Antheil, who claimed that his *Jazz Symphony* of 1927 represented "a reaction toward Negro jazz as away from sweet jazz."[18] Antheil successfully sought to have this piece premiered by W. C. Handy's orchestra, not by Paul Whiteman's, which had premiered George Gershwin's *Rhapsody in Blue* in 1924. As for the *Rhapsody*, by far the most popular product of American jazz-age modernism, Gershwin conceived of it as the epitome of the national style. But in saying what that involved, he included the modern equivalent of Emerson's log rollers and stumps, but left out the Negroes and Indians:

> It was on the train, with its steely rhythms, its rattlety-bang that is
> often so stimulating to a composer. . . . I frequently hear music in the
> very heart of noise. And there I suddenly heard . . . the *Rhapsody*,
> from beginning to end. . . . I heard it as a sort of musical kaleidoscope
> of America—of our vast melting pot, of our unduplicated national pep,
> of our blues, our metropolitan madness.[19]

"Our blues": Gershwin's invocation of the melting pot ideal is unquestionably bound up with his own "racial" position as a Jewish upstart. But the complexities of that position, as of Gershwin's later effort to identify openly with black music in *Porgy and Bess*, are more than I can deal with here.[20]

In the view widely shared by highbrow critics in the 1920s, jazz, as Deems Taylor put it, was "spontaneous, noisy, and barbaric." Even those who liked it distrusted its low social origins; it was backstreet "dross" waiting to be transformed into symphonic gold.[21] The waspish British composer Constant Lambert made the point most candidly, blurting out the racialist truth disavowed by many of his American colleagues: "Jazz is not raw material but half-finished material in which European sophistication has been imposed over coloured crudity. . . . The jazz composer is . . . bound to a narrow circle of rhythmic and harmonic devices. . . . It is up to the highbrow composer to take the next step."[22] *Rhapsody in Blue*, a piece Lambert scorned as insufficiently barbaric, famously took that step by combining jazz with an easygoing version of Lisztian romanticism, hybridizing the elements that Ives's still unknown First Piano Sonata had segregated. Other notable works of the decade, the piano concertos of Gershwin and Aaron Copland, and Copland's *Music for the Theatre*, won critical esteem by subjecting jazz materials to traditional high-art techniques of thematic and motivic development, cyclical thematic integration, contrapuntal combination, and sonata-style conflict and resolution.

As Oja observes, Copland was often used as a stick with which to beat the *arriviste* Gershwin. Copland, said one contemporary, was "the young man who seems to hold out the greatest hopes for a jazz that shall be music as well."[23] But it was Gershwin whose piano concerto ends with something like a classical rondo, replete with a punchy little fugato in the middle and a broad, *Eroica*-style apotheosis before the close. The Copland-Gershwin polarity was clearly prompted in part by an anxiety over the boundaries of high-art music. Copland's more "advanced" modernist techniques tend to support the perception that he is trying to sublimate his jazz-derived materials within a "higher" artistic synthesis. Gershwin, in contrast, seems indifferent to questions of stylistic hierarchy; he just takes it for granted that the "cultivated" and "vernacular" styles on which he draws are mutually permeable. That does not mean that Gershwin's concert pieces are free of citational distance or aspirations to highbrow prestige, but it is consistent with Wynton Marsalis's judgment that "there's no condescension or fear in any of his music."[24]

BABYLON REVISITED

What Copland and Gershwin were to American jazz-age modernism, Darius Milhaud and Maurice Ravel were to the French variety, even though Milhaud's contribution amounts to only a single work, the ballet *La Création du monde*. The musical context for both Ravel's and Milhaud's interest in jazz is a cosmopolitan aesthetic oriented toward the present rather than the past, especially the Germanic past. "The world we live in," wrote Ravel in an article entitled "Take Jazz Seriously!" "is an auspicious one for composers. . . . changing and contradicting itself as never before."[25]

Jazz seemed to embody this general ferment and could be both imitated and emulated by other forms of music seeking to do likewise.

The social context is more complicated. The French government exploited the wealth of its colonies in equatorial Africa at second hand, by means of concessionary companies that routinely depended on brutal forced labor to extract ivory, rubber, and mahogany from the jungle and to work on the railway running from the Atlantic to Brazzaville.[26] An uneasy awareness of the abuses, together with the need to turn a blind eye to them, probably helped shape a countervailing Africanist fantasy widely current in Paris during the 1920s and early 1930s. The fantasy pictured black Africa as a primitive Eden, a scene of ecstatic ritual, sexual rapture, and what Marianna Torgovnik describes as "transcendence and renewal."[27] The chief medium for this fantasy, however, was not African at all, but American; it was jazz. According to the writer and ethnographer Michel Leiris, his post–First World War generation found in jazz "an abandonment to the animal joy of experiencing the influence of a modern rhythm. . . . In jazz, too, came the first public appearance of *Negroes*, the manifestation and the myth of black Edens which were to lead me to Africa."[28] But the fantasy also has a lining of ambivalence. "Under this vibrant sign of jazz," writes Leiris, "whose frivolity masked a secret nostalgia," he found both his sexual initiation and an impotence "with a little American Negro dancer" (shades of Josephine Baker) which sent him reeling into a year of psychoanalysis.[29] The nostalgia enervates the secretive desire it serves.

The fit between this fantasy and Milhaud's *La Création du monde* is so perfect it is almost disconcerting. With a scenario based on African creation myths, the ballet depicts the movement from primordial chaos to the rapturous first kiss of the first man and woman. Basic to this process is the emergence of the Edenic couple from a whirling mass of bodies, first animal, then human, abandoned to the joy of experiencing a modern rhythm. In keeping with the westward displacement of the fantasy, the music for all this is classic blues and New Orleans jazz, as heard during visits to Harlem that Milhaud made in 1922. Or, to be more exact, the music is high-art modernism saturated by jazz and blues citation and bent on "elevating" the black vernacular into universal, mythographic art. (In contrast to Copland's implicit, culturally more saturated version of this project, Milhaud's is programmatic and highly distanced.) *La Création du monde*, especially in the concert suite by which it is usually represented, makes a point of combining its scandalously "low" and "wild" expressivity with studied, impeccable "high-art" technique. The show of technique seems both to legitimate the expressive content and to keep it without bounds. The music is tautly motivic and highly contrapuntal, with a form so cyclical as to be almost Franckian. Its hottest, most "barbaric" jazz takes the form of a fugato, and the energy of its fugal subject, associated with the untamed mass of bodies, is eventually sublimated when an augmented form of the subject appears in counterpoint with the blues theme that opens and closes the work. The fantasy of transcendence and renewal becomes operative only by means of a double Africanist distancing that mediates Africa by jazz, and jazz by a "European sophistication" surpassing its own.

To some degree, Ravel also subscribed to the aesthetic of this distancing, but with an important difference. Commenting on the slow movement, entitled "Blues," of his Sonata for Violin and Piano (1927), he remarked:

> To my mind, the "blues" is one of [America's] greatest musical assets, truly American despite earlier contributory influences from Africa and Spain. Musicians have asked me how I came to write "blues." . . . While I adopted this popular form of [American] music, I venture to say that nevertheless it is French music, Ravel's music, that I have written. Indeed, these popular forms are but the materials of construction, and the work of art appears only on mature conception where no detail has been left to chance. Moreover, minute stylization in the manipulation of these materials is altogether essential. To understand more fully what I mean by the process to which I refer, it would be sufficient to have these same "blues" treated by some [American] musicians and by musicians of other countries than France, when you would certainly find the resulting compositions to be widely divergent, most of them bearing the national character of their respective composers, despite the unique nationality of their initial material, the American "blues."[30]

Ravel maintains the musical polarity of the vernacular and the artistic, but he declines to encode in it either a social polarity of low and high or a racial polarity of black and white. What he encodes instead is a polarity of origins that can be read off in a series of forms meant to be taken as parallels: material versus conceptual, foreign versus national, generic versus individual. The new polarities are not exactly unhierarchical, but neither do they produce a fantasy space in which the privileged term desires and dreads its Other. Instead they define the continuum from which style emerges as Roland Barthes would later construe it, "[the] image, delivery, vocabulary [that] springs from the body and the past of the writer . . . a self-sufficient language which has its roots only in the author's personal and secret mythology."[31] The transformative effect of style in this sense depends on a cosmopolitan openness to the artist's materials; to be worked into the "mature conception" of the work of art, the popular form must be stylized, but only minutely. The result is a stylistic plurality that, ideally at least, is organized by the artist's nationality and / or individuality but without rigidity or defensiveness.

Ravel's concept of minute stylization opens up the possibility of a minimal Africanist distance, and thus the possibility of a (nearly) non-Africanist concert blues or jazz. Of the four pieces that explore this possibility—the violin sonata, the opera *L'Enfant et les sortiléges* (1925), and the two piano concertos (1929–31)—it is perhaps the G-major concerto and the sonata that realize it most fully.

The first movement of the concerto combines three very different musics, each with a signature theme: a diminutive carnivalesque type, its percussive texture initiated by the crack of a whip, high, bitonal piano arpeggios, and jaunty piccolo and trumpet solos, all as if *Petrushka* were being recomposed for wind-up toys; a brooding, emotionally complex jazz; and an impressionist lyricism that splits off from a bluesy transition. Although the movement feints at a vestigial sonata form, the musics that compose it form neither a structural hierarchy nor a dynamic process of conflict and resolution. Nor are they treated to traditional techniques of development, which in any case were Ravel's *bête noire*. Instead, they are continuously varied and juxtaposed in segments both large and small with scant regard for any projection of continuity. The result is a kind of mosaic or collage texture, a pure surface without depth. There is no enclosure, no frame to turn the jazz into citation; either nothing on the surface is citation, or, more likely, everything is. The surface, it is worth adding, extends throughout the concerto as a whole, which also collages three different musics: the heterogeneous mix of the first movement; a pure, avowedly Mozartian lyricism in the second; and a fragmented, accelerated mix of the earlier carnivalesque and jazz types in the third.

A similar refusal to construct racialized hierarchies informs the "Blues" movement of the Violin Sonata and helps give the music the open, urbane, cosmopolitan character evoked by Ravel's description. The movement combines the concerto's collage technique with a linear, goal-directed process aimed at embracing the blues idiom without rationalizing it by appeal to a higher principle.

Four compound episodes fill out the form. The first two simply make a full statement of the Ravelian blues followed by a passage of classicizing impressionism. The contrast plays on the cliché of lowdown versus high-toned expression, but it is drawn so broadly that both styles seem the object of an ironic or playful citation. The high-low distinction progressively comes apart in the remaining episodes, which begin with alternating fragments of the two styles and end with blues passages. Episode three jumbles a diversity of fragments together; as they interrupt and intrude on each other, the blues fragments become more refined and the classicizing ones less so, a process already astir in the classicizing half of episode two. After the blues climax of episode three, episode four renews the stylistic jostling but confines it to the abrupt alternation of just two small fragments, as if the process had been pared down to its essence. At this point, the fragments refer to the two styles more by association than by any sonorous quality. Sheerly as sound, there is not much to choose from between them; each consists of vigorous piano figuration backed by percussive figures on pizzicato violin. After a climax based on the blues fragment, the movement ends with a return of the original blues theme, but in a pointedly rarefied form. With its quiet phrases divided between unaccompanied lines on violin and piano, the blues ends the movement not as something cited, but as a reflective self-citation.

Both as collage and process, Ravel's "Blues" absorbs and displays cultural difference without grounding it in the familiar order of the same. At no point does it make any effort to synthesize or reconcile two styles it conjoins. As collage, it amalgamates the blues with the modernist techniques of juxtaposition, nonsubordination, and the display of disparate, quasi-autonomous episodes. As I've suggested elsewhere, this kind of heterogeneous display allies Ravel's music with the modern consumer culture centered in one of his favorite haunts, the Parisian *grands magasins*, which, like the blues, were a hallmark of modern urban life.[32] The impetus of the music is not to contain or depict the forms of that life from a safe distance but to participate in them. As process, the movement is "analytic"; it breaks down its own materials to reach a double conclusion. The first is the tumble and jumble of the fourth episode, where representatives of both the blues and "French music, Ravel's music" reveal an essential identity that is hard to distinguish from sheer musical energy. The second is the close, which calls on the blues idiom to convey the very contemplative detachment it was widely thought to obliterate. Far from civilizing the blues, this movement is educated by them.

By disabling the framing, citational power of the high-art style, Ravel encourages his listeners to enjoy the jazz of the G-major concerto and the blues of the Violin Sonata without ambivalence or racialized fantasy. Another way to make the same point is to say that he cuts the pleasure loose from the tradition of blackface minstrelsy. The politics of that pleasure is my concluding topic.

BEHIND THE PLEASURE PRINCIPLE

Slavoj Žižek has recently theorized that ethnic and national identities are based on the fantasmatic possession of a definitive core pleasure. This pleasure, though, becomes fully available only when someone other is conceived of as stealing it. The other is necessary in order to embody an excess of the pleasure itself; the guilt or fear (Žižek says hatred) induced by the excess is projected outward as hatred of the other.[33] As Eric Lott has shown, Žižek's model is very useful in elucidating the social mechanism of blackface minstrelsy.[34] My own comments will follow his cue, but with a reservation that jams the mechanism of projection. The thief of pleasure cannot just be any old other, a convenient tabula rasa; the identity of this other is always historically specific, always already present to the self. It is only in such a figure, inescapably a part of the self's story, that the self's core pleasure appears as excess. The result is that there is not one thief of pleasure but two: the self becomes the guilty thief of the other's pleasure-as-excess, and accordingly makes the other the object of envy, desire, mimicry, and ritual debasement.

Lott suggests that the pleasure minstrelsy offered to its original audiences, mostly white working-class northern men, was partly unstructured and threatening, partly structured and reassuring. The "black fun" called forth an oscillation between abject self-abandonment and privileged self-control. Musically, this opposition played itself out between two types of repetition: a prolonged, unvaried, circular type involving small riff-like units or refrains, and a more cultivated type involving sequences and parallel phrase structures relieved by contrasting material.[35] The second type acted as a curb on the excess pleasure of the first, which it made available in regulated form, or, as I would construe things, constituted as an excess in the process of regulating it. The structure of this opposition, though not its specific musical content, recurs throughout the history of blackface and surrogate-blackface performance, and I would suggest that it also recurs in the Africanist practice of modernist concert music. The structural usages that we have seen shaping subjectivity and cultural identity clearly play a role in this process, but even more important is the role played by the qualitative feel, the characteristic sonority, of the music involved.

To make the point crudely, Antheil and Lambert were not wrong when they complained that symphonic jazz was too pretty. What one does *not* hear in blues or jazz citation is the material character, and especially the bodily character, of blues or jazz proper. The instruments' vocal inflections and voice-derived gestures, the varied degrees of bending into blue notes, the call-and-response patterns, the registral heights and depths, the "dirtying" of intonation and texture, the swing, the pulse of the rhythm section—they are all somewhere else. These traits do not necessary signify pleasure as excess within the discourse of jazz itself, but they readily do so in the discourse (including the musical discourse) of jazz citation. Their palpable absence, or sometimes their rationed presence, is the most common basis of the citational process. Like minstrels in blackface, musical Africanisms seek what might be called a relationship of intimate detachment with imaginary black bodies and voices—bodies and voices that have been decontextualized both musically and socially so that they can be deeply invested with fantasmatic powers. Thus Ives's "Elegy" reinscribes pleasure-as-excess as plantation sentimentality in the blackface of "Old Black Joe"; thus Milhaud's ballet relentlessly classicizes the "savage" expression of an appropriated negritude and encases even real dancing bodies in a wrapping of racial fantasy. It is striking that when *La Création du monde* does incorporate a few physically raw jazz sonorities, they are so isolated within the texture that they sound from within virtual quotation marks as primitivist shock effects. The Africanist distance becomes greatest where it appears to be least.

Most modernist Africanism harbors an element of defensive gentility. It flirts with pleasure as excess, and the attendant racialized fantasy, by representing that pleasure as an absence, something safely curbed in the very act of being invoked. Musical Africanisms arise in the place that pleasure as excess is felt to have vacated. Normally an imaginary event, this replacement becomes audible and emblematic in *Rhapsody in Blue:* the whole piece can be heard as a rationalization of the physically gripping gesture that begins it in "the very heart of noise," the combination of a low bluesy growl and wailing glissando ascent on the clarinet. The rationalizing effect is subdued, almost offhanded, in the original jazz-band orchestration of the piece, but so marked in the symphony-orchestra version—prepared by the same arranger, Ferde Grofé—that intimations of timidity, defensive refinement, and even an un-Gershwinian condescension are hard to fend off. Critical response to the *Rhapsody*, even in its original version, reflected the same tensions. Olin Downes, reviewing the premiere for the *New York Times*, felt free to describe the music of the Whiteman band (which he enjoyed) in terms suggestive of minstrelsy, noting the "odd, unseemly, bushman sounds" of the instruments and the rocking and toe-tapping of the players' bodies. But his description of the *Rhapsody* emphasizes the logic of its construction in the wake of the "outrageous cadenza of the clarinet."[36] For Downes, Gershwin's achievement lay precisely in regulating the irregular pleasures that Downes himself found captivating. The fact (now well known) that the "outrageous cadenza" was actually the invention of a white musician, Ross Gorman, only reinforces the Africanist point.

The problem of pleasure as racialized excess informs both the piece that effectively opens the era of Africanist modernism and the piece that effectively closes it. Claude Debussy's piano prelude "Minstrels," composed in 1909 and conspicuous as the endpiece to Debussy's first collection of twelve preludes, refers most immediately to a cakewalk revival that had become an international dance craze some years earlier. But the piece also contains prominent percussive passages that seem to mimic the bones and tambourine of classic minstrelsy (see ex. 9.1); another point of reference is a performance by an outdoor minstrel troupe that Debussy heard in 1905 in Eastbourne, England.[37] The drumming effect of the "tambo" passage (marked *quasi tamburo*, i.e., "like a drum," on its first appearance) may owe something to this performance, as may the oscillating movement—the clacking—of the "bones," which may also suggest the strumming of a banjo. Both passages are nonthematic, the "bones" consisting of alternating major-second clusters, the "tambo" of a repeated note punctuated by minor-second clusters. From one standpoint both passages are expressions of pure sonority and rhythm, conduits for the material pleasure of Africanized bodies in song and dance. From another perspective, however, the same passages are disciplined elements of structure, the "bones" a lightly disguised dominant and the "tambo" an emphatic dominant. It remains, and is meant to remain, unclear whether sonority as pleasure is being curbed by the dominant function, or the dominant function is being undone by sonority as pleasure. Debussy hints at the latter by recapitulating the "tambo" passage in a low bass register, where tonal function is almost lost in the darkness, as it were the blackness, of the sound. But it is not so easy to make a dominant disappear, and the question remains open at the end.

Turning now from a miniature to a monolith, Michael Tippett's Third Symphony, premiered in 1970, is an explicit modernist reply to the social vision of Beethoven's Ninth Symphony, one that seeks to put the blues in the exact place where Beethoven had put his "Ode to Joy." Tippett's finale first erupts with an exact quotation of the "horror fanfare" that opens Beethoven's, then proceeds, after a brief interlude, to introduce the voice just as Beethoven does. But where Beethoven calls for a bass to sing his quasi-popular, quasi-national tune, Tippett calls for a soprano to sing the blues. His purpose here is not to elevate a black vernacular into high, universal art, but rather to suggest that the universal can be found, in our time,

Example 9.1. Debussy, "Bones" and "Tambo" passages from "Minstrels"

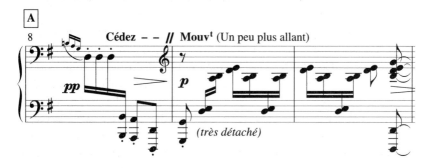

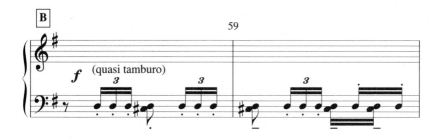

only in this underacinated vernacular.[38] To that end, he declines to write a generic concert blues, and instead models his blues (actually the first of three) on a classic recording of "The St. Louis Blues" made by Louis Armstrong and Bessie Smith in 1925. The result, to my ear, is music of great fervor and dignity, but it is not the blues. Tippett suffers a slippage from writing to citing a blues because the sonority he devises sounds, despite itself, like a curb on pleasure as excess.

As Ian Kemp observes, "the harmonium accompaniment of the [Smith-Armstrong] original is transferred to trombones and tuba (plus supporting bassoons) and the cornet solo to flugelhorn" (452; see ex. 9.2). The result,

Example 9.2. Tippett, "Slow Blues" from Symphony no. 3 (doublings by bassoons and contrabasson omitted)

Example 9.2. (continued)

especially given the plangency of the text (by Tippett himself), is slightly mannered, more distant from its model than it means to be. The harmonium's association with church services takes on an almost Brucknerian solidity in the trombone-tuba quartet, the movement and texture of which are those of a solemn four-part chorale. The flugelhorn solo, compelling in its melodic fluidity, still takes the edge off Armstrong's cornet solo, even if its provenance also includes the playing of Miles Davis. And the vocal line combines the rhythms and melismatics of the blues with a characteristically modernist angularity of contour. The shape of the line virtually compels the voice to produce the most telling effect of distance in this episode. Even miked, as Tippett instructs, the voice cannot sound anything like Bessie Smith's; it has to sound like a classically trained soprano's. Heather Harper, who sang the premiere, recorded the work that way, presumably with Tippett's approval; a slightly roughened but transparently pure intonation replaces, even as it signifies, the blues singer's urgent exploration of vocal grain and timbre.

Tippett's Third Symphony was something of a throwback. The era of symphonic Africanism had found a kind of closure thirty years earlier in Tippett's own oratorio *A Child of Our Time*, which used spirituals where Bach, in his Passions, had used congregational chorales. (The spirituals are like silk flowers, their "spontaneous" musical gestures fully composed.) In France and America, the heart had gone out of things with the deaths of Ravel and Gershwin. Copland, meanwhile, had turned to the new, non-Africanist national style that would make him famous. His success suggests a resurgent impulse in the United States to divide its two nations, black and white, an impulse perhaps embodied by the huge successes, in the early 1940s, of a complementary pair of musical theater works, the revived *Porgy and Bess* and the new *Oklahoma!* The squat figure of Rod Steiger's Jud in the film version of *Oklahoma*, talking funny and clothed in black, suggests the buried persistence of the racial fantasies and anxieties of blackface.

Yet in a sense there has been no closure at all, and not only because the issues raised by this body of music are far from being settled. Morrison, Lott, Gates, Rogin, and others have fostered a new awareness of both the extent and complexity of racialized discourses in modern culture. Because music informs those discourses through and through, the study of musical Africanisms should help lead to the heart of the labyrinth. Let me close with a personal allegory. One effect of my work on this chapter was an unexpected jogging of boyhood memories. The televised version of *Amos 'n'*

Andy cropped up first, followed by Walt Disney's proud broadcasting of *The Song of the South* and *Dumbo,* the latter still going strong at your video store with its literalized Jim Crow fantasy. Finally, in classical Freudian style, the earliest memory appeared, a memory involving someone I never saw or heard. It was a memory of my family's obituary tribute to the man they called the greatest entertainer who had ever lived. "When he sang 'Mammy,' " they said of Al Jolson, " *'s gar nischt helfen,* grown men cried like babies." So there I was, right back where I started from: back at blackface.

10
Long Ride in a Slow Machine
The Alienation Effect from Weill to Shostakovich

BERLIN REVISITED

Recently I saw an advertisement for a compact disc entitled *Ella Fitzgerald: Complete Ella in Berlin—"Mack the Knife."* The ad promised that the listener would be drawn into the "palpable" excitement of the live concert audience, especially in the "rollicking title track." Fitzgerald keeps this promise brilliantly, especially when she forgets the words after the third chorus and begins to improvise, explicitly "signifying" on earlier recordings by Louis Armstrong and Bobby Darin and conflating the figure of Mack the Knife with that of the singers who tell his story. It might be supposed that if Bertolt Brecht could have heard this performance, he would have admired its self-reflective irony and its "alienation effect." The only trouble is that the performance does not sound in the least alienating: it really does rollick. And of course an "authentic" performance of "Mack the Knife"—or more exactly of Brecht and Kurt Weill's "Moritat von Mackie Messer," the opening number of *Die Dreigroschenoper* (Threepenny Opera)—is not supposed to rollick at all. It is supposed to repel empathy and prod the listener into reflecting on its social character. In other words, it is supposed to produce precisely what Brecht would eventually call the alienation effect. This is, of course, very well known. Music in Brecht's theater is supposed to do the opposite of what it traditionally does best: it is supposed to keep you at a distance. From this point of view, the collaboration of Brecht and Weill on the Moritat, by far their most popular song, is actually their most spectacular failure.

The most obvious explanation for this is that the song needs to be heard in context. As the prelude to a theater piece, the Moritat is ironic and reflective. Taken by itself, however, it returns—or can be made to return—to the expression of emotion that Brecht considered to be the bourgeois function of music.[1] The fact that the song can be put to these different uses raises an important question that has not, perhaps, been asked very often. It is also a question that places the music at the core of this book's concern with the vicissitudes of musical meaning and the art of the remainder.

To what extent is the alienation effect actually built into the music of a song like "Mack the Knife"? Or, to go a step further, to what extent does music in general produce an alienation effect comparable to that of Brecht's epic theater? Because the alienation effect is primarily a modernist phenomenon, this last question should primarily be addressed to modernist music. I would like to suggest some answers to it by examining a small group of musical works composed between 1925 and 1960. The results will show, I hope, that modernist music does produce a type of alienation effect, and one with a definite character, both musical and social.

Part of that character, already indicated by Ella Fitzgerald's recording, is that the musical alienation effect, unlike its theatrical counterpart, involves an ambiguity that is always capable of collapsing reflective distance into palpable excitement. This is not to say that the theatrical effect is unambiguous, just that its ambiguity is different. In fact, a leitmotif of the critical reception of *Die Dreigroschenoper* is that the bourgeois audiences with whom it was so successful must have misunderstood its debunking of them as romance or light satire—a problem the play itself poses by ending with an absurd *deus ex machina,* a mounted messenger who arrives at the last moment to avert a seemingly tragic outcome. But the musical effect is more immediate and more pervasive, most likely forming the main vehicle for the theatrical one, which is why Brecht's theater is so often musical theater. The audience hums the tunes and buys the recordings, which both form a symbolic distillate of the play and stand on their own as sources of musical pleasure. The "misunderstanding thesis" itself (as Stephen Hinton calls it) originated primarily in relation to the music, which Theodor Adorno and Ernst Bloch thought was being popularly enjoyed as if it embodied the very musical and social styles that it alienated.[2]

For Adorno the powers of alienation and demystification in *Die Dreigroschenoper* flow from the music into the drama; their engines are the "unrelated juxtaposition of . . . banal sonorities, their alteration with wrong notes, the photographic, almost pornographic glibness of the rhythmic motion; the incessant mobilization of a musical expression that would like nothing better than to gush into complete inanity." The possibility of misunderstanding arises because the artist—by which Adorno means the composer, thinking of both Weill and the Stravinsky of *L'Histoire du soldat*—"who dares to enter [the] demonic world of decay [i.e., of out-moded bourgeois sensibility] . . . all the more perilously succumbs to it, the deeper he goes."[3] Adorno comes close here to recognizing what his own ideological commitments force him to miss, what he masks with the epic metaphor of catabasis, the hero's journey to the underworld: namely that the "succumbing" he describes is not the result of a mere reception mistake but a condition of possibility for hearing any musical alienation effects at all. The music's ambiguity is even more deeply historical than Adorno acknowledges. It is a specific manifestation of the a priori ambiguity of modern Western music in general, here poised between social contingency and emotional autonomy.

STRANGE ATTRACTORS

At this point some further questions arise. If we can indeed identify both a theatrical and a musical alienation effect, how are the two related? Do they always go together? If not, are they linked by imitation, independent resemblance, or coincidence? These questions can be dealt with in more than one way. At a documentary level, they can be answered by tracing sources and influences, for example by looking into Brecht's musical activities and associations, or by trying to support the conjecture that composers such as Bartók and Shostakovich were interested in reproducing Brechtian gestures. At a hermeneutic level, the existence of both theatrical and musical alienation effects can be taken to point to a wider phenomenon, to be a symptom of something in the larger culture or history of modernity.

In my view the documentary level is meaningful only in the context of the hermeneutic, and it is therefore the latter that concerns me here. At this level, Brecht's alienation effect can be put into a "genealogical" relationship on the modernist time line with other, similar effects in various media. At least two of these seem indispensable to understanding both Brecht's initiative and its musical parallels.

The first is Victor Schklovsky's concept of *ostranenie*, usually translated as "defamiliarization" in English; Brecht's *Verfremdung* is a possible rendering in German. Schklovsky proposed in 1917 that literary language functions by making what is familiar strange, renewing perceptions dulled by routine; one basic technique in this process is "laying bare the device," exposing the usually invisible machinery of representation.[4] Brecht's familiarity with this concept is a matter of dispute, but regardless of documentary questions, Schklovsky's *ostranenie* has a structural similarity to the family of concepts that Brecht developed from the mid-1920s to the mid-1930s, including the epic style, the gestic, and finally the alienation effect.[5] Brecht's *Verfremdung* is sometimes said to politicize Schklovsky's *ostranenie*, but a more accurate statement might be that it makes the political implications of Schklovsky's concept manifest. Once the essentially habitual and artificial character of perception becomes clear, the possibility of changing the objects of perception, together with the social order that supports them, becomes clear as well. Brecht sought to produce both types of clarity by "stripping the event of its self-evident, familiar, obvious quality and creating a sense of astonishment and curiosity."[6] The resulting necessity to reperceive the event would submit perception itself to critical reflection and expose it as a social process through and through. Once made perceptible in its own right, perception would display its historical, constructed, contradictory, and above all changeable character. This type of defamiliarization later became important to Roland Barthes, much of whose work from the 1950s to the 1970s sought to expose the mechanisms by which ideologically constructed signs were passed off as natural formations. Signs that had been "natural-ized" to produce the "mythologies" of modern society could once again be denaturalized, alienated, laid bare as devices.[7]

Barthes's concept can be said to realize the semiotic implications of Brecht's as Brecht's realized the political implications of Schklovsky's. One result was that Barthes produced a reinterpretation of Brecht's concept that may be taken to "lay bare" the general form of the modernist device exemplified variously by defamiliarization, alienation, and denaturalization.

According to Barthes, Brecht's technique consists simply of "detaching the sign from its effect." The alienation effect, in other words, consists precisely in one's alienation from an effect. When the imaginary unity of the sign and its effect is broken, both halves of the former unity appear differently. The effect now invites critical reflection by presenting itself as one of many possible outcomes of signification regarded as a sociocultural function. This function, in turn, assumes the quality that J. L. Austin found in performative speech acts such as "I sentence you to death" when they appear in literary or theatrical settings. Austin described these "nonserious" (i.e., fictitious) utterances as "in a peculiar sense hollow or void." His description has become best known for Jacques Derrida's critique of it, which holds that the possibility of being hollow or void in the same peculiar sense is inherent in all speech acts.[8] I would like to rehabilitate Austin's description here by taking it to apply not to fictitious speech acts in general but to signifying acts submitted to the alienation effect. This hollowing-out of the sign, moreover, is not without its own perceptual consequences. In many cases, the alienated sign conveys a sense of damage or injury, as if willingly yielding itself to harm as a way of testifying that the world is out of joint. Barthes points to this quality when he speaks of Brechtian alienation as a "shock practice . . . a critical art that lacerates, that crackles the smooth surface, that fissures the crust of languages."[9]

The three qualities of reflectiveness, hollowing out, and damage form the profile of what I will call the general modernist trope of estrangement. If to these three is added a seemingly innate oscillation between the possibilities of alienation and emotive expression, the profile becomes that of the musical alienation effect. To explore this idea, I will now turn to compositions by Schoenberg, Bartók, and Shostakovich—but not before I have set the stage by turning back to my point of departure, Brecht and Weill's "Moritat von Mackie Messer."

M

As is well known, the Moritat was a great last-minute idea. According to Lotte Lenya, Weill's widow, Brecht wrote the text overnight after Harald Paulsen, the original Macheath, lobbied for an introductory ballad; Weill then matched Brecht by writing the tune overnight as well, with the intention of having it ground out on a hand organ. Brecht and Weill, who knew how to put on a show, obviously realized they had stumbled onto a gold mine. They gave the Moritat to a ballad singer instead of to Macheath and thus gave their play its epitomizing moment.[10]

From a theatrical standpoint, the Moritat prefigures everything to follow by producing alienation effects at several levels. As the audience quickly comes to realize, the events described in the ballad have no connection to the plot of the play. Similarly, the ballad's Mack the Knife, a cross between Professor Moriarty and Jack the Ripper, bears little resemblance to the play's Macheath, who, depending on which version of the playtext one follows, is either an enterprising criminal or a criminal entrepreneur, but no serial killer. (The difference is culturally marked; serial killers such as Peter Kürten, the child-murderer fictionalized in Fritz Lang's *M*, haunted the imagination of the Weimar Republic. Like *M*, however, the original 1928 production of *Die Dreigroschenoper* signaled the entrances of its outlaw protagonist with a musical motif—there Grieg's "From the Halls of the Mountain King," here the "Moritat" theme—that refers more to myth than to "reality.")[11] The Moritat thus comes to produce, not the mythic figure of a romantic outlaw, but a glimpse of the way that a society based on the twin pillars of need and greed mythifies itself by constructing the romantic outlaw as a self-image. One good fiction, moreover, deserves another, so the idea of Mackie Messer is shown to be the fantasy promoted, indeed sold, by a ragged underclass figure who recounts Mackie's deeds of acquisition (the murders are just business) with a mixture of awe and envy. In the original production, the actor who sang the Moritat also played the police chief Tiger Brown, thus creating another perspective: the servant of the law is shown to fill up the emptiness of that servitude by his abject, eroticized infatuation with the romantic outlaw. Brown's temptation, it should be added, is better supported in the original playtext than in the revision published by Brecht in 1931. The original Macheath, though ruthless enough, was more like a "real" romantic hero than the bourgeois gangster of the later version.[12]

The reflective, critical effect of the Moritat comes to a head in a brassy coup de theatre inserted in that version, possibly on the basis of the way the play's prologue was staged; the effect was incorporated in the last verse of the Moritat itself in the off-Broadway version of the 1950s in which Lotte Lenya reprised her role as Jenny from the original production.[13] As the singer finishes the ballad, there is a burst of laughter from a group of whores; a man emerges from the group and passes quickly across the stage. "Look!" someone cries—it will turn out to have been Jenny, Macheath's betrayer—"that was Mack the Knife." The audience is thus invited to recognize the unbridgeable gap between the man Macheath and the myth of Mack the Knife; we have been looking right at Mackie as his deeds are recounted, and we have not recognized him.

From a musical standpoint, all that is needed for Weill's Moritat to support these theatrical alienation effects is that the song be performed correctly, which is to say, unmusically. "The actor," Brecht stipulates, "must not only sing but also show someone singing."[14] In addition to the song, the performance itself must be performed. Emotional expression is not to be avoided (after all, the actor does sing), but it is to be demoted, detached from its usual effect, which is to identify the singer with the song. That identification breaks down when the technical devices that support it are exposed, through either default or exaggeration. Curiosity overtakes empathy when the act of singing sets the song askew. The effect is like a carnivalesque inversion of a certain operatic ideal in which only a transcendental technique can prevent the song from going askew.

At a minimum, then, all Weill needed to meet this requirement was to write an ostentatiously easy tune, so that its "good" performance would be unremarkable and its "bad" performance clearly deliberate. And he did. Even more than the show's other numbers, the Moritat is what Weill categorized as "music that could be sung by actors, that is, by musical amateurs."[15] It is music ideally suited to show singing itself as an act in every sense of the term. When, for instance, Wolfgang Neuss sings the Moritat in the 1958 recording produced by Lenya, he emits what can only be described as a nasal croak that not only renders the song stagy but almost upstages it.[16] Brecht's prescription could hardly be filled better. But Weill went much further than merely providing the opportunity to fill it; he built an alienation effect of his own into the design of the song. This musical effect, moreover, not only supports but also reinterprets the theatrical effect produced by Brecht. It is consistent with Brecht's purposes (as of 1928), but also bent on Weill's own project of establishing a new mode of opera distinguished by "generally valid themes that no longer deal with private ideas and emotions but with larger relationships." For Weill, music in "the new operatic theater" works precisely by laying bare the devices that support the illusion of private ideas and emotions. The music "renounces pumping up the action from within, glazing over the transitions, supplying the background for events, and stirring up passions." By alienating itself from these effects, the music preserves an "absolute *concertante* character" that is, paradoxically, both "purely musical" and a means of reporting on "man, his actions, and what impels him to commit them."[17]

The key to Weill's design is the hand organ. During the first production, a specially made hand organ was used to accompany the Moritat's first two strophes. Weill's score further instructs that the song be accompanied "In der Art eines Leierkasten" [in hand-organ style].[18] The accompaniment continuously mimics the rotary motion of the instrument with ostinato basses in rocking fourths and fifths; these are assigned to the piano alone, which thus "plays" the hand organ as the actor plays the ballad singer. The net effect is one of mechanical repetition, the working of a tireless automaton, and it is this automatism with which Weill interprets the ideological work displayed by the Moritat.

In the cultural climate of 1928, the choice of figure seems highly overdetermined. The association of the hand organ with urban street life was stereotypical, as was the association of mechanical motion with modernity. Just a few years earlier, Thomas Mann's *The Magic Mountain* had personified the modern worldview in a character, Ludovico Settembrini, "leitmotivically" referred to as "the hand-organ man." As a mechanical instrument, moreover, the hand organ could invoke the terms of a debate over musical automatism that had begun in the Romantic era and renewed itself in the 1920s in relation to the "mechanical music" produced by player pianos and the phonograph. The terms of this debate were surprisingly durable. From E. T. A. Hoffmann in 1814 to H. H. Stuckenschmidt in

1926, the key question was whether musical mechanisms preserved or destroyed the spiritual element in music.[19] For Theodor Adorno, the trope of the hand organ in modern music registered the alienation of the human subject in a world of mechanical authority both social and technological, and at the same time—in the figure of the hand-organ man, "the *imago* of the shabby, fallen individual"—offered a nostalgic defense against that very alienation, "a remedy against decay."[20] By playing on this sort of ambiguity in the context of the modern street scene, Weill's music for the Moritat could both convey the charisma of Mack the Knife and conduct a critical reflection on it.

The quality of automatism is worked into the song's phrase structure and from there works its way into the strophic form. The Moritat theme consists of two groups of four brief phrases, all but one of which are versions of the same basic idea (ex. 10.1). In the first half, all four phrases have the same shape and end on the same note, the A on the treble staff. This ending gives a distinctly "mechanical" impression, and not just because it is so regular. Phrase 1 harmonizes the closing A as the embellishing note of a C-major added-sixth chord; phrases 2 and 3 provide alternative harmonizations; phrase 4 returns to the original added-sixth. The first half of the theme thus executes a melodic-harmonic rotation geared to a "tonic" chord that leans more toward motion than rest. And not just any chord: although the added-sixth would eventually become a familiar signature of jazz-inflected popular music, in the Berlin of 1928 its primary associations are still with Wagner (especially the Wagner of *Tristan*) and Mahler. The "mechanization" of this particular chord via the hand-organ style signals the palpable collapse of a subjectivity-laden romantic sound world into a disenchanted modernity.[21]

As if to acknowledge this, the second half of the theme begins to contort the basic melodic idea, but it too rotates around a single note, apparently—but only apparently—a new one. Phrase 1 reaches up a third to close on C; phrases 2 and 3 peak on this note and single it out registrally, closing and continuing in the octave below. Phrase 4 begins on the C and descends by step to close on the original A; melodically speaking, the phrase acts in lieu of a $\hat{3}$-$\hat{2}$-$\hat{1}$ cadence formula. The whole second half thus reveals itself as intent on producing that surrogate formula, the impetus to which is conveyed through the C—a decidedly unstable C, one never harmonized as $\hat{1}$ of the nominal tonic, C major. If the first half of the theme suggests a tendency to rotate through and to the final A, the second half suggests that this tendency is self-perpetuating and irrepressible. The melodic contortions act as the mechanism of the note's palpable displacement and

Example 10.1. Weill, "Moritat von Mackie Messer," first verse. From Kurt Weill/
Bertolt Brecht, *Die Dreigroschenoper*. Vocal score © 1928 by European American
Music Corporation, copyright renewed. Orchestration © 1972 1928 by European
American Music Corporation, copyright renewed. All rights reserved. Used by
kind permission of European American Music Corporation.

inevitable return. The effect is heightened by the fact that phrase 4 is a
brand new one, retaining nothing of the basic idea *except* the original closing note.

Ironically, however, this note is still harmonized so that it provides no
sense of closure. On the contrary: it provides the potential energy for a new

rotation of the musical flywheel. The final A returns at last, not just in its own person, but in the same added-sixth harmony that framed its original cycle of appearances; the second half of the theme is less an answer to the first than a continuation of its rotary motion. The stage is thus set for the small-scale rotation of the first half to be repeated by the full theme at a higher level, that of the song as a whole. Following the basic principle of strophic song, each successive strophe holds out the possibility that a second ending will emerge to set things straight with an unvarnished cadence. This is a purely formal possibility that persists no matter how often it is denied—and it is always denied. Each new strophe ends with the same inconclusive sonority; the mainspring of musical motion never unwinds. This rotary process takes up a full six strophes. When the song finally ends, by arbitrarily repeating the sixth strophe's second half, the inconclusive conclusion is still the same. Weill was careful to preserve this effect when he adapted the Moritat for a concert suite, the "Kleine Dreigroschenmusik," even though in this version the Moritat theme is heard only twice and ironically combined with "The Vanity of Human Effort," a song associated with Macheath's antagonist Peachum.

The two-tiered system of added-sixth endings formally installs the trope of damage in this music, which the strophic cycle seeks in vain to repair. Traditionally, strophic repetition involves the humanization of its own potentially mechanical character by expressive vocalization, a technique that even the Moritat singer is expected to use in measured doses. But the technique courts failure here because it appears so patently as one technique resisting another: not an expression of subjectivity, but a contrivance of it meant to cover a lack. That the strophic process has lost all organic significance and become mere mechanism is further brought out by the way each new strophe begins on the heels of the last with scarcely a pause for breath. The crank of the hand organ just keeps turning.

The rotary process, however, is coupled with a contradictory linear process at the level of musical texture. As the voice proceeds from strophe to strophe, the Moritat's accompaniment grows progressively richer in both sonority and expressive gesture, as if it were responding empathetically to the seductive call of the outlaw myth. At first just the bare hand-organ imitation, it becomes an evocation of cabaret music—first in isolation in strophe 3, then continuously in 5 and 6. The feeling of mechanism fades increasingly into the background of a sophisticated social allusiveness, which is no doubt why Weill curtailed the original hand organ after the first two strophes, even though strophe 4 returns to hand-organ style. Yet just as the transformative process reaches its peak in the positively lush strophe 6—

just when the exposed automatism of the hand organ is about to be fully sublimated into the concealed automatism of the cabaret ensemble—the song abruptly runs out of steam. In the final, "extra" half strophe, the cabaret sound fades away on saxophone over the piano's tireless hand-organ effect, conceding its own illusory character as a social mechanism. One might even hear the piano's final measures as a distant echo of the "hand organ" accompaniment in Schubert's "Der Leiermann," the final song of *Winterreise,* as if the Moritat had become "Der Leiermann" stripped of all pathos, emptied of emotional appeal.

The Weill Moritat thus fulfills all the requirements of the general alienation effect: reflective distance, the hollow or void quality, and damage. Yet the musical means by which this is done also create the possibility of the very opposite effect, the rollicking ballad of the outlaw hero. The rigid phrase structure and strophic fixity of the song create the opportunity for singers—singers with musical voices—to inject expressive variations, to reshape the raw material of the song in order to express emotion and affirm their own subjectivity. This is precisely what happens in both the carnivalesque recordings of Ella Fitzgerald and Frank Sinatra (who restages "Lady Ella's" self-reflective improvisation as his own) and the more straightforward versions by Louis Armstrong and Bobby Darin that sustained a virtual "Mack the Knife" craze during the long off-Broadway run of *Threepenny Opera* from 1954 through 1961. It can also happen in the show itself or in the audience's memory of the show. The romanticizing effect is enhanced by the use of Marc Blitzstein's very free translation of Brecht's "Moritat," which subordinates the portrayal of Macheath as a self-employed hit man to his charms as a lady killer, a leather-jacketed Don Giovanni. The singer, a new Leporello, winds up by telling the listener—defined as a woman and repeatedly addressed as "dear"—where to stand in line for service.[22] Blitzstein's Mack the Knife and Brecht's Mackie Messer do the same fell deeds, more or less, but Blitzstein's language is insinuating where Brecht's is deliberately flat; where Brecht's text inventories Mackie's crimes with pokerfaced irony, Blitzstein's reels them off like an accomplice basking in secondhand notoriety. The crimes of Mack the Knife are thus easily subsumed under his charisma by the structure of repeated address to the awestruck "dear," which just happens to occur at prominent phrase endings. Both Armstrong and Sinatra nudge this process along by tweaking Blitzstein's text; the shift in accent becomes a complete reversal in Bobby Darin's version, which quickly converts the "dear" into a "babe" and progressively embroiders on the text until it becomes a flat-out celebration of Mack the Knife's phallic prowess.

Weill's attempt to articulate "generally valid themes" thus slips back toward the fiction of "private ideas and emotions" it was supposed to surmount. The song's Depression-era social mythology becomes a vehicle for shaping 1950s sex appeal. This is not to say that the song is being travestied, whatever one may think of this particular sexual ideal; as Adorno had cautioned in 1929, it is a mistake to underrate the "erotic charm" of the "dashing Mackie Messer."[23] But Weill and a singer like Bobby Darin, whose "Mack the Knife" was the most popular fifties version, differ sharply in the way they play out the ambiguity built into the song's alienation effects.

What seems unavoidable is the playing-out itself. Weill may be exemplary in the way he composes this process directly into the Moritat, but he is not alone. Nor are the alienation effect and its consequences confined to theater music or song; as the Moritat itself suggests, they belong to a general "structure of feeling" that can be realized in a diversity of media and social practices, both musical and otherwise.[24] To tease out more of the formal and social themes involved, we can turn to a series of concert pieces by Schoenberg, Bartók, and Shostakovich, with emphasis, respectively, on the qualities of hollowing out, critical reflection, and damage.

THE CHAIRMAN DANCES

In 1925, Schoenberg made an arrangement of Johann Strauss's "Kaiserwalzer" (The Emperor Waltz) for string quartet, flute, clarinet, and piano. The transcription is scrupulously faithful to Strauss in its melodic surface and overall design, at times even imitating Strauss's tone colors, but it is subtly contrarian beneath the surface. Schoenberg detaches Strauss's musical sign from its effect by making every structural element of the music transparently audible; nothing blends. Strauss's melodic art is reconstituted as a display of contrapuntal craft. Where Strauss's texture is smooth, unified, sensuous, and seemingly effortless, Schoenberg's is rugged, fragmentary, intellectual, and strenuous. Where Strauss evokes the material and cultural wealth of imperial Vienna, Schoenberg suggests the friction and complexity of the post-imperial city. At some points the nubby texture of his arrangement exfoliates into reworkings and "analytic" elaborations meant to bring out the motivic design of the waltz. As Schoenberg wrote of some Bach transcriptions he made about the same time: "Our modern conception of music demanded clarification of the *motivic* procedures in both horizontal and vertical dimensions. . . . A 'pleasant' effect originating in an ensemble of skillfully constructed parts is no longer sufficient for us. We need transparency, that we may see clearly."[25]

The arrangement may thus be said to reveal the intellectual labor, and with it the economics of composition, concealed beneath the grace and charm of Strauss's orchestration. Also revealed are the economics of performance; the material luxury of Strauss's orchestra stands out from the very cleverness by which Schoenberg's reduced ensemble replaces it. By these means, the Schoenberg exposes the Strauss as ideology and suggests that the sensuousness and social cohesiveness represented by the original is no longer available except in an alienated, disassembled form. These features still inhere in the music, but are in a peculiar sense hollow or void. Schoenberg's "own" music of the period, especially the Serenade Op. 24 and Suite for Piano Op. 25, conveys a similar message by combining early serial technique with traditional dance forms.

In keeping, however, with the ambiguous character of musical alienation effects, the critical message also harbors the potential for empathy. The "Kaiserwalzer" in particular risks losing itself in a warm bath of nostalgia. Schoenberg's contrapuntal elaborations do nothing overtly subversive; his "analytic" additions, to the extent they are even noticeable as such, claim to be more true to the original than the original is to itself. The technique of the arrangement paradoxically multiplies the pleasures of the original "Kaiserwalzer" by investing it with distance and an air of unreality, like an affectionate rather than disenchanted version of Ravel's later "La Valse." It is as if each contrapuntal strand concentrated, even as it alienated, the pleasures formerly diffused throughout the work as a whole. And those pleasures are substantial, more than enough to cast doubt on Theodor Adorno's near-contemporary claim that "dated" musical idioms are only permissible because one no longer believes in them.[26] The piece might even be heard as acting out Schoenberg's own stubborn clinging to those pleasures in spite of his self-appointed artistic mission. "Light music," he wrote in 1934, after praising Brahms's appreciation of the *Blue Danube* waltz,

> could not entertain me unless something interested me about its musical substance and working out. And I do not see why, when other people are entertained, I should not sometimes be entertained; I know indeed that I really ought at every single moment to behave as my own monument; but it would be hypocritical of me to conceal the fact that I occasionally step down from my pedestal and enjoy light music.[27]

As a Strauss impersonator, Schoenberg takes a further step down and realizes the ambition of a true son of modernism, though with the slight stiffness of a statue brought to life: he becomes an entertainer.

SEPTEMBER SONG

Where Schoenberg's "Kaiserwalzer" foregrounds the hollow character of the "nonserious" speech act, Bartók's Sixth String Quartet concentrates on the production of reflective distance. That distance emerges from the contrast between the two entirely different types of music whose combination—perhaps it would be better to say collision—gives the quartet its unusual design. Both the design itself and its historical roots are well known. The quartet begins with a lively sonata-allegro movement and continues with two scherzo-like character pieces. Each of these movements is preceded by a slow introduction marked *Mesto*, "sad." The fourth and final movement seems at first to be following the same pattern, but this turns out to be true only in a negative, dialectical sense. The fourth Mesto now fills up the whole space of the movement it is supposed to introduce; although the expectation of a standard finale is formally invoked, that finale never appears. As it happens, Bartók actually composed the first ninety bars of an energetic folk-style finale, then abandoned it. His probable reason for doing so has the same roots as the general recurrence of the Mesto music. This quartet was composed between August and November 1939 and is commonly taken to reflect Bartók's dismay over the outbreak of war, the prospect of Nazi domination over Europe, and, in more personal terms, the inevitability of his own exile. That his mother was dying at the same time suggests that the quartet incorporates a lament both for her loss and for Europe's—an elegy for both mother and motherland.

The most obvious point of contrast between the Mesto segments and the self-contained movements is expressive. The Mesto segments are slow, uniform, emotional, and unusual; the independent movements are fast, varied, vigorous, and conventional. In Brechtian terms, one might call the Mesto segments "empathetic" and the independent movements "epic" or "gestic." This particular contrast, however, is purely relative: the mournful intensity of the Mesto sections serves to accentuate the witty or ironic detachment of the independent movements, and vice versa.

Underneath these contrasts in expression lies a more important contrast in musical process. Like Weill in the Moritat, but on a larger scale and in a far darker mood, Bartók produces an ongoing contradiction between rotary and linear planes of action. The Mesto segments carry on an additive, open-ended process. They are all based on the same theme, which the first Mesto states on unaccompanied viola; the subsequent Mestos add one contrapuntal voice at a time until a four-part texture is achieved in the fourth movement. One consequence of this process is that each Mesto segment is longer than the last. The independent movements are written in closed three-part forms; they all consist of an opening section, a contrasting or developmental middle section, and a recapitulation of the opening. As the quartet proceeds, and the Mesto sections grow in scale and contrapuntal weight, they seem to drain the independent movements of real importance. The impression is one of an implacable lament that grows fuller and keener even when it is not being heard. The independent movements may take up considerably more clock time, but they matter far less. As the quartet comes increasingly to be governed by the Mesto process, the closed forms of the independent movements become alienated; they look more and more like the mechanical applications of a formal principle that, in the historical crisis of 1939, has lost all credibility. It is no wonder that the finale cannot, so to speak, bear to show its face. Ultimately, and especially in the aftermath of that nonappearance, the music seems to have detached the independent movements from its core identity, to have reinterpreted them as mere appendages or remainders. Unlike tangibly unassimilated or abject remainders, moreover, these remainders with pretensions to be wholes lack the power either to disrupt or to stabilize the symbolic order that produces them. What they have lost is precisely the ability to pass themselves off as representing that kind of order.

But the process of alienation does not stop there. Bartók has apparently structured the ambiguity typical of musical alienation effects so that the price of distancing the independent movements is upholding the empathetic character of the Mestos. Yet the Mestos themselves are also ambiguous. Their reliance on strict counterpoint, plus their arithmetical addition of one voice per segment, gives their lamentations a studied, even a ritualized character. The Mestos thus assume a neo-Baroque quality that is not different in kind from the neo-classicism of the independent movements. Although the emotional power of its laments is never compromised, the quartet ultimately seems to be ransacking the musical past for a means of expression adequate to the historical present, and failing to find one. If the series of Mestos is meant to suggest a process of mourning, then that process, too, is a failure. The quartet ends, not by finding a gesture of resignation, acceptance, or, least of all, consolation, but by falling apart. The viola returns to its original theme at pitch, but can manage only the first two phrases before breaking off on a "false" note, a semitone higher than its original keynote. A moment later, with the viola now withdrawn from the ensemble, a gapped, rhythmically distorted version of the theme's first phrase sounds indistinctly atop a series of soft pizzicato chords on the cello. And the piece is over.

Before we take leave of the Sixth Quartet, however, one further aspect of its finale deserves mention. With this movement, the open-ended Mesto process allows itself to slip into the very kind of closed ternary form that it has worked so steadily to estrange. Yet it does so only to complete the work of estrangement. At the point where the conventional fast finale "ought" to begin (and would have, in Bartók's original version), a "middle section" emerges consisting of three reprises of themes from the first movement. These are arranged, ironically, in a ternary pattern: first theme in ascending form, second theme, first theme in descending form. But the themes move slowly now, too slowly; as Stephen Walsh has observed, they are "stripped of their erstwhile vitality and protean energy, . . . uninvited guest[s] at [their] own funeral."[28] In the sections devoted to it, the first theme is rewritten so that its incipit reproduces the rhythmic figure (a dotted quarter tied into a triplet) that begins the Mesto theme; the figure has been heard in other contexts, but at the new tempo it seems to assimilate the once bright theme into the dark one. When the Mesto theme subsequently crumbles away in the "reprise" of the finale's own first section, the Mesto process is simply turning on itself the alienation effect it has just used to complete the repudiation of the rest of the quartet by reducing it, literally, to a remainder.

One way to describe the auto-critique thus culminated is as a failure of symbolization. The quartet's initial gesture is one of abandonment or bereavement, and it is so in "mixed-media" terms, produced not only by the sound of the solo viola, but also by the sight of the other musicians sitting motionless while the viola plays, imaging the force of isolation. (The viola: normally a "social" instrument, in relay between other voices.) The gradual accumulation of a four-part texture would enact the process of mourning, and hence of renewal, but only in order to demonstrate the futility of its own effort. The formal aim of the quartet is the ironic reversal whereby the completion of the texture, and therefore of wholeness and symbolic authority, coincides with emotional depletion and the negation of the finale music that is "proper" to the close.

This outcome can be explicated with a concept developed by Slavoj Žižek from suggestions by Jacques Lacan, the concept of symbolic debt.[29] Žižek suggests that when the consistency of reality, which rests on symbolic constructions, is ruptured by a traumatic event, the trauma can be healed only by being symbolized. But it often happens that the very trauma that imposes this demand also renders it next to unfulfillable, a condition reflected by the continual return into the symbolic order of some disfiguring trace of the original trauma that reimposes the demand, as if a debt had not been paid. Bartók's Mesto segments can be said to act this way, both in their devaluing of the formal, that is symbolic, integrity of the independent movements and even more in their negation of the symbolic functions of the first-movement themes in the finale. On this view, the Mesto segments identify themselves not as a ritualized response to trauma, but as trauma itself. In so doing, they repel the Romantic trope that otherwise might be applied to them, that of a deep subjective integrity whose anguish is the measure of injustice or loss. This music seeks to suggest, on the contrary, that there is no such measure and no such subject. The damage is itself objective and for the music to internalize it would be both glib and false. The very sense of internality, we might surmise, is an effect of the civilized institutions in whose imminent collapse the music is grounded. The quartet—which was indeed followed by years of silence from its composer—seems to be showing by example that musical "expression" is impossible when the likes of Hitler and Stalin are calling the tune.

SONGS AND DANCES OF DEATH

Where Bartók thus emphasizes a dismaying reflective distance, Dmitri Shostakovich in his Eighth Quartet dwells on the sense of damage. This work has become the most famous of Shostakovich's fifteen quartets, leading their recent climb to the top of the twentieth-century quartet canon. Its fame is due in no small part to its autobiographical character and its implication in the much discussed question of closet dissidence in Shostakovich's music.[30] True to the spirit of the alienation effect, the following pages will adopt the pretense that the familiar features of the Eighth Quartet are still quite strange in order to see them again in their actual strangeness. Peeling the onion, the discussion will try to slip beneath questions of supposed dissidence in order to catch a glimpse of the hard conditions in which such questions become thinkable, if not resolvable.

Composed in Dresden in 1960, a city still in ruins from its firebombing fifteen years before, the Eighth Quartet is dedicated to "The Memory of the Victims of Fascism and War." In his memoir, *Testimony*, Shostakovich declares the dedication to be an obvious sham, and although the memoir's authenticity is questionable, the sham really is obvious.[31] The work, indeed, is a kind of meditation on shamming, understood as a necessary means of personal and aesthetic survival in a totalitarian state, but one with a heavy cost. In form and expression, the quartet intimates a tragedy, which

Shostakovich—this time verifiably—would also identify as a sham, though an affecting one. Behind the facade of historical tragedy is an autobiographical *cri de coeur*; the fact that the composer's personal misery must hide itself behind the misery of millions is one sign of the bizarre dystopia in which he lives. The self compelled to hide, however, even with the transparency of an open secret, may not survive the act of hiding. The deeper dystopic effect of this quartet, which should perhaps cast a pall over the recent eagerness to embrace it as confessional, is the realization that behind the facade there is nothing—nothing left—at all.[32]

The autobiographical "testimony" begins with the use of musical cryptograms and allusions. The quartet is pervaded by a four-note motto that signs Shostakovich's name in German musical notation: D. S. C. H. (D-Eb-C-B). The motto opens the work as the subject of a slow fugue in a minor key, and in this guise it clearly alludes to the famous B. A. C. H. motto of J. S. Bach's *The Art of Fugue*. The two figures also set up similar rhythmic profiles. At the same time, a slow opening fugue in the minor with a four-note incipit alludes with equal clarity to an antecedent quartet, Beethoven's Op. 131 in C♯ Minor. Shostakovich's subject is like a distorted memory of Beethoven's; both are symmetrical, rising then falling by a single interval, and both end on a melodic dissonance followed by a half-step resolution. This reference is continued by the way the first movement of Shostakovich's quartet evolves into the second and by the seamless linkage among the individual movements generally. All of these allusions are painfully ironic. Whereas Bach and Beethoven could employ their musical techniques to mirror a viable world order, Shostakovich can only mirror the collapse of that order into chaos, brutality, and dissimulation. Whereas for them form is self-validating, for him it is self-damaging. His allusions have the feel of self-inflicted wounds. Thus Shostakovich begins and grounds his piece in emulation of the signature by which Bach involuntarily ended his incomplete magnum opus, the composer's death supposedly stopping the work just after the signature motive appears; the terms of identity, origin, and death become hopelessly confused. Thus also Shostakovich imitates the reduction to a single note by which Beethoven crosses over from his opening fugue to the subsequent fast movement. But whereas Beethoven makes the transition by the rise of a half step, suggesting a new phase in an ongoing process, Shostakovich stays with the "leftover" note, suggesting a condition of immobility or entrapment.[33]

Perhaps the most striking overall feature of the quartet, and the main medium of its sense of damage, is something we have seen before: rotary motion. The five-movement scheme of the work forms a kind of downward spiral marked by a rigid, if complex, symmetry. The opening fugue, as just noted, leads to a fast movement, a furiously sputtering moto perpetuo that culminates with outbursts of lamenting melody. The middle movement is a sardonic waltz that acts as a hollow core or danse macabre. Symmetrical in itself, the three-part form of this movement mirrors the larger symmetry for which it forms the pivot; the waltzing outer sections surround a middle section marked (among other things) by self-mocking distortions of the D. S. C. H. figure. The fourth movement is a kind of photographic negative of the second, a slow lament framed and bisected by violent hammerblows, percussive chords extrapolated from the second movement. The evenly spaced recurrence of these chords within the movement forms yet another mode of implacable rotation. The finale is a second slow fugue on the D. S. C. H. motto, this one more mournful than the first. It begins as the first fugue did, with the solo cello on the motto, and ends with a fadeout on muted strings—"Not with a bang but a whimper."

A listener who wanted to could certainly hear this pattern "straight" as an instance of motivically unified cyclical form.[34] As I hear it, however, the music courts a different kind of description. Its cyclical form is more facade than structure, and one so badly damaged as to be nearly meaningless. The D. S. C. H. motto, in particular, may sometimes act as a melodic cell and sometimes as the source of traditional thematic metamorphosis, but neither of these is its primary role. Its primary role is just to keep coming back in its own person, which, fugal answers aside, is virtually always the original D. S. C. H. The motto returns at pitch in all five movements. Its insistence, or more properly perhaps its insistence on itself as a motto, a cryptogram, might be heard as a demand for full recognition that can never quite be satisfied. Unlike Schumann's "sphinxes," discussed in chapter 5, Shostakovich's cipher is an actual musical motive; the expressivity of its repetitions asks, even pleads, for the verification of subjective truth that the abstractions of *Carnaval* dispense with. (In the language of chapter 7, the D. S. C. H. motto can draw unlimited meaning from the semantic loop created by its encipherment, but never just the right meaning, and never meaning enough.) As already noted, Žižek has suggested that this type of recurrent unconditional demand is the effect of a disturbance in the process of symbolization; that which keeps returning does so because it represents a trauma that has not been reconciled with the symbolic tradition. The quartet may be premised on the failure or impossibility of any such reconciliation. The ending suggests as much: the motto is at its most insistent in the closing fugue, where it rotates through an almost continuous cycle of restatements before its deterioration brings the work to a close.[35]

The issue comes to a head at the level of form in the relationship between the last two movements. The large-scale symmetry introduced by the finale endows the quartet with the kind of suite-like "arch" form familiar from Bartók's Fourth and Fifth Quartets; it is in the context of this form that the fourth movement appears as a "negative" of the second. But the fourth movement also breaks with the convention of arch form by departing in tempo and character from its counterpart. As a slow movement in penultimate position, it would seem to anticipate a fast finale. Had one followed, the quartet would have resembled a standard four-movement form with the opening fugue as an extended introduction. The actual finale, piling one mournful slow movement on another, not only forms a gesture of great gravity, but also, like Bartók's Sixth Quartet, specifically declines to put a dynamic, up-tempo finale in the place usually appointed for one. Like the Bartók, too, the Shostakovich grounds this decision in a cumulative process: in Bartók's case the recurrence and expansion of the initial slow music, in Shostakovich's the implacable production of a symmetrical rotation. One might describe this by saying that the convention of cyclical return in the Shostakovich overrides the convention of contrast between adjacent movements.

This decisive last turn of the downward spiral follows a path set by the D. S. C. H. motto. The motto sounds only once amid the miseries of the fourth movement, and it sounds wrong. Intoned in soft bass octaves by the viola and cello, it comes in a whole tone off-pitch, as if it were forgetting its own name, losing its subjective value. The impression is confirmed by the treatment of the last note, which petrifies into a pedal point sustained for a full twenty-nine bars under mournful broken figures on the violins. At the very end of the movement, two consecutive statements of the motto at pitch make an attempt at recovery. The first, though, chokes up at the point of completion; its last note is replaced by a full bar of silence, leaving the subject's mantra on the edge of a void. The second statement does reach the last note, but only as the transition to the overwhelming sadness of the final fugue. Each of these statements is for first violin alone, as if the singular voice of the subject had momentarily become audible in the prevailing silence. And each, in its own way, fails.

At this point the effect of damage takes over. Instead of resolving the impasse of the fourth movement, the closing fugue compounds it. Instead of transfiguring the anguish of the opening fugue, the closing fugue heightens it. Instead of progressing along a dialectical spiral from one fugue to another, the quartet turns around on itself and swallows its own tail. Compare, as the music seems to invite, the linear progress of the Beethoven

Quartet in C♯ Minor, which ends by arriving at the place where most classical quartets begin, a sonata-allegro movement. The only "progress" in the Shostakovich is a movement of depletion or entropy that occupies the three inner movements: the passage from the rapid-fire moto perpetuo to the stumble-footed waltz to the dragging lament. In this context, the concluding return to the slow fugue is not a new beginning but a dead end, the notice of an unpaid symbolic debt.

The significance of this self-consuming process, and for that matter its existence, becomes fully apparent only in connection with the melodic means used to articulate it. Within the rotary motion of the whole there lies yet another cycle of rotations, this one operating at the level of self-citation and allusion established by the D. S. C. H. motive. This new cycle *in der Art eines Leierkasten* is also a new vein of autobiographical testimony. The Eighth Quartet is threaded by a pastiche of quotations from Shostakovich's earlier works representing every decade of his career: the First Symphony (1924–25), his first great success; *Lady MacBeth of the Mtensk District* (1930–32, premiered 1934), the opera that unexpectedly offended Stalin after two years of successful performances and left Shostakovich in official disfavor and fear of his life; the Second Piano Trio (1944), the Tenth and Eleventh Symphonies (1953, 1957), and the First Cello Concerto (1959). Even the D. S. C. H. motive is a self-citation rather than a gesture "original" to this quartet; the monogram actually hails from the third movement of the Tenth Symphony, the finale of which it subsequently caps at the close with a loud flourish, the way one signs an important document.

As what Shostakovich called this "little miscellany" feeds into the quartet's large-scale rotation, the music appears to be bound on the wheel of a form that has lost its capacity for meaning, but that clings desperately to the exhausted signifiers of past meaning. Everything here is recollection at best, and what is recollected is everything at its worst. Leading the way, the D. S. C. H. motive is a pale shadow of its former symphonic self, to whose character, impish and defiant by turns, it gives the lie. (The motive, we might say, rejects as fantasy the symphony's claim to have won symbolic recognition.) A similar etiolation turns the opening fanfare from the First Symphony into a whispery avowal of disillusionment; an extended quotation from *Lady MacBeth*, a lyrical melody on solo cello—the favored image of personal voice in Shostakovich's quartets—suggests the ache of an injury never mended.[36]

What is surely the most damaged of these recollections appears amid the violence of the second movement, which culminates by quoting from the finale of the Piano Trio. Based on Jewish themes, this finale was composed in 1944 in response to the horrors of the Nazi death camps, several of which had just been liberated by the Russians. The Trio thus became the first of a series of "Jewish" pieces that occupied Shostakovich in the late 1940s and early 1950s, among them the Fourth Quartet, the First Violin Concerto, and the song cycle "From Jewish Folk Poetry." In the autobiographical context of the Eighth Quartet, the quotation of the Jewish theme—heard twice, with mounting intensity—is disturbingly equivocal. It may commemorate a defining moment of allegiance that put Shostakovich at odds with Russian as well as German anti-Semitism, or it may convert genuine empathy for the victims of atrocity into a spurious identity, at worst appropriating the enormity of the Holocaust as a metaphor for one man's personal plight.[37] I doubt whether these possibilities can be disentangled, either from each other or from a fantasy of what might be called transcendental victimization. The quartet certainly forces the issue: on both of its appearances the Jewish theme bursts forth clamorously as the climax of a rapid-fire series of reiterated D. S. C. H. motives.

Like those motives, the theme makes a symbolic demand that cannot possibly be met; it lodges in the music like a foreign body. In contrast, say, to Schoenberg's cantata *A Survivor from Warsaw* (1946–47), which quotes the "Sh'ma Yisroel" at the moment when its narrator recalls—relives— singing the anthem with a doomed group of fellow Jews, the quartet simply jumps the gap between one shibboleth of identity and another. The gesture calls for a validation that its own arbitrariness blocks. "I wrote this" is not enough; "I am this" is too much. For whatever it's worth, *Testimony* ascribes a statement to Shostakovich that associates Jewishness with the shamming technique of the Eighth Quartet: "There should always be two layers in music. Jews were tormented for so long that they learned to hide their despair. They express despair in dance music" (156). But if shamming is a paradoxical kind of authenticity learned from the persecuted Jews, does it stretch to cover the shamming of persecuted Jewishness? Whatever the answer, the quotation of the Jewish theme sounds and feels traumatic, something, indeed, like a frenzied dance. When its recapitulation is abruptly curtailed to end the movement with a shocking silence, the trauma feels unassimilated, a toxic substance that can be neither absorbed nor expelled.

Another kind of traumatized recollection rotates through the fourth movement, the hammerblows of which are coupled with a lamenting three- note figure on the low strings. The lament is a slowed and heavily scored version of the theme from the Cello Concerto, which has been quoted and lightly bandied about during the waltz movement. In its new articulation, the theme becomes a distorted memory of the similarly shaped and articu-

Example 10.2. Shostakovich and Beethoven, slow cello themes from Quartets no. 8 and no. 16, respectively

a. Beethoven, "Muss es sein?"
  motive with answer

b. Shostakovich, Cello
  Concerto Variant

lated motto that opens the finale of Beethoven's F-Major String Quartet, Op. 135, over which Beethoven wrote the words "Muss es sein?" (Must it be?). The hammerblows correspondingly form a distorted memory of the rhythmically similar groups of repeated chords that cut across the "Muss es sein?" figure during Beethoven's introduction (ex. 10.2). Like Beethoven's, Shostakovich's answer, repeated over and over, is as clear as it is brutal. But decidedly unlike Beethoven's, it is final and unalterable—the more so because a hint dropped elsewhere by Shostakovich suggests that the hammerblows also form a mock-heroic allusion to Siegfried's funeral music in Wagner's *Götterdämmerung*.[38] The boundaries of memory and identity here cannot be fixed, and neither can those of travesty and allusion. The only thing clear, perhaps, is that memory is implacable: its content aside, the insistence of musical memory here acts as a metaphor that identifies memory in general with a fatality by which the subject is both formed and felled.

Combined with its self-damaging form, the allusions and self-citations of the Eighth Quartet add up to another empty ritual. Like the Mesto segments of the Bartók Sixth, this music seems to engage in a mourning process that is unable to complete itself. Perhaps this is because it goes without saying, without even thinking, that the music's self-representations can appear only under false pretenses; the most "authentic" thing about them is that they are shams. Shostakovich made doubly sure that the requisite fiction was firmly in place, announcing the quartet's dedication in an interview a month before its premiere. The device succeeded: the work was immediately hailed as a masterpiece and its autobiographical element recognized in the Soviet press as an expression of Shostakovich's lifelong "struggle against the dark forces of reaction."[39] The one explicit quotation in the quartet from a work not by Shostakovich, the revolutionary song "Exhausted by the Hardships of Prison," seemed to authorize this reading. As Richard Taruskin reports, the song was widely reputed to have been a favorite of Lenin's and thus helped force (or at least shape) the quartet's official acceptance.[40] It is too easy, though, just to wink at this as a mere cover story for Shostakovich's own sense of bondage. Heard ironically, the quotation turns an anthem of the regime against the regime itself, but the language and the authority of the regime penetrate the work on the back of that very irony. The quotation is a conspicuously planted clue to the self-corrosive force of the quartet's practice of shamming.

Perhaps in anticipation of this outcome, Shostakovich responded to the Eighth Quartet with a strange combination of self-gratification and self-loathing, as if he were pleased at his success at passing off his personal grievance as a historical lament, and at the same time disgusted by the political necessity of doing so. In a letter to a friend, he identified the quartet as an essay, not in autobiography but in auto-obituary, and suggested (with hints of suicide) that it would be his final work. (The "Muss es sein?"-cum-Siegfried allusion takes on added resonance in this context, reinforcing the mortuary associations of D. S. C. H. as a memory of B. A. C. H.; where this music "speaks," it speaks in epitaphs.) But Shostakovich also rejected his own claims to pathos as both squalid and false, how wholeheartedly it is impossible to say. His letter continues: "The pseudo-tragedy of the quartet is so great that, while composing it, my tears flowed as abundantly as urine after downing half a dozen beers. On arrival home, I have tried playing it twice, and have shed tears again. This time, not because of the pseudo-tragedy, but because of my own wonder at the marvelous unity of form."[41] The rhetorical passage from tears to urine to beers both equates the falsification of tragedy with a loss of spirit and compensates the loss with a transgressive pleasure of the body that literally turns being emptied into a gain: embarrassing but true, life-affirming but degrading.

The desperation of these measures is deepened rather than relieved by the uplifting cliché about unity of form. It suggests that, for its composer at least, the Eighth Quartet has resolved the ambiguity typical of musical alienation effects and resolved it in the negative. The element of damage has gone so far that reflective distance collapses—but not into the pleasures of empathy. Unlike Bartók's, Shostakovich's quartet cannot secure a detached perspective, even temporarily, by rejecting a portion of itself as a mere remainder; everything in it is just a remainder. The quartet's overabundance of self-citation and allusion might, of course, be taken otherwise—for instance as an act of covert defiance. It might convey an assertion of bourgeois individuality against the Soviet construction of the self as the subject of the class struggle in history. But the citations and allusions are too numerous to carry conviction; their multiplication suggests a depth of anxiety that might be glossed by Freud's wry observation that the multiplication of phallic symbols in dreams is a sign of castration. The self here exists in memorial fragments that become more fragmentary the more one seeks to make them cohere, which is just the task the quartet assigns itself. Denied an ordinary life, which is to say, a life that can aspire to be ordinary, the self secures its boundaries against colonization by an oppressive state only by collapsing into a wild marionette-theater of former identities and alter egos. The multiplication of these abandoned forms becomes the one resource of self that state power cannot control and abuse. Yet insofar as they require camouflage from the victims of Fascism and war, these old shards of selfhood are controlled and abused already. That, perhaps, is why the mourning process in this music is both keen and unachieved: it has no object. The quartet is in mourning for something that its auto-obituarizing subject has never truly had, a free subjectivity that should be his by right but that something—history, life, fate, the state—has denied him, leaving him nothing but a cipher.

With Shostakovich's Eighth Quartet, alienation as estrangement passes over into alienation as dispossession. The difference between these terms may have a certain diagnostic value. It may help define the spectrum within which musical alienation effects typically operate, and therefore help indicate the role these effects play in the history of modernity. Estrangement postulates an independent self that can both produce and undo a critical detachment from social deformation. The Moritat can both travesty the outlaw ballad and be one; Schoenberg's "Emperor" Waltz can both wish away Strauss's dreamworld and wish it back. Dispossession postulates the sacrifice of independent selfhood to a deformation so extreme that no lesser effect can bear witness to it. Bartók's Sixth Quartet ends in this extremity—

in every sense its terminal condition—and can be said to dramatize the emergence of dispossession from the collapse of mere estrangement, its less harassing cousin. Shostakovich's Eighth Quartet simply lives out the aftermath of that collapse; its true tragedy is that it can never be other than a pseudo-tragedy. The Eighth Quartet thus makes a fitting close to this selective survey, if not a happy end. But unlike *The Threepenny Opera*, the history of modernity cannot necessarily summon up a mounted messenger to reverse its fortunes.

11
Chiaroscuro
Coltrane's American Songbook

"Eddy is white," writes Toni Morrison of a Hemingway character, "and we know he is because nobody says so."[1] The same can be said for Mack the Knife, by whom I do not mean Brecht and Weill's Macheath (of whom "The Cannon Song" does say so), but the protagonist of the American hit song based on Marc Blitzstein's loose adaptation of "Moritat von Mackie Messer." As noted in the last chapter, Blitzstein's text turns the ambiguous Macheath into a period-specific romantic outlaw, a Brandoesque tough cookie with great sexual magnetism. This Mack the Knife is white, and we know he is because nobody says so, including Ella Fitzgerald and Louis Armstrong. Not that the question ever came up.[2] What would it have meant, in 1950s America, to take seriously the question of Macheath's race? The absence of the question is a good part of its answer: a black Mack the Knife would have been mantled in fear, not roguish charisma. But were those black artists—including also jazz musicians like Oscar Peterson and Coleman Hawkins who made instrumental versions—really celebrating a white cultural icon, the nonconformist rebel with a slouch, a hooded glance, and a girl on each arm?

Behind this question stands another, more fundamental one. What does it mean for a sociocultural group to have its "own" expressive style? What would it mean for a black artist to sing about a white Macheath, and what would it mean for one not to? What does "blackness" mean as an expressive category, and how does it relate to blackness as a social or racial category? As exemplified already by the Africanisms of modernist concert music, music is a venue in which this question has historically been raised with particular urgency. In what follows, I would like to pursue the question from, so to speak, the other side of the mirror, asking not what is sometimes done to black music but what it sometimes does. My point of departure will be to consider more seriously than usual a classic jazz usage, the taking of a pop standard as the basis of improvisation, the standard being (as is often the case) by a white composer while the improvisers are, as the musical genre is, black. This musical chiaroscuro is one of the issues raised by John Coltrane's landmark 1960 album *My Favorite Things*, which addresses itself to standards by George Gershwin, Cole Porter, and Richard Rodgers—a kind of holy trinity of American popular song—and seeks to refashion their music into an American songbook of a different color.

In negotiating the space between these socially or racially marked compositions, I will draw on a concept that has proven useful in negotiating the similar space between works in different media. (Part of my effort is, indeed, to show precisely that these spaces are similar, portions of the general space of mixed signification and expression: the communicative economy.) The concept is that of structural, or, alternatively, cultural tropes. These are patterns of action and signification that can be realized equally well within diverse artistic media, and that can be interpreted both as affecting artistic form (they are structural tropes) and as responding to questions of value, identity, and historical location (they are cultural tropes). Such tropes are understood to form part of a general habitus (see chap. 7): an ensemble of "structuring structures" that enable the members of a cultural group to respond coherently to the constantly changing texture of experience; they are, in effect, principles of improvisation. Numerous cultural tropes have come up in the course of this book without being named as such, from mirror effects in Schumann to the alienation effect in modernist music. With African American culture, the paradigmatic example is perhaps the pattern of call and response, a structuring structure (with roots in both African ceremony and the labor of American slaves) that is at once social, religious, ethical, and aesthetic.[3]

Not all structural tropes, however, are as readily identifiable as these, and not all medium-neutral effects function as structural tropes. It may be useful to make a distinction here, knowing, of course, that there will be many circumstances in which the distinction breaks down. Some medium-neutral effects seem primarily to emerge as stylistic traits, and to become analytically significant when we recognize them as typical; stylistic traits represent cultural traits when they are disseminated over a multiplicity of works, media, and contexts. For instance, one might find a controlled but propulsive kineticism in both the classic jazz rhythm section and the "jazz poetry" of Langston Hughes. Where the music simultaneously couples metronomic statement and off-beat counterstatement, the poetry binds together short, irregular lines with "syncopated" verbal repetition and "off-beat" rhyme:

> Sleek black boys in a cabaret.
> Jazz-band, jazz-band
> Play, plAY, PLAY!
> Tomorrow . . . who knows?
> Dance today!

("Harlem Night Club," 1–5)[4]

The point is not so much that Hughes is imitating jazz rhythms, although he is, but that this kind of kinetic energy is widespread in African American forms of expression and that its various manifestations may have common cultural origins, in this case, perhaps, in certain types of oral performance. At the same time, one could look at the stanza-like grouping of short, irregular lines in the poetry of William Carlos Williams and see it as linked, not to jazz, but to the techniques of Precisionist painters like his friend Charles Demuth, who drew on Cubist geometries to depict "the machine in the garden" of industrialized America:

> Where a
> waste of cinders
> slopes down to
> the railroad and
> the lake
> stand three children
> beside the weed-grown
> chassis
> of a wrecked car

("View of a Lake," 7–15)[5]

One reason for the difference of feeling, the difference in cultural trait, is that Hughes sticks with rhyme and verbal repetition while Williams abandons them. Hughes superimposes a quasi-musical rhythm on speech, while Williams evokes a more splintered, more linear impetus that he associates with the vernacular rhythms of speech itself.

Other medium-neutral effects seem to emerge less as traits than as processes; they are not stylistic or sensuous effects offered to immediate perception, but patterns or tendencies that must be inferred, divined, interpreted. Their relationship to cultural forms is less qualitative than performative. Because medium-neutral processes exist at one remove from immediate perception, because they are tacit, implicit tendencies, they are harder to exemplify than medium-neutral traits. The readiest examples may come from certain well-delimited genres of narrative whose narrativity (principles of purpose and direction) can travel from one medium to another: quest narrative, slave narrative, coming-of-age narrative, and the like. Coltrane's Gershwin-derived composition "Summertime" (one of two in *My Favorite Things*) exhibits this sort of narrativity, which I will later take up in some detail. It contains an extended passage suggestive of the process of dwelling on and then crossing a threshold that is characteristic of both heroic quest narrative and the coming-of-age story. But this is only true if one listens, not only sensuously, aesthetically, but also interpretively, semantically. The processes disclosed to such listening are cultural tropes.

The basis of what follows is one such trope that I do not think has been previously recognized, although I would welcome the discovery that, in one way or another, it has been. I call this trope either "disassemblage" or "debricolage" and offer it for consideration as something with special relevance to African American artistic practices.

As the term *debricolage* suggests, what is involved here is a variant of the technique of bricolage that became famous after Claude Lévi-Strauss proposed it as a key component in mythical thinking.[6] The enhanced concept of bricolage survived the obsolescence of classical structuralism and passed into common usage. The term literally means "tinkering," in the sense of adapting old materials to new uses; if you don't have a string bass handy, rig up a washtub. In this example, bricolage figures as both a response to scarcity and a measure of inventiveness. The inventiveness begins as a compensation for the scarcity but ends by taking on a life of its own.

My notion of debricolage retains the element of inventiveness but replaces real scarcity with a fictitious or travesty scarcity. Debricolage adapts old materials to new uses for reasons of desire, not of need. Instead of assemblage, its basic principle is disassemblage, and what it disassembles are the norms and forms of a dominant culture. In debricolage, these appear in bits and pieces, but so articulated that their original wholeness remains perceptible; they are not just strewn about, but carefully disassembled. A classic example of this process is the three-part epigraph that begins Toni Morrison's novel *The Bluest Eye* (1970). The first part is an excerpt from *Fun with Dick and Jane*, the once-ubiquitous primary school reader that was, of course, always illustrated by drawings of a white middle-class family. The black schoolgirls whose story the novel tells would have been taught to read with this text. The second part is a word-for-word repetition of the first but with all the punctuation removed. The third part is a word-for-word repetition of the second but with all the spaces between the words removed. As one passes through the sequence, the cultural non-sense of the original is exposed by its transformation into verbal nonsense. This is a nonsense, however, that both preserves the substance of the original text and becomes a counter-text, a rush of pure oral and textual energy, in its own right. A fictitious scarcity—here a cultural rather than a material scarcity, a faked linguistic incompetence—becomes an actual abundance. The effect striates the book as a whole thanks to a further deformation: chapter heads consisting of unspaced and unpunctuated fragments of the *Dick and Jane* text with all the letters shifted from their original lower case to upper case, the equivalent in print of a shouting or wailing voice.

At one level, Morrison's disassemblage of *Fun with Dick and Jane* is a symbolic condensation of the tragic story she has to tell—of incest, madness, and the desire of a little black girl for blue eyes—but at a deeper level it is a symbolic reversal of that story. Placed at the margins of society, the characters of *The Bluest Eye* are undone by the link between social and symbolic order; placed at the margins of the text, the epigraphic sequence undoes the link between social and symbolic order. Morrison draws no conclusions from this reversal, holds out no dialectical promise on its basis. She simply suggests to the reader that it might be best to read her text, as well as its paratext, as a disassemblage rather than a traditional narrative.

In this respect her practice differs, perhaps dissentingly, from the model set in 1903 by W. E. B. Du Bois in *The Souls of Black Folk.* This book, a series of essays on the theme that "the problem of the twentieth century is the problem of the color line," is both deliberately structured and pieced together from miscellaneous, previously published materials.[7] Each chapter but the last begins with a double epigraph consisting of the musically notated theme of an unidentified Negro spiritual set underneath a quotation from a white poet. The juxtaposition forms a paratextual image of Du Bois's famous concept of "double consciousness," the ambivalent awareness of being both African and American, subaltern and citizen, that for Du Bois defines the phenomenology of African American spirit after Reconstruction. My allusion to Hegel points to a dialectical turn made by the final chapter, the epigraph of which anticipates a healed and whole black consciousness by conjoining the musically notated spiritual with an anonymous lyric identified as a "Negro song." As the chapter proceeds, words and music coalesce for the first time as the previously quoted spirituals are identified and excerpts from several others appear in musical notation with textual underlay. The last and longest excerpt, with obvious symbolic intent, is written out in full four-part harmony; sung in octaves until its last phrase, it closes on a fully harmonized C-major cadence. Less hopeful than Du Bois, or maybe just more realistic, Morrison prefers her dissonances unresolved. She declines to trace the outline of an autonomous subjectivity amid the debris of racial history. Instead she settles for a disassemblage that exposes the racial contingency of what passes for autonomous.

Those who have been historically excluded from the privileges of a dominant culture can redefine their relationship to it through such disassemblage, which transforms the instruments of exclusion into a means of self-definition and self-creation. Insofar as this process involves symbolically taking control of one's own history, it becomes a means to the construction and performance of collective identity—in the context of black expressive culture, what Kimberly Benston has termed the performance of blackness.[8] One result is the production of a repertoire of expressive styles that signify group membership and in which accordingly the evolving group identity can solidify. These styles are, nonetheless, highly individualized, and there is nothing paradoxical in the fact. If Houston Baker is right that African American cultural expression in the past century has often arisen out of a vernacular "blues matrix," then it may also be true that the trope of debricolage belongs to a complementary matrix, that of a black high culture.[9] The example from Toni Morrison might suggest as much; what Morrison's text disassembles is not only the covertly racialized language of Dick and Jane, but also the experimental technique of high-modernist fiction, with a more than casual backward glance at the beginning of James Joyce's *Portrait of the Artist as a Young Man*.

A similar effect occurs in Coltrane's "Summertime"—also, intriguingly enough, at the very outset. The music starts abruptly with an unprepared tenor sax solo, Coltrane giving out George Gershwin's famous melody at what might be called the vanishing point. The listener seems to break in during a process of melodic transformation that has already begun, is already well advanced, and that in the very next moment will carry the melody beyond recognition—which is indeed what happens, as Coltrane proceeds into the proliferating roulades of his "soundsheet" style. Furthermore, as with Morrison, the initiating moment of disassemblage affects not only the particularity of a single text, but a whole realm of technique. Gershwin's combination of pentatonicism and blues inflection evokes an image of idyllic rural contentment and black simplicity. The invocation is ironic in both the song itself and its operatic context in *Porgy and Bess*, but the irony is a poignant one, and the image is suffused rather than undercut by it. Coltrane's rapid and highly complex version of the melody superimposes a second image of urban turmoil and black sophistication. The second image is the first disassembled.

Coltrane's "Summertime" is one of the topics touched on by another literary example of debricolage, A. B. Spellman's elegiac poem, "Did John's Music Kill Him?" The text is pieced together from impressions and reflections joined without transition. Gradually, a recollection of what it was like to be there when Coltrane played becomes a testimony to the power of his playing to perform the listener's identity—indeed, to confront the listener with an identity otherwise evaded. The issue is blackness, which finds its voice in Coltrane's horn. In return, the listener, as poet, uses his own voice to secure Coltrane's presence. Prosopopoeia, the classical trope of speech exchanged between the present and the absent, the living and the dead, becomes a means of refusing absence, denying death, in full awareness of the ultimate futility of the gesture[10]:

> jimmy'd bow a quarter hour
> till Mccoy fed block chords
> to his stroke. elvin's thunder
> roll & eric's scream. then john.
>
> then john. *little old lady*
> had a nasty mouth. *summertime*
> when the war is. *africa* ululating . . .
> into knots paints beauty black.
>
> trane's horn had words in it
> i know when i sleep sober & dream
> those dreams i duck in the world. . . .
>
> > so beat john's death words down
> > on me. . . . o john death will
> > not contain you death
> > will not contain you
> > (6–12, 14–17, 26–27, 32–34; ellipses added)[11]

The debricolage of this poem appears most overtly in its systematic deformation of standard English spelling and punctuation. Sentences always begin with a small letter, not a capital; the first person pronoun is always spelled with a small letter, not a capital; names are not capitalized, either, except for "Mccoy," which in context reads like a misprint; "and" is always written as an ampersand—that is, as a punctuation mark, not a word; and the only other punctuation mark applied to sentence structure is the period, which divides the text less into grammatical units than into orally conceived breath units. The most important periods, moreover, are the ones that are not there: after the key sentences "trane's horn had words in it" and the double "death will not contain you": both statements of sheer virtuality, defying absence, statements that want no closure and therefore receive none. Instead of closure, the poem offers a symbolic shift to a new, "uncontained" frame of reference by justifying the margin of the final stanza to a deep indent rather than to the left margin. The nominal poem space, the space occupied by the first four stanzas, is unable to contain the passions of the last, which are "fermenting & wanting to explode" like Coltrane's music. The last stanza defies the absence its move makes visible on the page. The doubling of its final words, "death will/not contain you," suggests that the speaker has merged his voice with that of Coltrane's horn, so that his apostrophic call to Coltrane becomes its own response.

Many modern poems, of course, jettison standard spelling and punctuation, but it is striking how many black and other minority poets have been drawn to the device since the 1960s; Amiri Baraka, Ishmael Reed, Nikki Giovanni, Don L. Lee, Michael Harper, and Sonia Sanchez are among many other practitioners of this sort of disassemblage. Writing "incorrectly" most often signifies either resistance (the norms are used oppressively) or authenticity (the poem springs from types of experience the norms can't comprehend); either way, it suggests the abandonment of rules. A notable poetic subgenre takes Coltrane in particular to embody the spirit of this technique, a role spelled out imitatively, with multiple layers of "signifying," at the beginning of Sanchez's "a/coltrane/poem":

> my favorite things
>> is u/blowen
>>> yo/favorite things.[12]

In Spellman's poem, though, the same technique is studied, systematic; the poem makes up its own rules, improvising a counter writing as Coltrane improvises a counter music. The formality of the poem's writing system also resonates strongly with its ritualistic invocation of the key elements of traditional elegy, namely memory, music, the journey through death, and the promise of new life, all of which are transposed from their traditional moorings in a timeless pastoral world to the modern urban world of jazz performance.

Coltrane, as we saw earlier, effects a similar transposition at the beginning of "Summertime." In so doing, he also initiates a larger process of debricolage that unfolds across the composition as a whole. The process can be described in terms of narrativity—almost, indeed, in the elegiac terms of a descent to a kind of underworld and a return to life. The narrative impulse, in turn, can be described as a gradual reshaping of the music's initial disassemblage of Gershwin's melody. Closure is achieved by means of a partial reassemblage that is also a new and more stable disassemblage.

As noted earlier, Coltrane's opening solo takes wing less from a preliminary statement of the "Summertime" melody than from an already advanced transformation of it. The transformation, moreover, is aggressive and hard driving, far removed from the poignant languor of the original. Coltrane sustains the transformative impetus for almost four minutes of unremitting high-voltage playing. Spellman is right when he says that trane's horn had words in it; the words here, contrary to those of the song, are unspoken but unmistakable: it may be summertime, but the livin' is far from easy. Spellman's allusive phrase, "summertime when the war is," can be taken to suggest both a creative conflict between Gershwin and Coltrane and the destructive conflicts that erupted in American inner cities during more than one summertime of the mid-1960s. The music can be heard as an effort to work through the violent impulses that initially impel both conflicts and to achieve some sort of reconciliation, however tentative.

Coltrane, or more exactly Coltrane's horn, the personification of a suffering, heroic, questing subjectivity in this piece as in others—Coltrane's horn makes this effort in a most remarkable way, not by action but by suffering, not by sound but by silence. It's as if for much of the piece the horn merely listens. Following the long opening solo, McCoy Tyner's piano takes over. Calming the embattled atmosphere but with no loss of energy, it quickly settles on the texture it will sustain throughout its solo: a nonmelodic skittering in the upper registers punctuated by emphatic chordal figures. Unlike the sax, which seems to have been trying (in vain) to rid itself of Gershwin's melody, the piano absorbs a key feature of the melody, the interval of a third, and repeatedly builds phrases and figures around it. In this synoptic guise "Summertime" becomes the kernel of an intensive contemplation, but one that the piano can only foster, not complete. A great deal will depend on what happens when the tune is eventually rearticulated—in particular when trane's horn once again has words in it.

What follows is both the narrative pivot of the piece and its emotional nadir. Against a light background from the percussion, Steve Davis begins a double-bass solo in the instrument's low register. The texture is thick, almost inarticulate; there is no trace of melody; the overall effect is of a kind of blind groping. The music dwells in this space of privation as on a threshold, as if dwelling there were something that had to be endured in order to move on. That onward motion eventually evolves as the piano combines with the bass and the percussion (by Elvin Jones) begins to dominate, finally cutting loose into a powerful statement of "elvin's thunder" that breaks the spell of agonized inaction. After more interjections from the piano, Coltrane's saxophone, so long silent, finally speaks out.

Recalling its opening solo, the sax again combines free commentary on the theme with rapid-fire figuration, but the mood is noticeably different. The theme feels more fully present, for one thing, both in itself and as a melodic resource; the nonmelodic skeins spun out from it are briefer and less extreme; and, most importantly, its paraphrases and offshoots are now brushed with some—only some—of the mellowness of the original. This is still not Gershwin's "Summertime" by a long shot, but it is a Coltrane "Summertime" in which aggressive appropriation has been replaced by a kind of cultural and emotional dialogue. The livin' may still not be easy, but it has become easier to live. The end of the piece goes even further in this direction, with a really mellow saxophone statement of a phrase of Gershwin's melody that has been sidestepped or brusquely dismissed on its earlier appearances. The phrase is Gershwin's own close, to the words "Hush little baby, don't you cry." When trane's horn has these words in it, the sense of reconciliation already achieved heightens into a sense of consolation, perhaps the one sense above all to which the sax had seemed impervious in its opening solo. The end of Coltrane's "Summertime" thus becomes a significant moment of self-overcoming and self-creation by transforming and completing, not only the implication-laden melody on which it is based, but also its own initial debricolage on that melody. Such moments of wholeness are always precarious; one never knows if they can be fully believed. But when they are so hard won, they are always moving to witness.

A similar moment forms the conclusion to the title track of *My Favorite Things*. Here, too, a combination of liminality and disassemblage works to correct, transform, and finally reclaim an initially false image of innocent happiness. The stakes here, however, are somewhat different than in "Summertime," and in a sense are higher. Gershwin's *Porgy and Bess* may be problematical in some of its representations, but it does seek to pay tribute to the presence of black people in American life. Rodgers and Hammerstein's *The Sound of Music*, the source of the catchy waltz "My Favorite Things," studiously ignores that presence, as do all of their musicals. (The shows deal instead with safely remote cultural Others: in *The King and I*, a nineteenth-century Siamese ruler whose death in the last act marks the beginning of his country's westernization; in *South Pacific* two beautiful Polynesian women, one of whom dies beforehand leaving her husband to find love and marriage again with the white heroine, and the other of whom loses her white fiancé in battle. Both shows carry an overt message of racial tolerance that is compromised both by such plot devices and by the evasion of its real referent, the color line in America.) *The Sound of Music* is particularly problematical because it identifies the values of its American audiences with those of a fairytale alpine paradise mysteriously uninfected by a Nazism shown to overrun it from without.

Coltrane's "My Favorite Things" can be said to seek the remedy for these multiple acts of bad faith, which in musical terms means that it seeks to make the archaic (Phrygian) modality of the first half of Rodgers's tune the basis of something more than a nostalgic *Schlagober*. But Coltrane does not condescend to the tune, as commentators on his piece would make a habit of doing; instead, he carefully disassembles it to unfold previously unsuspected expressive possibilities.[13] His later takes on it—he could not seem to leave the tune alone—would be longer and fiercer, as if he were trying to wrest something from it that constantly eluded him, or as if the tune's claim of unassailable innocence were in the long run too hard to tolerate. In the short run, however, Coltrane is content just to sing the tune in his own way. The 1960 version is punctuated by multiple statements of it in lightly jazzed-up form; these support complex improvisatory episodes grounded in a pair of rhythmic motives, one devised to introduce the tune and comp with it, the other drawn from the tune itself. The piece thus alternates between reminiscences of the tune and transformations of it, or, more exactly, from it, the tune becoming the kernel of a freewheeling musical energy it cannot hope to contain. Most of the improvisatory episodes, the ones for Coltrane's alto sax, are full of a kind of quicksilver dynamism. One of them, however, for McCoy Tyner's piano, is very different.

Like the bass solo in "Summertime," the piano solo here creates a sense of threshold. Framed by statements of the tune, it occurs fairly early in the piece, so that when it has been dwelt on and crossed over, the release of creative energy that follows can appear, not as a single consummating moment, but as a viable state of being. The episode is virtually static, consisting primarily of repetitions of the three-note comping figure heard at the outset of the piece. It goes on this way for a palpably long time, evoking a sense that time itself has slowed or even stopped, and that the sax, here as in "Summertime" cast in a listening role, is lost in contemplation. It is as if the subjectivity embodied by the sax were being formed or tested in the threshold experience, which requires of it an ascetic (rather than an ecstatic) self-forgetting. This emptying-out of the self as a prelude to fullness may even be inscribed in the shape of the comping figure, which incorporates a moment of delay and anticipation between its first two notes (on the beat) and its third (behind the beat).

When the sax resumes after this rite of passage, we are free to imagine that its creative energy is centered in and invested by the unconditioned musical-psychological-spiritual potentiality, part void and part patient calm, to which it has just submitted. The solo at this point is the longest in the piece, the most free, and the most purposeful. It turns the static rhythmic abstraction of the piano solo into a dynamic principle. Where the first saxophone solo took off from the tune of "My Favorite Things," this one seems to be seeking a transfigured version of it, which emerges late in the game and immediately receives a bouncy variation. The story thus told is that favorite things, which the song lyric defines as consoling things, are not something one has but something one seeks; the sense of having is an illusion, and perhaps one fostered by complacent social privilege. The seeking requires patience, emotional mobility, and transformative energy, and even so its outcome is never quite sure. The saxophone solo suggests as much near the close, much as its counterpart does in "Summertime," by turning to a neglected portion of the tune, this time a still unheard portion: the bridge that ends—trane's horn again has words in it—with the statement of consolation: "And then I don't feel so bad." That the phrase implicates the burden of a long tradition of Negro spirituals suggests both irony and revaluation. The sentiment may be vacuous in the original tune (that is, in the tune's fictitious world), but it fills with meaning when filtered through the black experience that the tune so obliviously denies. The meaning is tentative, wise in its insecurity, as much resigned as hopeful; the melodic phrase takes a sober, low-voiced turn at the end, and is followed by a brief, brooding epilogue that calls for suspended judgment. But something has been accomplished. Without resorting to rancor or mockery, the series of solos has both disassembled the original tune in a critical spirit and, in the disassemblage, found something of value.

This process may seem complete at the end of "My Favorite Things," but—nothing being that easy—it starts over again in "Summertime" where the saxophone must repeat and enhance its earlier passage to self-affirmation through patient self-abnegation. In the interim, however, the illusion of fulfillment is sustained by "Every Time We Say Goodbye," a short idyllic interlude the bliss of which is that it can merely be itself, whatever it wants to be. The piece is a "classically" simple A B A form, with a pair of soprano sax solos framing a solo for piano. The outer sections are dreamy and reflective, alternately caressing and departing from Cole Porter's melody; tension and urgency are nowhere within earshot. The middle section is a model of restraint, modestly faster and more active, but content to serve as a lightly glittering foil for the sections that frame it. Coltrane's solos ignore the melancholy of Porter's song, approaching and then refusing a melodic cadence every time the song would say "goodbye." Slow, thoughtful, and marked by a liquid, classical purity of tone on the sax, the solos seem bent on carrying Porter's music into depths of feeling that are foreign to it, or least characteristically veiled by the pretense of being foreign to it. After the dissolving close of this number, the hard-driving opening of "Summertime" comes as a rude awakening.

As we've seen, however, "Summertime" closes in reconciliation, and this time the achievement seems durable, at least for the time being. "But Not for Me" closes the album by showing what that achievement makes possible. In mood, like all the tracks on the album, it goes against the grain of its original; what's "not for me," it seems to be saying, is once again the romantic melancholy of a love song. Coltrane's "But Not for Me" is about creativity, and more particularly about a creative energy that continually acknowledges a source outside its own milieu but that in the very course of acknowledgment becomes self-sustaining.

In form, the track replicates the classical simplicity of "Every Time We Say Goodbye," with two Coltrane solos framing one by Tyner, but the solos are much longer and very different in character. Their interest in the source melody focuses mainly on its title phrase, for which they continually devise substitutes; the phrase thus becomes a residual presence throughout the solos, especially the sax solos. Coltrane begins by fragmenting Gershwin's tune, throwing off substitutes for its incipit and title phrase and juxtaposing them with more literal recollections of what follows, a pair of phrases (model and sequence) centered on long-breathed blue notes, a passage later retouched to give Gershwin's song its hook. That done, the first solo alludes to the tune only through the substitutive phrasing, which is used to anchor the improvisation. The solo itself becomes increasingly exuberant, freewheeling, and virtuosic, and it gives way to a similar statement by Tyner in which even the substitutive phrasing seems to vaporize. Tyner, however, does close with a title-phrase substitute, and Coltrane, in another classicizing gesture, begins his second solo with a recapitulation: a double statement of the tune with substitutes for the incipit and title phrase and literal recollections of the blue-note passage, pointedly including Gershwin's hook. The context and fullness of the gesture effect a transformation: what sounded like fragmentation earlier now sounds like a reconstruction. The reconstructed tune, however, is only another point of departure; it shatters quickly as the solo gathers energy. Its appearance here provides a full but final acknowledgment of an original that now serves best by being left behind: goodbye and thanks, says the sax, I can take it from here. And it does. Unlike the three previous tracks, "But Not for Me" ends without a decisive reference to its original, which bows out on yet another substitute phrase. The difference signifies. *My Favorite Things* confirms its status as a new American songbook by concluding on its own.

In its blend of tenacity and forbearance, fierceness and generosity, Coltrane's debricolage in this album illustrates the sheer difficulty of the problem of appropriation: of how engaging with, transforming, respecting, and disrespecting the cultural style of one group can produce a cultural style that "belongs" to another. To suggest a fuller sense of what is at stake in that difficulty, both aesthetically and ethically, a wider historical perspective (and even a historical detour) may prove useful.

For African Americans, gaining a share in cultural production has often depended on an ability to translate a despised or envied subaltern discourse into forms that make manifest their own distinct rationality, their mastery of a codifiable technique and their possession of a symbolic tradition, all on terms that differ from the norms that depreciate them for lacking just those qualities. One thing this might mean is a deformation of standard models so thoroughgoing that the models are lost. For Zora Neale Hurston, writing about the evolution of the spirituals, this process "negroises" its models without hesitation or apology, especially by enhancing the role of the body and breath in singing and by refusing to subordinate the individual to the group.[14] As David Metzer observes, Hurston's term "negroising" is a neologism that "captures what it describes: the bringing together of fragments—words or music of white origin—to create new compounds that declare black creativity."[15]

A contrary possibility is an identification with standard white models that simply refuses to acknowledge racial boundaries, a tack most notably pursued early in the century by Du Bois. The penultimate chapter of *The Souls of Black Folk*, "Of the Coming of John," is structured around a double musical climax that, prompted by this type of identification, temporarily obliterates the condition of double consciousness. Du Bois's title suggests the story of a sacrificial precursor, a latter day John the Baptist. The hero, John Jones, a young educated black man whose name also makes him a kind of everyman, blindly follows a New York crowd into the Metropolitan opera where—before being politely ejected—he is sent into transports of rapture by Wagner's *Lohengrin* Prelude: "A deep longing swelled in all his heart to rise with that clear music out of the dirt and dust of that low life that held him prisoned and befouled." The longing is doomed from the start; the story will end with John's lynching. But his violent death becomes a scene of personal transfiguration mediated by memories of Wagner's music: "He leaned back and smiled toward the sea, whence rose the strange melody, away from the dark shadows where lay the noises of horses galloping, galloping on."[16] It is not supposed to matter here that Lohengrin is a racially charged image of a Teutonic knight, an image that might even be said to overlap with that of the galloping horsemen, presumably White Knights of another kind. The transcendental scene seeks to negate Wagner's racial standpoint by making his music speak for Du Bois's.

A similar use of the *Lohengrin* Prelude appears in Charlie Chaplin's film *The Great Dictator* (1940). This anti-Nazi satire initially associates the music with Hitler, known here as Adenoid Hynkel, but ends by transferring it to Hynkel's double and antithesis, a Jewish barber. Midway through the film, Chaplin as Hynkel follows up an injunction to "kill off the Jews" by performing a balletic pantomime to the first few minutes of the Prelude, tossing, kicking, and butting an inflated globe of the world like a giant soap bubble—until it bursts. Later, Chaplin as the barber mistaken for Hynkel gives an impassioned anti-Nazi radio address from a Nuremberg-style rally, ending with a direct appeal to Hannah, his refugee beloved. Initially shown lying prostrate in a field, Hannah stands and gazes upward as the sound of the Prelude miraculously descends to her from on high, ending the movie by ironically realizing Wagner's own program for the music with a Jewish exile in the place of a Grail knight. This musical frame structure seeks to turn Wagner against both Hitler and himself, beginning by invoking Wagner's anti-Semitism but ending by dismissing it, effectively dividing Wagner into contrary personae in parallel with Hynkel and the barber. Hynkel's pantomime is ambiguous, both a perversion of what the movie takes to be the spirit of the Prelude and a demonstration that the historical nexus of Hitler, Wagner, and anti-Semitism lays that spirit under a cloud of suspicion. The redemptive return of the music is also the means of the music's own redemption, its disengagement from historical reality and its enlistment in the service of utopian hope. For Chaplin as for Du Bois, the outcome hinges on a faith in the capacity of applied meaning to strip the artwork of its exclusionary and rejecting powers.

Debricolage like Coltrane's can be understood as a reaction to the historical collapse of that faith, which tends to survive, where it does survive, only among the groups least affected by exclusion and rejection. Debricolage cuts against the grain of Du Bois's unqualified idealism without rejecting it altogether, as Hurston's "negroisation" tends to do. It acknowledges that any sense of self, dominant or marginal, citizen's or subaltern's, contains an indispensable nucleus of otherness that may be controlled, demonized, or idolized only in fantasy. On that basis, it goes about its work. It sets out in search of its favorite things.

As embodied in Coltrane's *My Favorite Things*, that search depends on the acknowledgment that identification with a cultural style neither requires nor supports claims of authenticity or dogmatic understanding.[17] Traits or tropes associated with one cultural position may always be, have always already been, transferred to, imitated by, and appropriated to other positions. The sense of group identity or "ownness" in a given work thus comes from the process of installing the cultural-structural trope over against the embodied history of its other uses with little, or only a little, attempt to hide the effort. The openness concedes or affirms that this processual "ownness" is itself porous, incessantly open to further processes of hybridization, amalgamation, negotiation. Its "ownness" is a trope, a figure, in its own right that is constituted not as a possessable quality but as an attitude conveyed through continual reworking and revisitation.

These conclusions can serve as a bridge to the next, and final, chapter, which begins by taking up the question of ownness or authenticity in a narrow aesthetic space, the idea and ideal of creative originality. The chapter spins off from there to adjacent fields of larger questions. Entry into those fields, it will claim, is open with life-enhancing effects if only, and only if, one refuses the suppositions behind such an idea, the lure of such an ideal.

12
Ghost Stories
Cultural Memory, Mourning,
and the Myth of Originality

The Mirror Stage. There is a strange place found in some clothing stores, a kind of dormer constructed of three full-length mirrors. A central mirror stands opposite the customer and two flanking mirrors spread out at equal angles like wings. When you pass before this compound mirror to try something on, the multiplication of your image is both magical and disturbing. The wings fling you into a vertiginous opening where there are just too many of you, and at the same time enfold you in a womblike tent where there are just enough of you, where even the walls are you. The images, the repetitions of your figure, of you as a figure, are all different because they are differently angled and set at different depths, some of them as reflections of reflections. But they are all the same. In their sameness they lure you to a narcissistic pleasure—one result of which is that you buy the clothes. In their difference they throw the comforting notion of your sameness, your identity with yourself, into doubt, or rather into a kind of spectral suspension in which seeing yourself is like seeing a ghost.

The dormer of mirrors is a locus of what might be called the deconstruction of everyday life, the innumerable small dislocations of mind and body that disclose one's subjectivity to be infinitely divisible. In remembrance and self-reference, in desire and discomfiture, the self is forever liable to get lost amid the wilderness of its own identities. Like the figures in the dormer wings, it multiplies indefinitely, each of its avatars simulating all the others without any one standing firm as the others' origin. The effect is a kind of subjective polyphony, and the metaphor is no accident. Musical subjectivity is my topic in this chapter, both in its own right and in relation to subjectivity in general, and my starting point is the idea that this subjectivity, too, takes the prismatic shape of the dormer glass.

For many listeners, music offers a connection to a pure source of subjectivity, be it high emotion, the charisma of the composer or performer, the bonds of group identity, or the like. Yet this subjectivity has no single origin or locale; it does not belong to any of the persons, living or dead, real or imaginary, engaged in the occasion of music, yet it belongs to all of them at once. The subjectivity called forth musically in each of these figures stands as a simulacrum for an original subjectivity that appears only in the multiplication of simulacra. Unlike a fictional character, the musical subject does not present the appearance of a concrete individual identity; even in vocal music, dramatic character tends to become transparent to a musical character that envelops and exceeds it. Like the dormer of mirrors, but of course with immeasurably greater impact, music both gathers and scatters subjectivity in the same gesture.

The customary ways of thinking about music tend to flatten out its subjective multidimensionality by focusing on a single originating agency, usually the composer if the music is "classical." Although this focus on individuals has been all but annihilated in many academic circles, if not in the intellectual public sphere, it has proven exceptionally resistant to critique or deconstruction in relation to music, especially to the canonical art music of the last three centuries. I want to ask what happens when we understand such music while also understanding that its composer is not a controlling origin translatable into a controlling musical persona, but, like the persona itself, a relay in a series of shimmering simulacra, a kind of revenant on the mirrored stage. It may even turn out that the music itself can be understood to transcribe the process of this simulacral repetition, not simply in relationship to its composer but in general. The music may in some sense be about the uncanny replication of one subject in or by another.

In making this suggestion, however, I do not myself want to speak as the kind of originary subject I am trying to subvert, and "I," accordingly, will make several spectral appearances in what follows as my own simulacrum, recalling episodes from the history, and prehistory, of my own musical subjectivity in ways that cut across the grain of the argument. At stake here, I hope, is more than just the fin-de-siècle academic fashion for first-person statements and more than just self-regard, both of which are real enough possibilities. The other "I" who visits and revisits this text is meant to speak from a position of genuine perplexity that both enriches and questions what it means to make knowledge claims about something as imponderable as music.

The Condition of Music. In saying that music may be "about" revisitation, about the experience of the general form of the uncanny, I will be making a pair of claims that depart from the established canons of explanation for the origins of the musical artwork. Music arises, the story goes, from musical technique; it becomes new, becomes original, when it breaks through from known to unknown technique, and thereby gives technique a history. My first claim is that compositional decisions on matters of technique are indeed to be understood as a response to musical ideas, but that these musical ideas are not necessarily technical ideas. The context of the musical work is musical experience, but a musical experience always already permeated by a prismatic irradiation of imaginary, symbolic, and hermeneutic experiences. Technique is, or may be, the vehicle of musical experience, but it is not necessarily, perhaps not even often, the source or content of musical experience. The second claim is that the musical artwork can be timely without being, or seeking to be, original in a technical sense. Twentieth-century convention takes such originality as the indispensable sign of responsiveness to changing times, and therefore of seriousness and artistic integrity. I would like to set up a counter position from which the technical originality of the work appears only as a contingent by-product of the prismatic irradiation just now invoked, a by-product of the way that the work, even despite itself, overflows its boundaries into multiple contexts of meaning, cultural practice, communicative action, and the construction of subjectivities. Technical innovation may contribute to this process, but it need not. Construed as a prerequisite for the serious artwork, such innovation is little more than a means of accumulating prestige value, or, as Pierre Bourdieu calls it, cultural capital.[1]

It follows from these claims that the question of musical originality is not narrowly aesthetic; it is a symptomatic or threshold question "sounding out" a host of historical, philosophical, and ethical issues. One corollary, and to me an important one, is a demonstration that thinking about and through musical questions is not just a specialist interest, but a way of thinking about and through fundamental questions of knowledge, culture, and value. The point of this chapter is not whether to prefer Schoenberg or Shostakovich, modernist heroics or postmodernist pastiche, the classical canon or a wide-open world of plural musics, but to open the question of what we do when we ground any work of music, or for that matter anything else, in the transcendental subjectivity postulated by the ideal of originality and the associated concepts of genius, voice, and artistic integrity.

This ideal is protean, and once produced on the historical stage it comes back in new guises as rapidly as it disappears in old ones. It is, for example, now widely felt that the heyday of the original artist-genius is over. As Michael Lind put it in an essay in the *New York Times Book Review*, "For the

better part of two centuries, the artist stepped into the roles made available
after revolutions stripped the aristocracy and the clergy of legitimacy. Our
aristocracy today is made up of movie stars and pop musicians, not classical
music composers and conductors. Our clerisy contains journalists and pun-
dits and think-tank experts and political historians, but not novelists or
poets."[2] But Lind's rhetorical choices say more than they mean to: the
celebrity and the expert do not replace the figure of the charismatic artist but
reincarnate it. And their aura sometimes seems just as inescapable, just as
much a sticky web that clings more tightly the more one tries to remove it,
as that of the charismatic heads of state who, in a part of the story Lind leaves
out, also stepped into the post-Enlightenment power vacuum. The reflections gathered in this chapter take off from a particular modernist myth that
may now be "over" in its most literal form, though its residual power and
sub rosa returns should not be underestimated. But they are meant to move
in an outward spiral—percephonically, in the nonce-phrase of chapter 8—to
take in basic questions about changing social-cultural forms and valuations
hidden in plain sight behind the apparatus of artistic authority.

Starting Over. A revenant is a specter, a ghost, a phantom, one who haunts,
who returns, who walks again. Such visitants may be ghastly, of course, but
they may also be genial, beguiling, seductive; the only things they all have
in common are an aura of ambivalence and an attraction to lack. The
revenant appears to point at a known lack or point out one unknown. It
embodies a condition of loss, self-division, or desire that it may both worsen
and alleviate, invest with either regret or acceptance. Tropes or spirits of the
dormer glass, revenants are peculiar mixtures: both elusive and insistent,
misplaced in time and right on time, inevitable creatures of chance.
Consider, for example,

It's a question of genealogy in reverse, legacies willed by the heirs rather
than the bequeathers, the use and abuse of the past. It's a question

the *Goldberg Variations* of J. S. Bach. Writers on this work tend to be deeply
impressed by its close, which, after nearly an hour of music, reprises the aria
on which the variations are based. The effect, for many, is as if Bach had
revealed the aesthetic equivalent of a sacred truth. The classic statement is
by Donald Tovey:

The Aria returns in its original shape, with a strangely new and yet familiar effect. Its numberless trills and graces no longer seem curious and posing, and its harmonies are now revealed as what they really are, the support of the whole mighty design, not merely the bass of a delicately-ornamented sarabande. As the Aria gathers up its rhythms into the broad passage . . . with which it ends, we realize that beneath its slight exterior the great qualities of the variations lie concealed, but living and awake; and in the moment that we realize this the work is over.[3]

As someone who has always enjoyed the aria in its own right—better, even, than some of the variations—I take a certain pleasure in shredding the rhetoric of this passage: in suggesting that the aria is only curious and posing for someone who needs a mighty design to redeem it from that condition, that the breathless admiration of monumentality is tinged by authority worship and the correlative dismissal of lightness, delicacy, and ornament by a dread of effeminacy, and that the language of revelation belongs to a modernist religion of art that Bach himself would have abhorred. My deeper interest, however, is drawn by the strain placed on these values by unacknowledged strains within the rhetoric itself.

By calling the effect of the reprise "strangely new and yet familiar," Tovey acknowledges that this effect is initially disorienting, somehow in excess of the manifest intention to frame the set of variations. The subsequent image of a mighty design revealed serves to set things straight; the aesthetics of design contains the unaccountable dynamics of return. Gradually we realize that beneath the slight exterior there lie great qualities, which is to say, the qualities of greatness. The moment of realization, however, is postponed until the last moment of the piece, which itself turns out to repeat, in more rarefied form, the interplay of disorientation and containment produced by the reprise of the aria. Disorientation returns in the seemingly gratuitous irony by which the music ends at the very moment of revelation. Yet this irony restores the very balance that it disturbs; it elevates the material return of the aria into the manifestation of an ideal aesthetic form, something reassuring precisely in being impalpable. All of this goes forward in Tovey's text—and perhaps in Bach's music— with a stately eloquence that masks the tensions being negotiated. The turns from unaccountable disorientation to aesthetic containment are made to seem so natural that they can hardly be recognized. But what would happen if, having recognized them after all, we decided to do without them?

The reprise of the aria is literal, and its literalism suggests something more boxy than organic. Its neat, perhaps overanxious orderliness can be taken to pose the question of whether the theme is the true source of the mighty design or merely the pretext for a musical abundance that may or may not be contained by that design, or any other. The design itself, driven by a series of canons, is conspicuous, even pedantic. But in what sense does the aria contain a canon in embryo, let alone a whole canonic matrix, let alone the other variations placed within the matrix? Does a mass of traces from the aria, or rather from its bass line, really constitute a relationship of coming-from? Can't a group of fundamentally different pieces have much the same bass line? And isn't it possible that the variations too fully negate the expressive values of the theme in the course of appropriating its bass, and that this negation is cause for regret? Is that why the variation process actually concludes with a pastiche of popular tunes, as if it were trying to anchor itself in the convivial uses of music? Has the process produced a gap which the theme returns to bridge?

Perhaps what Bach has discovered here is not the divine circle of musical unity but the compulsive recurrence of the musical revenant. That would help explain the curious and certainly inadvertent coincidence of Tovey's description of the effect of the reprise and Freud's famous definition of the uncanny as something strangely new and yet familiar: familiar because long established in the mind and yet estranged by the process of repression.[4]

Revenants. In 1806, Beethoven composed a set of thirty-two variations in C minor, which he published the following year but later declined to honor with an Opus number. In fact, it's said that when he heard the music performed some time after its publication, he failed to recognize it. Perhaps this is because the piece, which revives a baroque variation form, the passacaglia, struck him as a ghostly reminiscence of Bach, whose keyboard music he knew well. The number 32 is particularly significant in relation to the *Goldberg Variations*, which Beethoven's twelve concentrated minutes of music neither emulates nor seeks to rival, but in some sense reanimates. (Or not: the variations are so minuscule, so fleeting, that they never become fully animate, or only mimic animation, like little clockwork figures of another age.) By taking this path, Beethoven's piece frees itself from any supposed anxiety of influence. It can work on a small scale and do whatever it likes. It does not even have to remain Beethoven's own. That's how you recognize a revenant: it takes the privilege of a ghost and does whatever it likes. It follows a body of rules, no doubt, but not the rules of those from whom it derives or to whom it appears.

Revenants do not have to worry about originality. What they bring is not difference, but that estrangement within sameness by which sameness becomes compelling. Not difference, but what Derrida named *différance*, the continuous distinction and deferral of the same from itself.[5] Musical

revenants throw into question the romantic and modernist ideal of originality. They suggest that there is no need to seek difference from the past
because that difference is always already present, in the present. The sameness of the revenant is the form in which that difference is overcome, the
form in which the past lives on—but not as it was, not exactly. The same
returns in order to live on—differently.

Pleintes d'un Troubadour. But it is not by accident that I am writing about
ghosts. The living on I spoke of, at its outer limit, occurs in the closest proximity to death. Perhaps this is because death above all is what mandates living on, what necessitates it: if the same were not fated to disappear, to be
absent not from one place but from every place, there would be no need to
demand the return of the same to its own place, no need to piece together
the traces of the same like Isis patching together the bits and pieces of the
dismembered and disseminated Osiris.

The first composer to realize this fully was probably Schubert, whose
revenants, snatches of song transplanted to instrumental works, are all
imbued with the melancholy of absent voice and nearly all topically laden
with themes of loss: a beautiful world now vanished; the solitude of a wanderer for whom the world has no beauty left; the meeting of Death and the
Maiden.[6] These revenants seem to summon up a melancholy latent in all
forms of citation, even self-citation, and at the same time seek to temper
that melancholy with the warmth of its relationship to subjectivity, of
which the revenant in the Romantic era is a familiar image.

The slow movement of the String Quartet "Death and the Maiden"
(1824–26, D. 810) is a set of variations on a melodic revenant, Death's theme
from Schubert's own earlier setting of a Matthias Claudius poem (1817,
D. 531) in which the doomed maiden's fears are set to rest by Death himself
in the guise of a comforter/bridegroom/father. The quartet's outer movements are full of a turmoil suggesting mortal terror in excess of anything con-
ceivable in the song. The trio of the third movement, in D major, forms a
romance interlude, but its dream of life is crushed between two statements of
a very violent D-minor scherzo. To the extent that the terror has a counter-
weight, it appears during the variations movement, a kind of Isis fantasy based
on continual changeovers from minor to major. The spectral theme plus variations 1, 2, and 5 begin in minor and end in major; this pattern repeats itself
at a higher level between variation 3, all minor, and 4, all major. The returns
of the theme within this pattern, revenants of a revenant, are as much irradi-
ant as they are spectral, or rather they become so each time the music turns

from minor to major, as if the unrepresented voice of the Maiden, whose stilling the theme in the song both imposed and consoled, were taking on a new, uncanny life. Only at the end does this fantasy prove too ungrounded to sustain; the final variation and coda grow equivocal, wraithlike, even bleak, despite the major close of the one and the major mode of the other.

This ending casts a retrospective pall over the whole movement, which in turn seems doomed from the start. As noted in chapter 7, Jane Campion's film version of Henry James's *Portrait of a Lady* uses excerpts from this movement to evoke the fatality by which the heroine Isabel Archer's desire pursues its own death and symbolically drains her of life. The film ends with Isabel's solitary passage through in a bleak snowscape, turning her story into a revenant for another Schubertian paradigm, a *Winterreise*.

The revenant's tale in Schubert's late E♭ Piano Trio (1828, D. 929) ends with a spirit less severe, more autumnal than wintry. (I have written elsewhere about this music, in an essay entitled "Revenants"; the text you are reading now may be taken as a double of that other one, an image in one of the wings of the dormer glass.)[7] This visitation is both doubled and redoubled: the dirge-like main theme of the second movement, sung by the cello, incorporates bits and pieces of the Swedish folksong "The Setting Sun"; the same theme returns both to interrupt the lighthearted course of the finale and to conclude it. Here, though, a new piano accompaniment exchanges the funereal for the ethereal and transforms the theme, sung just the same as before, from a threnody into a ballad, its melancholy made half pleasing by a fusion between the over-closeness of the uncanny and the distance of nostalgia. Like the theme (re)cited and varied in the "Death and the Maiden" Quartet, this song is haunting, but it suffers no retrospective chill. On the contrary, it regains traces of its "timeless" folk origins that were missing in its first apparition. The revenant returns to live on—differently.

—no, not a question, a stake: something at risk, ventured or invested, the marker of a boundary or claim, a post at which to burn, a heart-piercing weapon.

The stake is cultural memory, something the ideal of originality effaces and supplants. This process dates from the mid-eighteenth century, when the work expected of the artist began to change from imitation and emulation to original creation. The artist as original genius siphons off collective memory into his own charisma. In its later combination with modern communications media, this charismatic channeling of cultural authority would create the star system, the world of the celebrity idol whose singular presence masks a silent host of persons and technologies engaged in its production. As chapter 4 noted with respect to Liszt, nineteenth-century creative artists were the first beneficiaries of this system, which has since, as Michael Lind says, put them in the shadow of pop singers, movie actors, and sports heroes. (It is no accident that the Orpheus and Eurydice of Salman Rushdie's *The Ground beneath Her Feet,* noted in chapter 8, are rock stars.) The charisma-bearers function both to inspire and to intimidate the normative subject of culture—a subject meant to be authenticated by having its own measure of charisma and originality, but not in large doses. The stars absorb the excess and display it in the form of public pleasure and suffering.

As original genius, the figure of the artist has acted historically, and in high-culture venues still acts, like an elevated version of the doorkeeper in Kafka's famous parable of the Law.[8] A man who seeks admission to the Law repeatedly fails to get the doorkeeper's permission to enter. He remains outside though the door is open and the keeper does nothing to obstruct him. Years go by; finally, just before the man dies, he is told that the entryway has been reserved all along for him alone, but that the doorkeeper (who makes this revelation) is now going to shut it. The man's illusion is that the Law is independent of both his will to uphold it and his desire to please its official guardian, beneath which lies a failure to recognize that these motives are actually in conflict. The corresponding aesthetic illusion is that cultural memory is independent of both one's will to preserve it and one's desire to idolize—symbolically speaking, to please—its official embodiments, together with the failure to recognize that these motives, too, are in conflict. The desire, in both cases, blinds the will. Whoever seeks entrance to the Law, which is also cultural memory—at this point there's no telling them apart—confuses the authority of the goal with the ability to persuade the doorkeeper, and even more to persuade oneself, that one is the right kind of person to enter, that one's identity is not so impoverished or so alien (the man in Kafka's parable is from the country, a metaphysical bumpkin) that one has no right to enter. The only way out of this dilemma is to realize that the doorkeepers do not derive their power of intimidation from the Law or cultural memory, but the reverse. You can be yourself and pass right by these phantasms and not come to any harm. *After*

The End of the Origin. I would like to bury the concept of a constitutive originality, an originality synonymous with seriousness and "greatness" in art. If I could have my way, I would bury it so deep it could never return. Revenants are not original; let's not have originality as a revenant. We do not need more tales from this crypt. Originality in this sense is based on a conception of sovereign, self-possessed subjectivity that is no longer viable, no longer even appealing to those of us tired of its cultic aspect, its encrypted version of unquestionable sociopolitical authority. This original-ity condemns us to valorizing tawdry Oedipal scenarios of rivalry and sym-bolic parricide.[9] And it conduces, has for a long time conduced in the world of art music, to a suicidal reduction in the audience for new composition. The public, the so easily vilified bourgeois public, is excluded from listening by a cult of enhanced difficulty and esoteric order.

This claim is likely to incur strenuous denials, so it is worth illustrating with an anecdote. Charles Rosen tells the story as part of an article written in defense of difficult musical modernisms:

> Nothing is more comic than the resentment of contemporary art, the self-righteous indignation aroused by its difficulty. I remember once being invited to lecture in Cincinnati on the music of Pierre Boulez and Elliott Carter. In the question period afterward, a woman posed what she evidently conceived not as a question but as an aggressive and defi-ant challenge: "Mr. Rosen, don't you think the composer has a respon-sibility to write music that the public can understand?" On such occasions I normally reply politely to all questions, no matter how foolish, but this time I answered that the question did not seem to me interesting but that the obvious resentment that inspired it was very significant indeed.[10]

I agree with Rosen that the questioner's resentment is significant. But even more significant, I would say, is the staggering condescension with which he treats it. Even though the woman's question cannot have the simple answer she clearly wants, the question itself is not prima facie foolish. And what is so contemptible about the desire to *feel addressed* by new music? Isn't the position of addressee precisely the one that Rosen is reserving for knowl-edgeable lovers of Boulez and Carter?

Admittedly, the impulse behind the cult of exclusion is understandable. Modernist aesthetics is based in part on a justifiable repulsion from the power of mass culture to appropriate cultural forms in the service of pro-ducing inflated commodity values for everything on its market—and everything *is* on its market.[11] The cultic solution, however, is as literal-minded as mass culture at its worst is purely figurative. There is little point in resisting commodification by producing things that no one desires. A less Draconian choice, literally a more aesthetic choice because a more pleasurable one, would be to look for ways to frame, to present, to experience desirable things in excess of their commodity value. Resistance neither requires nor implies an impossible place beyond the system of economic and symbolic exchange; it is always already built into the system itself. Consider, for example, the case of

The Emperor's New Clothes. I'm picking up a remainder from chapter 10, Arnold Schoenberg's arrangement of Johann Strauss's "The Emperor Waltz" for string quartet, flute, clarinet, and piano. The arrangement, as we saw, is like an X ray of the "original" music, which is also to say that it is like an X ray of originality in music. (Schoenberg probably wouldn't have wanted this second exposure; he sought above all to be original, a musical Moses. But the Moses of his own unfinished opera and self-portrait, *Moses und Aron*, expresses himself only in *Sprechstimme*, the alienated modernist version of recitative. He cannot sing.) In Schoenberg's arrangement, the silken homogeneity of Strauss's orchestration breaks down into a nubby diversity, something rigorous and effortful and individualistic; Strauss's refined sensuality becomes intellectual, his sophisticated self-possession turns into self-consciousness.

How, then, are we to hear this arrangement—which, it has been my experience repeatedly, audiences like very much, as they do not very much like Schoenberg's "own" pieces? Should we hear it as proposed before, as a laying-bare of the productive mechanisms that give the illusion of effortless luster in Strauss's original, the hard technique that supports the artifice of social ease? Or should we, rather, take the Schoenberg as a reassurance that our slightly guilty pleasure in the Strauss (just entertainment music for the well-off, after all) is esthetically well founded, since we can now hear in clarity what we must only intuit in the original orchestration, namely that the "Emperor Waltz" actually forms an organic work of art, that all its elements are mutually implicative, that it grows generatively out of pregnant musical motives? Or, again, should we take Schoenberg's version as a historical expression of nostalgia, an acknowledgment of loss: a recognition that for a modern listener, the only legitimate "Emperor Waltz" is the X-rayed one, its sensuousness and social cohesiveness available only in the alienated form of disassembled counterpoint, fragmented effect, the shape of the bone rather than the sheen of the flesh? In that way Schoenberg would be able to write a piece that acknowledges modern alienation without forfeiting musical pleasure—or rather, without demanding that his audiences forfeit what most of them still think of as musical pleasure. He would be able to do what he elsewhere could do so rarely, despite his obvious genius: he could write music that people like.

The high-modernist ideal of originality is directly at risk here: the notion that to be "absolutely modern" one must be difficult, off-putting, esoteric, and thus incorruptible in one's resistance to the blandishments and debasements of modern life. Schoenberg staked most of his career on this ascetic ideal, which has endeared him to a small band of mostly academic admirers, but to almost no one else. Still, the tendency to define authentic modernity with a repudiation of pleasure (or, worse, with a second-order pleasure in contemplating that repudiation) was too much even for him. His "Emperor Waltz" was composed in 1925, after four years spent working on the twelve-tone system by which he hoped to restore a musical order he felt had been shattered, not least by himself. His reversion to Strauss (whose original "Emperor Waltz" was then only thirty-six years old) comes almost as a sigh of relief. Unlike Schoenberg's slightly earlier arrangement of "Roses from the South," composed for a fundraising event, the "Emperor Waltz" is an "autonomous" composition. It is as much a bouquet to a lost world as the *Rosenkavalier* of another Strauss, though it is also a bouquet of dried flowers, as befits one gathered after the great caesura of the World War. (When Ravel wrote "La Valse" a few years later, the bouquet had become a mockery.) Still, dried flowers make nice arrangements—and they last. Could it be, then, that this arrangement, this revoicing of another man's notes, is Schoenberg's most profound piece, his most lighthearted and most serious, his most enjoyable and most—original?[12]

"Revenants." One August morning a few years ago, I went to the piano directly after waking and began to compose a set of variations entitled—I knew this right off—*Revenants.* The title suggested the variation process as a musical image of a procession of revenants, "A second-sight procession, such as glides/Over still mountains, or appears in dreams,"[13] and as the variations accumulate they seek to build up that image. (I have no interest in the paranormal but can easily be fascinated by figurative hauntings. "Revenants" was partly inspired by an image from Carl Dreyer's classic silent movie, *Vampyr:* a band of shadows whirling in a dance, but with no dancers to cast the shadows. I have always associated the image with the fantasmic "imperial palace about the year 1855" that Ravel depicted in "La Valse": a scene in which "from time to time, through rifts in turbulent clouds, waltzing couples can be glimpsed."[14] The rifts in the clouds suggest tears in the swirling fabric of time itself.) The music tries to sound like

something you must have heard before but can't quite place. The underlying pattern of notes is not a melody, though it sounds in the melodic line and is easy to hear; nor is it motivic, though it breaks up easily enough into bits that sound like motives. It is just what I called it, a pattern of notes. It sounds the way a piece of paper looks after it has been folded in two, had curves and triangles cut out at various points along the fold, and been unfolded again. This pattern recurs in most of the variations, now in strong profile, now in shadow, amid stylistic "bendings" or allusions that invite an awareness of past musics. The variations inhabit a variety of different sound worlds, some readily locatable on the time chart of musical history, some less so. What varies is not so much the pattern of notes but its idiom, its dialect, its accent. What returns is not just the past within the music but the past of music.

My piece, however, also had a subtitle: *32 Variations in C Minor*. The piece was not only about revenants, it was a revenant itself, a reanimation of Beethoven's variations in key, scope, size, mood, and shape. How postmodern of me to rifle the past so shamelessly! Even if the past I was rifling was canonical, Eurocentric, masculinist, and metaphysical. What was I thinking of? Beethoven, of course, has always haunted other composers; it's one of the things he does best. Being successfully haunted by Beethoven is even something of an accomplishment. Not that my piece sounds like Beethoven—would that even be possible at this date except as parody?—but it's obvious that he's there in spirit. And because the chain of revenants is endless, because even the "original" of a revenant may be a revenant itself, behind both Beethoven's piece and mine hovers the ghost of Bach's, which my set resembles in its frequent use of canons, melodies that return like revenants to nip at their own heels. (Besides, look at the company I get to keep: the guest list reads Bach, Beethoven, and—who? "Just reeling off their names," wrote W. H. Auden, "is ever so comfy.")[15] Still, in the age of multimusics from Cage to Coleman, Reich to rap, on the very eve of the new millennium, could one still write like this?

Well: in an age when movie companies spend small fortunes to create meticulous simulacra of Jane Austen's England, when the first word that comes to mind in connection with "reality" is "virtual," why not? Why not write a piece that is neither original nor unoriginal, but simply indifferent to originality as a value? The idea would be to occupy an intermediate zone between the equally dubious categories of "original work" and "pastiche," and in so doing to acknowledge as fully as possible the network of dependencies and alliances that both categories necessarily dissemble. The state of mind involved would be good to imagine, even if the piece itself were not good.

A computer realization of "Revenants" can be heard on the CD included with this book. The sonoric image is the right one, askew in an acoustic dormer mirror. Although as a practical matter the piece is "for" piano, the faux-piano version is in a sense the more authentic because of its alienation from the sonority usually associated with this kind of music. What the CD presents is not a piano piece called "Revenants" but a revenant by that name, the ghost of a piano piece in a machine.[16]

The Origin of the End. As is well known, the cult of originality, which is also the cult of technical innovation, reached its apogee in the era of figures like Schoenberg, Joyce, and Picasso, an era that tended to identify modernist esthetics with a quasi-heroic, quasi-hieratic ethics. In music this era was carried forward after the Second World War by the rise of the academic avant garde. The result was what Susan McClary has called "terminal prestige" in the sense of terminal illness; music written to this order reaches its appointed terminus in an arcane hinterland, and is there terminated.[17] More recently, many composers have taken to writing more "accessibly," most familiarly in minimalist and neo-romantic styles, but their efforts may have come too late. The aesthetics of modernism are still being used to characterize and evaluate compositions that no longer conform to those aesthetics. This process is in many cases internal to the music itself, which often uses technically inflated means to reach the end of listenability. Like rock songs, postmodernist concert pieces often find complex ways to sound simple; unlike rock songs, they make a point of showing it. The result of this residual modernism is that audiences still cannot hear the music, no matter how eager it is to be heard. What they hear is the apparatus: is modernism. There is little value in changing the picture without also changing the frame. But that change, too, may come too late. The thought is unpleasant, worthy of the people whom the musical mentors of my youth taught me to think of as the enemies of progress, but it may nonetheless be true that high modernism was the death knell of classical music.[18]

all my ancestors when B. (either B.) wrote his so-compelling set of variations were forcibly unassimilated Jews herded into the Pale between Kiev and Odessa, bones stuck in the throat of European Russia. The only music they knew was davening and cantillation. What did they have to do with the highfalutin' or even workaday musical life, the churches and salons, klaviers and hammerklaviers, of Leipzig or Vienna? (Some—not all—

made it outside the Pale during the mid-nineteenth century, converted pro forma to Christianity, and entered professions. Some—not all—were eventually herded back; some kept moving westward until they reached New York. Legend has it that a later precursor came to America in disgrace after sharing in the defeat of the Russian navy in the Russo-Japanese war. His wife was said to have smuggled jewels out in her vagina. Legend has it that another crisscrossed America in freight cars raising money for Leon Trotsky and was murdered in Jerusalem on the same day Trotsky was assassinated in Mexico.) Once set up in America, my forebears listened to swing bands and borscht belt Heldentenors; I heard not a note of Beethoven—never heard of Beethoven, period—until I was fifteen. Ah, but

The End of Influence. Decline, destruction, drowning; a ruin going to earth, a celestial body passing below the horizon: all are embraced by the German word *Untergang,* which Nietzsche's Zarathustra invokes as the motto of human self-overcoming. I like the image in this context: originality "going under" so that something better can come up.[19]

But if originality goes under, it will, it should, take influence along with it. Like originality, its sibling, influence is an ideologically charged concept, successful to the degree that its ideology is invisible. Traditionally thought of as a failure of individuation, a form of imitation that does not differ enough from its model, influence has more recently been thought of as a struggle for priority, in which guise it has been, well, influential in musicological circles. In either version, the concept of influence presupposes that the artist must be a certain kind of autonomous subject, a subject authentic to the degree that it resists the subjectivity of others. In the climate of postmodernism, we can surely at least surmise that both influence and the subject it enjoins on us are fictions, created partly by critical understanding, partly by works of art, and partly by the correlative fiction that art takes the form of quasi-autonomous "works." The process of exhibiting and escaping influence is a major means by which the modern artwork situates itself or is critically situated as the expression of a master-subject in relation to transcendental objects. The artist's precursor is not a person but a trope that guarantees personhood. The great myth of originality requires the continual possibility of unoriginality in order to flourish.

The fiction of influence becomes the vehicle of that possibility by exaggerating the latent melancholy of citation and casting intertextuality, the very condition of possibility for representation and expression, as a kind of affliction. The results play themselves out in two broad scenarios, spun from two tropes, that may seem antithetical but are at bottom the same, differing only in where they locate a certain inferiority.

One scenario produces influence as a by-product of canon-formation; only "major" figures are understood, that is, appointed, to wield it, to inspire an imitation that they also forbid. Though Beethoven may sometimes have sounded like Clementi, or Chopin like Kalkbrenner, the resemblance, if noted at all, is used only to mark the superiority of the great composers over their models. But to have sounded like Beethoven or Chopin, even for Chopin to have sounded like Beethoven, is to have been an epigone. In some circumstances, even *not* sounding like Beethoven can mark a subjective default; hence Slavoj Žižek, in a weak moment, can repeat with assurance the sub-Wagnerian bromide that the beginning of Mendelssohn's Violin Concerto "marks a clear melodic regression with respect to Beethoven's violin concerto."[20]

This remark offers a transition to the second scenario, which shifts the burden of unachieved subjectivity from the receiver of influence to its transmitter. Here one is supposed to detect illegitimate influence in supposedly glib, unoriginal, meretricious works, interlopers in the canon that succeed by virtue of their very shallowness. The results can be ugly: for Wagner to brand Mendelssohn as the exemplar of a "Judaism in music" that threatens (but by threatening covertly guarantees) the universal validity of German genius, it was necessary only to brand Mendelssohn's music as cleverly imitative, and therefore as all too likely to be imitated: a bad influence.[21]

D. S. C. H. In Shostakovich's Third String Quartet, composed in the aftermath of Russia's Pyrrhic victory in the Second World War, the penultimate movement (the fourth) is a keen lament, almost a ritual keening, plainly a mourning song for the countless million Russians whose death made even "Pyrrhic" too gaudy a term to couple with "victory." (In Shostakovich's autograph it carries the title "Homage to the Dead.")[22] The movement comes to no conclusion. Instead a meandering transitional passage carries it into what soon comes to sound like a common or garden variety finale, faintly folksy, faintly sardonic: nothing special. The ordinariness is intolerable in this context. Its appearance imputes bad faith to the very concept of the ordinary and at the same time gives cause to question whether an apparently extraordinary finale would be any better. Midway through the actual finale, following a sudden wave of intensity, a gap tears open and the mourning song breaks out anew, a double of itself at double its "original" intensity. Unlike Schubert's threnody, Shostakovich's does not flicker or shimmer when it returns; it burns.

The re-arisen lament finally exhausts itself in a series of quasi-vocal cries, broken by silences, on the unaccompanied cello, the last of them a drawn-out, fading moan. It would seem crass, even indecent, to go on from this point. When the finale tries to do so anyway, it sounds like a revenant itself, washed out, empty; before long it ebbs away, subsides into its own impotence. What lives on, what has returned to live on, is only the lament. The dead return—not survive, but return—in the return of the mourning revenant. Forlorn though it is, this revenant is welcome. It must be made welcome.

what a note changed all that! A note of liberation, anthem of joyful defiance: by sheerest contingency it was Beethoven's Egmont Overture, *that great galumphing paean to political liberty, to choosing a destiny and living it out to the last breath, breathless with having been there, triumphant in having run the course. I found this treasure on a scratchy LP my mother brought home from the supermarket, they had a special on culture with the groceries, only, excuse us, the piece is a little long, we've cut out a lyrical passage for woodwinds exchanging a tune in unforced amity, you'll never miss it, but I did miss it, even knowing nothing of it, and now the passage always sounds like the mending of a broken promise. What I heard became the listener, assumed new form, new life, in the listening, which was palpably mine, all mine, but only because the music was so palpably not mine, something I could only make mine by letting it remake me a little and living with the difference. So it's a question after all:*

Danse macabre. On the imaginary horizon of music history there flits, to the one who knows how to eye it rightly askance, a procession of specters like the enchained silhouettes composing a dance of death, hands joined as they follow the king of shadows—who, unlike Death in the famous image from Ingmar Bergman's *The Seventh Seal* that is reanimated in this sentence, turns out to be a fiddler. The spooky, mock-lyrical second movement of Mahler's Fourth Symphony lets you hear him playing—*Freund Hein spielt auf,* Mahler explains—his instrument mistuned to give the impression of a cheap country fiddle, of death as a counterfeit of life. Sometimes this shadowy figure of death seems to wear the features of Bach or, especially, Beethoven, but more often it has no features at all, being a trope for the curiously memorial function of all composed, all written music, the mere performance of which according to the score constitutes an attempt to reanimate something always already fleeting, disappearing, lost, dead. All such music is memorial; all such music is necromantic. Even where it mourns, it forms an attempt to transcend or undo mourning.

One impetus behind specific, self-identified musical revenants, figures of nameable return, an impetus in excess of all concrete musical meanings, is to make audible the general scheme whereby music, precisely insofar as it is not original, reanimates the dead: music as magic, animal magnetism, healing touch, resurrection, life-support technology. But since we don't believe—of course we don't; never mind the New Age section at Barnes and Noble, the whole premise of the post-Enlightenment culture in which these phenomena take place and on which they are premised is that we don't believe, that no one right in the head could believe—since we don't believe that the dead return, that the past returns, we need to theorize this impetus in less credulous terms. We need to treat of these things rationally, if for no other reason than to give ourselves a good cover for an irrationalism that we will not, because we cannot, let go.

Considered apart, then, from its particular ghostly determinants, the musical revenant is an instance of what can be called, in Derridean style, the general process of citation, the (re)iteration of a statement, a gesture, a figure, an expression, in a new context. Citation is a process that both preserves sameness and, by relocating it, undoes sameness.[23] What Derrida might call the metaphysics of art would mandate that citation be concealed, denied, or repressed by the artwork. The deepest convention is the forgetting of convention, the willing suspension, not of disbelief, but of familiarity. Some expressive forms, however, including the musical revenant, take the opposite tack. They display citation, stage it and mirror it, unfurl and unveil it, let it imitate its former incarnations as a mime imitates events that have never occurred.[24] (My "Revenants" mean to do that: to form a procession most of whose members are mime variations, simulations of recognizable but nonexistent originals, true, each of this kind, to a model it does not have.)

Philosopher's Tone. When do we judge an expression to be original? One answer may be suggested by the Wittgensteinian notion of the language game, a figure for the enabling and prohibiting effects of discrete, small-scale language systems on particular speech acts.[25] Important here is the practical fact that the rules of a language game tend to go without saying until something throws them into doubt. A sentence like "It's raining" falls well within a language game known by anyone able to read this text; we do not need to ask what kind of a subject would utter it. In contrast, a sentence like "I have my right hand today but I don't remember whether I had it yesterday" is either nonsensical or pathological; the game does not allow for a kind of subject who would utter it. Some sentences, however, fall neither clearly within the rules of the game nor clearly outside them. Confronted, say, with an utterance like "Thou still unravished bride of quietness, / Thou foster-child of silence and slow time," we are constrained to ask what kind of a subject would utter it.[26] We are, to go further, constrained to construct a subjectivity for such a subject, and for ourselves insofar as we can communicate or identify with that subject. Originality is one of the concepts in which such constructed subjectivities have commonly been grounded. It is an appearance, a prop or stage set, by means of which the indeterminacy that compels the act of construction is disavowed.

Originality is thus the reified, positive form of the break in sense that the indeterminate utterance produces. Just a few such utterances scattered across a text suffice to pose the question of the subject. Some artistic traditions—high modernism, for example—have demanded more than just a few. Either way, the break in sense must be closed so that the game can continue: that, too, is one of the rules. That does not mean, of course, that the break necessarily produces anxiety or vertigo. We may even court it. The rhythm of break and closure often gives pleasure. But in general this pleasure has tended to depend on the tether of closure; the break tosses us into space, into a free fall of unmeaning, unreason, transgression, thrill, but not for too long. Our fall is protected, like a bungee-jumper's, by a long cord.

It may be, of course, that a self-contained, originary subjectivity is indeed the source of "original," that is, indeterminate utterances. The existence of the utterance, however, is not itself evidence for the existence of the subject. What clearly exists is the process of construction, the possibility of which is intrinsic to every language game. The rest is an act of faith, a Kantian leap into the freedom of the noumenal world.

During the nineteenth century, the originality posited in that leap took music, or rather a certain concept of music, as its paramount medium. The process involved at least two different domains of subjectivity. On the one hand, purely instrumental music, untexted and without representational content, was understood to have installed a break in sense not in a single language game, but in the game of language in general. The result for some listeners, Hegel notably among them, was something very much like anxiety or vertigo; as indeterminate utterance, purely instrumental music had plenty of detractors.[27] As a discourse without speech, such music emanated from a subjectivity without borders. It could be understood in radically opposed terms: either as an exercise in technique that tended to empty itself of spirit or as the gateway through which the self-positing noumenal subject enters historical time. As the aesthetician Theodore Vischer put the paradox in 1857, "[Music] is the richest art: it expresses inmost things, utters the unutterable; yet it is the poorest art, [it] says nothing."[28] Perhaps in order to fend off the charge of emptiness, instrumental music recognized a need to appropriate its technique to the service of noumenal expression. A requirement was widely accepted: such music had to testify at every moment to its own originality. In practical terms, this meant that the music could contain none of the conventionalized "filler" common in earlier eras.[29] The result was to raise the technical stakes in composition, and to keep on raising them, a process that would lead in the twentieth century to the identification of musical originality with technical innovation.

On the other hand, and perhaps as a means of deflecting the anxiety and vertigo that could always ripple through a borderless subjectivity, musical originality in the nineteenth century came to be vested in the figure of the great composer, in the first instance Beethoven. And here, perhaps, the break in sense hovers precariously between something experienced and something imposed. The rules of music games tend to be even fuzzier than those of language games; it is not always clear when a musical utterance is indeterminate. Take the first movement of the "Moonlight" Sonata, for example: as we saw in chapter 2, it's an example par excellence of what I have elsewhere called a musical "subject image," an expressive kernel about which a certain subjectivity, here dreamy, romantic, erotic, profound, mysterious, has repeatedly been constructed.[30] But as we also saw in chapter 2, this construction has a complex cultural history and is largely ex post facto. The depth of subjectivity so often ascribed to this music is not required to make sense of it; Beethoven himself offered an alternative with the label "quasi una fantasia," where the fantasy is a musical, not a psychological form. (But just try to keep the two apart.) The fantasy genre carries with it a model of subjectivity involving the public display of musical invention based on familiar emotions spontaneously expressed. Yet something about this music, something perfectly obvious—perhaps its simple insistence, the studied monotony that links it to the "pathetic" mode of the sublime—chafes against the fantasy model, producing a break in sense that for generations of later listeners seemed to grow wider the more "moving" the music was found to be. The connections documented in chapter 2, that for a century or so grounded the music in narratives of sexual love mediated by the genius of the composer, made this break intelligible, bearable, pleasurable. Or did they, rather, produce the break in sense in order to remedy it, make the "Moonlight" Adagio more "original" that it claims to be in order to install the very effect of subjective depth with which the music now seems synonymous? The point of asking this question is to indicate that there is no way to answer it. Even if there were, it would not settle the question of whether the subject who "speaks" in this Adagio is familiar or uncanny, reasonable or excessive, intelligible or unfathomable.

Cenotaphs. Music often seems to seek or express the presence of a single originating voice, but this presence is always spectral no matter how real it may seem in the moment. The separation of musical utterance from any voice that might claim the utterance as its own is basic to many kinds of music qua music, and this to a degree that exceeds comparable separations in language.

In particular, melody has become the Western trope of self-expression par excellence. When played or, especially, sung "with feeling," a melody can seem to make another subjectivity nakedly present to the listener, who may respond with an equally immediate sense of involvement—absorbed, aroused, captivated, desirous. The self thus expressed may belong, or seem in the dormer mirrors of the musical moment to belong, to any or all of several persons: the composer, the performer, a dramatic character, someone for whom these figures come consciously or unconsciously to stand, or a nonspecific imaginary other who may envelop or supplant the rest, and who need not or cannot be explicitly recognized, localized, or identified.[31] Melody in these cases is a quasi-material medium of intimacy and, through intimacy, of contact with subjectivity as origin and truth. Yet melody, nonetheless, is grounded in the capacity to be reproduced without regard for individual subjects. Anyone can sing or play a tune; anyone can listen. When a melody becomes popular, everyone hums it, sings it, mangles it, varies it, covers it, cites it, hears it in the mind's ear and in various public spaces. No matter who its original audience may have been, it addresses itself to anyone within earshot; no matter how famous its composer may be, its origin becomes anonymous, or rather, it becomes omninonymous, it becomes everybody. "White Christmas" is no longer written by Irving Berlin. Thanks to the European Union, the "Ode to Joy" is no longer even by Beethoven.[32]

Certain snatches of poetry may achieve the same status, but the phenomenon is far more common in music. Derrida argues that sentences are characterized by a capacity to be understood afresh when repeated in a wide variety of contexts, but this notion—he calls it "iterability," which is first cousin to citationality[33]—applies equally to the most banal and the most poetic utterances, few of which, in any case, circulate with the kind of sustained vitality and self-renewing energy that are routine for famous tunes. One might say that linguistic iterability is a lesser form of a specifically musical capacity, or, alternatively, that musical iterability is the superlative degree of a linguistic capacity that mostly lacks the superlative degree. When someone composes a melody, his or her disappearance from the melody is always already invoked; it is, indeed, the very condition of possibility for melody, the condition that the melody arises, in part, to remedy. The melody arises where whatever subject enunciates it has departed, or may depart, or will have departed, and arises, moreover, imbued with both the pathos of this departure and its mitigation. Such pathos, the pathos of a half-open wound, is perhaps a primary part of what we feel when we find a melody "moving," or when even a playful or exciting melody seems to have something poignant about it, or at least to evoke a poignancy in us. Melody is therefore an essentially cenotaphic form, memorializing the absent dead—which may be one reason that melody is so readily associated with persons in musical theater or movies and so effectively evokes them in their absence from the scene, perhaps before they arrive, perhaps after they have died. At what seems a more clichéd level, this evocativeness may be involved when romantic lovers associate the history of their love with a melody: "our song." More soberly, the absence of self inscribed within melody may come to the fore in liturgical chant as a mark of spiritual power.

The voicing of a melody is never other than divided, its movement never other than a continuous flowing away from any possible origin. Melody is practical necromancy. It can come to life either as an extension or a surplus of the subjectivity of anyone in the community of listeners or performers, a fully present, deeply meaningful expression of feeling, a prosthetic sentience, or, on the contrary, as an automaton wandering within the subject, a simulacrum of feeling repeating itself with the meaninglessness of a talking doll. Melody is more "iterable" than the sentence because it does not mean but precedes meaning. It is the substrate or material form of a meaning immediately known, and therefore that which can either preserve the meaning as a precious object or annul it in an expressive taxidermy. Music means by many means—as process, action, behavior, usage, performance, narrativity, cultural trope, summons to subjectivity—but melody, the sine qua non of so many musics, constantly offers to rise above or sink below meaning, to enter an ideal plane of autonomy or ineffability, a wellspring of felt life, or an abyss or funerary space of life-less forms, a wax museum of the spirit. Coleridge perhaps testifies to this division at or of the origin when, elaborating on "Pindar's fine remark respecting the different effects of Music, on different characters, . . . [that] as many as are not delighted by it are disturbed, perplexed, irritated," he declares that "The beholder either recognizes it as a projected form of his own Being, that moves ahead of him with a Glory round its head, or recoils from it as from a Spectre."[34]

Explicit divided voicings offer to haunt the ear with these alternatives, to undo the seemingly natural relation of utterance to origin by producing a sonoric vision or visitation. We have encountered several in these pages.

When the finale of Michael Tippett's Third Symphony (chap. 9) begins with the *Schreckensfanfare* of Beethoven's Ninth, Tippett's music appears not to notice how startling the gesture is. When this music speaks in voices not its own, it does so with little or no sense of citational distance. The *Schreckensfanfare* will eventually precede each of the three sections of Tippett's finale, bringing with it a process that emulates, quotes, or alludes to Beethoven's movement at every turn, including the turn to the blues. One might almost think that the Ninth was the citing voice, not the cited one; "I can't reinvent the archetype" was Tippett's own comment.[35] The "non-original" voices of Tippett's finale thus form its very conditions of possibility. They act as what Slavoj Žižek calls "the little piece of the real" in which any imaginary or symbolic formation must anchor itself: something that seems found without having been sought, something met with involuntarily, of necessity, even though from a certain point of view it can only have been planted by design.[36]

When John Coltrane's "Summertime" (chap. 11) yields at its close to a "voice" more like Gershwin's than Coltrane's "own," at the same time bringing in a phrase of music so far suppressed, the listener cannot know who speaks more clearly: the revenant Gershwin or the Coltrane who has now reconciled with and absorbed him on the complex terrain of racial, national, and musical identities. Unlike Tippett, for whom quotation imposes itself as an origin, Coltrane searches for a way to reach it as an end.

When Steve Reich's *Different Trains* (chap. 8) incorporates both taped fragments of speech and their instrumentally realized "melodies," the peo-ple whose voices are on the tape have known identities; the listener has access to their names and something of their history. Yet the voices con-tinually escape this origin. As musical sounds they no longer speak "as" anyone in particular, and their instrumental doubles—revenants—can speak as anyone at all. As figures in a narrative these voices are caught up in a complex "train" of symbolic relationships. Even the testimony of holocaust survivors is generalized, depersonalized, as the work of memory ironically recapitulates the depersonalization of the speakers by their Nazi persecutors in the very process of bearing it witness.[37] Each voice becomes all voices—not as an abstract or sentimental testimony to common humanity, but as a force dispossessing the listener. These voices break the shell of subjectivity. They are not to be heard in the ear, but felt in the throat.

At successive points of historical self-reflection, often stung by injustice or worse, music willingly or willfully loses its voice.

the question of whether cultural memory has to travel in a direct line of descent from some identifiable origin—both the proponents and critics of specific traditions tend to share this view—or whether it travels, and survives, by continually falling into the hands of strangers, all of us being such strangers even when we most fervently think otherwise. Which might be condensed into a simpler, more direct question:

Replique. Many of those who love music can recall a moment of initiation after which nothing else is quite the same, an incident of listening that goes beyond the voluntary in which one first comes to espouse a certain sonorous world. Like any initiation, this one marks a transition in the subject's relation to culture, but it is important not to find a premature closure in it. Does the initiate enter a fixed and mysterious order, like Tamino and Pamina at the end of *The Magic Flute*? Or does the initiation reveal that the order one thought was one's own is different from anything one thought, part of a larger and stranger condition to which the initiatory experience can promise but not deliver entrance?

Both outcomes are obviously possible, but it may be that the former most often serves to screen or rationalize the latter. When George Eliot's Daniel Deronda is transfixed by the music in a Leipzig synagogue (chap. 3), the result is not his acquisition of the Jewish identity that in nineteenth-century terms is his by blood, but the beginning of a process of cultural and personal transformation that requires work, courage, and no small amount of sheer dumb luck, and that is far from complete when the novel ends. When W. E. B. Du Bois's John Jones is transfixed by the *Lohengrin* prelude (chap. 11), the result is not a synthesis of African- and European-derived identities, but a new sense of self for which no outward realization is possible. What John hears at the opera produces an ecstasy that crosses two kinds of social boundary, one musical, the other—as he inadvertently touches a white girl seated next to him—racial. The initiatory act of listening is countermanded by the taboo (and quickly punished) act of touch, an act that is at one level an accident, but at another the inescapable symbolic equivalent of the musical initiation. The two levels combine at the end of the story when John's consciousness floats serenely above the violence of his own lynching, buoyed by the imaginary sounds of the opera's unconsummated bridal scene.

Music in initiatory moments can acquire an ethical dimension by offering to chasten the arrogance of identity, both that of the initiate and that of the initiator. The moment of initiation has the capacity to break down the very illusions of identity as a prize and a possession that it may seem to support.

Sphinxes. The musical subject has a vivid personality but a nebulous identity. It can be endlessly impersonated but never identified with a person. It appears as a visitor or a visitant within anyone—listener, performer, composer, any or all—who adopts a subject position that some musical work or event can be felt to address, to uphold, to call forth. But any such position is a simulacrum, a reflection without an original, and the person who adopts it becomes for the time being a revenant in a dormer-glass relay. Music has no true first-person form.

The character of the musical subject throws light on the character of subjectivity in general precisely by this lack of the definite content and history usually felt to be necessary to subjectivity, and usually enshrined in musical aesthetics by identifying the musical subject with the historical subjectivity of the great musician, whether composer, performer, or both. Perhaps the most rewarding musical experiences arise when such identifications are cast off, regardless of what may be said about them afterwards. What matters in the musical subject is not its identification but its disposition, in all senses of the term: its tendency, arrangement, relatedness, position among a field of possibilities, all conditions that may express themselves in psychological, social, or cultural terms with a high degree of interchangeability. Subjectivity is defined by the historical possibilities and limits of such positionality in relation to other subjectivities. It is precisely this condition of incessant relatedness that gives subjectivity its density, vitality, and tangibility. And in music this condition appears—can appear, if only we let it—

in something like its own right, independent of the personifications that both realize and conceal it.

Citation for Originality. My title here plays on the multiple meaning of citation as a reference, an award, and the record of an infraction. Consider once more the sets of thirty-two variations by Bach and Beethoven to which these remarks of mine stand, in some sense, as a set of discursive variations. What actually occurs when each of these works cites or reanimates its antecedents? Bach's work is a strongly centripetal act of organization, a quasi-geometric structure that orders the full conspectus of baroque keyboard possibilities into a system. The music forms a kind of encyclopedia, an image of world order that is also the image of a learned book. Thus every third variation is a canon; every canon begins its imitative process at an interval one step or half step higher than the last. The profusion of expressive segments is, so to speak, always indexed; the ear always knows where it has been, where it is going, where to turn. Beethoven's piece is like a single page from the Bachian encyclopedia, a page that has been torn off and for which no context survives; it is a fragment of a world order that can be maintained only by implication, and only by an act of individual will. Beethoven's piece records the shift of position of the Bachian encyclopedia from an object of faith to an object of nostalgia or fantasy. Thus the piece is strangely self-divided, self-divided to make a hospitable place for the sense of strangeness. It is, on the one hand, as noted already, a passacaglia, an old form that, like the *Goldberg Variations*, retains the harmonic but not the melodic contour of its theme. But it is also a modern ternary structure, A-B-A-coda, with its contrasting sections (minor versus major, predominantly dramatic versus predominantly lyric) marked off by thematic reprises. The highly colored, highly volatile variations are thus clenched, leashed, by a doubly controlling hand. One mode of order supplements another, although it is not clear what is the supplemented, what the supplement; the ear is always sure it is going somewhere, but does not know where that is, nor can it recognize the place upon arrival.

My own "piece," this verbal reanimation of these and other earlier compositions that I have so often enjoyed, is neither structured nor directional. Like "Revenants," its musical double and namesake, my text dwells on the citational basis—but it is not a basis—on which both structure and direction depend, and through which all structure reveals itself as the trace of a past direction, all direction as the trace of a past structure. Both the musical and the verbal "Revenants" simply gather their variations piecemeal, assembling them—to borrow one of Derrida's images for the effect of *différance*—into a sheaf.[38] Like all sheaves, this one—either one—is loose, so loose it continually threatens to fall apart and scatter. Like all sheaves, too, this one has no noncontingent identity, no "itself" or "per se"; it can be uttered, but it is not an utterance. It is, rather, a set of interstices through which both music and history are reanimated in spectral form, a site where memory, or perhaps only the intention of memory, is summoned to appear despite its stubborn subterfuges and persistent denials.

What are you willing to remember? What are you unwilling to forget?

Playing Ostrich. In the waning days of World War II, the aged Richard Strauss wrote a threnody for strings, *Metamorphosen*, which assigns a key expressive and structural role to the main theme of the funeral march from Beethoven's *Eroica* Symphony. One of Strauss's themes, which increasingly comes to dominate his piece, is a distorted reminiscence of Beethoven's. It is difficult to know whose voice is speaking in this music. Strauss himself claimed not to have recognized Beethoven's theme in his own until late in the process of composition; the belated recognition is dramatized at the end of the work when the two versions of the theme appear in counterpoint together. The mourning voice is surely not Strauss's own: his theme chokes over Beethoven's as if it had swallowed something bad, and stammers through three preliminary attacks, each a full beat long, before reaching its headnote, as if the Straussian voice had continually to overcome a tremendous lethargy of spirit just to enunciate its motto of grief. But the voice is not Beethoven's either, not only because the theme is distorted but because the sacrificial death the *Eroica* had in mind was surely less annihilating, less apocalyptic, than the one mourned here—the immediate historical referent of the *Metamorphosen* is the firebombing of Dresden. Quoted at the end on a band of double basses, the original theme is depleted of expressivity; it has burned out, been burned out. And surely, too—but this is by no means so sure—the voice is not that of the Third Reich itself at its last gasp, even though in one sense it sounds exactly like it: when the news of Hitler's death was broadcast over German radio, what followed was the funeral march from the *Eroica*.[39] But surely that was a perversion of everything about the *Eroica* that means anything. Surely, one would like to say, Strauss's ventriloquism is different.

But it is not so sure. When I first became familiar with Strauss's piece, I found it moving in its bleakness and resignation, but a subsequent hearing, the one that has stuck with me, unexpectedly filled me with a rage I could not understand. Oh, I knew what I now condemned about the piece, but I couldn't explain the sheer intensity of my feeling. On this occasion I simply became aware that what Strauss was mourning was not what Germany had done, but what had been done to Germany. A program note set me off; it had told of Strauss's anguish at the loss of the Munich opera houses where his father had played and his own early career had flourished, of his birthplace in the same city, of "Goethe's House, the holiest house in the world," of "Dresden—Weimar—Munich, all gone!"[40] It was impossible not to honor this anguish, but equally impossible not to be shocked by its moral blindness. I realized I had been hearing the piece in the spirit of Thomas Mann's Serenus Zeitblom, the narrator of *Doctor Faustus*, whose anguish is all too clear-sighted about the enormity of both the loss and its cause: "Our 'thousand-year' history, refuted, reduced *ad absurdam*, weighed in the balance and found unblest, turns out to be a road leading nowhere, or rather into despair, an unexampled bankruptcy, a *descensus Averno* lighted by the dance of roaring flames. . . . [But] to recognize because we must our infamy is not the same thing as to deny our love."[41] There was nothing of this spirit in Strauss's lament, no recognition of the ills that had wrought so much ill. And you could hear the absence right there in the music, which for all its desolation was just too delicate, too nobly pathetic, too sensitive—just too damned pretty. Perhaps I was more angry at myself for filling the gap than at Strauss for leaving it. But the force of my rage (its traces are here in this prose) still seemed unexplained.[42]

Later still, I found the missing connection, or so I believe. Mann's Zeitblom provides a clue, too indirectly, with his reference to "those incredible photographs . . . [that surpass] in horribleness anything the human imagination can conceive" (481). I first encountered those photographs in the attic of my great-aunt's house some ten years after the war, when I was about ten myself. My family never talked about the war, although it had not apparently suffered from it much: no casualties from the American branch, no known relatives in Russia to have been exterminated. The attic, though, was a treasure trove of war memorabilia, together with a pictorial history that I was secretly studying, though I couldn't be said to be learning much, since the pictures were accompanied with almost no text at all. Toward the end of the last volume I came across the photos of the crematoria and the mass graves and could not grasp what I was looking at—my imagination couldn't conceive it. But when I sought for explanation from my family I met only with silence. I was told I should not have looked. I was told not to ask. The truth before my eyes, before everyone's eyes, could not be seen because it was posited as literally unspeakable. Remembering this, I discovered the source of my rage. What I heard in the Strauss, and especially in its contorted cover of Beethoven's voice, which could not have conceived of this either but at least had been plain spoken within the limits of the tragedies of its age, was the silence of my family, the silence of those who above all should speak.

Deep Postmodernity. The condition of postmodernity is often held to spin us across the slick surface of a lifeworld that is depthless and ahistorical, a distended televisual screen on which empty simulacra jostle, overlap, and usurp each other's places.[43] Many of us seek to reject or escape this novum orbis, people, often enough, with nothing else in common: New Age seekers and religious fundamentalists and white supremacists and ordinary middle-class citizens at the gym who understand that the resistant materiality of their bodies is their last refuge even as they work out on machines, cyborgs in spite of themselves. But the condition prevails, invisible as the fiber optic cable that enlaces the globe, whispery as the static that precedes the burst of the image on the screen or as the omnipresent tinnitus of the keys on computer keyboards interfaced with who knows whose fingers.

The condition of postmodernity is both archaic and timeless: we gibber like Homeric ghosts, asking for the tribute of blood from a solid Odyssean figure who never arrives, and we chatter in a dimensionless cyberspace, cut off even from the primordial satisfaction of hearing our own voices in what we say. Another way to describe this condition is to say that it makes us live explicitly the movement of nonpresence, the spill without a cup, that deconstruction has shown to be the implicit condition of all discourse. It is a condition we can no longer hide from ourselves, and it declares itself repeatedly in the paradox of the origin: the experience, on the one hand, of having no place of origin to which we can refer or aspire, of being part of a universal diaspora from nowhere, and the experience, on the other hand, of living in a whirligig of repetitions, citations free to become endless recitations, pasts that are constantly re-presenting themselves.

Musical revenants form the soundtrack of that lifeworld, and their sound is surprisingly uncoercive. When you play or hear them, you will not find your subjectivity shattered or scattered, nor summoned by the fiction of originality to break with a past from which you have neither the ability nor the desire to break. Everything that postmodernity has emptied of substance is still there, only with a difference, a *différance*, the trace of the impossible but improbably successful effort to reanimate the sense of substance without its essence, to defer the endless irony of postmodern post-consciousness in an interval of pleasure, of reflection, of absorption. The musical revenant, as both event and concept, is one small means by which the lifeless past can revive within the "life" half of my deliberately loaded term "lifeworld." Unoriginal music is one resource by which even the living may discover their capacity to live on in the present—only differently.

Notes

INTRODUCTION: SOUNDING OUT

1. Ludwig Wittgenstein, *Philosophical Investigations*, trans. G. E. M. Anscombe, 2d ed. (New York: Macmillan, 1958), 194.

2. Eric Santner, "Freud's *Moses* and the Ethics of Nomotropic Desire," *October* 88 (1999): 18.

3. Apart from my own work, some of it discussed later in this introduction, see inter alia Richard Leppert, *The Sight of Sound: Music, Representation, and the History of the Body* (Berkeley and Los Angeles: University of California Press, 1993); Susan McClary, "Constructions of Subjectivity in Schubert's Music," in *Queering the Pitch: The New Gay and Lesbian Musicology*, ed. Philip Brett, Elizabeth Wood, and Gary C. Thomas (New York: Routledge, 1994), 205–34, and "Narratives of Bourgeois Subjectivity in Mozart's *Prague* Symphony," in *Understanding Narrative*, ed. Peter J. Rabinowitz and James Phelan (Columbus: Ohio State University Press, 1994), 65–98; Rose Rosengard Subotnik, *Deconstructive Variations: Music and Reason in Western Society* (Minneapolis: University of Minnesota Press, 1996); and Gary Tomlinson, *Music in Renaissance Magic* (Chicago: University of Chicago Press, 1993).

4. Scott Burnham, "How Music Matters: Poetic Content Revisited," in *Rethinking Music*, ed. Nicholas Cook and Mark Evarist (Oxford: Oxford University Press, 1999), 215.

5. Stanley Cavell, *A Pitch of Philosophy: Autobiographical Exercises* (Cambridge: Harvard University Press, 1994), 129–69; Lydia Goehr, *The Quest for Voice: Music, Politics, and the Limits of Philosophy* (Berkeley and Los Angeles: University of California Press, 1998); Gary Tomlinson, *Metaphysical Song: An Essay on Opera* (Princeton: Princeton University Press, 1999).

CHAPTER 1. HERMENEUTICS AND MUSICAL HISTORY

1. Ned Rorem, *Pure Contraption: A Composer's Essays* (New York: Holt, Rinehart and Winston, 1974), 7. "A songwriter . . . [joins] music, which is

289

inherently meaningless in the intellectual sense of the word, to poetry, which is inherently meaningful." "Non-vocal music has no meaning literally, or even physically. It cannot say happiness, or hot and cold, or death . . . except by association. It says whatever its composer tells you, in words, that it says" (122).

2. G. W. F. Hegel, *Aesthetics: Lectures on Fine Art*, trans. T. M. Knox (Oxford: Oxford University Press, 1975), 954. Hegel's language implicitly sets up an aesthetic Scylla and Charybdis: ghostly insubstantiality for the amateur, mere mechanism for the expert.

3. Eduard Hanslick, *On the Musically Beautiful*, trans. Geoffrey Payzant (Indianapolis: Hackett, 1986), 57.

4. C. S. Lewis, *The Allegory of Love: A Study in Medieval Tradition* (1936; reprint, New York: Oxford University Press, 1958), 60.

5. Quoted from "Beethoven's Heroic Symphony," in Richard Wagner, *Judaism in Music and Other Essays*, trans. W. Ashton Ellis (1894; reprint, Lincoln: University of Nebraska Press, 1985), 222–23, 224. I've retained Ellis's archaizing translation as a means both of capturing Wagner's own bardic tone and of retaining a sense of historical "alienation" in the account; the original is conveniently available on the Web at "The Wagner Archive," *http://users .utu.fi/hansalmi/texts/eroica.html*.

6. My translation of "Nur in des Meisters Tonsprache war aber das Unaussprechliche kundzutun, was das Wort hier eben in höchster Befangenheit andeuten konnte."

7. Wilhelm Dilthey, "Die Entstehung der Hermeneutik," in *Gesammelte Schriften*, 4th ed. (1921; reprint, Stuttgart-Göttingen: B. G. Teubner, 1964), v; for discussion, see Paul Ricoeur, "The Problem of Double Meaning," in *The Conflict of Interpretations: Essays in Hermeneutics* (Evanston, Ill.: Northwestern University Press, 1974), 62–78. On the relevance of Dilthey and the concept of lived experience to postmodernist thinking, see Victor Turner, *The Anthropology of Performance* (New York: PAJ Publications, 1987), 84–98.

8. On ekphrasis and the theory of representation, see W. J. T. Mitchell, "Ekphrasis and the Other," in *Picture Theory: Essays on Verbal and Visual Representation* (Chicago: University of Chicago Press, 1994), 151–82. As well as a literary technique—and genre—ekphrasis was the basic expository technique of traditional art history until it was displaced by photographic reproduction. See Robert S. Nelson, "The Slide Lecture, or The Work of Art History in an Age of Mechanical Reproduction," *Critical Inquiry* 26 (2000): 414–34, esp. 430–32.

9. The paraphrase is partly obscured by the density of Wagner's parabolic language, which binds his text to the earlier phases of the hermeneutic tradition. Nonetheless, his narrative of gender fusion incorporates, and appeals to, a certain characterization of the variation process: "Around [the utterly simple, *höchst einfachen*] theme, which we may regard as the firm masculine individuality, there wind and cling [*winden und schmiegen*] from the very outset of the movement all the softer and more tender feelings, evolving to a proclamation of the purely feminine element" (*Judaism in Music*, 224, translation modified).

10. Edward T. Cone, "Schubert's Promissory Note: An Exercise in Musical Hermeneutics," in *Schubert: Critical and Analytical Studies*, ed. Walter Frisch (Lincoln: University of Nebraska Press, 1986), 24.

11. Mitchell, "Ekphrasis and the Other," 153–56. Mitchell also postulates a moment of indifference that my account omits.

12. Donald Francis Tovey, *Essays in Musical Analysis: Symphonies and Other Orchestral Works*, new ed. (London: Oxford University Press, 1981), 196.

13. Another common objection is that hermeneutics continues the traditional concentration on the musical work, thus still losing too much in the way of context and at the same time overinvesting in a restrictive canon. What this argument ignores, or chooses to ignore, is the thoroughgoing critical-hermeneutic effort to restructure concepts such as "the work" and "context" precisely so as to avoid the difficulties in question. On the canon question, see Katherine Bergeron and Philip Bohlman, eds., *Disciplining Music: Musicology and Its Canons* (Chicago: University of Chicago Press, 1992), and my essay-review "Charging the Canons," *Journal of the Royal Musical Association* 119 (1994): 130–40.

14. See Michel Foucault, *The Archaeology of Knowledge*, trans. A. M. Sheridan Smoth (New York: Pantheon, 1972), esp. 31–49.

15. For a concise overview of the socio-medical history, see Linda Hutcheon and Michael Hutcheon, *Opera: Desire, Disease, Death* (Lincoln: University of Nebraska Press, 1996), 68–83, 95–106. See also Barbara Maria Stafford, *Body Criticism: Imaging the Unseen in Enlightenment Art and Medicine* (Cambridge: MIT Press, 1991), 297–300; Sander Gilman, *Disease and Representation: Images of Illness from Madness to AIDS* (Ithaca: Cornell University Press, 1988); and Claude Quétel, *History of Syphilis*, trans. Judith Braddock and Brian Pike (Cambridge: Polity, 1990).

16. Otto Erich Deutsch, *Schubert: A Documentary Biography*, trans. Erich Blom (London: Dent, 1946), 339.

17. On the poisoning fantasy, see Elizabeth Norman Mackay, *Franz Schubert: A Biography* (Oxford: Clarendon Press, 1996), 205.

18. Michel Foucault, *The History of Sexuality*, vol. 1, *An Introduction*, trans. Robert Hurley (New York: Random House, 1978), 140–41.

CHAPTER 2. HANDS ON, LIGHTS OFF

1. *Allgemeine Musikalische Zeitung* 4: 40 (30 June 1802), col. 650.

2. Christian Friedrich Michaelis, "The Beautiful and the Sublime in Music," *Berlinische musikalische Zeitung* 1 (1805): 179–80; Aubin Millin, "Le Sublime," in his *Dictionnaire des beaux-arts* (Paris, 1806), 202–3; reprint in *Music and Aesthetics in the Eighteenth and Early Nineteenth Centuries*, ed. and trans. Peter le Huray and James Day (Cambridge: Cambridge University Press, 1988), 207–9.

3. Hector Berlioz, *A Travers Chants* (Paris: Michael Lévy Frères, 1862), 62–

63, and *The Art of Music and Other Essays,* trans. Elizabeth Csicsery-Ronay (Bloomington: Indiana University Press, 1994), 39.

4. Friedrich Schiller, "Über Matthissons Gedichte," *Werke und Briefe,* ed. Otto Dann et al., 12 vols. (Frankfurt am Main: Deutscher Klassiker Verlag, 1992), 8: 1024–25.

5. Carl Czerny, *On the Proper Performance of All Beethoven's Works for the Piano,* trans. unattributed, ed. Paul Badura-Skoda (Vienna: Universal Edition, 1970).

6. *Journal des Debats,* 12 March 1837. For a discussion of this passage in relation to Berlioz's aesthetics and gender ideology, see Katharine Kolb Reeve, "Primal Scenes: Smithson, Pleyel, and Liszt in the Eyes of Berlioz," *Nineteenth-Century Music* 18 (1995): 229.

7. For Legouvé's account, see Alan Walker, *Franz Liszt: The Virtuoso Years, 1811–1847* (New York: Knopf, 1983), 182. Berlioz's later account appeared in *A Travers Chants,* 63 (*The Art of Music,* 39).

8. Slavoj Žižek, *Looking Awry: An Introduction to Jacques Lacan through Popular Culture* (Cambridge: MIT Press, 1993), 83–84. The sublime object will return as a topic in chapter 7.

9. John Field began publishing piano works entitled "Nocturne" in 1812, but as Jeffrey Kallberg ("'Voice' and the Nocturne," in *Pianist, Scholar, Connoisseur: Essays for Jacob Lateiner,* ed. Bruce Brubaker and Jane Gottlieb [Stuyvesant, N.Y.: Pendragon Press, forthcoming]) has noted, the genre was not recognized as an independent entity until the 1820s and 1830s.

10. Alexandre Oulibicheff [Alexander Ulibyshev], *Beethoven, ses critiques et ses glossateurs* (Paris and Leipzig, 1857); quoted by Harold C. Schonberg, *The Great Pianists* (New York: Simon & Schuster, 1963), 127.

11. Richard Leppert, *The Sight of Sound: Music, Representation, and the History of the Body* (Berkeley and Los Angeles: University of California Press, 1993), 119–88.

12. Wilkie Collins, *The Woman in White* (Harmondsworth: Penguin, 1974), 81. For more on music in this novel, see Nicky Lossoff, "Absent Melody and *The Woman in White,*" *Music and Letters* 81 (2000): 532–50.

13. Leo Tolstoy, *Great Short Works,* trans. Louise Maude and Aylmer Maude (New York: Harper & Row, 1967), 24.

14. My translation, from Christopher Middleton, ed. and trans., *Friedrich Hölderin, Eduard Mörike: Selected Poems* (Chicago: University of Chicago Press, 1972), 193.

15. On the romance of the Friend, with some further remarks on Mörike's poem, see my *Franz Schubert: Sexuality, Subjectivity, Song* (Cambridge: Cambridge University Press, 1998); on liquescence as a nineteenth-century trope for desire, my *Music as Cultural Practice: 1800–1900* (Berkeley and Los Angeles: University of California Press, 1990).

16. Adolph Bernhard Marx, *Ludwig van Beethoven: Leben und Schaffen* (Leipzig: Adolph Schumann, 1902), 2 vols., 1: 106–7. My translations.

17. Terry Castle cites this painting as an instance of what she calls the "spec-

tralization" of subjectivity in the post-Enlightenment era; see "Spectral Politics: Apparition Belief and the Romantic Imagination" in her *The Female Thermometer: Eighteenth-Century Culture and the Invention of the Uncanny* (New York: Oxford University Press, 1995), 168–89. Richard Leppert discusses the sexual politics of the painting in *The Sight of Sound*, 144–45. The refined-Gothic nexus of the apparitional and romantic desire was installed in English poetry in 1807 when Wordsworth published his poem "She Was a Phantom of Delight" (*The Oxford Authors: William Wordsworth*, ed. Stephen Gill [Oxford: Oxford University Press, 1984], 292), the first stanza of which reads:

> She was a Phantom of delight
> When first she gleamed upon my sight;
> A lovely Apparition, sent
> To be a moment's ornament;
> Her eyes as stars of Twilight fair,
> Like Twilight's, too, her dusky hair,
> But all things else about her drawn
> From May-time and the chearful Dawn:
> A dancing Shape, an Image gay,
> To haunt, to startle, and way-lay.

18. Maynard Solomon, *Beethoven* (New York: Schirmer, 1977) 151–52, 158–59.

19. Anton Schindler, *Beethoven as I Knew Him*, trans. Donald W. MacArdle (London: Dent, 1966), 101. Alexander Wheelock Thayer, *The Life of Ludwig van Beethoven*, 3 vols. (Carbondale: Southern Illinois University Press, 1960), 1: 321–23.

20. Thus Paul Bekker in his *Beethoven*, trans. and adapted by M. M. Bozman (1911; rpt. London: Dent, 1925), 109: "Certain foolish legends have gathered about the [C♯-minor Sonata] ... which attribute to it a definite autobiographical significance. ... Although Beethoven's art is autobiographical in general ... to attach anecdotes to individual works—as, for instance, that the C♯-minor Sonata tells of a love affair—is manifestly absurd. ... [The] popularity of [this work] probably accounts for the growth of the legends attached to it. ... A purely artistic impulse of reaction from the preceding work [Op. 27.1] is sufficient, without romantic fiction, to account satisfactorily for the birth of the C♯-minor Sonata." The underlying opposition of art and legend is a quintessentially modernist gesture

21. Vincent D'Indy, *Ludwig van Beethoven* (1911; tr. 1913 by Theodore Baker, reprint, 1973, New York: Da Capo), 49.

22. William Behrend, *Beethoven's Pianoforte Sonatas*, trans. Ingeborg Lund (New York: Dutton, 1927), 76.

23. Romain Rolland, *Beethoven the Creator*, trans. Ernest Newman (1929; reprint, New York, Dover, 1964), 109.

24. Figgis's film supplements the Beethoven Adagio with other music, most notably by Chopin, as Tolstoy's text supplements it with Mozart; the process of

supplementation suggests the tendency to form a stable network of romantic mood pieces with the "Moonlight" Adagio at or near its nucleus. The Paderewski film uses bravura pieces by Chopin and Liszt to supplement the Adagio in a contrastive pattern typical of nineteenth-century virtuoso pianism (of which Paderewski, at 78, was still an exponent); the pattern and its cultural contexts will concern us in chapter 4.

Another film worth noting is the Russian *Chapiev* (1934), a classic of socialist realism in which a villainous White Russian leader, representing bourgeois culture, is observed unawares playing the "Moonlight" Adagio by his orderly, whose brother has just been executed. The orderly is cleaning the floor with rags attached to his shoes; with the music sounding, his movements suggest a tortured dance linking the oppressor and the oppressed in a strange intimacy, a negative form of the communion at the Liszt performance described by Berlioz. (Mark Slobin introduced me to this film in his paper, "Beethoven's Shadow in Soviet Film," delivered in Toronto at the year 2000 "megameeting" of North American Musical Societies.) This example indicates that the reception history of the Adagio is not—of course—confined to the sphere of romance, but also that its contingency is limited, as the elements of masculine intimacy and bourgeois identity testify.

25. Olivia Hensel [Mary Alice Seymour], *Life and Letters of Louis Moreau Gottschalk* (Boston: Oliver Ditson, 1870), 13.

26. Michel Foucault, *The History of Sexuality*, vol. 1, *An Introduction*, trans. Robert Hurley (New York: Random House, 1978), 124, 120, 122.

27. On the social and sexual scenarios enveloping the "Kreutzer" Sonata— both the story and the music—see my *After the Lovedeath: Sexual Violence and the Making of Culture* (Berkeley and Los Angeles: University of California Press, 1997) and Leppert, *The Sight of Sound*, 153–88.

28. Gustave Chouquet, quoted in Katharine Ellis, "Female Pianists and Their Male Critics in Nineteenth-Century Paris," *Journal of the American Musicological Society* 50 (1997): 369.

29. Roland Barthes, *A Lover's Discourse: Fragments*, trans. Richard Howard (New York: Hill and Wang, 1978), 106–10, 132–33.

CHAPTER 3. BEYOND WORDS AND MUSIC

1. George Eliot, *Daniel Deronda* (Baltimore: Penguin, 1967), 250.

2. On Victorian theories of infantile consciousness, see Ekbert Faas, *Retreat into the Mind: Victorian Poetry and the Rise of Psychiatry* (Princeton: Princeton University Press, 1988), 71–73.

3. My attention was drawn to the musical instructiveness of *Daniel Deronda* by Ruth Solie's paper, "'Tadpole Pleasures': *Daniel Deronda* as Music Historiography," presented at the 1997 meeting of the American Musicological Society.

4. On the acoustic mirror, see Kaja Silverman, *The Acoustic Mirror: The Female Voice in Psychoanalysis and Cinema* (Bloomington: Indiana University

Press: 1988), 72–100, and David Schwarz, *Listening Subjects: Music, Psycho-analysis, Culture* (Durham: Duke University Press, 1997), 1–22.

5. For illustrative discussions, see Edward T. Cone, "Words into Music: The Composer's Approach to the Text," in *Sound and Poetry*, ed. Northrop Frye (New York: Columbia University Press, 1957), 3–15; my *Music and Poetry: The Nineteenth Century and After* (Berkeley and Los Angeles: University of California Press, 1984), 125–70; Steven Paul Scher, "Comparing Music and Poetry: Beethoven's Goethe Lieder," in *Sensus Communis: Contemporary Trends in Comparative Literature*, ed. Janos Riesz, Peter Boerner, and Bernhard Scholz (Tübingen: Gunter Narr, 1986), 155–65; Walter Bernhart, "Setting a Poem: The Composer's Choice for or against Interpretation," *Yearbook of Comparative and General Literature* 37 (1988): 32–46; Kofi Agawu, "Theory and Practice in the Analysis of the Nineteenth-Century Lied," *Music Analysis* 11 (1992): 3–36; and Richard Kurth, "Music and Poetry, a Wilderness of Doubles: Heine—Schubert—Nietzsche—Derrida, *Nineteenth-Century Music* 21 (1997): 3–37.

6. See "The Signification of the Phallus" in Jacques Lacan, *Écrits: A Selection*, trans. Alan Sheridan (New York: W. W. Norton, 1977), 288–90.

7. Roland Barthes, "The Grain of the Voice" (1972), in *The Responsibility of Forms: Critical Essays on Music, Art, and Representation*, trans. Richard Howard (Berkeley and Los Angeles: University of California Press, 1985), 267–77.

8. My thanks to Steven Paul Scher, Walter Bernhart, and Werner Wolf for suggestions that enabled me to address the questions raised in this paragraph.

9. In my translation:

A boy saw a little rose growing,
Little rose on the heath,
So young and fair as morning,
He swiftly ran up to be near her,
Gazed at her with much joy,
Little rose, little rose, little rose red,
Little rose on the heath.

Boy spoke: I'll pick you,
Little rose on the heath.
Rose spoke: I'll prick you,
You'll remember me forever,
And I won't suffer the picking.
Little rose, little rose, little rose red,
Little rose on the heath.

And the wild boy picked
Her, little rose on the heath,
Little rose fought back and pricked,
But her "woe" and "ah!" did no good,

She had to suffer regardless.
Little rose, little rose, little rose red,
Little rose on the heath.

10. Refined, because the eighteenth-century *volkstümlich* ideal tended to center on unaccompanied melodies that could be sung in unison by convivial groups without musical training. Around 1815, just about the time Schubert turned his hand to the type, the ideal shifted to accompanied song with folk-like qualities. On this topic, see Arnold Feil, *Franz Schubert: Die Schöne Müllerin, Winterreise*, trans. Ann C. Sherwin (Portland, Ore.: Amadeus Press, 1988), 11–21.

11. On Schlegel's irony and its relation to nineteenth-century music see John Daverio, *Nineteenth-Century Music and the German Romantic Ideology* (New York: Scribner's, 1993), esp. 1–18, together with the review essay by Marshall Brown in *Nineteenth-Century Music* 18 (1995): 290–303.

12. See my *Franz Schubert: Sexuality, Subjectivity, Song* (Cambridge: Cambridge University Press, 1998), 130.

13. Agawu, "Theory and Practice," 30.

14. In my *Music and Poetry*, 132.

15. Mikhail Bakhtin, "Discourse in the Novel" (1934–35), in *The Dialogic Imagination*, ed. Michael Holquist, trans. Caryl Emerson and Michael Holquist (Austin: The University of Texas Press, 1981), 342.

16. Slavoj Žižek, *The Indivisible Remainder: An Essay on Schelling and Related Matters* (London: Verso, 1996), 154.

17. Richard Wagner, "Judaism in Music," in *Judaism and Music and Other Essays*, trans. W. Ashton Ellis (1894; reprint, Lincoln: University of Nebraska Press, 1995), 91.

CHAPTER 4. FRANZ LISZT AND THE VIRTUOSO PUBLIC SPHERE

1. From an account of a Liszt recital in Andersen's *A Poet's Bazaar*, reprinted in full in James Huneker, *Franz Liszt* (New York: Scribners, 1911), 230–34. The quoted phrase appears on p. 232; the Orpheus metaphor is one of the leitmotifs of the essay.

2. Ibid., 233.

3. Max Kallbeck, *Johannes Brahms*, rev. ed., 4 vols. (Berlin: Deutsche Brahms-Gesellschaft, 1913–22), 1:90.

4. On the significance of the piano as machinery, with specific relation to Liszt, see Richard Leppert, "Cultural Contradiction, Idolatry, and the Piano Virtuoso: Franz Liszt," in *Piano Roles: Three Centuries of Life with the Piano*, ed. James Parakilas (New Haven: Yale University Press, 1999), 252–81.

5. The first statement (from 1842) is quoted in Eleanor Perenyi, *Franz Liszt: The Artist as Romantic Hero* (New York: Little, Brown, 1974), 209; the second

is from a letter to Mendelssohn's mother, 30 March 1840, in *Felix Mendelssohn, Letters*, ed. G. Seldon-Goth (New York: Pantheon, 1945), 289.

6. Quoted in Perenyi, *Franz Liszt*, 206; Mendelssohn made the remark to Robert Schumann. A small episode at Mendelssohn's home in 1840 is revealing about his ambivalence toward Liszt. After hearing the latter play a Hungarian folksong with variations, Mendelssohn impishly imitated the performance in every detail, complete with Liszt's "grandiose movements and extravagant gestures." Liszt was reportedly delighted with the impersonation, which, however, suggests that Mendelssohn could "do" Liszt's act whenever he wanted to, but wanted to only in jest. Reported by Max Müller, *Signale für die musikalische Welt*, 2 January 1902.

7. For Andersen, see Huneker, *Franz Liszt*, 230–31; for Heine, *Poetry and Prose of Heinrich Heine*, ed. and trans. Frederic Ewen (New York: Citadel Press, 1948), 635: "No one in the world knows how to organize 'successes' as well as Franz Liszt—or better, how to stage them. In that art he is a genius." For an account of advertising and self-promotion in Paris during the early nineteenth century, see Paul Metzner, *Crescendo of the Virtuoso: Spectacle, Skill, and Self-Promotion in Paris during the Age of Revolution* (Berkeley and Los Angeles: University of California Press, 1998), 273–90.

8. Hallé, from Sir Charles Hallé, *Life and Letters*, ed. C. E. Hallé and Marie Hallé (London: Smith and Elder, 1896), quoted by Perenyi, *Franz Liszt*, 63; Chopin, from a letter to Julian Fontana, 11 September 1841, trans. by Jeffrey Kallberg from *Korespondencja Fryderyka Chopin*, ed. Bronistaw Edward Sydow, 2 vols. (Warsaw: Panstwowy Institut Wydawnicy, 1955), 2: 34. My thanks to Jeffrey Kallberg for providing me with the exact sense of the passage.

9. Working on the same principle, and at times on the same touchstone passages, Susan Bernstein formulates a reading of virtuosity that complements the one offered here; see her *Virtuosity of the Nineteenth Century: Performing Music and Language in Heine, Liszt, and Baudelaire* (Stanford: Stanford University Press, 1998).

10. Donald Francis Tovey, *Essays in Musical Analysis: Concertos and Choral Works* (1935; new ed., Oxford: Oxford University Press, 1981), 95.

11. Robert Schumann, *On Music and Musicians*, ed. Konrad Wolff, trans. Paul Rosenfeld (1946; reprint New York: W. W. Norton, 1969), 156; translation modified.

12. Ibid., 160. The concert took place in 1840.

13. For a reading of the cultural construction of the virtuoso Liszt as a generally military and specifically Napoleonic figure, see Dana Gooley, "Warhorses: Liszt, Weber's *Konzertstück*, and the Cult of Napoleon," *Nineteenth-Century Music* 24 (2000): 62–88.

14. Quoted by Peter Ostwald, *Schumann: The Inner Voices of a Musical Genius* (Boston: Northeastern University Press, 1985), 162.

15. It was, in fact, the size, pomp, and circumstance of one of Liszt's audiences, as reported in the *Revue et Gazette musicale de Paris* (5 September

1841), 407, that prompted Chopin's remarks: "The Liszt article from the concert at the Cologne Cathedral greatly amused me: and the fifteen thousand people counted, and the president, and the vice president, and the secretary of the phil[harmonic] society, and that calèche (you know what the fiacres there are like), and that port, and that ship!" *Korespondencja*, 2: 34.

16. Perenyi, *Franz Liszt*, 63.

17. On photography as the objective form of "natural," "neutral," or "chaste" vision, see Mary Warner Marien, *Photography and Its Critics: A Cultural History, 1839–1900* (Cambridge: Cambridge University Press, 1997), 2–8, 39–42.

18. Heinrich Heine, "Über die Französische Bühne, Zehnte Briefe" (1837), *Sämtliche Werke in vier Bänden*, vol. 3, *Schriften zu Literatur und Politik I*, ed. Uwe Schweikert (Munich: Artemis u. Winkler, 1996), 761; my translation. The pianist Alexander Siloti later wrote similarly that "when Liszt played there was no sound of the instrument . . . [only] music such as no one could form any idea of without hearing it"; quoted by Perenyi, *Franz Liszt*, 204. For a critic in the *Manchester Morning Post*, reviewing a recital of 1840 or 1841, Liszt's technique "made his efforts seem rather like the flight of thought than the result of mechanical exertion, thus investing his execution with a character more mental than physical" (quoted in Huneker, *Franz Liszt*, 316).

19. Heine, "Über die Französische Bühne, Zehnte Briefe," 761.

20. Quoted in Huneker, *Franz Liszt*, 285.

21. Richard Leppert, *The Sight of Sound: Music, Representation, and the History of the Body* (Berkeley and Los Angeles: University of California Press, 1993).

22. In his *Nineteenth-Century Music* (Berkeley and Los Angeles: University of California Press, 1989), 138–42, Carl Dahlhaus constructs a useful opposition between virtuosity and interpretation in nineteenth-century pianism, but on strictly technical grounds and in binary rather than dialectical terms. (Dialectic is reserved for his account of form and technique in Liszt's E♭ Piano Concerto.) In her *The Quest for Voice: Music, Politics, and the Limits of Philosophy* (Berkeley and Los Angeles: University of California Press, 1998), 132–73, Lydia Goehr discusses a similar opposition in nineteenth-century music generally between the ideals of expressive performance and truth to the work. The opposition I discuss here is framed somewhat differently from Goehr's, but the most important—most indicative—difference between them is that the mode of virtuosity I am concerned with lies at the outer limit of her performative ideal, to the point of disrupting the broader duality entirely; this virtuosity lodges like a fatal flaw in the more moderate "doubling" she describes. One might put this by saying that Goehr is concerned with the opposition of music and visibility, whereas Lisztian virtuosity disrupts its containment within that opposition by creating an opposition of music and visuality, as it were, the libidinal form of the visible.

23. Ewen, *Poetry and Prose*, 634. The concert took place in 1844.

24. Slavoj Žižek, "Grimaces of the Real, or When the Phallus Appears,"

October 58 (1992): 44–68, and *Looking Awry: An Introduction to Jacques Lacan through Popular Culture* (Cambridge: MIT Press, 1993), 3–47.

25. Heine, "Über die Französische Bühne, Zehnte Briefe," 761.

26. Amy Fay, *Music Study in Germany* (Chicago: McClurg, 1880), 214; reprint in *Strunk's Source Readings in Music History*, ed. Leo Treitler et al. (New York: W. W. Norton, 1998), part VI: "The Nineteenth Century," ed. Ruth A. Solie, 1246.

27. Ibid. (McClurg edition), 214, n. 23.

28. From an anonymous review in *L'Illustration*, 18 May 1844; quoted by Metzner, *Crescendo*, 229.

29. "Liszt's 'Programme-Symphonies' . . . denied to music more completely than ever before its independent sphere, and dosed the listener with a kind of vision-promoting medicine," Hanslick, *The Beautiful in Music*, 7th ed., trans. Gustav Cohen (1891; reprint, Indianapolis: Bobbs Merrill, 1957), 5–6. The quotations from the review of Liszt in concert (1874) are from Hanslick, *Music Criticisms, 1846–99*, trans. and ed. Henry Pleasants (Harmondsworth: Penguin, 1963), 110. Hanslick's earlier review of the symphonic poems (1857), a severe attack but not (for once) a hatchet job, appears on pp. 53–57.

30. Hanslick makes a little addendum here—"especially his female listeners"—that is also worth noting. The familiar trope of Liszt's sex appeal is gratuitous in this context; Hanslick may be using it to contain the emotional and erotic charge of Liszt's facial display by assigning the display to the sphere of femininity. Susan McClary calls attention to the influence of gender anxiety on Hanslick's music criticism in her "Constructions of Subjectivity in Schubert's Music," in *Queering the Pitch: The New Gay and Lesbian Musicology*, ed. Philip Brett, Elizabeth Wood, and Gary C. Thomas (New York: Routledge, 1994), 225–27.

31. Quoted in Derek Watson, *Liszt* (New York: Schirmer, 1989), 100, from Evans's/Eliot's collected recollections of her three visits to Weimar, *The Liszt Society Journal* 8: 26–32, reprint in Huneker, *Franz Liszt*, 258–62.

32. Anonymous, *Manchester Morning Post*, ca. 1840, quoted in Huneker, *Franz Liszt*, 316.

33. Quoted from Andersen's *A Poet's Bazaar* in both Huneker, *Franz Liszt*, 231, and Alan Walker, *Franz Liszt*, vol. 1, *The Virtuoso Years, 1811–1847* (New York: Knopf, 1983), 290. The translation here is from Huneker, with two changes (the substitution of "personality" for "individuality" in the first sentence and of "demon" for "demonia" at the word's last appearance) borrowed from Walker.

34. Compare Schumann's account of Liszt playing Weber's *Konzertstück* (discussed earlier) where the auditory reference is retained. When, following this passage, Andersen alludes for the only time to actual music, he again renders the music visual—at best a background noise: "[Liszt's] Valse Infernale is more than a daguerreotype from Meyerbeer's Robert. We do not stand before and gaze upon the well-known picture. No, we transport ourselves into the midst of it. We gaze deep into the very abyss, and discover new, whirling forms.

It did not seem to be the strings of a piano that were sounding. No, every tone was like an echoing drop of water" (231–32).

35. Johann Wolfgang von Goethe, *Wilhelm Meister's Apprenticeship*, trans. Thomas Carlyle (1824; reprint, New York: Collier Books, 1962), bk. 8, 486; translation slightly modified. For the original text see *Goethes Werke, Hamburger Ausgabe in 14 Bänden*, ed. Erich Trunz (Munich: C. H. Beck, 1982), 7: 543. I've kept Carlyle's "awkward," translating *seltsam* ("peculiar," "odd"), for its suggestion that particularity is not only innately strange but also clumsy. Similarly, Carlyle's "uses," translating *hervorbringt* ("produces") to express the relation of the singer to a fine voice, brings out the transcendental autonomy implicitly ascribed to the voice itself.

36. Huneker, *Franz Liszt*, 427–28.

37. Thomas Mann, *Buddenbrooks*, trans. H. T. Lowe Porter (New York: Random House, 1961), 206.

38. Joachim quoted in Perenyi, *Franz Liszt*, 322; Brahms quoted in Hans Gal, *Johannes Brahms: His Work and Personality*, trans. Joseph Stein (London: Weidenfield and Nicolson, 1963), 33–34.

39. Friedrich Nietzsche, *The Case of Wagner*, sec. 11, quoted from *The Birth of Tragedy and the Case of Wagner*, trans. Walter Kaufmann (New York: Random House, 1967), 179. Nietzsche is nonetheless ambivalent about Liszt, who he elsewhere says "surpasses all other musicians in his noble orchestral accents" (from *Ecce Homo*, in *The Genealogy of Morals and Ecce Homo*, trans. Walter Kaufmann [New York: Random House, 1967], 251).

40. Nietzsche's anti-theatricalism registers the beginnings of an important offshoot of the antinomy between music and visuality first cultivated by the virtuoso, its transplantation—to continue the metaphor—to the operatic stage. As opera after Wagner focused increasingly on metaphysical themes, the contrast between the mystique of invisible music and the all too visible mechanism of stage production gave the issue a heightened urgency (and a rather heavy Schopenhaurean afflatus) that persisted well into the twentieth century. The actual playing out of the problem, though, continually confounds any neat distinction between theatrical embodiment and disembodied music. For discussions, see Gary Tomlinson, *Metaphysical Song* (Princeton: Princeton University Press, 1998), and Christopher Morris, *Opera between the Lines: Musical Interludes and Cultural Meaning* (Cambridge: Cambridge University Press, forthcoming).

41. Freud's concept is too familiar to require specific citation; for Foucault's, one must track the index entries in his *The Archaeology of Knowledge*, trans. A. M. Sheridan Smith (New York: Pantheon, 1972), but a cognate account (with different key terms) appears synoptically in "Nietzsche, Genealogy, History," in Michel Foucault, *Language, Counter-Memory, Practice: Selected Essays and Interviews*, ed. Daniel Bouchard, trans. Daniel Bouchard and Sherry Simon (Ithaca: Cornell University Press, 1977), 139–65.

42. See Simon Schama, *Citizens: A Chronicle of the French Revolution* (New York: Knopf, 1989), 504–12, and Metzner, *Crescendo*, 221–31.

43. On these and other details of the coronation, see Paul Johnson, *The Birth of the Modern: World Society, 1815–1830* (New York: HarperCollins, 1991), 955–56. Rossini's *Il Viaggio a Rheims,* cannibalized by the composer for other works and not given a modern staging until 1984, had an ear-popping ten principal roles; reviewing a New York City Opera production in 1999, Alan Kozinn describes the result as a "nonstop stream of ambitiously florid arias and ensembles"—each offering tribute to the king in a different national style. ("In Long Lost Rossini, Tributes to a French King," *New York Times,* Thursday, 16 September 1999, E5.)

44. Johnson, *Birth of the Modern,* 954–55.

45. On carnival, the cancan craze, and Philippe Musard, see Johannes Willms, *Paris, Capital of Europe: From the Revolution to the Belle Epoque,* trans. Eveline L. Kanes (New York: Holmes and Meier, 1997), 231–35. Heine includes a satirical discussion of the cancan craze in an 1842 article for the *Allgemeine Zeitung,* reprint in part in Ewen, *Poetry and Prose,* 802–3: "You ask 'What is the cancan?' Holy heavens! do you expect me to define the cancan for the *Allgemeine Zeitung? . . .* [Suffice it to say that] the reserve recommended by the late Victris is not needed and that the French are often disturbed by the police when dancing this dance."

46. Delphine de Girardin in 1839; quoted in Willms, *Paris,* 383 n.179.

47. Arséne Houssaye in a memoir of 1885; quoted in Willms, *Paris,* 384 n.180.

48. Anonymous, quoted in Huneker, *Franz Liszt,* 253.

49. Quoted in Willms, *Paris,* 235.

50. Heine, "Mademoiselle Laurence" (from *Florentine Nights,* 1837), trans. Frederic Ewen, in Ewen, *Poetry and Prose,* 551.

51. Norbert Elias, *The Civilizing Process* (1936), trans. Edmond Jephcott (New York: Urizen Books, 1978).

52. Mikhail Bakhtin, *Rabelais and his World* (1964), trans. Helene Iswolsky (Bloomington: Indiana University Press, 1984), 1–44.

53. "B. W. H.," identified as "an American Lady" who saw Liszt in Weimar in 1877, quoted in Huneker, *Franz Liszt,* 278.

54. Delphine de Girardin, quoted in Willms, *Paris,* 384 n.179.

55. Heine, "Paganini" (from *Florentine Nights*), in Ewen, *Poetry and Prose,* 614–21. The flavor can be gleaned from a brief extract: "When Paganini began to play again, my eyes grew dim. The sounds were not transformed as before into bright shapes and colors. On the contrary the master's form was enveloped in gloomy shades, from the depths of which his music wailed in rending accents" (618). The performance is described as culminating with a demonic cacophony suggestive of the Last Judgment, upon which "the tormented violinist drew his bow across the strings with such frenzy and desperation" that the pandemonium vanished (619).

56. János Jánko, "Franz Liszt at the Piano," caricature series, from *Borsszem Janko* (6 April 1873). Photo: Yale University Library. See also Leppert's discussion of this cartoon in "Cultural Contradiction."

57. The actor is Noah Taylor (in the role of the young Helfgott). On "le trait unaire," see Ellie Raglund-Sullivan, *Jacques Lacan and the Philosophy of Psychoanalysis* (Chicago: University of Illinois Press, 1987), 224–26. "Unary" suggests the opposite of "binary"; "le trait unaire" is a play on the French phrase for the hyphen (i.e., a linking mark), *trait d'union*, as well as on the multiple meanings of *trait* in general.

58. From Huneker, *Franz Liszt*, 231, 232.

59. Žižek, *Looking Awry*, 69–83, 130–53; Lacan, *Tarrying with the Negative: Kant, Hegel, and the Critique of Ideology* (Durham, N.C.: Duke University Press, 1993), 69–79, 120–24. As I use it here, the concept of the big Other has some key features not pursued by Lacan or Žižek. First, it is constitutively incomplete, a cipher that requires historical specification before it can be effective in either action or interpretation. Second, and in partial disharmony with the first point, the big Other typically becomes effective precisely as a cipher: it works primarily by being embodied in representation, and in particular by being personified, as the term "big Other" suggests.

60. See Julian Johnson, *Listening in Paris: A Cultural History* (Berkeley and Los Angeles: University of California Press, 1995), 182–83.

61. For a brief account (with emphasis on music), see Johnson, *Listening*, 126–29; for more detail, see Schama, *Citizens*, 746–50, 778–79, 830–36.

62. Anonymous, originally published in German; quoted by Huneker, *Franz Liszt*, 253.

63. Salman Rushdie, *The Ground beneath Her Feet* (New York: Henry Holt, 1999), 424. Interestingly enough, Ormus and Vina perfect their powers not only by their voices (and their long-deferred marriage) but also by "reinventing" their stage act to include spectacular visual effects that cause some of their former admirers to accuse of them of "selling out" for the sake of effect.

64. Metzner, *Crescendo*, 158.

65. Alan Walker, *Franz Liszt*, vol. 2, *The Weimar Years, 1848–1861* (New York: Knopf, 1989) 280, 321.

66. Metzner, *Crescendo*, 127.

67. Lawrence Levine, *Highbrow/Lowbrow: The Emergence of Cultural Hierarchy in America* (Cambridge: Harvard University Press, 1988), 108.

68. Johanna Keller, "In Search of a Liszt to Be Loved," *The New York Times*, Sunday, January 14, 2001, AR 35.

69. Quoted in Walker, *Franz Liszt*, 2: 346–47.

70. Žižek, *Looking Awry*, 3–20.

71. "Sonata deformation" derives from James Hepokoski; see his "Fiery-Pulsed Libertine or Domestic Hero? Strauss's *Don Juan* Reinvestigated," in *Richard Strauss: New Perspectives on the Composer and His Work*, ed. Bryan Gilliam (Durham: Duke University Press, 1992), 135–76, esp. 143–44.

72. The cadential reprise of the percussive theme is colored by nonharmonic dissonance and subsequently clarified in bar five of an eight-bar statement. The declamatory theme is harmonized with diminished seventh chords grounded by the keynote in the deep-bass register of the percussive theme. This note now

sounds only briefly, however, and only twice, so that the resolution of the declamatory theme remains uncertain. Even so, the diminished-seventh harmony unmistakably represents a dominant minor-ninth minus its root, and it leads into an important clarification, a passage affirming G♮ (the off-tonic note with which the sonata begins) as the upper neighbor to the fifth scale degree, F♯. The subsequent semi-scalar theme ends on C♮, an upper leading tone also found in the recapitulated percussive theme. This note finds a deferred resolution after a chordal passage the heart of which is a soft series of sustained six-four chords. The last note in the piece, the lowest B on the keyboard, both resolves the hanging C♮ (which is the lowest C) and links with the bass of the six-four chords to form a solid V-I profile with which to close.

73. Jürgen Habermas, *The Structural Transformation of the Bourgeois Public Sphere*, trans. Thomas Burger with the assistance of Frederick Lawrence (Cambridge: MIT Press, 1991), 14–42. See also Metzner, *Crescendo*, 213–21.

CHAPTER 5. RETHINKING SCHUMANN'S 'CARNAVAL'

1. Franz Liszt, "Robert Schumann" (1855), in *Schumann and His World*, ed. and trans. R. Larry Todd (Princeton: Princeton University Press, 1994), 356.

2. Carl Dahlhaus, *Nineteenth-Century Music*, trans. J. Bradford Robinson (Berkeley and Los Angeles: University of California Press, 1989), 145.

3. Ibid., 147.

4. Katerina Clark and Michael Holquist, *Mikhail Bakhtin* (Cambridge: Cambridge University Press, 1984), 300.

5. Carl Kossmaly, "On Robert Schumann's Piano Compositions," trans. Susan Gillespie, in Todd, *Schumann and His World*, 311.

6. Naomi Schor, *Reading in Detail: Aesthetics and the Feminine* (New York and London: Methuen, 1987). See also Jeffrey Kallberg, "The Harmony of the Tea Table: Gender and Ideology in the Piano Nocturne," in his *Chopin at the Boundaries: Sex, History, and Musical Genre* (Cambridge: Harvard University Press, 1996), 30–61, esp. 38–40, and Katharine Ellis, "Female Pianists and their Male Critics in Nineteenth-Century Paris," *Journal of the American Musicological Society* 50 (1997): 353–86.

7. Peter Ostwald, *Schumann: The Inner Voices of a Musical Genius* (Boston: Northeastern University Press, 1985), 146.

8. Liszt quoted by the editor, in Robert Schumann, *On Music and Musicians*, ed. Konrad Wolff, trans. Paul Rosenfeld (New York: W. W. Norton, 1969), 163n.

9. It is worth pausing to reflect on one further aspect of musical gender mobility. As we will see in connection with *Dichterliebe*, circularity at the end of a composition is by no means invariably coded as masculine. Circularity is a contested term in nineteenth-century discourse; its gender affiliation derives from the work it does. Musical circularity is masculine when it projects analogues to, and so annexes the authority of, sonata form. The same circularity is feminine when it projects an image of self-enfoldedness or the cyclicity of

nature. Many other terms were subject to similar contestation during the period; for a discussion of contestatory representations of sexual desire, see my *Music as Cultural Practice: 1800–1900* (Berkeley and Los Angeles: University of California Press, 1990), 137–45.

10. On the artist as cult figure, see Jochen Schulte-Sasse, "The Prestige of the Artist under Conditions of Modernity," *Cultural Critique* 12 (1989): 83–100, and the discussion of the star in Jacques Attali's problematical but suggestive *Noise: The Political Economy of Music* (1977), trans. Brian Massumi (Minneapolis: University of Minnesota Press, 1985), 68–81. On the feminization of art, see Carol Christ, "The Feminine Subject in Victorian Poetry," *ELH* 54 (1987): 385–402, and my "Music and Cultural Hermeneutics: The Salome Complex," *Cambridge Opera Journal* 2 (1990): 269–95.

11. Text from Johann Wolfgang von Goethe, *Werke: Hamburger Ausgabe in 14 Bänden*, vol. 1, *Gedichte und Epen*, ed. Erich Trunz (Hamburg: Wegner, 1948); my translation.

12. Choderlos de Laclos, *Les Liaisons Dangereuses*, trans. P. W. K. Stone (Harmondsworth: Penguin, 1961), 109–10.

13. William Butler Yeats, *Collected Poems*, 2d ed. (London: Macmillan, 1950).

14. Friedrich Nietzsche, *Beyond Good and Evil*, trans. Marianne Cowan (Chicago: Henry Regnery, 1955), sec. 238.

15. Ostwald, *Schumann*, 38.

16. Ibid., 42; my translation.

17. Ibid., 55.

18. Ibid., 146.

19. Ibid., 87, 138, 140, 173. My impression is that Schumann's use of tropes like this falls off after 1841 or 1842, perhaps as a result of his increasing allegiance to the role of manly husband. The change is partly prompted by his musical ambition to master the "higher" forms and partly by a defensive reaction to his financial dependence on Clara's performing career (the tensions of which also undermined the ideal of partnership / identification). For details on the Schumanns' marriage, see *The Marriage Diaries of Robert and Clara Schumann*, ed. Gerd Neuhaus, trans. Peter Ostwald (Boston: Northeastern University Press, 1993), and Nancy B. Reich, *Clara Schumann: The Artist and the Woman* (Ithaca: Cornell University Press, 1985).

20. Franz Brendel, "Robert Schumann with Reference to Mendelssohn-Bartholdy and the Development of Modern Music in General" (1845), reprint in Todd, *Schumann and His World*, 329.

21. Ruth Solie, "Whose Life? The Gendered Self in Schumann's *Frauenliebe* Songs," in *Music and Text: Critical Inquiries*, ed. Steven Paul Scher (Cambridge: Cambridge University Press, 1991), 219–40.

22. Ostwald, *Schumann*, 39; translation modified.

23. Frederick Niecks, *Robert Schumann* (New York: Dutton, 1925), 87.

24. See Mikhail Bakhtin, *Rabelais and His World* (1964), trans. Helene Iswolsky (Bloomington: Indiana University Press, 1984), 1–44.

25. Terry Castle, *Masquerade and Civilization: The Carnivalesque in Eighteenth-Century English Culture and Fiction* (Stanford: Stanford University Press, 1986), 4; see 2–6, 26–51 for a general discussion. For a discussion of *Carnaval* in relation to unitary notions of the self, see my *Music as Cultural Practice*, 210–13; several of the technical points raised in that book also appear below for reconsideration in relation to gender.

26. Brendel, "Robert Schumann," in Todd, *Schumann and His World*, 325.

27. Ostwald, *Schumann*, 115.

28. Slavoj Žižek, "Robert Schumann: The Romantic Anti-Humanist," in *The Plague of Fantasies* (London: Verso, 1997), 192–212, at 207. I'm not sure about the squid, but the performance of *Sphinxes* certainly suspends for a moment the "lifelike" quality of the carnival procession. On impossible objects, see my *Music as Cultural Practice*, 85–93; for the association of *Sphinxes* with moths as well as the figures of ancient myth (also noted by Žižek), see Eric Jensen, "Explicating Jean Paul: Schumann's Program for *Papillons*, Opus 2," *Nineteenth-Century Music* 22 (1998), 135–36.

Žižek gives problematical accounts of several of the musical numbers in *Carnaval* (e.g., *Lettres Dansantes, Reconaissance*) but his description of the moment of reanimation after *Sphinxes* is telling: "In 'Papillons,' a dynamic piece which immediately follows 'Sphinxes,' it actually seems as if a butterfly has got rid of the inertia of a larva, and started to fly wildly" (207). The symbolic value of the sequence is also noted by Jensen, 136.

29. On this subject see Nina Auerbach, *Woman and the Demon: The Life of a Victorian Myth* (Cambridge: Harvard University Press, 1982); Terry Castle, "The Pleasure Thermometer," *Representations* 17 (1987): 1–27; my *Music as Cultural Practice*, 117–24; and the illustrations in Bram Dijkstra, *Idols of Perversity: Fantasies of Feminine Evil in Fin-de-Siècle Culture* (New York: Oxford University Press, l986), 133–34, 235–71.

30. Franz Liszt, "Robert Schumann," in Todd, *Schumann and His World*, 355–56.

31. Nietzsche, *Beyond Good and Evil*, sec. 245, 181.

32. Schumann, *On Music and Musicians*, 143.

33. Leo Treitler, "History and Archetypes," *Perspectives of New Music* 35 (1997): 123.

> Think of the interpretive moves that must be supposed to find that meaning in the music: the listener apprehends the structural relationship—the symmetry in the harmonic movement of the two pieces—as a salient property; the symmetry registers as a juxtaposition of mirror images (this is to say that the listener executes cognitively the metaphor entailed in denoting that symmetrical relation with the word "mirror," rather than "crab," for example); and the listener, aware from the titles that the pieces are meant to characterize women, makes the leap from a musical "mirror" relationship to the associations of the woman in the mirror that are described in the preceding paragraph. The harmonic symmetry is interpreted as the symbol of the mirror imagery and as the linch-pin for the connection. There is no inquiry aimed at learning whether the apprehension of this, or any other piece at the time, would have entailed such recognitions and thought processes. . . . [W]here the critic takes such pains to link the musical

structure to contemporaneous psychological themes and ideological issues and social structures in the sense that it expresses, represents, or embodies them, there is not only an implication that the music itself . . . participates in the practice of this social expression, there is a positivistic implication that such meaning is imprinted on the musical structure, and can be read off from it. (123–24)

In fairness to Treitler, his complaint about contemporary thought processes has some weight—there's substantially more ascriptive history in this version of my essay than in the first. In fairness to me, I never rested my claims about *Chiarina* and *Estrella* solely on their harmonic symmetry. The important issue here, however, is not the evidentiary basis of the meanings in question but the characterization of meaning per se.

34. Quoted in Simon Schama, *Landscape and Memory* (New York: Knopf, 1995), 496.

35. On this topic see Jenijoy La Belle, *Herself Beheld: The Literature of the Looking Glass* (Ithaca and London: Cornell University Press, 1988).

36. Text from Arthur Symons, *The Collected Works of Arthur Symons*, vol. 2, *Poems* (London: M. Secker, 1924).

37. Charlotte Brontë, *Villette* (Harmondsworth: Penguin, 1979), 551, 584.

38. Mary Elizabeth Coleridge, *Poems by Mary E. Coleridge* (London: Elkin Matthews, 1908), 8–9. In *The Madwoman in the Attic: The Woman Writer and the Nineteenth-Century Literary Imagination* (New Haven: Yale University Press, 1979), Susan Gubar and Sandra Gilbert cite this poem to illustrate the affirmation of resistant feminine rage, but in so doing they choose to ignore the last stanza, which seeks to reject equally both the conventional and the disfigured images (15–16). A latter-day descendant of Coleridge's poem is Sylvia Plath's "Mirror" from her *Crossing the Water: Transitional Poems* (New York: HarperCollins, 1971), 34. Compare: "A woman bends over me, /Searching my reaches for what she really is" (ll. 10–11).

39. On Lady Hawarden, see Virginia Dodier, *Clementina, Lady Hawarden: Studies from Life* (New York: Aperture, 1999), and Carol Armstrong, "From Clementina to Käsebier: The Photographic Attainment of the 'Lady Amateur,' " *October* 91 (2000): 101–39. Armstrong discusses the photograph in fig. 5.2, one of many Hawarden images of her daughters at mirrors, in mirrored poses, or at windows, on 114–15 (but misidentifies the daughter).

40. Ostwald, Schumann, 122.

41. Schumann thus subtly suggests how mirroring both preserves and loses the object mirrored; the A B A form of the piece can be rewritten a b a/b a/b a.

42. Charles Rosen has suggested that the characters of Pantaloon and Columbine are assigned to the "soprano" and "bass" parts that mimic each other throughout this piece rather than to its contrasting staccato and legato sections; to be more exact, he has declared that anyone familiar with the commedia dell'arte would hear the piece this way ("Music a la Mode," *New York Review of Books*, 23 June 1994, 57). I would not be inclined to call this reading "quite wrong" (Rosen's phrase for the alternative); there is no reason not to hear a travesty *pas de deux* in the music. But Schumann's practice elsewhere in

Carnaval is invariably to portray each character with a single distinctive texture. That practice invites us to hear *Pantalon et Columbine* as depicting the dance of desire from the contrasting points of view of the characters involved: one frantic in pursuit, the other self-assured in eluding it.

43. Schumann on Paganini and Liszt, in Robert Schumann, *On Music and Musicians*, ed. Konrad Wolff, trans. Paul Rosenfeld (New York: W. W. Norton, 1969), 156.

44. Alfred, Lord Tennyson, "The Lady of Shalott" (1832, rev. 1842), in *Poems of Tennyson*, ed. Jerome H. Buckley (Boston: Houghton Mifflin, 1958), ll. 115–17.

45. Kossmaly, "On Robert Schumann's Piano Compositions," in Todd, *Schumann and His World*, 316; Kossmaly is actually describing the later companion piece to *Carnaval*, "Faschingsschwank aus Wien," Op. 26, but his remarks make it clear that the same description applies to *Carnaval* itself.

46. See R. Larry Todd, "Quotation in Schumann's Music," in idem., *Schumann and His World*, 84–85, 100 nn. 8–10.

47. Robert Browning, *Fifine at the Fair*, excerpts from sections 93, 95, 96, in *The Complete Poetical and Dramatic Works of Robert Browning*, Cambridge Edition (Boston and New York: Houghton Mifflin, 1895).

48. Treitler, "History and Archetypes," 122, 124.

49. The staccato-legato comment refers to *Pantalon et Columbine*, which it subjects to a role reversal, switching the musical textures between the title characters. The error has implications for musical hermeneutics, discussed in the section of chapter 7 entitled "The Nest."

CHAPTER 6. GLOTTIS ENVY

1. On modernism high and low, see Andreas Huyssen, *After the Great Divide: Modernism, Mass Culture and Postmodernism* (London: Macmillan, 1986).

2. Walter Benjamin, "The Work of Art in the Age of Mechanical Reproduction" (1936), in *Illuminations*, ed. Hannah Arendt, trans. Harry Zohn (New York: Schocken, 1969), 217–52.

3. In his "Leaving the Movie Theater" (1975), Roland Barthes succumbs to the same assumption. Sound, he suggests—meaning the combination of sound-effects, music, and speech—is "merely a supplementary instrument of representation" conceived to support the "lifelikeness" of the image. In describing the image as a "lure," a source of fascination, however, Barthes parenthetically includes sound *within* the image, as if to admit backhandedly that if the image were stripped of its sound, its lifelikeness would erode: not disappear, to be sure, but begin to exert a demand precisely for the supposed supplement of sound. "Leaving the Movie Theater," in Barthes, *The Rustle of Language*, trans. Richard Howard (Berkeley and Los Angeles: University of California Press, 1989), 345–49.

4. On desire and "the vocal object," see Michel Poizat, *The Angel's Cry:*

Beyond the Pleasure Principle in Opera, trans. Arthur Denner (Ithaca: Cornell University Press, 1992), and Jeremy Tambling, "Toward a Psychopathology of Opera," *Cambridge Opera Journal* 9 (1997): 263–79.

5. On the quest for sound, see David A. Cook, *A History of Narrative Film* (New York: Norton, 1981), 233–57.

6. John Baxter, *Hollywood in the '30s* (New York: A. S. Barnes, 1968), 23.

7. Stanley Cavell, "Nothing Goes without Saying," *London Review of Books* 16, no. 1 (6 Jan. 1994): 3.

8. Mikhail Bakhtin, *Rabelais and His World*, trans. Hélène Iswolsky (Bloomington: Indiana University Press, 1984). My account of the logic of castration is indebted to the theories of Jacques Lacan; for an introduction, see Juliet Mitchell and Jacqueline Rose, eds., *Female Sexuality: Jacques Lacan and the École Freudienne* (New York: W. W. Norton and Pantheon Books, 1985).

9. On the innate theatricality of phallic display, see Marjorie Garber, *Vested Interests: Cross-Dressing and Cultural Anxiety* (New York: Routledge, 1992), 118–27.

10. Bakhtin, *Rabelais and His World*, chapter 6.

11. My allusions to Nietzsche (transvaluation) and Rimbaud (disorganization) are only half in jest; these figures really are forerunners of the Marx Brothers on the other side of the "great divide." In the episode of Harpo's beard, Roland Barthes finds an allegory of the clash between signifying and nonsignifying energy, in which, unusually, he sides with the former. The Marx Brothers side with the latter, which may appear in the overflow not only of zaniness or, as for Barthes, speech, but also of (operatic) music. See "Writers Intellectuals Teachers," in Barthes, *The Rustle of Language*, 313.

12. Slavoj Žižek, *Looking Awry: An Introduction to Jacques Lacan through Popular Culture* (Cambridge: MIT Press, 1993), 128–30. Žižek tends to emphasize the "obscene" side of unsymbolizable pleasure, perhaps because to acknowledge its wider range of inflections would bring it in dangerous proximity to the symbolic. This is a problem that may need to be worked out ad hoc.

CHAPTER 7. HERCULES' HAUTBOYS

1. Hans-Georg Gadamer, *Truth and Method*, trans. Joel Weisheimer and Donald G. Marshall, 2d ed. (New York: Continuum, 1975), 401. Gadamer's statement is a carefully toned-down paraphrase of Martin Heidegger's remarks in "Hölderlin and the Essence of Poetry," trans. Douglas Scott, in *European Literary Theory and Practice*, ed. Vernon W. Gras (New York: Dell, 1973), 31: "Language is not a mere tool, one of many which man possesses; on the contrary, it is only language that opens the possibility of standing in the openness of the existent. Only where there is language, is there world."

2. Gilles Deleuze, *Foucault* (Minneapolis: University of Minnesota Press, 1988), 60.

3. W. J. T. Mitchell, *Picture Theory: Essays on Verbal and Visual Representation* (Chicago: University of Chicago Press, 1994), 5; on the imagetext, 83–107.

4. Lawrence Kramer, *Classical Music and Postmodern Knowledge* (Berkeley and Los Angeles: University of California Press, 1995), 1–66.

5. Gadamer, *Truth and Method*, 274–78.

6. Text from William Shakespeare, *The Complete Works* [The Pelican Shakespeare], ed. Alfred Harbage et. al. (Baltimore: Penguin, 1969).

7. Nicholas Cook, *Analyzing Musical Multimedia* (Oxford: Clarendon Press, 1998), 112–13.

8. My formulations here are indebted to (but do not exactly reproduce) those of Michel Foucault in his *The Archaeology of Knowledge*, trans. A. M. Sheridan Smith (New York: Pantheon, 1972), 107–17.

9. Arthur Schopenhauer, *The World as Will and Representation*, trans. E. F. J. Payne, 2 vols. (New York: Dover, 1969), 1: 261–62, translation slightly modified. Both Carl Dahlhaus and Lydia Goehr also call attention to this passage in, respectively, *The Idea of Absolute Music*, trans. Roger Lustig (Chicago: University of Chicago Press, 1989), 130–31, and *The Quest for Voice: Music, Politics, and the Limits of Philosophy* (Berkeley and Los Angeles: University of California Press, 1998), 86.

10. Henry James, *Portrait of a Lady* (1880; reprint, Boston: Houghton Mifflin, 1963), 150. James does not identify the piano music; the film represents it by excerpts from two of Schubert's Impromptus, which also recur on the soundtrack during a crucial episode.

11. Jacques Derrida, "Signature Event Context" in *Margins of Philosophy*, trans. Alan Bass (Chicago: University of Chicago Press, 1982), 314–21.

12. Derrida, "The Pit and the Pyramid: An Introduction to Hegel's Semiology," in *Margins*, 82n., 83–84.

13. Thomas De Quincey, *Confessions of an English Opium-Eater*, ed. Alethea Hayter (Harmondsworth: Penguin Books, 1971), 79.

14. Ibid.

15. This account of musical presence runs counter to that of Scott Burnham, for whom music evokes a presence that is continually renewable: "we can listen to the music we value so often" because "it always brings us back to the same place, always invokes the same uncanny presence" (Burnham, *Beethoven Hero* [Princeton: Princeton University Press, 1995], 165). For me, this account both overstabilizes musical sound and musical experience and underestimates their semantic fluidity—which is not to deny that the desire for renewable presence plays a significant part in some Western musical traditions.

16. Kevin Barry, *Language, Music, and the Sign: A Study of Aesthetics, Poetics, and Poetic Practice from Collins to Coleridge* (Cambridge: Cambridge University Press, 1987).

17. Claude Lévi-Strauss, "Overture" to *The Raw and the Cooked: Introduction to the Science of Mythology*, vol. 1, trans. John Weightman and Doreen Weightman (New York: Harper and Row, 1969), 18.

18. "Als dämmernde Vermittlerin steht sie zwischen Geist und Materie; sie ist beiden verwandt und doch von beiden verschieden; sie is Geist, aber Geist, welcher eines Zeitmasses bedarf; sie is Materie, aber Materie, die des Raumes entbehren kann." Heinrich Heine, *Sämtliche Werke in vier Bänden*, vol. 3,

Schriften zu Literatur und Politik I, ed. Uwe Schweikert (Munich: Artemis u. Winkler, 1996), 743. My translation.

19. Bruce R. Smith, *The Acoustic World of Early Modern England: Attending to the O-Factor* (Chicago: University of Chicago Press, 1999), 9; the quotation from Serres is from his *Genesis*, trans. Geneviève James and James Nielson (Minneapolis: University of Minnesota Press, 1995), 7.

20. See Kaja Silverman, *The Acoustic Mirror* (Bloomington: Indiana University Press, 1988), and David Schwarz, *Listening Subjects: Music, Psychoanalysis, Culture* (Durham: Duke University Press, 1997), esp. 7–22.

21. Oliver Sacks, *Seeing Voices* (Berkeley and Los Angeles: University of California Press, 1989), 4–8; David Wright, *Deafness* (New York: Stein and Day, 1969), 22, quoted by Sacks, 5. Sacks notes further that even the congenitally deaf "do not experience or complain of silence. . . . [They] may hear noise of various sorts and may be highly sensitive to vibrations of all kinds" (8n.), their vibration-perception coming to form an "accessory sense" that can substitute for the sonorous envelope.

22. Wallace Stevens, "Description without Place," sec. iii, in *The Collected Poems of Wallace Stevens* (New York: Knopf, 1954), 341.

23. Jacques Lacan, "The Agency of the Letter in the Unconscious or Reason since Freud," in *Ecrits: A Selection*, trans. Alan Sheridan (New York: W. W. Norton, 1977), 154–55.

24. Pierre Bourdieu and Loic J. D. Wacquant, *An Invitation to Reflexive Sociology* (Chicago: University of Chicago Press, 1992), 16–19, 92, 128–29.

25. Stevens, "Description without Place," sec. iii.

26. In a certain sense, therefore, all music can be regarded as "multimedia" (Cook, *Analyzing Music Multimedia*, 270) or as "texted" (my statement in "Dangerous Liaisons: The Literary Text in Musical Criticism," *Nineteenth-Century Music* 13 [1989]: 167). These statements hover somewhere between the literal and the figurative, "pushing the envelope" to draw attention to the inevitable implication of music in the general communicative economy.

27. E. M. Forster, *Two Cheers for Democracy* (New York: Harcourt Brace Jovanovich, 1951), 126–30; quotations at 127–28, 128, 129.

28. Forster's discussion of associative and structural listening harks back to that of Robert Schumann a century earlier; in his famous essay on Berlioz's *Symphonie fantastique* (1835; in *On Music and Musicians*, ed. Konrad Wolff, trans. Paul Rosenfeld [1946; reprint New York: W. W. Norton, 1969]), Schumann raises the issue in terms of the nineteenth-century dialectic of sound and vision discussed in chapter 4. "Many," he writes,

> are too conservative in their approach to the difficult question of how far instrumental music may go in the representation of thoughts and events. . . . [W]e must not too lightly estimate outward influences and impressions. Unconsciously an idea sometimes develops simultaneously with the musical image; the eye is awake as well as the ear; and this ever-busy organ sometimes follows certain outlines amid all the sounds and tones, which, keeping pace with the music, may form and crystallize. . . . The more imaginatively or keenly the musician grasps these [possibilities], the more his work will uplift and move us. Why should [it] not . . . ? (181)

Nonetheless, Schumann maintains the capacity of music to "stand alone, without text or explanation," as his aesthetic gold standard; ideas and images, the stuff of the imagetext, are still ultimately on the "outside." Schumann takes this position, which runs counter to his main rhetorical impetus in this passage, because he regards the two types of listening as fixed types related by difference rather than as variable modes related by mutual implication, or the continual interplay of difference and identity that Jacques Derrida calls *différance*. The whole question is more deeply implicit in Schumann's text than in Forster's, and therefore further removed from the key recognition that—to paraphrase Derrida—each mode of listening is the other different and deferred. Schumann, *On Music and Musicians*, 181, 182; Jacques Derrida, "Différance," in *Margins*, 1–28.

29. Michel Foucault, *The Care of the Self*, trans. Robert Hurley (New York: Pantheon, 1986).

30. On designators, see my *Classical Music and Postmodern Knowledge*, 68–71, part of a chapter that examines a problem impossible to address here without unwieldiness, that of music seeking to be explicitly representational—aspiring, so to speak, to the condition of the imagetext.

31. Slavoj Žižek, *Looking Awry: An Introduction to Jacques Lacan through Popular Culture* (Cambridge: MIT Press, 1993), 83–84.

32. Leo Treitler, "Gender and Other Dualities of Music History," in *Musicology and Difference: Gender and Sexuality in Music Scholarship* (Berkeley and Los Angeles: University of California Press, 1993), 23–45. The concept of a subject with wide latitude within its subject positions implies a rejection of what Stanley Fish calls the authority of interpretive communities; for a compelling discussion, based on the work of Donald Davidson, see Reed Way Dasenbrock, "Do We Write the Text We Read?" *College English* 53 (1991): 7–18.

33. N. Katherine Hayles, "Simulating Narratives: What Virtual Creatures Can Teach Us," *Critical Inquiry* 26 (1999), 9.

34. Ludwig Wittgenstein, *On Certainty*, ed. G. E. M. Anscombe and G. H. von Wright, trans. Denis Paul and G. E. M. Anscombe (New York: J. and J. Harper, 1969), 30.

35. Robert Browning, *Fifine at the Fair*, section xcii, in *The Complete Poetical and Dramatic Works of Robert Browning*, Cambridge Edition (Boston and New York: Houghton Mifflin, 1895), 725–26.

36. For further discussion of this point, see my "Subjectivity Rampant!: Hermeneutics and Musical History," in *The Cultural Study of Music*, ed. Martin Clayton, Trevor Herbert, and Richard Middleton (New York: Routledge, forthcoming); further historical illustration appears in my "Primitive Encounters: Beethoven's 'Tempest' Sonata, Musical Meaning, and Enlightenment Anthropology," in *Beethoven Forum* 6, ed. Glenn Stanley (Lincoln: University of Nebraska Press, 1997), 31–66.

37. Roger Scruton, *Aesthetics of Music* (Oxford: Clarendon Press, 1997), 130–33. Scruton's argument presupposes but does not actually refer to the remainder, for which his aesthetics has no category; the phenomenon of ineffa-

bility, which he deals with at some length, is a kind of second cousin. In general, Scruton's challenging and wide-ranging text seeks to uphold the position that "The meaning of a piece of music is what we understand when we understand it as music" (344); the "as-music" proviso turns out to distinguish musical understanding fundamentally from all other kinds. This is scarcely the place for a detailed riposte. Suffice it to say that, although Scruton does not simply beg the question, his efforts to separate musical from what amounts to imagetextual understanding virtually all presuppose music as the Other of the imagetext while overlooking the historicity of that otherness and depreciating the cultural and historical practices by which it is as much broken down as built up.

38. See, for example, Carl Dahlhaus, "The 'Relative Autonomy' of Music History," chapter 8 of his *Foundations of Music History*, trans. J. Bradford Robinson (Cambridge: Cambridge University Press, 1983), and James Hepokoski's discussion in his "The Dahlhaus Project and Its Extra-Musicological Sources," *Nineteenth-Century Music* 14 (1991), 221–46, esp. 227–30, 244–46.

39. On this dimension of fantasy, see Žižek, *Looking Awry*, 6–8.

40. Yve-Alain Bois, Denis Hollier, and Rosalind Krauss, "A Conversation with Hubert Damisch," *October* 85 (1998), 12. Damisch, I should add, denies the existence of musical remainders on the familiar ground of music's immediate power of "self-constitution," a point on which he and I obviously part company.

41. Jacques Lacan, *Four Fundamental Concepts of Psychoanalysis*, ed. Jacques-Alain Miller, trans. Alan Sheridan (New York: Norton, 1981), 61–62, 83, 168, 179–80, 196–99; Žižek, *Looking Awry*, 1–12.

42. Burnham (*Beethoven Hero*, 158), following Kevin Korsyn ("Brahms Research and Aesthetic Ideology, *Music Analysis* 12 [1993]: 91–92), suggests (rightly, I think) that traditional musical aesthetics has been preoccupied with organic unity because it anxiously takes the organic work of art as a substitute for the unified subject. Surely the problem here, however, is not subjectivity per se, but an inadequate conception of it. Korsyn follows Terry Eagleton, *The Ideology of the Aesthetic* (New York: Routledge, 1990), see esp. 1–30, 70–101; but what Eagleton argues is not that the identification of the work of art as a kind of subject is a mere mystification, but that it is a specific historical formation (dating from the mid-eighteenth century) susceptible of mystification among other vicissitudes.

CHAPTER 8. THE VOICE OF PERSEPHONE

1. Nicholas Cook, *Analyzing Musical Multimedia* (Oxford: Clarendon Press, 1998).

2. E. M. Forster, "Art for Art's Sake," in *Two Cheers for Democracy* (New York: Harcourt, Brace, and World, 1951), 88–94.

3. Some starting points for tracking this process include John Brewer, *The Pleasures of the Imagination: English Culture in the Eighteenth Century* (New York: Farrar, Straus and Giroux, 1997, esp. 3–71); Michelle Perrot, ed., *A His-*

tory of Private Life: From the Fires of Revolution to the Great War, trans. Arthur Goldhammer (Cambridge: Belknap Press of Harvard University Press, 1990); and Leo Charney and Vanessa P. Schwartz, eds., *Cinema and the Invention of Modern Life* (Berkeley and Los Angeles: University of California Press, 1995).

4. Jean-Jacques Rousseau, *Essay on the Origin of Language*, in *The First and Second Discourses and Essay on the Origin of Languages*, ed. and trans. Victor Gourevitch (New York: Harper and Row, 1990), 287.

5. Slavoj Žižek, *Looking Awry: An Introduction to Jacques Lacan through Popular Culture* (Cambridge: MIT Press, 1993), 93.

6. Jacques Derrida, "Tympan," in *Margins of Philosophy*, trans. Alan Bass (Chicago: University of Chicago Press, 1982), ix–xxix.

7. Stravinsky's Persephone can be thought of as a modern counterpart to the Persephone of Monteverdi's *Orfeo*, who, true to her intermediary character, intercedes with Plutone on behalf of Orfeo and Eurydice. Monteverdi's Persephone is unique in her mode of singing as Stravinsky's is in her mode of speech. As Susan McClary notes, she combines music reminiscent of Orfeo's own with the rhetoric of seduction, but without incurring "a sense of shame or impending punishment"; what in another feminine voice would be transgressive is in hers both pleasurable (both musically and erotically) and generous. (*Feminine Endings: Music, Gender, and Sexuality* [Minneapolis: University of Minnesota Press, 1991], 44–46.) Persephone's intervention, however, may succeed too well; it moves Plutone so much that he asks her to renounce the dual identity that is (as he fails to see) the source of her power.

8. A further dimension of this force is suggested by the status of Nellie—particularly the original Nellie, Mary Martin, whose Broadway roles also included Peter Pan—as an icon for some gay men.

9. Salman Rushdie, *The Ground beneath Her Feet* (New York: Henry Holt, 1999), 479.

10. On Whitman, see my *After the Lovedeath: Sexual Violence and the Making of Culture* (Berkeley and Los Angeles: University of California Press, 1997), 55–59, 148–51; on the femininity of "transcendental voice," see David Lewin's "Women's Voices and the Fundamental Bass," *The Journal of Musicology* 10 (1992): 464–82, and the concluding pages (154–57) of my "The Waters of Prometheus: Nationalism and Sexuality in Wagner's *Ring*," in *The Work of Opera: Genre, Nationhood, and Sexual Difference*, ed. Richard Dellamora and Daniel Fischlin (New York: Columbia University Press, 1998), 131–60; on the history of constraining the transcendental or otherwise incalculable dimension of the female voice, see McClary, *Feminine Endings*, 80–111.

11. Notes to a recording of *Different Trains*, Elektra/Nonesuch 9-97176-4 (1989).

12. Nietzsche, *Daybreak*, part 2, sec. 30. This passage is quoted by Luce Irigaray in her *Marine Lover of Friedrich Nietzsche*, trans. Gillian C. Gill (New York: Columbia University Press, 1991), 111, where it becomes the prompt for a series of lyrical speculations on the figure of Persephone and her "experience

of the two veils, the two blinds, the two edges, the two cracks in the invisible. . . . Crossing ceaselessly, aimlessly back and forth through the frontier of these abysses" (115). For more on *Different Trains* as holocaust commentary see Naomi Cumming, "The Horrors of Identification: Reich's *Different Trains,*" *Perspectives of New Music* 35 (1997): 129–52; David Schwarz, *Listening Subjects: Music, Psychoanalysis, Culture* (Durham: Duke University Press, 1997), 18–20; and Richard Taruskin, "A Sturdy Musical Bridge to the Twenty-First Century," *New York Times,* 24 August 1997, 2: 29–30.

13. Sigmund Freud, *Group Psychology and the Analysis of the Ego,* trans. James Strachey (1922; reprint London: Liveright, 1967), 37–48, 61–65.

14. Mary Douglas, *Purity and Danger: An Analysis of the Concepts of Pollution and Taboo* (London: Routledge and Kegan Paul, 1966), 114–28.

15. Some rerun episodes condense the sequence by cutting the series of images from the radar screen through the silent scream; the result sacrifices some suggestiveness (presumably for commercial reasons) but also provides an even more concentrated distillation of the show's primary themes. Occasionally, too, the closing legend is varied, suggesting the remoter depths of the truth that is "out there."

16. Mulder's absence for much of the subsequent season, the result of a contract negotiation by the actor David Duchovny, necessitated some changes in the title sequence. The most interesting is that the falling figure is now explicitly Mulder himself, who plummets into what proves to be the iris of an open eye—shades of *Un chien Andalou.* On the show itself, Scully, given a stolid new partner, increasingly identifies with Mulder's position as she nears the term of a mysterious pregnancy. Mulder/Duchovny exits the series with the words "The truth I think we know"—announcing his paternity, by sperm donation, of Scully's child—upon which he kisses his partner romantically for the first time.

17. The exact content of this sequence has changed over the years to accommodate cast changes. Although most of what I have to say has general applicability, the closest fit is with the versions of the sequence ca. 1997–2000.

18. Michael Beckerman, "Capturing the Pounding Pulse of New York City," *New York Times,* 19 June 1994, 2: 31.

CHAPTER 9. POWERS OF BLACKNESS

1. Michael Rogin, "Blackface, White Noise: The Jewish Jazz Singer Finds His Voice," *Critical Inquiry* 18 (1992): 417–53, at 421.

2. Quoted in ibid., 434, 446.

3. Ibid., 447.

4. Toni Morrison, *Playing in the Dark: Whiteness and the Literary Imagination* (Cambridge: Harvard University Press, 1992), 66.

5. Stephen Whicher, ed., *Selections from Ralph Waldo Emerson* (Boston: Riverside Editions, 1957), 238.

6. Dvořák quoted in William Austin, *"Susanna," "Jeannie," and "The Old*

Folks at Home": The Songs of Stephen C. Foster from His Time to Ours (New York: Macmillan, 1975), 294.

7. Ibid., 296–97.

8. Huneker quoted in ibid., 296.

9. Michael Rogin, "'The Sword Became a Flashing Vision': D. W. Griffith's *The Birth of a Nation*," *Representations* 9 (1985): 130–95.

10. W. E. B. Du Bois, *The Souls of Black Folk*, in *Three Negro Classics*, ed. William Hope Franklin (1903; reprint, New York: Avon, 1965), 382.

11. On signifying—intertextual play based on black vernacular traditions—see Henry Louis Gates Jr., *The Signifying Monkey: A Theory of African-American Literary Criticism* (New York: Oxford University Press, 1988). William Grant Still's ballet *Lenox Avenue* (1938) raises the issue of Africanism in a modernist composition by an African-American composer; for a reading, see my "Consciousness Redoubled: Music, Race, and Three Riffs on Lenox Avenue," *Lenox Avenue: A Journal of Interartistic Inquiry* 4 (1998): 12–16.

12. Wilfred Mellers, *Music in a New Found Land: Themes and Developments in the History of American Music* (New York: Hillstone, 1975), 57.

13. Charles Ives, *Memos*, ed. John Kirkpatrick (New York: W. W. Norton, 1972), 56.

14. Charles Ives, *Essays before a Sonata, the Majority, and Other Writings*, ed. Howard Boatwright (New York: W. W. Norton, 1962), 94.

15. Mikhail Bakhtin, *Rabelais and His World*, trans. Hélène Iswolsky (Bloomington: Indiana University Press, 1984).

16. Eric Lott, *Love and Theft: Blackface Minstrelsy and the American Working Class* (New York: Oxford University Press, 1995), 141–53.

17. Austin, "*Susanna*," 321–22. Ives also used "Old Black Joe" in what he called his "Black March," a commemoration of the Civil War's Massachusetts Fifty-Fourth Infantry Regiment, which became the first movement of his First Orchestral Set under the title, "The 'St. Gaudens' in Boston Common: Col. Shaw and his Colored Regiment." For more on Ives's treatment of racial issues, see my *Classical Music and Postmodern Knowledge* (Berkeley and Los Angeles: University of California Press, 1995), 176–83.

18. Carol Oja, "Gershwin and American Modernism," *Musical Quarterly* 78 (1994): 656.

19. George Gershwin quoted in Edward Downes, *The New York Philharmonic Guide to the Symphony* (New York: Walker and Company, 1976), 352.

20. For more on this topic, see Rogin, "Black Face, White Noise."

21. Oja, "Gershwin," 665 n.34, 666 n.54.

22. Constant Lambert, *Music, ho! A Study of Music in Decline* (London: Faber and Faber, 1934), 228. Lambert was anticipated in 1925 by the American composer Louis Gruenberg, who regarded jazz through the lens of romantic primitivism as a "primitive" and "undeveloped" resource awaiting "exploitation" by "the white man with his superior knowledge." See Louis Gruenberg, "Jazz as a Starting Point," *The Musical Leader* 29 (28 May 1925): 594–95, and

David Metzer, "'A Wall of Darkness Dividing the World': Blackness and White-ness in Louis Gruenberg's *The Emperor Jones*," *Cambridge Opera Journal* 7 (1995): 55–72.

23. Oja, "Gershwin," 658.

24. *Newsweek* 132 (5 October 1998), 82.

25. Arbie Orenstein, ed., *A Ravel Reader: Correspondence, Articles, Inter-views* (New York: Columbia University Press, 1990), 391.

26. Thomas Pakenham, *The Scramble for Africa: The White Man's Con-quest of the Dark Continent from 1876 to 1912* (New York: Random House, 1991), 639–40.

27. Marianna Torgovnik, *Gone Primitive: Savage Intellects, Modern Lives* (Chicago: University of Chicago Press, 1990), 275.

28. Ibid., 111.

29. Ibid., 111–12.

30. Orenstein, *Ravel Reader*, 46.

31. Roland Barthes, *Writing Degree Zero*, trans. Annette Levers and Colin Smith (New York: Hill and Wang, 1967), 10.

32. In my *Classical Music and Postmodern Knowledge*, 201–25.

33. Slavoj Žižek, *Tarrying with the Negative: Kant, Hegel, and the Critique of Ideology* (Durham: Duke University Press, 1993), 200–237.

34. Lott, *Love and Theft*, 148–53.

35. Ibid., 174–76, drawing on Richard Middleton, "In the Groove, or Blow-ing Your Mind? The Pleasures of Musical Repetition," in *Popular Culture and Social Relations*, ed. Tony Bennett et al. (Milton Keynes, Eng.: Open University Press, 1986).

36. Downes, *New York Philharmonic Guide*, 354–55.

37. Robert Orledge, "Debussy's Piano Music," *Musical Times* 122 (1981), 27.

38. Ian Kemp, *Tippett: The Composer and His Music* (London: Eulenburg Books, 1984), 439–40.

CHAPTER 10. LONG RIDE IN A SLOW MACHINE

1. Bertolt Brecht, "Aus der Musiklehre," *Schriften zur Literatur und Kunst 1: 1920–1932* (Frankfurt am Main: Suhrkamp, 1967), 111–14.

2. On the "misunderstanding thesis," see Theodor Adorno, "The Three-penny Opera" (1929) and Ernst Bloch, "The Threepenny Opera" (1935), both trans. Stephen Hinton, and Stephen Hinton, "Misunderstanding the *Three-penny Opera*," all in Hinton, *Kurt Weill: The Threepenny Opera*, Cambridge Opera Handbooks (Cambridge: Cambridge University Press, 1990), 129–33, 135–37, 181–92.

3. Bloch, "The Threepenny Opera," in Hinton, *Kurt Weill: The Threepenny Opera*, 132.

4. See Victor Schklovsky, "Sterne's *Tristram Shandy*: Stylistic Commen-tary" and "Art as Technique," in *Russian Formalist Criticism: Four Essays*,

trans. and ed. Lee T. Lemon and Marion J. Reis (Lincoln: University of Nebraska Press, 1965), 27–57; and Fredric Jameson, *The Prison-House of Language: A Critical Account of Structuralism and Russian Formalism* (Princeton: Princeton University Press, 1972), 49–54, 75–82; with reference to Brecht, 58–59.

5. For the opposing positions on Brecht's familiarity with *ostranenie*, see John Willett, *Brecht in Context: Comparative Approaches* (New York: Methuen, 1983), 218–21, and Peter Brooker, *Bertolt Brecht: Dialectics, Poetry, Politics* (Sydney: Croom Helm, 1988). See also Fredric Jameson, *Marxism and Form* (Princeton: Princeton University Press, 1971), 372–74.

6. Brecht, "On Experimental Theater," *Gesammelte Werke* 15 (Frankfurt am Main: Suhrkamp, 1967), 301; trans. from Keith A. Dickson, *Towards Utopia: A Study of Brecht* (Oxford: Clarenden Press, 1978), 250.

7. See in particular Roland Barthes's *Mythologies* (1957), trans. Annette Lavers (New York: Hill and Wang, 1972), and the later essay "Change the Object Itself: Mythology Today" in Barthes's *Image Music Text*, trans. Stephen Heath (New York: Hill and Wang, 1977), 165–69.

8. J. L. Austin, *How to Do Things with Words*, ed. J. O. Urmson and Marina Sbisà (Cambridge: Harvard University Press, 1975), 21–22; Jacques Derrida, "Signature Event Context" in *Margins of Philosophy*, trans. Alan Bass (Chicago: University of Chicago Press, 1982), 309–30. In *A Pitch of Philosophy: Autobiographical Exercises* (Cambridge: Harvard University Press, 1994), 53–128, Stanley Cavell in effect argues that Austin was more Derridean than Derrida recognized; in "Sounding Serious: Cavell and Derrida," *Representations* 63 (1998): 65–92, Gordon C. F. Bearne argues—rightly, I think—that Derrida's critique holds up nonetheless.

9. Roland Barthes, "Brecht and Discourse: A Contribution to the Study of Discursivity," in *The Rustle of Language*, trans. Richard Howard (Berkeley and Los Angeles: University of California), 213.

10. Lotte Lenya, "Foreword: August 28, 1928," to Bertolt Brecht, *The Threepenny Opera*, English book by Desmond Vesey, English lyrics by Eric Bentley (New York: Grove Press, 1964), xi–xii. For a different version of the story, see Hinton, "'Matters of Intellectual Property': The Sources and Genesis of *Die Dreigroschenoper*," in his *Kurt Weill: The Threepenny Opera*, 22–23.

11. On the figure of the serial killer, see Maria Tatar, *Lustmord: Sexual Murder in Weimar Germany* (Princeton: Princeton University Press, 1995), *passim*; chapter 7 (153–72) is devoted to M. The detail about the 1928 production is from Geoffrey Abbot, "The 'Dreigroschen' Sound," in Hinton, *Kurt Weill: The Threepenny Opera*, 168.

12. For a discussion of the different versions of the play, see Hinton, "'Matters of Intellectual Property,'" in his *Kurt Weill: The Threepenny Opera*, 27–33. Brecht's revision, together with a set of notes on its proper performance, represents his effort to contain *Die Dreigroschenoper* within the limits of his increasingly strict Marxist worldview. (He was, among other things, stung by bad reviews in the Marxist press.) These texts can be neither accepted as authoritative nor dismissed as politically motivated; they are both. With regard to

Macheath in particular, the 1931 character is, according to Brecht's notes, a "bourgeois phenomenon" *(bürgerliche Erscheinung)* ("Anmerkungen zur 'Dreigroschenoper,'" *Schriften zum Theater,* vol. 2 [Frankfurt-am-Main: Suhrkamp, 1963], 94, my translation). Yet this is not quite the character that held the stage so long in either Berlin (1928–33) or New York (1954, 1955–61)—and yet, again, he is not so different a character that one can speak confidently of two Macheaths, let alone of authentic and falsified ones. More broadly, there simply is no single, integral work entitled *Die Dreigroschenoper,* only a family of works grouped under that name.

13. In their translation of the 1931 version (Methuen, 1993, 123), John Willett and Ralph Mannheim state that the prompt book of the original production includes the Moritat with no stage directions. It is plausible to conjecture that Brecht based the stage directions of the published text on practices developed for the production, but the facts remain uncertain. The interpolation "Look, that was Mack the Knife!" can be heard, minus the laughter, in the original-cast album of the off-Broadway production; *The Threepenny Opera,* MGM E3121.

14. Bertolt Brecht, "Anmerkungen zur 'Dreigroschenoper,'" *Schriften zum Theater,* vol. 2 (Frankfurt-am-Main: Suhrkamp, 1963), 101. My translation. My use of the "Anmerkungen" is subject to the cautions described in note 12 to this chapter; in this case the idea at hand is very characteristic of Brecht.

15. Kurt Weill, "Correspondence about *The Threepenny Opera,*" *Musikblätter des Anbruch* 11 (11 January 1929), 24–25; reprint and translation in *The Weimar Republic Sourcebook,* ed. Anton Kaes, Martin Jay, and Edward Dimendberg (Berkeley and Los Angeles: University of California Press, 1994), 576–78; quotation, 578.

16. Neuss can be heard on *The Threepenny Opera,* Columbia 02L-257; Gerald Prince's performance in the original cast album (MGM E3121) is in the same spirit, but less raucous. By contrast, Reinhold Firchow's performance on the 1997 Capriccio recording (60 058–1) is smooth and operatic, as if reluctant to mar what has now been upgraded from a stage show to a work of high art.

17. Kurt Weill, "Zeitoper," *Melos* 7 (March 1928), 106–8; reprint and translation in *The Weimar Republic Sourcebook,* 572–74; quotations, 573.

18. Kurt Weill, *Die Dreigroschenoper; A Facsimile of the Holograph Full Score,* ed. Ed Harsh (New York: The Kurt Weill Foundation for Music, and Valley Forge, Pa.: European American Music, 1996).

19. E. T. A. Hoffmann, "Automata," in *Best Tales of Hoffmann,* ed. E. F. Bleiler, trans. Alexander Ewing (New York: Dover, 1967), 71–103, esp. 93–97; H. H. Stuckenschmidt, "Mechanical Music," *Der Kreis* 3 (Nov. 1926), 506–8, in *The Weimar Republic Sourcebook,* 597–600. A remark by Hegel is (as usual) also pertinent: "The executant artist . . . must submit himself entirely to the character of the work. . . . [But] he must not, as happens often enough, sink to being merely mechanical, which only barrel-organ players are allowed to be. If . . . art is still to be in question, the executant has a duty to give life and soul to the work." G. W. F. Hegel, *Aesthetics: Lectures on Fine Art,* trans. T. M. Knox (Oxford: Oxford University Press, 1974), 956.

20. Theodor W. Adorno, *Philosophy of Modern Music* (1948), trans. Anne G. Mitchell and Wesley V. Blomster (New York: Seabury Press, 1973), 144–45. Adorno is writing with specific reference to Stravinsky.

21. As David Drew observes ("Motifs, Tags, and Related Matters" in Hinton, *Kurt Weill: The Threepenny Opera*, 149–60, esp. 150f.), Weill plays with added-sixth sonorities throughout the opera. Insofar as they mediate between this technique and the older romantic sound world, the "signature" added-sixth chords of the Moritat are not unlike Debussy's quotation of the opening of the *Tristan* Prelude in "Golliwog's Cakewalk," except that the Moritat's technique (unlike that of other numbers in the opera, such as Lucy's aria and the third finale) is not parodic.

22. An added complexity, pointed out by Kim Kowalke in *"The Threepenny Opera in America,"* in Hinton, *Kurt Weill: The Threepenny Opera*, 78–119, is that the version used on the cast album was bowdlerized at the insistence of MGM, so that "innocuous, nearly meaningless verses replaced those chronicling Sloppy Sadie's knife wound and Little Susie's rape in 'Mack the Knife'" (112). The characterization of Macheath in "Mack the Knife" could vary depending on both the verses used and the style of performance.

23. Theodor Adorno, "The Threepenny Opera," *Die Musik* 22 (1929): 424–28, reprint in Hinton, *Kurt Weill: The Threepenny Opera*, 129–33; quotation, 133.

24. For structures of feeling, the social organization that gives the sense of a lived present, see Raymond Williams, *Marxism and Literature* (New York: Oxford University Press, 1977), 128–35.

25. On Schoenberg's additions, see Horst Weber, "'Melancholisch düstrer Walzer, kommst mir nimmer aus den Sinnen!' Anmerkungen zum Schönbergs 'soloistischer Instrumentation' des Kaiserwalzers von Johann Strauss," *Musik-Konzepte* 36 (1984): 86–100. Weber also suggests that Schoenberg integrates contrapuntal lines from Haydn's Kaiserhymne. This extends the historical self-consciousness of the arrangement from one imperial era to another, but does so at an esoteric rather than a sonoric level—in Schoenberg's terms as idea rather than style. The Bach arrangements date from 1922; Schoenberg's statement about them is quoted in Josef Rufer, *The Works of Arnold Schoenberg*, trans. Dika Newlin (London: Faber and Faber, 1962).

26. Theodor Adorno, "Mahagonny," *Musikblätter des Anbruch* 14 (Feb./Mar. 1932), 12–15; in *The Weimar Republic Sourcebook*, 588–593. The citation is to p. 592.

27. Arnold Schoenberg, "Why No Great American Music," in Schoenberg, *Style and Idea*, ed. Leonard Stein, trans. Leo Black (Berkeley and Los Angeles: University of California Press, 1984), 178.

28. Stephen Walsh, *Bartók: Chamber Music* (London: BBC, 1982), 82.

29. Slavoj Žižek, *Looking Awry: An Introduction to Jacques Lacan through Popular Culture* (Cambridge: MIT Press, 1992), 21–23.

30. This question dominated the reception of the Emerson String Quartet's widely remarked performance of a complete Shostakovich cycle in the spring of

2000; for sharply contrasting views of the debate thus revived, see Joseph Horowitz, "A Moral Beacon amidst the Darkness of a Tragic Age," *New York Times*, Sunday, 6 February 2000: AR 34, and Richard Taruskin, "Casting a Great Composer as a Fictional Hero," *New York Times*, Sunday, 5 March 2000: AR 43.

31. Dmitri Shostakovich, *Testimony: The Memoirs of Dmitri Shostakovich*, as related to and edited by Solomon Volkov, trans. Antonina W. Bouis (New York: Limelight, 1992), 156.

32. In *Defining Russia Musically* (Princeton: Princeton University Press, 1997), 493–95, Richard Taruskin suggests that the quartet presents Shostakovich as a victim in order to excuse his joining the Communist Party in 1960; Laurel Fay's recent *Shostakovich* (New York: Oxford University Press, 2000), 216–19, suggests that there was actually little external pressure on him to join. My own contention is that the quartet is more self-accusatory than self-exculpatory, and that it is addressed to the general condition of which Shostakovich's internalized compulsion to join the Party is just one symptom.

33. For a different (and perhaps forced) treatment of Shostakovich's allusions to Beethoven's Op. 131 and various fugues by Bach, see Timothy L. Jackson, "Dmitry Shostakovich: The Composer as Jew," in *Shostakovich Reconsidered,* ed. Allan B. Ho and Dmitry Feofanov (London: Toccata Press, 1998), 601–3, 612–13.

34. For some cautions about the concept of cyclical form, with particular reference to Shostakovich, see Patrick McCreless, "The Cycle of Structure and the Cycle of Meaning: The Piano Trio in E Minor, Op. 67," in *Shostakovich Studies*, ed. David Fanning (Cambridge: Cambridge University Press, 1995), 113–36.

35. Žižek, 21–23. Žižek is particularly concerned with demands "made" by the dead, a topic that will prove unexpectedly pertinent to the Eighth Quartet later in this chapter.

36. Shostakovich quoted the opera again in his Fourteenth Quartet (1972–73), by which time a revised, somewhat toned-down version had returned to the Soviet stage under the title *Katerina Ismailova;* vindicating this work in some form was obviously crucial to him.

37. On the problem of "victim empathy," see Dominick la Capra, "Trauma, Absence, Loss," *Critical Inquiry* 25 (1999): 696–727.

38. Elizabeth Wilson, *Shostakovich: A Life Remembered* (Princeton: Princeton University Press, 1994), 340.

39. Fay, *Shostakovich*, 220.

40. Taruskin, *Defining Russia Musically*, 494.

41. Wilson, *Shostakovich: A Life Remembered*, 340.

CHAPTER 11. CHIAROSCURO

1. Toni Morrison, *Playing in the Dark* (Cambridge: Harvard University Press, 1990), 72.

2. An all-black troupe tried to get permission to revive the play in the early 1940s, but nothing came of it, and the idea seems to have disappeared thereafter. In 1946, *Beggar's Holiday,* a racially integrated adaptation of John Gay's *The Beggar's Opera* (Brecht and Weill's source) opened on Broadway with music by Duke Ellington, but closed after only fourteen weeks. (For details, see Kim Kowalke, "*The Threepenny Opera* in America," in Stephen Hinton, *Kurt Weill: The Threepenny Opera* [Cambridge: Cambridge University Press, 1990], 90–99). Armstrong is said to have based his performance on some criminal figures he knew as a young man, but this fact, if it is one, was not for public consumption. The appeal of "Mack the Knife" to an unusually large variety of white audiences can be measured by the existence of recordings by the likes of Wayne Newton, Lester Lanin, and Liberace.

3. On structural / cultural tropes, see my *Music as Cultural Practice: 1800–1900* (Berkeley and Los Angeles: University of California Press, 1990), and *Classical Music and Postmodern Knowledge* (Berkeley and Los Angeles: University of California Press, 1995); on call and response, see Samuel A. Floyd Jr., *The Power of Black Music* (New York: Oxford University Press, 1995).

4. Langston Hughes, *Collected Poems of Langston Hughes,* ed. Arnold Rampersad (New York: Knopf, 1994).

5. William Carlos Williams, *Selected Poems,* ed. Charles Tomlinson (New York: New Directions, 1985). Like the Precisionists, but with some ambivalence, Williams embraced the intrusion of modernity and machinery on the supposedly Edenic landscape of the nation—the topic of Leo Marx's *The Machine in the Garden: Technology and the Pastoral Ideal in America* (New York: Oxford University Press, 1964).

6. Claude Lévi-Strauss, *The Savage Mind,* trans. George Weidenfeld (Chicago: University of Chicago Press, 1966), 16–36.

7. W. E. B. Du Bois, *The Souls of Black Folk* (New York: Dover, 1994), v.

8. Kimberly W. Benston, "Performing Blackness: Re/Placing Afro-American Poetry," in *Afro-American Literary Study in the 1990s,* ed. Houston A. Baker Jr. and Patricia Redmond (Chicago: University of Chicago Press, 1989), 164–84.

9. Houston A. Baker Jr., *Blues, Ideology, and Afro-American Literature: A Vernacular Theory* (Chicago: University of Chicago Press, 1984).

10. For prosopopoeia in this sense (rather than the more general sense of personification), see Paul de Man, "Autobiography as De-Facement," in his *The Rhetoric of Romanticism* (New York: Columbia University Press, 1984), 67–82, at 75–78.

11. The full text appears in Benston, "Performing Blackness," 177–78, and in Stephen Henderson, *Understanding the New Black Poetry: Black Speech and Black Music as Poetic References* (New York: William Morrow, 1972), 261–62.

12. Sonia Sanchez, "a/coltrane/poem," in *Understanding the New Black Poetry,* 274. Benston, "Performing Blackness," 176, identifies "the Coltrane poem" as "that genre of modern black poetry in which the topos of performed blackness is felt most resonantly." If this is right, the existence of the genre may

suggest that Coltrane's music, especially as mediated by his untimely death, impressed many listeners as a paradigmatic performance of black identity.

13. This reading of "My Favorite Things" runs counter to that of Ingrid Monson in her "Doubleness and Jazz Improvisation: Irony, Parody, and Ethnomusicology," *Critical Inquiry* 20 (1994), 292–300.

14. Zora Neale Hurston, "Spirituals and Neo-Spirituals" (1934), in *Negro: An Anthology*, ed. Nancy Cunard (New York: Frederick Ungar, 1970), 223–25.

15. David Metzer, "Shadow Play: The Spiritual in Duke Ellington's 'Black and Tan Fantasy,'" *Black Music Research Journal* 17 (1997), 147; Metzer alters Hurston's term to "negroidisation."

16. Du Bois, *The Souls of Black Folk*, 146, 153. For more on this episode, with discussion of the apparent inconsistency between the music John hears at the opera and at his death, see my "Consciousness Redoubled: Music, Race, and Three Riffs on Lenox Avenue," in *Lenox Avenue: A Journal of Interartistic Inquiry* 4 (1998), 16–17.

17. For more on this question, see [Kwame] Anthony Appiah, "The Uncompleted Argument: Du Bois and the Illusion of Race," *Critical Inquiry* 12 (1985), 21–37; Stuart Hall, "What Is This 'Black' in Black Popular Culture?" in *Black Popular Culture*, ed. Gina Dent (Seattle: Bay Press, 1992), 21–33; Ross Posnock, "How It Feels to Be a Problem: Du Bois, Fanon, and the 'Impossible Life' of the Black Intellectual," *Critical Inquiry* 23 (1997): 323–49; and my "Consciousness Redoubled."

CHAPTER 12. GHOST STORIES

1. Pierre Bourdieu, "The Forms of Capital," in *Handbook of Theory and Research for the Sociology of Education*, ed. John C. Richardson (New York: Greenwood Press, 1983), 241–58.

2. Michael Lind, "Defrocking the Artist," *New York Times Book Review*, 14 March 1999, 32.

3. Donald Francis Tovey, *Essays in Musical Analysis: Chamber Music* (Oxford: Oxford University Press, 1978), 72–73.

4. Sigmund Freud, "The Uncanny," trans. Alix Strachey, in *Studies in Parapsychology*, ed. Philip Rieff (New York: Macmillan, 1963), 19–60.

5. Jacques Derrida, "Différance," in *Margins of Philosophy*, trans. Alan Bass (Chicago: University of Chicago Press, 1972), 1–27.

6. Schubert uses the accompaniment to the line "Schöne welt, wo bist du?" (Beautiful world, where are you?), from his setting of Schiller's "Die Götter Griechenlands" (The Gods of Greece), D. 677, in both the minuet of his A-Minor String Quartet, D. 804, and the finale of his Octet in F, D. 803; his setting of G. P. S. von Lübeck's "Der Wanderer," D. 489, gives its name to the "Wanderer" Fantasy for piano, D. 760, where it supplies the theme of the slow variations movement. "Death and the Maiden" is discussed in the text. Schubert also wrote two sets of virtuosic variations on loss-related song themes: "Trockne Blumen" (Withered Flowers) for flute and piano, D. 802, from *Die*

Schöne Müllerin, D. 795, and "Sei mir gegrüsst," D. 794 (Receive my greeting), in the Fantasy for Violin and Piano, D. 934. On the "Sei mir gegrüsst" variations, see Patrick McCreless, "A Candidate for the Canon? A New Look at Schubert's Fantaisie in C Minor for Violin and Piano," *Nineteenth-Century Music* 20 (1997): 205–30. On the complexities of Schubert's self-citation in the obvious exception to the rule of loss, the variations movement of the "Trout" Quintet, see "Mermaid Fancies: Schubert's Trout and the 'Wish to be Woman,'" in my *Franz Schubert: Sexuality, Subjectivity, Song* (Cambridge: Cambridge University Press, 1998), 75–92.

7. "Revenants: Masculine Thresholds in Schubert, James, and Freud," in my *Franz Schubert,* 152–72.

8. Franz Kafka, "Before the Law," trans. Willa Muir and Edwin Muir, in Kafka, *The Complete Stories,* ed. Nahum Glatzer (New York: Schocken, 1971), 3–4.

9. For a critique of these paradigms in music criticism and analysis, see Lloyd Whitesell, "Men with a Past: Music and 'The Anxiety of Influence,'" *Nineteenth-Century Music* 18 (1994): 152–67. Also pertinent is Richard Taruskin, "Revising Revision," *Journal of the American Musicological Society* 46 (1993): 114–38.

10. Charles Rosen, "Who's Afraid of the Avant-Garde?" *New York Review of Books* 45, no. 8 (14 May 1998): 21.

11. Theodor Adorno, "On the Fetish Character of Music and the Regression of Listening," in *The Essential Frankfurt School Reader,* ed. Andrew Arato and Eike Gebhardt (Oxford: Basil Blackwell, 1978), 270–99.

12. It's worth adding explicitly that the issue of Schoenberg's unpalatability to audiences is anything but dead. The emblematic year 1999, for example, saw empty seats at the Metropolitan Opera during its well-reviewed production of *Moses und Aron,* controversy in the pages of the Sunday *New York Times* (see particularly Michael Steinberg's pro-Schoenberg "Toward Fresh and Friendly Concerts," Sunday, 13 June 1999, and the letters to the contrary by James Sellars and Roger Kolb, Sunday, 27 June), and perhaps most notably, the promotional brochure for the tenth annual Bard Music Festival, *Schoenberg and His World,* 13–15 and 21–22 August. The brochure is admirably forthright. It begins with the statement that "In the final year of this century, the time has come to challenge unfounded prejudices" about Schoenberg, and goes on to claim that, viewed in cultural and historical context, Schoenberg "turns out to be an approachable and compelling personality whose work is truly accessible, suffused by emotion and an overriding conviction in the power of art." My sympathy with the contextual approach is unqualified, and that Schoenberg's creative personality is (or was) compelling is a historical fact. But approachable? accessible? emotional?—as, say, Puccini or Shostakovich are emotional? I'm not sure that the long history of audience failures to find these traits in Schoenberg's music (except for *Verklärte Nacht*) can be written off as the results of unfounded prejudice. And it may be that an overriding conviction in the power of art is more the problem than the solution. Might it not be that Schoenberg's

legacy is precisely the difficulty that most listeners have in liking his music—a difficulty full of social and aesthetic significance that would better be served by recognition and interpretation than by hortatory claims of original genius?

13. William Wordsworth, *The Prelude* (1805), vii.601–2.

14. Quoted from Arbie Orenstein, *Ravel: Man and Musician* (New York: Columbia University Press, 1975), 188.

15. W. H. Auden, "Lakes" (no. 4 of *Bucolics*), from *Collected Shorter Poems, 1927–1957* (New York: Random House, 1967).

16. For further comments on the music, see the University of California Press Web site, http://www.ucpress.edu/books/pages/9293.html. A copy of the score may be found in the research collection of the New York Public Library of the Performing Arts at Lincoln Center.

17. McClary, "Terminal Prestige," *Cultural Critique* 12 (1989): 57–82.

18. Lest there be any doubt about the persistence of the ideas at issue here or their standing as doxa, witness the following from a 1998 column by Paul Griffiths in the Sunday *New York Times*. The topic is the list of candidates for best classical composition at the year's Grammy awards:

> In their substance, most of these pieces make their homage to the past . . . explicit. Four of them . . . seem to unfold in a world where the clock stopped in about 1942. The great influences on them are composers from the first half of the century: Mahler, Prokofiev, Bartok, Sibelius, Rachmaninoff, Stravinsky. They could easily have been written at that time, except that [in some] a heavy pulsation . . . suggests rock music of a later date. And even this is moderated by Wagner and, again, Stravinsky. The four works imply a new way of appealing to traditional measures. Music is valued not because it lives up to a tradition but because it relives that tradition. Uniqueness, which had been a hallmark of importance in classical music, becomes an impossibility. The composer's job is to make effective simulacra.

"Are Grammy Write-Ins Possible?" Sunday, 22 February 1998, AR 33. Griffiths reiterates similar themes in the same prestigious forum in "With a New Century, a Promise of New Sounds," Sunday, 19 December 1999, AR 1, 41.

19. Friedrich Nietzsche, *The Gay Science* (1887), trans. Walter Kaufmann (New York: Random House, 1974), 274–75 [section 342]; Nietzsche reused this passage as the prologue to his next book, *Thus Spoke Zarathustra*.

20. Slavoj Žižek, *The Plague of Fantasies* (London: Verso, 1997), 194.

21. Richard Wagner, "Judaism in Music," in *Judaism in Music and Other Essays*, trans. W. Ashton Ellis (1907; reprint Lincoln: University of Nebraska Press, 1995), 75–122.

22. The autograph gives titles to all five movements, suggesting a narrative of the war from "Calm Unawareness of the Future Cataclysm" to "The Eternal Question—Why? And for What?" It's likely that publishing the titles would have been politically dangerous; the finale poses the "eternal question" in despairing terms that could easily be read as unpatriotic in Stalin's Russia.

23. See "Signature Event Context" in Derrida, in *Margins of Philosophy*, trans. Alan Bass (Chicago: University of Chicago Press, 1978), 307–30.

24. On the mime, see Derrida, "The Double Session," in *Dissemination*, trans. Barbara Johnson (Chicago: University of Chicago Press, 1981), 173–286.

25. Ludwig Wittgenstein, *Philosophical Investigations*, 2d ed., trans. G. E. M. Anscombe (New York: Macmillan 1958), 2–50.

26. John Keats, "Ode on a Grecian Urn," ll. 1–2.

27. On Hegel's qualms, see chapter 1; on the complex history of purely instrumental music, see Carl Dahlhaus, *The Idea of Absolute Music* (1978), trans. Roger Lustig (Chicago: University of Chicago Press, 1989), and *Esthetics of Music* (1967), trans. William Austin (Cambridge: Cambridge University Press, 1982), and, in part as a corrective, Mark Evan Bonds, "Idealism and the Aesthetics of Instrumental Music at the Turn of the Nineteenth Century," *Journal of the American Musicological Society* 50 (1997): 387–420.

28. Quoted in Dahlhaus, *Esthetics of Music*, 51.

29. A point emphasized by Dahlhaus; see his *Between Romanticism and Modernism: Four Studies in the Music of the Later Nineteenth Century* (1974), trans. Mary Whitall (Berkeley and Los Angeles: University of California Press, 1980), 97–99.

30. On the subject image, see my *Franz Schubert*, 157.

31. This unlocatability of the musical subject is qualitative, not substantive; it does not and cannot negate the historical specificity of the imaginary others to whom historically situated listeners may be drawn. On the question of unlocatability, see Naomi Cumming, "The Subjectivities of 'Erbarme Dich,'" *Music Analysis* 16 (1997): 5–44; on historicity, see my *Classical Music and Postmodern Knowledge* (Berkeley and Los Angeles: University of California Press, 1995), 19–25, 119–21.

32. On the "decomposition" of the finale of the Ninth into the European anthem, see Caryl Clark, "Forging Identity: Beethoven's 'Ode' as European Anthem," *Critical Inquiry* 23 (1997): 789–807.

33. Jacques Derrida, "Signature Event Context," *Margins of Philosophy*, 315–19.

34. *Aids to Reflection* (London, 1825), 220, cited by Coleridge himself in a footnote to his poem "Constancy to an Ideal Object" (also ca. 1825).

35. For a detailed account of the infiltration of Tippett's movement by Beethoven's, see Ian Kemp, *Tippett: The Composer and His Music* (London: Eulenberg, 1984), 449–56, tabulated on 450; the quotation from Tippett appears on 449.

36. Slavoj Žižek, *Looking Awry: An Introduction to Jacques Lacan through Popular Culture* (Cambridge: MIT Press, 1993), 29–34.

37. For more on questions of depersonalization in *Different Trains*, see Naomi Cumming, "The Horrors of Identification: Reich's *Different Trains*," *Perspectives of New Music* 35 (1997); on subjectivity in the work's listener, see David Schwarz, *Listening Subjects: Music, Psychoanalysis, Culture* (Durham: Duke University Press, 1997), 18–20.

38. Derrida, "Différance," 3.

39. David B. Dennis, *Beethoven in German Politics, 1870–1989* (New Haven: Yale University Press, 1996), 174. The broadcast occurred on 30 April 1945.

40. Quoted by Michael Kennedy, *Richard Strauss* (New York: Schirmer, 1976), 106.

41. Thomas Mann, *Doctor Faustus*, trans. H. T. Lowe-Porter (New York: Random House, 1966), 452.

42. Others, notably Timothy L. Jackson ("The Metamorphosis of the *Metamorphosen:* New Analytical and Source-Critical Discoveries," in *Richard Strauss: New Perspectives on the Composer and His Work*, ed. Bryan Gilliam [Durham: Duke University Press, 1992], 193–241), have suggested that in *Metamorphosen* Strauss does express his guilt and remorse at having been involved with the Third Reich. The argument seems untenable to me, but one might say that it's unclear whom I disbelieve, Strauss or his apologists or both.

43. See Fredric Jameson, *Postmodernism; or, The Cultural Logic of Late Capitalism* (Durham: Duke University Press, 1991), esp. 1–66, 297–418; and Jean Baudrillard, *Simulacra and Simulation*, trans. Sheila Faria Glaser (Ann Arbor: University of Michigan Press, 1994).

Index

Text: 10/13 Aldus
Display: Aldus
Compositor: BookMatters, Berkeley
Printer and Binder: Sheridan Books, Inc.